Linguistic Choices in the Contemporary City

Linguistic Choices in the Contemporary City focuses on how individuals navigate conversation in highly diversified contexts and provides a broad overview of state of the art research in urban sociolinguistics across the globe. Bearing in mind the impact of international travel and migration, the book accounts for the shifting contemporary studies to the workings of language choices in places where people with many different backgrounds meet and exchange ideas. It specifically addresses how people handle language use challenges in a broad range of settings to present themselves positively and meet their information and identity goals.

While a speaker's experience runs like a thread through this volume, the linguistic, cultural and situational focus is as broad as possible. It runs from the language choices of Chinese immigrants to Beijing and Finnish immigrants to Japan to the use of the local lingua franca by motor taxi drivers in Ngaoundéré, Cameroon, and how Hungarian students in their dorm rooms express views on political correctness uninhibitedly. As it turns out, language play, improvisation, humour, lies, as well as highly marked subconscious pronunciation choices, are natural parts of the discourses, and this volume provides numerous and extensive examples of these techniques. For each of the settings discussed, the perspective is taken of personalised linguistic and extra-linguistic styles in tackling communicative challenges. This way, a picture is drawn of how postmodern individuals in extremely different cultural and situational circumstances turn out to have strikingly similar human behaviours and intentions.

Linguistic Choices in the Contemporary City is of interest to all those who follow theoretical and methodological developments in this field. It will be of use for upper level students in the fields of Sociolinguistics, Pragmatics, Linguistic Anthropology and related fields in which urban communicative settings are the focus.

Dick Smakman is an Assistant Professor at the Leiden University Centre for Linguistics in the Netherlands. He specialises in the sociolinguistics and sociophonetics of both first-language use and second language acquisition and use.

Jiří Nekvapil is an Associate Professor at Charles University in Prague. His specific research interests lie in the issues of language interaction, Language Management Theory, language diversity in multinational companies and the ethnomethodologically based analysis of media discourse.

Kapitolina Fedorova is a Professor of Russian Studies at Tallinn University in Estonia. Her research interests include language contacts, intercultural communication, migration and border studies, and register variation in everyday communication.

Routledge Studies in Language and Identity
Series Editor: Reem Bassiouney

The Routledge Studies in Language and Identity (RSLI) series aims to examine the intricate relation between language and identity from different perspectives. The series straddles fields such as sociolinguistics, discourse analysis, applied linguistics, historical linguistics and linguistic anthropology. It aims to study identity and language by utilizing novel methods of analysis as well as ground breaking theoretical approaches.

Titles in Series:

Language, Identity, and Syrian Political Activism on Social Media
Francesco L. Sinatora

Mixing and Unmixing Languages
Romani Multilingualism in Kosovo
Amelia Abercrombie

Research Companion to Language and Country Branding
Edited by Irene Theodoropoulou

Translation as a Set of Frames
Ali Almanna and Chonglong Gu

Languages, Identities and Intercultural Communication in South Africa and Beyond
Russell H. Kaschula

Linguistic Choices in the Contemporary City
Postmodern Individuals in Urban Communicative Settings
Edited by Dick Smakman, Jiří Nekvapil and Kapitolina Fedorova

For more titles, please visit: www.routledge.com/Routledge-Studies-in-Language-and-Identity/book-series/RSLI

Linguistic Choices in the Contemporary City
Postmodern Individuals in Urban Communicative Settings

Edited by
Dick Smakman, Jiří Nekvapil and
Kapitolina Fedorova

LONDON AND NEW YORK

Cover image: © praetorianphoto / Getty Images

First published 2022
by Routledge
4 Park Square, Milton Park, Abingdon, Oxon OX14 4RN

and by Routledge
605 Third Avenue, New York, NY 10158

Routledge is an imprint of the Taylor & Francis Group, an informa business

© 2022 selection and editorial matter, Dick Smakman, Jiří Nekvapil and Kapitolina Fedorova; individual chapters, the contributors

The right of Dick Smakman, Jiří Nekvapil and Kapitolina Fedorova to be identified as the authors of the editorial material, and of the authors for their individual chapters, has been asserted in accordance with sections 77 and 78 of the Copyright, Designs and Patents Act 1988.

All rights reserved. No part of this book may be reprinted or reproduced or utilised in any form or by any electronic, mechanical, or other means, now known or hereafter invented, including photocopying and recording, or in any information storage or retrieval system, without permission in writing from the publishers.

Trademark notice: Product or corporate names may be trademarks or registered trademarks, and are used only for identification and explanation without intent to infringe.

British Library Cataloguing-in-Publication Data
A catalogue record for this book is available from the British Library

Library of Congress Cataloging-in-Publication Data
Names: Smakman, Dick, 1970– editor. | Nekvapil, Jiří, editor. |
Fedorova, Kapitolina, editor.
Title: Linguistic choices in the contemporary city :
postmodern individuals in urban communicative settings /
edited by Dick Smakman, Jiří Nekvapil and Kapitolina Fedorova.
Description: London ; New York : Routledge, 2022. |
Series: Routledge studies in language and identity |
Includes bibliographical references and index.
Identifiers: LCCN 2021043813 (print) | LCCN 2021043814 (ebook) |
ISBN 9780367366766 (paperback) | ISBN 9780367366735 (hardback) |
ISBN 9780429348037 (ebook)
Subjects: LCSH: Urban dialects. | Sociolinguistics. |
Languages in contact. | Language and languages–Variation. |
Identity (Philosophical concept) | Multilingualism. |
Immigrants–Language–Social aspects.
Classification: LCC P40.5.U73 .L43 2022 (print) |
LCC P40.5.U73 (ebook) | DDC 306.44/6–dc23/eng/20211217
LC record available at https://lccn.loc.gov/2021043813
LC ebook record available at https://lccn.loc.gov/2021043814

ISBN: 978-0-367-36673-5 (hbk)
ISBN: 978-0-367-36676-6 (pbk)
ISBN: 978-0-429-34803-7 (ebk)

DOI: 10.4324/9780429348037

Typeset in Bembo
by Newgen Publishing UK

Contents

List of tables	viii
List of figures	x
List of contributors	xii

1 Introducing city people and their communicative challenges   1
  D. SMAKMAN, J. NEKVAPIL AND K. FEDOROVA

PART I
Innovative language uses   13

2 Marginal spaces in small urban areas: Evidence from a refugee centre in Southern Italy   15
  L. IEZZI

3 Urban language practices online? Multilingualism among German-Namibians in computer-mediated communication   30
  H. RADKE

4 Motorcycle taxi drivers in Ngaoundéré, Cameroon: Communication in a diffuse multilingual setting   49
  K. BEYER

PART II
Competing identities   65

5 Language choices and language identities of Finns in Japan   67
  LIISA-MARIA LEHTO

6 PC goes East-Central Europe: Enregistering politically
   correct language in Budapest university dormitories   83
   CSANÁD BODÓ, R. K. TURAI AND G. SZABÓ

7 The Haarlem legend: The unpredictable formation of a
   national language norm   100
   D. SMAKMAN

8 The sociolinguistic situation in Hradec Králové, the best
   researched town in the Czech Republic   114
   J. NEKVAPIL

PART III
Multilingual strategies   139

9 The social linguistic soundscape and its influence on
   language choice in Stornoway   141
   I. BIRNIE

10 Bilingualism, ideology and identity: Change in the
   Finland-Swedish variety   154
   J. A. E. STRANDBERG AND C. GOOSKENS

11 Trasyanka as a dying phenomenon of urban speech in the
   city of Minsk   172
   I. LISKOVETS AND K. FEDOROVA

12 Language problems in interactions between locals
   and foreign tourists in the city of Prague: A language
   management study   193
   V. DOVALIL

PART IV
Linguistic landscapes   211

13 'Non-identical twins': Monolingual bias and linguistic
   landscapes of the twin cities of Ivangorod/Narva   213
   K. FEDOROVA AND V. BARANOVA

14 'Nothing personal, just business': Individuals as actors in changing monolingual linguistic landscapes in Vyborg, Russia   239
V. BARANOVA AND K. FEDOROVA

15 Behind the linguistic landscape: An interview-based study of business owners' reasons for choosing business names in the German city of Mainz   260
F. VAN MEURS, B. PLANKEN AND N. LASARZEWSKI

PART V
Global processes and sound change   273

16 Rhotics frequency in Beijing   275
H. HU AND D. SMAKMAN

17 Reacting to urbanisation in Morocco: New language practices, old discourses?   287
J. FALCHETTA

18 The dynamic sociophonetics of Bulgarian /l/: The quiet transition from [l] to [ŭ]   304
S. MITSOVA, G. PADAREVA-ILIEVA AND D. SMAKMAN

Index   322

Tables

2.1	Adaptation of the model proposed by Mioni (1988: 300) for African countries. The diglossic model (H language and L language), is further expanded with the addition of a M language that serves as lingua franca	22
3.1	Distribution of place of origin among users and their comments	34
3.2	The four participants	35
3.3	Standard German in German Namibian CMC (n = 2,178)	37
3.4	Population size and frequency of Namibia-specific comments	41
4.1	Linguistic variables and their values as used in the Ngaoundéré study (adapted from Kramer 2018)	52
4.2	Age groups among the MTDs of Ngaoundéré	53
4.3	Distribution of ethno-linguistic background among MTDs	54
8.1	Foreign nationals, February 2020, Hradec Králové district	125
8.2	Residents of Hradec Králové district according to their mother tongue (as of March 2011)	125
9.1	Language use survey locations and observation results	145
11.1	Utterances in Trasyanka	175
11.2	Russian stems in Trasyanka	176
11.3	Belarusian stems in Trasyanka	176
11.4	Paraphones	176
11.5	Differences in syntax	177
12.1	Foreign tourists in the Czech Republic in 2019 and in 2018 (top 10 countries)	195
15.1	Characteristics of the businesses whose owners were interviewed	263
16.1	The speaker groups ($N = 76$), split up on the basis of gender, age and dialect background	277
16.2	Number of rhotics ($N = 3,402$) per 1,000 words for the various speaker groups ($N = 76$)	278
16.3	Summary of the independent t-test on the number of rhotics types by female and male *Beijing* native speakers	281
16.4	Summary of the independent t-test on the number of rhotics by female and male *Beijing* native speakers ($N = 31$)	282

16.5	p-values of pairwise comparisons of three age groups of *female Beijing* native speakers ($N = 15$)	282
16.6	p-values of pairwise comparisons of three age groups of *male Beijing* native speakers ($N = 16$)	282
16.7	p-values of pairwise comparisons of *Beijing* native speakers ($N = 31$) and *With-r* speakers ($N = 22$) of three generations	284
17.1	Evolution of the population in four central Moroccan cities	288
17.2	The chosen lexemes	292
17.3	Frequency of each allophone in the two age ranges	292
18.1	Formant frequencies (mean value F1 and F2) of [l] (isolated from the word [lampə]), [ŭ] (isolated from the word [ŭampə]) and [u]	308
18.2	Realisations of /l/ in prevocalic position. The pluses show the possibility of appearance of the specific /l/ allophones in prevocalic position and the minuses show the absence of such a possibility	310

Figures

2.1	Language choices by the informants	23
4.1	ECN of Ego1 (University student originally from Chad)	56
4.2	ECN of Ego2, native Fulfulde speaker of Ngaoundéré	58
4.3	ECN of Ego3, a Kolé-speaker from the northern borderland of Cameroon, Chad and Nigeria	59
7.1	Location of the city of Haarlem	101
8.1	A door sign of the Indian-Nepalese restaurant *Tandoor* (*zavřeno* English: closed; *otevřeno* English: open). December 2018	129
8.2	*Rychlý kafe* (A quick coffee). June 2020	130
8.3	A blackboard on the wall of *Rychlý kafe*. January 2019	131
8.4	A shop window of the travel agency *Votrok*. June 2020	132
10.1	Map of Finland highlighting bilingual municipalities with Finland-Swedish minority (light grey) or Finland-Swedish majority (dark grey), as well as monolingual Finland-Swedish municipalities on the Åland islands (black). Data source: Kuntaliitto 2017	157
12.1	Foreign tourists in the Czech Republic since 1989 (in thousands)	194
13.1	Ivangorod Fortress and Narva Castle facing each other across the Narva river	219
13.2	Tourist map of Ivangorod	222
13.3	Poster of Ivangorod Art Museum	223
13.4	Ivangorod Art Museum's entrance	224
13.5	Road sign near the border, Ivangorod	225
13.6	The advertisement of Narva hotel and restaurant 'King', Ivangorod	226
13.7	An entrance to an apartment building, Narva	227
13.8	Old street sign, Narva	228
13.9	Tourist map of Narva	229
13.10	Hand-written sign ('The shop is open') inside a local shop, Narva	230
13.11	Home-printed signs ('Glasses for vision', 'Glasses for 6.50 €') inside a local shop, Narva	231

13.12	Trilingual advertisement in a supermarket, Narva	232
13.13	Advertisements of cultural events on a billboard, Narva	233
14.1	Street sign for Shpalernaya str., St. Petersburg	241
14.2	Bilingual sign inside Central Market, Vyborg	245
14.3	Home-printed sign ('Fresh bread') inside Central Market, Vyborg	246
14.4	Hand-written sign ('We serve in Finnish') inside Central Market, Vyborg	247
14.5	Direction sign in Vyborg Castle	248
14.6	Trilingual souvenir shop's advertisement near Vyborg Castle	249
14.7	Trilingual menu, restaurant Вкус ('Taste'), hotel Victoria, Vyborg	250
14.8	Historic map of Vyborg on the wall of the restaurant Круглая башня ('The round turret')	250
14.9	Billboard near café Gloria, Vyborg, 2010	251
14.10	Official trilingual sign, Vyborg railway station, 2010	252
14.11	Bilingual sign for tourist information centre, Vyborg railway station, 2018	253
14.12	Car wash in front of the railway station, Vyborg, 2010	254
14.13	The same car wash in front of the railway station, Vyborg, 2018	254
16.1	Distribution of rhotics ($N = 3{,}402$) across the speaker groups ($N = 76$)	279
16.2	Number of rhotics ($N = 2{,}403$) of each gender (*female*, $N = 15$; *male*, $N = 16$)	280
16.3	Number of rhotics ($N = 2{,}403$) of each age group of *Beijing* Speakers ($N = 31$)	281
16.4	Number of rhotics ($N = 2{,}403$) of each dialect background group ($N = 76$)	283
17.1	Variation of phonological assignments between two generations of informants. The percentages indicate the frequency with which that particular lexeme was pronounced with a /g/ by any of the speakers of that generation	291
18.1	Articulatory configurations of [l], [ŭ] and [u]	307
18.2	Spectrogram of [l], [ŭ], and [u]	308
18.3	Лош & Гол	315

Contributors

Vlada Baranova graduated from St. Petersburg State University (Department of Russian), 2002, and European University at St. Petersburg (Department of Ethnology), 2005. PhD in anthropology (2007). Works at National Research University – Higher School of Economics, St. Petersburg and at Institute for Linguistic Studies, Russian Academy of Sciences. Research interests: sociolinguistics, language policy, minority languages, migration studies, Kalmyk, Chuvash.

Klaus Beyer is a researcher at the department of African Studies at Goethe-University, Frankfurt. His interests are in the fields of multilingualism, language contact theory, and the interplay of individual linguistic behaviour with complex language ecologies. By combining social network analysis with language contact theory, Beyer currently aims at modeling socio-psychological processes in multilingual speakers and developing new theoretical perspectives on ongoing variation in multilingual communities.

Ingeborg Birnie is a lecturer in Education and Gaelic Medium at the University of Strathclyde. Her research interests include the teaching and learning of minority languages within the education system and exploring different methodologies to evaluate the spoken use of different language in public spaces in bi- or plurilingual communities.

Csanád Bodó is Associate Professor in the Institute of Hungarian Linguistics and Finno-Ugric Studies at Eötvös Loránd University, Hungary. His research areas include critical sociolinguistics with particular focus on the impact of globalisation on the margins, the ethnography of language revitalisation, and language, gender and sexuality. He has published several books on multilingualism and language ideologies, as well as articles in the *Journal of Sociolinguistics*, *Discourse & Society* and *Open Linguistics*.

Vít Dovalil works at the Department of Germanic Studies at the Faculty of Arts of Charles University in Prague. His research interests include language management in the European Union with the focus on the case law concerning the language-related disputes. In addition, he explores language standardisation and pluricentric languages. He studies German grammar from structural and sociolinguistic perspectives as well as the status of German as a foreign and minority language in the Czech Republic.

Jacopo Falchetta graduated from Università di Bergamo (2008) and SOAS (2010). PhD in Arab, Islamic and Semitic Studies, with a thesis in Arabic Dialectology and Sociolinguistics (2019). He has fulfilled teaching positions in Arabic Linguistics, Dialectology and Sociolinguistics at the University of Bayreuth (2021–22), Moroccan Arabic at the INALCO in Paris (2021) and Modern Standard Arabic at the Università di Bergamo (2022). His main research interests are Urban Sociolinguistics, Arabic Dialectology, Arabic Linguistics, Interactionist Linguistics and Dialect Contact.

Kapitolina Fedorova graduated from St. Petersburg State University (Department of Russian and Department of General Linguistics), 1999, and European University at St. Petersburg (Department of Ethnology), 2001. PhD in philology (2002). In 2003–2018 worked at European University at St. Petersburg and then at Hankuk University of Foreign Studies in Seoul, South Korea. Since 2020, she has been Professor of Russian Studies at Tallinn University, Estonia. Research interests: sociolinguistics, language contacts, migration studies, border studies, linguistic landscape.

Charlotte Gooskens is associate professor of European Languages at the Center for Language and Cognition Groningen (CLCG) at the University of Groningen, the Netherlands. Her research is concerned with perceptual and communicative effects of language variation, e.g. language attitudes, speaker identity and mutual intelligibility of closely related languages. For her research she uses experimental methods and exact measurement techniques.

Hu Han is a PhD student at Leiden University Centre for Linguistics (LUCL), specialising in the sociophonetics of Beijing Mandarin.

Luca Iezzi is a PhD student at 'G. d'Annunzio' University of Chieti-Pescara (Italy). His primary research focus is on contact linguistics (especially with regard to migrants settled in refugee centres) and language maintenance and shift in new migrant communities in Italy. He is also particularly interested in Chinese dialectology and linguistics, language policy and planning, TESOL, translation and interpreting.

Nadine Lasarzewski graduated from Radboud University Nijmegen, the Netherlands, with a Master degree in International Business Communication. She holds a Bachelor degree in Linguistics and Economics at Johannes Gutenberg University Mainz, Germany. After spending one year in Japan, with a Heinz Nixdorf Program scholarship to promote Asia-Pacific related work experience of young professionals, she now works in international Sales and Marketing.

Liisa-Maria Lehto is a post-doctoral researcher at the University of Oulu, Finland. She works for LinBo-project (linguistic and bodily involvement in multicultural interactions) and is concentrated on discourses and ideologies amongst different multilingual groups. Her special interest is using corpus assisted methods to study discourses.

Irina Liskovets graduated from St. Petersburg State University (Department of Applied and Structural Linguistics), 1992, and European University at St. Petersburg (Department of Ethnology), 1999. PhD in linguistics (2006). Works at St. Petersburg State University of Industrial Technology and Design. Research interests: sociolinguistics, language contacts, language attitudes, urban multilingualism in Belarus.

Frank van Meurs is an Assistant Professor in the Department of Language and Communication and the Centre for Language Studies, Radboud University Nijmegen, the Netherlands. He has published on foreign languages in advertising and on the evaluation of foreign accents in advertising and in English Medium Instruction. With Jos Hornikx, he wrote *Foreign Languages in Advertising: Linguistic and Marketing Perspectives* (Palgrave Macmillan, 2020).

Sofiya Mitsova, Ass. Prof., PhD, Department of Bulgarian language, South-West University 'Neofit Rilski', Bulgaria. Scientific interests: Sociolinguistics, Intercultural communication, Conversation analyses, Language Management.

Jiří Nekvapil is Associate Professor at Charles University in Prague. His scientific interests include Language Management Theory, ethnomethodologically informed analysis of media discourse, and the use of languages in multinational companies.

Gergana Padareva-Ilieva, Assoc. Prof., PhD, Department of Bulgarian language, South-West University 'Neofit Rilski', Bulgaria. Scientific interests and expertise: Phonetics, Media speech, Applying phonetics and linguistics in communication disorders research.

Brigitte Planken is an Associate Professor in the Department of Language and Communication and the Centre for Language Studies, Radboud University Nijmegen, the Netherlands. She has published on English as a business lingua franca, the effects of language choice in advertising, and the evaluation of non-native (versus native) accent in functional communication contexts. She has published a number of textbooks, most recently *Teaching Business Discourse* with Cornelia Ilie and Catherine Nickerson (Palgrave Macmillan, 2019).

Henning Radke is a lecturer of German as a foreign language and sociolinguistics at Duitsland Instituut Amsterdam and the Universiteit van Amsterdam. He is currently writing a dissertation on the variation of the German language in Namibia. His previous academic activities include: lecturer of the German Academic Exchange Service (DAAD) at the Duitsland Instituut Amsterdam (2014–2020), guest lecturer at the University of Namibia (2018), DAAD teaching assistant at the University of Cape Town,

South Africa (2014), field research in Paramaribo, Suriname (2013). He holds a MA in 'European Languages' (2013) and a BA in Dutch Philology and Communication Science (2010) at Freie Universität Berlin.

Dick Smakman is lecturer at Leiden University Centre for Linguistics (LUCL) and specialises in sociolinguistics, sociophonetics and English language pronunciation teaching. With Patrick Heinrich (Ca' Foscari University in Venice) he edited *Globalising Linguistics. Challenging and Expanding Theory* (Routledge 2015) and *Urban Sociolinguistics. The City as a Linguistic Process and Experience* (Routledge 2018). He wrote *Clear English Pronunciation. A Practical Guide* (Routledge 2020) and *Discovering Sociolinguistics. From Theory to Practice* (Palgrave MacMillan, 2018).

Janine Strandberg is a doctoral candidate in Theoretical and Empirical Linguistics at the Center for Language and Cognition Groningen (CLCG) at the University of Groningen, the Netherlands. Focusing on bilingualism in the context of minority and heritage languages, her doctoral research project examines sociophonetic and lexical variation in the Finland-Swedish variety. She is also interested in language policy, the sociolinguistics of globalisation, and linguistic landscape research.

Gergely Szabó is a joint PhD Student in Hungarian Linguistics at ELTE Eötvös Loránd University and in Information and Knowledge Society at Open University of Catalonia. His doctoral project is an ethnographically informed critical sociolinguistic study of Hungarians in Catalonia with special attention to the (re)production of belonging. His research interests also cover the sociolinguistic aspects of transnational migration, linguistic ideologies, language and gender.

Ráhel Katalin Turai is a sociologist and gender expert with a PhD from Central European University, Budapest, Hungary. Ráhel taught sociology of gender and sexuality in the Eastern European context. She participated in research projects on language and masculinity, partnership violence, care work migration and gender inequalities in schooling/academia.

1 Introducing city people and their communicative challenges

D. Smakman, J. Nekvapil and K. Fedorova

1.1 Rationale behind this volume

Cities have always been an important focus in Sociolinguistics – from the study of the way people in Buenos Aires (Guitarte 1955), Tokyo (Sibata 1958) or New York (Labov 1966) speak to more recent studies into language use in Copenhagen (Holmberg 1991), Mannheim (Kallmeyer 1994), Tripoli (Pereira 2007) or South African townships (Brookes 2014). While a common interest was to highlight class-related linguistic patterns in big cities, more contemporary studies tend to focus on the language of and between individuals in places where people with many different backgrounds meet and communicate. Indeed, recent research has focussed specifically on high levels of diversity in cities nowadays and has moved away from the group approach to a more inter-individual and even intra-individual approach.

This volume addresses the theme of communication in the city in a broad way in one sense and in a very narrow way in another. The broad approach lies in the idea that communication (not language) is chosen as the theme, so that multiple communication tools are included as a focus. Although it can be qualified as sociolinguistic, and mainly focussed on language, this book takes a broader approach by acknowledging that there is no strict dividing line between the linguistic and non-linguistic, because communication might be in body movement, rituals and how objects are treated (Goodwin 2018; Pennycook 2018). Moving around the cities, people simultaneously make use of different communication channels: they look around and see street signs and advertisements in many colors and with every kind of images; they talk to strangers and text their friends on their smartphones; they listen to the noise and to the music of the city life. The specificity of the volume lies in the interest in individuals, specifically modern individuals. The idea behind the book is that interacting and co-operating individuals are increasingly less categorisable and are, in fact, in search of their own unique place in a generally diverse and often confusing societal urban structure. This leads to highly personalised styles and modes of communication. Narrow – or micro-level – approaches to such interactions within urban space make more sense than broad-scale surveys leaving individuals out of the picture. Methodologically, identities are no more conceptualised as fixed social categories useful for characterisation of linguistic details abstracted from complex semiotic behaviour. Due to the increased movement and contact of people, within the boundaries of states or transnationally, identities have become hybrid and less stable, which shifts the scholar's attention to their dynamic production and management in talk-in-interaction.

This book aims to demonstrate a sociolinguistics of mobile semiotic resources, both in and across particular interactions taking place in multiple territories worldwide. To gain a better insight into communicative factors, this book zooms in on the individual and how they treat the communicative commodities at hand in their daily lives within specific settings, amongst which shops, trains, skating ranges, youth hangouts, etc. Rather than addressing abstract group behaviour and the correlations between linguistic/communicative and social/situational factors, this book focusses on interacting and co-operating individuals with different life trajectories in a diverse urban context, and their language choices. It asks the question why people communicate the way they do in highly diverse public-space contexts. In such contexts, the individual is confronted on a daily basis with their communicative repertoire and skills and makes choices based on changes in context: interlocutor, setting, speaker intentions, identity, emotional moves and many more. Metaphorically speaking, the individual asks themselves: 'What do I want to achieve; amusement, money, food, a job, friendship, confrontation, love, attention, reassurance, or perhaps, identity expression?' That same individual needs to adjust to changes in interlocutor and social setting, and the urban communicator is therefore typically a flexible and innovative forerunner in post-modern language use and management (Neustupný 2006), which is characterised by the strongly self-conscious use and management of communicative tools from the past adjusted to and mixed with more contemporary ones. This typically leads to an amalgamation of styles and genres including codes; an almost artistic mixing of all the communicatively relevant resources and strategies that are available into a personalised set of communicative habits, which rejects conventions and focuses on the interacting and co-operating social actor and their practical and symbolical needs. This everyday creativity connects to an enhanced sensitivity to the use of language, such as noting and evaluating linguistic phenomena, and, as a result, frequent metalinguistic activities evident in the communicative behaviour of the individual managing his or her language (Nekvapil and Sherman 2015). This book tries to fathom individual agency and the resultant choices in various cities across the globe and draw conclusions on how individuals in such varied places share certain behaviours and management strategies, which then may be interpreted as being the result of modern globalising tendencies – the roles they play, the social categories they assume turn by turn, their sensitivity to these roles and categories, including their self- and other-perceived position in the flow of communicative behaviours.

In line with the concept of 'globalising sociolinguistics'(Smakman and Heinrich 2015, 2018), this book tries to give a central role to authors, places, approaches and theories that stem from outside the Anglo-western realm of sociolinguistic influence. Combined with research from within this realm, an insightful picture may be painted of the postmodern individual in the city and how they share habits and motivations with their equivalents in another urban context geographically far removed from them. It is true that in the global village of today's world similar processes can be found all over the globe – the same way as fast food and mass market franchises. However, being diverse does not necessarily mean the same for a German city and a small Russian border town, or for an expat living in Japan and a taxi driver in Cameroon, which this volume will demonstrate. Changing focus helps to refrain from generalisations and preconceptions based on one's own experiences and expectations, and to find better ways to deal with such diversities within diversities. The focus on postmodern individuals communicating in urban settings shouldn't prevent us from acknowledging that the contemporary globalised world also comprises features 'not so postmodern'– in other words, modern or even traditional – and the co-existence of the postmodern and modern may generate important research areas in present-day sociolinguistics.

1.2 The chapters

Part I of this volume is called *Innovative language uses* and describes such uses in urban contexts, and oftentimes involving the use of more than one language to get messages across. Urban communicative situations are known to be important places of linguistic innovation, both when it comes to changes to a broader language norm and to the upcoming forces through street-level use, where intuitive mixing of languages is practiced commonly. Massey (2005) described cities as 'peculiarly large, intense and heterogeneous constellations of trajectories, demanding of complex negotiation' (154). The dynamism of modern lifestyles, in which communication takes place in various languages with various types of speakers and is often not restricted to one language, results in interesting and often highly systematic language choices by ordinary speakers. In such superdiverse situations, linguistic resources are often freely borrowed from, resulting in heavy code-mixing and the rise of new systems, some of which could be referred to as languages in their own right. This first part illustrates how innovative language choices are not merely practical in nature but in the process naturally hold much identity expression.

The chapter by Iezzi, first of all, in a lively – and often confronting – manner describes how migrants find their way in a situation that they are not prepared for and in which the stakes are high and information communication may be life-changing. It illustrates the plight of Pakistani migrants in Italy in a small urban society that is culturally and linguistically foreign to them. Without documents or financial resources, linguistic resources are the main tool of these '*profughi*', immigrants, towards communication and persuasion of authorities. In-depth observations of discourse show how these migrants mix language resources to demonstrate their willingness to integrate into the new society and positively contribute to this new environment.

The chapter by Radke on multilingualism among German-Namibians in computer-mediated communication asks the question what the similarities and the differences are between rural and urban language practices in multilingual societies when speakers meet virtually in CMC while at the same time meeting each other face to face on occasion. The chapter describes the interconnection of urban and rural areas through 'rich networks of people, goods, and ideas' that have been common in history. CMC provides a platform for the urban and rural to meet in order to maintain both types of networks. This lays bare the multilingual practices that urban and rural individuals partake of. The outcome of such communication is in this chapter captured through the unique linguistic repertoire of the German-Namibians. This repertoire includes German, Afrikaans, English, indigenous Namibian languages and a non-standard variety of German commonly referred to as Namdeutsch. The chapter shows that multilingualism among German-Namibians is a trans-urban phenomenon fulfilling a wide range of pragmatic purposes but is also stylised in many cases.

A final example of language innovation and of diffuse language systems and solutions for communicative obstacles is the situation in Ngaoundéré, as described by Beyer. In this city in Cameroon, the linguistic innovations by motorcycle taxi drivers are outlined through network analysis. The chapter suggests that while identity construction seems to be mostly associated with social settings in the Global North it is also found in the Global South. In the end, these taxi drivers follow well-known mechanisms of simplification and reduction that are typical of urban linguistic settings worldwide. An important and highly useful contribution of this chapter is methodological, making the observation that urban contexts, especially those that hold languages that are not standardised in the European sense of the word, need to be analysed differently and that special attention should be paid to data collection methods. To demonstrate one way of going about this, Ego-Centred-Networks (ECN) are presented for the specific group of speakers under investigation.

Papers focusing on identity-work of various kinds have been collected in Part II; *Competing identities*. Here the authors, in multiple and divergent connections and contexts, deal with identity as a situated accomplishment. They examine competing ethnic and non-ethnic identifications, demonstrate how constructing social identities is tied to the operation of political or language ideologies, and address the mutual forming of city identity and language identity, approaching them not only as the work of urban people, but also of the researchers investigating language life in the city.

Lehto's chapter focuses on urban immigrants – Finns in Japan living in metropolitan areas. Through discourse analysis, her study demonstrates how identities are managed in talk of Finns in Japan who depict their multilingual lives. The author examines the identities of Japan Finns from two perspectives: firstly, she focuses on the reported language choices that they took in various domains; secondly, she pays attention to the categories and category-tied features that they choose to describe languages and their speakers during the research interview. As expected, the informants perceive Japanese as the language of the surrounding society, and hence important, while Finnish is seen as an index of heritage and the country of origin. The study reveals, however, that English works as a marker of identity as well. It connects the informants to the group of foreigners, which in the context of Japan may be more valued by them than being a Finn.

In their chapter, Bodó, Turai and Szabó seek to reveal local meanings and categories of political correctness in a contemporary East-Central European context, specifically, among university students in Hungary. Instead of focusing on the public sphere, the chapter examines individual understandings of political correctness. Dealing with everyday talk of students in Budapest, the capital city of Hungary, the authors demonstrate that individuals perceive political correctness as a constraint originated from an external (mainly Western) authority, and they negotiate this mode of expression in their ordinary talk. Drawing on the concepts of voice and enregisterment, the authors argue that political correctness in the metadiscourse among Hungarian students is assigned to the Other. Critiquing this political correctness contributes to individual self- and other-constructions by questioning Western modernist projects. Stances to political correctness serve as a means to work on individual and group identities. It should be mentioned that the chapter contains extracts of conversations the language of which may be offensive for those who belong to the groups concerned, such as black people and some ethnic groups.

The identity issue needn't apply only to humans, but also, for example, animals, toys, things, theories, institutions, languages or cities. Smakman's chapter on the 'Haarlem legend' clarifies how Haarlem, a Dutch town situated close to Amsterdam, is popularly associated with 'good' Dutch, that is, the national language norm in the Netherlands. This legend has been shaped and reproduced through continuous identity work both of Haarlem's residents and other Dutch people taking place in the course of more than one century. The author gives both historical and current reasons that maintain the popularity of the legend in the Netherlands. He shows that, as a 'totalizing vision' (Irvine and Gal 2000), it is resisting numerous counter-arguments based both on common-sense and scientific discourse. He concludes suggesting that vitality of the myth of the distinctive linguistic status of Haarlem may be sustained by the desire of postmodern individuals to find a stable norm to face the ever increasing diversity of present-day language life.

In his chapter, Nekvapil reports on the large body of sociolinguistic knowledge justifying his claim that the city of Hradec Králové may be 'the best researched town in the Czech Republic'. He draws attention to the research paradigms involved and seeks to present the conducted research as a coherent whole, addressing the issue to what degree the agenda of present-day sociolinguistics can profit from the sociolinguistic agenda of the past. In his methodologically oriented paper, city identity proves to be neither stable nor self-evident. Nekvapil demonstrates the ways city identity is constructed through various semiotic resources by various social actors living in the town. Moreover, he deals with how city identity works in the research design of the researchers – some fully acknowledge it and put it in focus of their research, some push it to the background while some even hide and mask the city identity, pursuing research with a more general super-local aspiration.

Part III of the book, titled *Multilingual strategies*, is, probably, closest to what was usually meant when talking about language choices and strategies employed by people to communicate in different situations, starting from pioneering works of Joshua Fishman (1965) and Susan Gal (1979). In multilingual settings, speakers can choose between different languages, varieties, registers, or individual language items, depending on what seems more appropriate for them in a given situation. Their choices, however, are neither free from societal constrains, nor, on the other hand, totally determined by them. Global processes of language maintenance, shift or language revival occur in countless everyday interactions when people give preference to one code over another, or use them both alongside each other.

Birnie's chapter on the use of Gaelic and English in Stornoway – the largest town in Comhairle nan Eilean Siar, the only region of Scotland where a majority of the population self-reported to be able to speak Gaelic – reveals exactly those complicated relations between individual strategies and societal norms. In the course of a unique multimodal study, the author has collected ethnographic data in a selection of public spaces in the town to evaluate how, when and by whom Gaelic is used in this community. Unsurprisingly, she finds that English is a default language for most public spaces despite rather strong positions of Gaelic in in-group communication. However, not all public places are totally dominated by English. Aiming to reverse the language shift, some Scottish organisations actively promote the use of Gaelic among their employees, and in such places – where speaking Gaelic has become a linguistic norm – it could be also used for communication with the members of the public.

Another chapter dealing with a community undergoing language shift, Strandberg and Gooskens's chapter on the use of Swedish in Finland, takes a somewhat different approach. It focuses on the changes resulting from urbanisation of historically Swedish-speaking coastal regions and the increase in bilingualism among their population. Finland-Swedes have traditionally held a strong linguistically anchored ethnic identity, but Finland-Swedish features in their speech are frequently stigmatised, due to being considered non-standard Swedish. There are evidences that (near-)native bilingualism may influence both vowel production and perception in Finland-Swedish. The chapter provides an overview of how regular the use of and switching between Finnish and Finland-Swedish encourages bilingual speakers to make adjustments to their Swedish as well as developing their new bilingual awareness.

The next chapter – Liskovets and Fedorova's longitudinal study of language use and speakers' attitudes in the Belarusian capital of Minsk – reveals a rather paradoxical situation: being an official state language of Belarus, Belarusian in

Minsk can be seen as a minority language although there are some evidences of its gaining more power recently, especially since for many citizens it has become the symbol of opposition to a politically oppressive regime. In most everyday situations, people use Russian or the so-called 'Trasyanka' variety, a mixed vernacular resulting from contacts between two closely related Slavonic languages, Russian and Belarusian. The chapter focuses on the use of this variety, which, due to its dubious status and low prestige, has become an instrument of social stigmatisation of its speakers. In the eyes of many Minsk citizens, Trasyanka is a corrupted version of either Russian or Belarusian, and thus, confronted by two strictly normative language ideologies, even speakers of this variety themselves see it as an objectionable phenomenon due to disappear in the near future.

The last chapter in this section – Dovalil's study on intercultural communication in the city of Prague – deals with communication strategies used in interactions between the local people working in tourist services, particularly cafés and restaurants, and foreign tourists. Based on ethnographic data structured along the analytical categories of Language Management Theory (Fairbrother, Nekvapil and Sloboda 2018), the research concentrates on how the Czech speakers and their foreign customers manage language, communicative and socio-cultural problems taking place in their encounters. The results show that both foreign tourists and the Czech staff predominantly use English as a lingua franca to fulfil basic communication functions in mutual interactions. In some situations, though, they resort to other languages (German, Russian, Czech, Slovak) and, importantly, to electronic devices. Such devices help to solve manifold difficulties in interactions by taking advantage of the written medium, thus making communication both transmodal and translingual.

Part IV of this volume, called *Linguistic landscapes*, may look like a step aside from individuals and towards a more 'impersonal' approach to sociolinguistic data. In fact, however, it pursues the same theme of linguistic choices made by individuals but with the focus on written use of languages in urban public spaces. Essentially, the studies in this part follow the tenets of Ethnographic Linguistic Landscape Analysis (Blommaert and Maly 2015) going beyond mere observations on language use on the public signs placed around the city and revealing more profound conclusions about the people who write and read the signs.

The first chapter by Fedorova and Baranova deals with the representation of foreign languages in the linguistic landscapes of the twin border cities of Ivangorod and Narva on the Russian-Estonian border. The authors focus on language ideologies and their impact on local communication practices. They find that both Russia and Estonia adhere to quite a strict monolingual policy, not favouring diversity in public language use. Narva, populated mostly by Russian speakers, reveals an evident mismatch between official language policy and actual communication patterns. The diversity of its linguistic landscape is created mainly by private actors, with businesses playing a major role. On the other hand, Ivangorod, despite being a border city, looks almost like an outpost of monolingualism. Both city officials and business actors totally avoid using Estonian. In the rare cases when they go beyond the strict one-language policy, they resort to English and not the language of the neighbouring country.

The next chapter, written by the same two authors, takes us up to the North, alongside the Russian border, where there is Vyborg, a small city situated very close to the border with Finland. In the 1990s, the town was quite popular among Finnish tourists but nowadays tourism is in decline, and the city's economy is in a rather poor state. In their research, the authors find that the use of languages other than Russian, especially in public places, is often limited and emblematic, both in official and in commercial signs. In some cases, Finnish is literally even erased from some signs in the city centre. However, local business actors use some Finnish in their commercial signs and advertisements. In the absence of official support to multilingualism, individuals responsible for creating commercial signs become principal actors in the changing of a monolingual façade, challenging gradually deepening patterns of language attitudes and monolingual ideology in general.

The third chapter, by van Meurs, Planken and Lasarzewski, goes further in studying individuals' agency in constructing meaning via linguistic landscape. Specifically, the chapter investigates the motivations underlying business naming practices. This is done through interviews with business owners in the city of Mainz, Germany. A qualitative analysis shows that these reasons can be classified as relating to presentation of self; theory of good reason (i.e., to create an effect on potential customers); properties of name (such as its 'good' sound or brevity); links between business name and products sold; trends in naming; references to owners' or family members' names; and references to the location of businesses. The authors suggest that each business owner's specific reasons for choosing a business name are a matter of individual agency which allows us to see the urban spaces as populated and signed by acting individuals rather than abstract social or ethnic groups.

Part V, *Global processes and sound change*, deals with a combination of the sociologically broad and the linguistically narrow, namely the phonetic. Global changes effectuate a growing interest in the city and spreading city norms. In the end, these developments inevitably bring about linguistic change, through choices – conscious and subconscious – that individuals make. An interesting area that deals with the conscious and subconscious is subtle pronunciation variation. A speaker may find herself changing her vowels and consonants, or others point out that she does (because she wasn't aware), and after awareness has settled, pronunciation choices become more pertinent. The final three chapters of this volume describe these low-level changes that often go from too small to notice, to noticeable and marked, and, finally, to noticeable and unmarked.

The chapter by Hu and Smakman discusses the tendencies of immigrants to Beijing adopting the salient and marked Beijing postvocalic /r/, even if their own dialect does not contain such an /r/. This radical pronunciation change by individuals is considered socially acceptable despite its salience. The chapter reminds us that studying a phoneme in a specific phonological context cannot be done without taking into consideration linguistic aspects. In other words, simply counting the occurrences of the phoneme in question and describing its acoustic features is not sufficient in the way that it was when Labov (1966) did his New York study. The Beijing results show a clear power struggle between the de-rhoticisation tendencies due to the influx of non-rhotic speakers and the official promotion of standard Chinese, which does not have this prominent feature.

The choice between /q/ versus /g/ and the option to affricate /t/ in the Arabic as spoken in the city of Temara, Morocco, is the next illustration of change at the semi-conscious pronunciation level. In this chapter, Falchetta explains how Temara men under 39 relatively often show innovative tendencies in these respects. The author links these linguistic choices to the evolution of the urban environment surrounding the younger informants. Older and younger generations Temareses have been raised in very different social and material contexts. However, Falchetta suggests that a relatively conservative stance is assumed by both older and some younger interviewees towards modernisation and that discourses may contribute to widening the gap between the evolution of social and linguistic habits, on the one hand, and the people's attitudes towards them, on the other.

Mitsova et al. explain how a language norm, namely unvocalised /l/, is promoted as a reality and a norm by ordinary Bulgarian speakers when asked about it. But these same speakers in their answers to this question do not systematically use the phoneme in question. Instead, vocalised /l/ is more or less a default unwritten norm, i.e. it is widespread in all social layers. This final chapter of the volume shows how individual speakers are struggling to find their way between proclaimed and real-life norms but find the proclaiming more important than the actual usage; they do not practice what they preach. Rather than viewing reality as it is, they prefer to say that they meet the norm.

1.3 Covid/Corona

Contributions to this volume are based on the presentations given at the *Globalising Sociolinguistics* conference held at the University of Leiden in December 2018, and their first drafts were submitted in the second half of 2019. Thus, in principle, the contributions to this volume reflect the linguistic or social situation as it was before the outbreak of the global Corona virus pandemic. So, it may be appropriate to pose the question whether or to what extent this pandemic may have changed the findings of the pre-pandemic research. Of course, an answer along these lines should be formulated on the basis of proper empirical research. Nevertheless, we would like to dare a few remarks based on general linguistic evidence and our knowledge of the research sites that we observe more or less continuously.

Obviously, some linguistic phenomena resist rapid social changes more and some less. For example, the sound phenomena in the linguistic behavior of the individuals that the authors addressed in the last part of this volume can hardly be expected to change during such a short period. On the other hand, change in communicative patterns might be pervasive. This could be observed, for example, in Prague, from where foreign tourists almost disappeared, and, as a result, for more than one year the communicative and management strategies addressed in Dovalil's chapter were suspended, and it remains to be seen how the situation will evolve. Or we could ask to what extent linguistic landscape has changed during the pandemic. This is closely connected to the economic measures of individual countries and their different attitudes to privately owned businesses such as shops, restaurants or cafes, that is, businesses that contribute a lot to the semiotic appearance of the city streets. The government of the Czech Republic supported private businesses on a vast scale, so most of them have survived. The linguistic landscape of Hradec Králové, examined in Nekvapil's chapter, has changed in some details but these are rather due to a usual dynamic of linguistic landscape in the market economy than to the Corona virus pandemic, and have not changed values of the 'perception scale of the representation of individual languages in the linguistic landscape of Hradec Králové' worked out on the pre-pandemic data collected in the city.

In the city of Haarlem, as for another example, change is not likely to have taken place, as the city is visited mainly by locals and long-time inhabitants of the Netherlands. Smakman's contribution presented a city that is not at the centre of attention and would like to remain in that position. What is true is that this city's centre was visited less than before during the pandemic, so intercultural contact as well as similar-culture contact will have been less than before. It is unlikely that this will have had an effect, and it is also unlikely that the city has changed its linguistic or other landscape in any serious way, except for the signs related to Corona.

The impact of Corona restrictions on border cities such as Narva and Ivangorod, as examined by Fedorova and Baranova, was rather severe. The constant flow of people and goods through the border literally stopped in March 2020, barring the city dwellers and their important economic resources. Deserted border check-points and closed shops, cafes, and car insurance agencies became a new reality. Even the sign showing the distance to the Estonian capital in Ivangorod was demolished, or simply fell down and is now placed on the ground near the bus station, looking as a sad symbol of the new world where destinations cannot be reached anymore.

At the same time, there are some evidences that while physical spaces became empty and their linguistic diversity may decline due to the lack of tourism and all the new difficulties migrants had to face, digital communication and virtual linguistic landscapes flourished. Unable to interact face-to-face, people more and more resorted to CMC of all possible kinds – texting and voice and video calls became a primary routine. Struggling to survive, shops and restaurants had to develop online ordering and delivery services, and adding options to use different languages helped to embrace a wider audience.

It seems interesting, in other words, to research how anonymous cities and well-known cities recover linguistically from the pandemic, because the pandemic is often said to have changed people's general outlook on life and living.

An important motivation behind this volume is bringing to the surface sociolinguistic situations in lesser known places. Such areas are receiving much attention but not the attention they deserve on the basis of their population size and general sociolinguistic uniqueness (Smakman 2015). Somehow, the corona situation emphasises the lack of urgency felt when it comes to lesser known areas, or areas lower on the Human Development Index (http://hdr.undp.org/en/content/human-development-index-hdi). For as this volume is being finalised, 'the West' has started to report triumphantly on having conquered the virus, and these reports are followed by reports on large places like India and South America, where the virus is peaking. This reporting on some non-Western areas illustrates once again how these areas are commonly treated as by-the-way rather than points of first concern. We would be happy if this volume became a small step in another direction, to a more open-minded, equal and inclusive approach in studies on languages, people and places.

1.4 Acknowledgements

We would like to thank all our contributors for the tremendous efforts they put into writing and revising their chapters. Special thanks are due to reviewers of individual chapters, including Marián Sloboda. We are grateful to the University of Leiden Centre for Linguistics (LUCL) for helping to organise the conference *Globalising Sociolinguistics: Communication in the City*, where earlier versions of most of the chapters in this volume were presented. The work on this volume was supported by the Strategic Partnership established between the Charles University in Prague and the University of Leiden.

June 2021

References

Blommaert, Jan, and Ico Maly. 2015. 'Ethnographic Linguistic Landscape Analysis and Social Change: A Case Study.' In *Language and Superdiversity*, edited by Karel Arnaut, Jan Blommaert, Ben Rampton and Massimiliano Spotti, 197–217. New York, London: Routledge.

Brookes, Heather. 2014. 'Urban Youth Languages in South Africa: A Case Study of Tsotsitaal in a South African Township.' *Anthropological Linguistics* 56(3–4): 356–388.

Fairbrother, Lisa, Jiří Nekvapil, and Marián Sloboda. 2018. 'Methodology in Language Management Research.' In *The Language Management Approach. A Focus on Research Methodology*, edited by Lisa Fairbrother, Jiří Nekvapil and Marián Sloboda, 15–39. Berlin: Peter Lang.

Fishman, Joshua A. 1965. 'The Relationship between Micro- and Macro-Sociolinguistics in the Study of Who Speaks What Language to Whom and When.' *Linguistics* 2: 67–88.

Gal, Susan. 1979. *Language Shift. Social Determinants of Linguistic Change in Bilingual Austria*. San Francisco: Academic Press.

Goodwin, Charles. 2018. *Co-Operative Action*. New York: Cambridge University Press.

Guitarte, Guillermo. 1955. 'El ensordecimiento del zaísmo porteño [The silencing of Buenosairean Zaísmo].' *Revista de Filología Española* 39: 261–283.

Holmberg, Henrik. 1991. 'The Sociophonetics of Some Vowel Variables in Copenhagen Speech.' In *The Copenhagen Study in Urban Sociolinguistics*, edited by Frans Gregersen and Inge Lise Pedersen, 107–240. København: C. A. Reitzels forlag.

Irvine, Judith T., and Susan Gal. 2000. 'Language Ideology and Linguistic Differentiation.' In *Regimes of Language. Ideologies, Polities, and Identities*, edited by Paul V. Kroskrity, 35–84. Santa Fe: School of American Research Press.

Kallmeyer, Werner, ed. 1994. *Kommunikation in der Stadt. Teil 1: Exemplarische Analysen des Sprachverhaltens in Mannheim [Communication in the City. Volume 1: Exemplary Investigations in the Linguistic Behavior in Mannheim]*. Berlin, New York: Walter de Gruyter.

Labov, William. 1966. *The Social Stratification of English in New York*. Washington, DC: Center for Applied Linguistics.

Massey, Doreen B. 2005. *For Space*. London: Sage.

Nekvapil, Jiří, and Tamah Sherman, eds. 2015. 'The Language Management Approach: Perspectives on the Interplay of Bottom-up and Top-down.' *International Journal of the Sociology of Language* (232).

Neustupný, J. V. 2006. 'Sociolinguistic Aspects of Social Modernization.' In *Sociolinguistics: An International Handbook of the Science of Language and Society*, edited by Ulrich Ammon, Norbert Dittmar, Klaus J. Mattheier and Peter Trudgill, 2209–2224. Berlin, New York: Walter de Gruyter.

Pennycook, Alastair. 2018. *Posthumanist Applied Linguistics*. Abingdon, New York: Routledge.

Pereira, Cristophe. 2007. 'Urbanization and Dialect Change: The Arabic Dialect of Tripoli (Libya).' In *Arabic in the City: Issues in Dialect Contact and Language Variation*, edited by Cathrine Miller and Enam Al-Wer. London, New York: Routledge.

Sibata, Takesi. 1958. *Nihon no hōgen [Dialects of Japan]*. Tokyo: Iwanami.

Smakman, Dick. 2015. 'The Westernising Mechanisms in Sociolinguistics.' In *Globalising Sociolinguistics. Challenging and Expanding Theory*, edited by Dick Smakman and Patrick Heinrich. London: Routledge.

Smakman, Dick, and Patrick Heinrich, eds. 2015. *Globalising Sociolinguistics. Challenging and Expanding Theory*. London: Routledge.

Smakman, Dick, and Patrick Heinrich, eds. 2018. *Urban Sociolinguistics. The City as a Linguistic Process and Experience*. London: Routledge.

Part I
Innovative language uses

2 Marginal spaces in small urban areas

Evidence from a refugee centre in Southern Italy

L. Iezzi

2.1 Introduction

2.1.1 The European migrant crisis

Within the past decade, migratory flows towards the European Union have acquired unique characteristics compared to previous movements, for example, with respect to the higher number of people involved, and the percentage of people who have lost their lives along the way in particular. An ever increasing number of migrants, here referred to as '*profughi*', people who leave their countries without documents and resources, and travel to Europe using precarious means of transport (Gentileschi 2009: 45–46), cross the Mediterranean or the Balkan peninsula to seek their fortune in the richer countries of the Union. Italy, due to its strategic geographical position, is often the first place of arrival for these people.

Until September 2018,[1] according to the 142/2015 legislative decree,[2] the reception system in Italy consisted of three phases:[3]

1. first aid and identification;
2. primary reception, provided by specific governmental centres for the time necessary to formalise their asylum or refugee request[4] and to officialise the identification and health status of the applicant;
3. secondary reception, provided by SPRAR (*Sistema di Protezione per Richiedenti Asilo e Rifugiati*, translatable as Protection System for Asylum Seekers and Refugees), whose aim is to promote integration of migrants within the host society.

Because of the high number of newcomers, the government has allowed Prefectures to establish additional temporary centres, the above-mentioned CAS, supervised by private organisations and institutions[5] which are given authority to manage these centres following a specific tender procedure.[6] These centres serve as temporary 'bridges' until migrants are sent to primary or secondary governmental reception centres. In contrast to the public centres, private CAS can accommodate a higher number of migrants, sometimes up

DOI: 10.4324/9780429348037-3

to a hundred, without having to distinguish them based on their origin or the type of request they want to make. Consequently, the CAS are multicultural and multilingual collective centres, where contact among different languages or varieties of languages is commonplace.

2.1.2 Research objectives

The present research concerns one of the numerous aspects regarding the European migrant crisis. Although different studies have been carried out in recent years, mainly concerning sociology, law and language acquisition within refugee centres, little attention has been given to sociolinguistic factors related to contact phenomena in speech within refugee centres. Therefore, this chapter aims to illustrate the preliminary outcomes of the analysis concerning the usage of the languages in the linguistic repertoire of a sample which includes migrants within a CAS, specifically the ones coming from Pakistan, who already come from a multilingual context where the use of at least three languages is commonplace. In particular, the author will provide an overview of the relationship between the languages involved, which role these languages play in the researched migrants' conversations, and what kinds of contact phenomena take place. Based on a qualitative analysis, I will identify general patterns and draw subsequent conclusions.

The data used for this research come from a corpus of 8 hours of recordings, made between May and September 2018 with a hidden voice recorder,[7] in a CAS located in a small *comune*[8] of Abruzzo, in southern Italy (3,049 inhabitants[9]). The Pakistani informants, who had been living in Italy for one and a half years at the time of the research, were aware of the investigation and the possible use of recording techniques (also in written form through a GDPR – General Data Protection Regulation – document), and they agreed to be recorded covertly. First, they were asked to complete an anonymous questionnaire about their Pakistani province of origin, linguistic background and self-evaluated knowledge of Italian. Second, spontaneous conversations both with and without fellow countrymen, and both with and without other refugees hosted in the centre or Italian workers or social assistants, were recorded in the absence of the researcher.[10] To analyse the recorded data, the researcher used the grammatical approach proposed by Muysken (2000), involving the three types of insertion on the one hand (which allows the researcher to identify the base language of interaction, and then the typology of mixing phenomena which take place), and the situational approach based on the concept of domain (Fishman 1972) described by Berruto (1990).

Since there is a lack of consensus on the nomenclature of contact phenomena in speech, the term 'code-mixing' will be used in the present study to refer to the grammatical analysis as proposed by Muysken. The term 'code alternation' will be used for the macro-sociolinguistic situational analysis, interpreted here as 'the alternation between two languages in accordance with, or in relation to, the speech event or the communicative context, or the interlocutor or addressee to whom you are talking'[11] (Berruto 1990, cited in Dal Negro and Guerini 2007: 39–40).

2.2 The sociolinguistic background

In order to understand the linguistic and sociocultural background of the subjects of this study, it is worth providing an overview of the historical and sociolinguistic context in Pakistan, the informants' birthplace.

2.2.1 Language policy and language use in Pakistan

The Islamic Republic of Pakistan is a federal republic composed of four provinces, namely Punjab, Khyber Pakhtunkhwa, Sindh and Balochistan, and three territories, namely the Islamabad Capital Territory, Gilgit-Baltistan and the disputed territory of Azad Kashmir. It is a multilingual country, with two official languages, Urdu and English (the first being national language too),[12] and more than seventy minority languages,[13] five of them spoken by the vast majority of the population of the country (more than 90%) as their mother tongue (Eberhard et al. 2019). Few of these languages are given the status of provincial languages, but, as Mansoor 2004 points out, they do not receive enough support by the state commissions set up by the government. While Urdu is the mother tongue of less than 8% of the entire population of the country (Rahman 2006), it was chosen as an official and national language (alongside English) to represent the symbol of identity in 1947, because it was the language of the powerful elite that guided the separatist rebellion. Even though it has been suggested that Urdu should have been kept as sole official and national language from 1971 (Baumgardner 1993), English was never abandoned because, as Baumgardner (1993: 14) points out, 'the anchorage of English in Pakistan is that the Constitution and the body of the law are codified in English, [...] and the large industrial and business sector operates in English', meaning that this language has kept its *status quo* of powerful and international language, highlighting the linguistic imperialism of English throughout the world (Phillipson 1992), and its symbolic power of globalisation and modernisation, making it a '*capital culturel*' (Bourdieu 1991). At the same time, the privileging and diffusion of Urdu has led to a paradoxical phenomenon: while before there was a quite stable diglossia (Ferguson 1959: 435), with Urdu and English being the high languages and the indigenous languages being the low languages, nowadays, even though there is still some ethnic resentment against the national language, the same indigenous people are favouring language shift. Young generations prefer to learn and speak Urdu, because it is seen as more important and useful, or, as Bourdieu (1991: 45) would put it, because '[the] state language becomes the theoretical norm against which all linguistic practices are objectively measured', meaning that heritage languages are implicitly given less importance and seen as not worth learning. This situation of *dilalia* (Berruto 1987: 61), in which a former high language is used in informal contexts alongside a low language, in combination with the strict language policy in Pakistan, has created a tripartite hierarchy. At the top there is the English language, as a result of the fact that imperialism still exerts some degree of influence; then there is the Urdu language (Rahman 2006), which ghettoises and devalues the minority languages, even the standardised and widely spoken ones, and paradoxically jeopardises multilingualism; at the bottom there are the 'minority languages' spoken all over the country.

2.2.2 The Punjabi language vitality

In the province of Punjab, in eastern Pakistan, Punjabi is the mother tongue of more than 75% of the population.[14] It is, however, not officially recognised in the Constitution of Pakistan and is seen as culturally inferior. For this reason, its use is prohibited in many Punjabi schools, not only by (head)teachers, but even by parents. The cultural shame in some urban areas is so high that if pupils speak Punjabi in school, they are quite vulgarly called *paindu*, an offensive term for people coming from the countryside or small villages which means 'rustic village yokel'. These explicitly authoritative language practices aggressively affect the language behaviour of the Punjabis, who think of their language as useless and prone to exclusion from the society (Rahman 2006).

This widespread feeling of inferiority by the population itself finds its roots in the language movements of the 1970s and 1980s, not supported by the Punjabi elites, that favoured the Urdu language, and whose followers forsook their ethnic identity (Punjabi) for a national identity (Pakistani) (Rahman 2006). Upon the partition of the British India (1947), even though Punjabi was the most spoken language not only in the Province but also in the country, it was not chosen as official or national language because the powerful elite behind the creation of the country did not want to support one indigenous ethnic group at the expense of others. In the early 1970s, Punjabi activists were in fact actively involved in such language planning decisions, although mainly concerning orthography and the compilation of modernised dictionaries, but this did not influence the final decision regarding the choice of national or official language. The Punjabi language movement continued through the 1980s and the 1990s, as Punjabis tried to obtain some sort of acceptance and acknowledgment of their language by the central government. However, to this day, the Punjabi language has not been recognised, and increasing numbers of Punjabi people nowadays despise their heritage language and see it as unimportant (Rahman 1997).

Even though the language policy into force risks marginalising Punjabi, the language is far from an endangered language. There are a number of reasons for this. First, it is the most spoken language in the country, with dozens of millions of speakers, even among younger generations, who speak it as their mother tongue. Second, even if not recognised and not used in high and formal contexts, Punjabi continues to be used as a low language in informal and domestic situations, and also in music, poetry and literature. Last but not least, the language has a very strong and powerful standardised form which is in official use in the bordering state of Punjab (India). As such, it is not in real and immediate danger, although it may be eventually.

2.2.3 The rise of a new variety

Analysing the questionnaire, it came out that all except three Pakistani informants of this study come from the same part of Pakistan. Six of them were born and grew up in the region of Punjab, and their mother tongue is (Western) Punjabi; of the other three, two were born in Azad Kashmir, and their mother tongue is a variety belonging to the Pahari macro-group, while the other was born in the city of Haripur in Khyber Pakhtunkhwa, and his mother tongue is a variety of (southern) Hindko. Even though the actual distance between their areas of origin is around 400kms, they all come from northern Pakistan, and the varieties of languages that they speak are closely related. Moreover, even the speakers coming from Azad Kashmir and Khyber Pakhtunkhwa spent some years in Gujranwala before leaving the country, and are fluent in Punjabi.

Gujranwala, the city where all of the informants grew up or spent some time before moving to Italy, is the fifth most populous city of Pakistan, situated some 80kms north of the Punjab provincial capital Lahore. The city has experienced a high degree of development and industrialisation in the past three decades, and thanks to its geographical and climatic features, it has seen a significant increase in urbanisation over the past years (Mirza et al. 2014). In fact, the flourishing growth of Pakistan's cities, both during the colonial period and after that, has led to a multiplicity of innovative and changing practices associated with urban life. Among these developing transformations, there is the emergence of new language varieties, stimulated by the complex linguistic situation of the contemporary cities, which attract a considerable number of people from rural areas, along with their linguistic and cultural background. Needless to say, another pivotal characteristic of the cities, and so also of Gujranwala, is that more people have access to schooling, which enhances the knowledge of the national language, namely Urdu, leading to some sort of Urduisation of the Punjabi spoken in cities and major towns. However, from a bottom-up perspective, even the varieties brought by people moving to these cities have an influence on the autochthonous variety, in terms of phonology, vocabulary and, when contact becomes more intense, even morpho-syntax. As in most post-colonial countries, and as already mentioned in the previous paragraphs, English maintains the role of official language of Pakistan as well, and it is used in the official domains of power (such as bureaucracy, government, etc.) as well as in private education. This situation has led to the creation of a language-based stratification, exacerbated by the two models of English-medium schooling and Urdu-medium schooling put in place by the first governors of Pakistan. This system favours only a small elite, and prolongs these inequalities by keeping the *status quo* of 'elite closure' (Myers-Scotton 1993) unchanged. The non-elitist classes in cities, who cannot afford to attend the expensive private English-medium schools and so attend the Urdu-medium ones, learn the English language as in any other country where it is not official, so as a foreign language; consequently their skills might or might not be very high, depending on what extent they find themselves exposed to it. This causes them to pick words and expressions from specific fields of knowledge, as well as common items, and make use of them in their conversations.

The above-mentioned linguistic environment has inevitably favoured the rise of a sort of new 'urban variety'. This 'urban variety' is nothing but a new variety of Punjabi with insertions from Urdu and English. While Punjabi provides most of the core vocabulary[15] and morpho-syntactic structures, Urdu provides lexical items referring to specific realities of Pakistan (like administrative subdivisions, legal procedures etc.), and only a few empty words[16] as a result of the centuries-old intense contact between the two languages; English, on the other hand, exclusively provides some nouns or some verbs (that are nominalised anyway), which are inserted seemingly without any specific socio-cultural reason.

From a sequential point of view, this new urban variety of Punjabi can be considered as an intermediate phase towards a 'mixed code' (Auer 1999), with the use of nonce borrowings[17] from English, and lexical items in Urdu instead of the corresponding ones in Punjabi.

As far as the nonce borrowings from English are concerned, considering the tripartite model proposed by Muysken (2000: 3), it is worth noticing that the subjects of this study make use of two types of insertions, namely single constituents, and morphological integrations.

In the recorded sample taken into account, the aforementioned new variety of Punjabi is the unmarked form chosen by the informants when talking to other people coming from Pakistan. The following extracts provide some examples of this new variety;[18] in all of the following situations, the speakers are from Pakistan, and there are neither refugees from other countries nor Italians. The letters representing the informants are casual and most of the time they are the first letters of their names.

(1) [A, B and D are sitting at the table and B is about to take a document and bring it with him]

    A: *Ai* **nā** *paipar* *nū* touch **nahiṇ** **kar-nā**!
       this not paper to   not to do-POT-M.SG
       Don't touch this piece of paper!

(2) [A and I are talking about job opportunities in Italy]

    A: **Har** *ćiz* *dī* **Terai** *ko* opportunity *ai*. [...]
       each thing of you-POSS to   to be-PRS.3SG
       Jithai **qānūn** **nahiṇ** *ai,*   *uthai* **terā**
       where law   not   to be-PRS.3SG there you-POSS

totally	**koi**	**vī**	**fāida**	**nahi̯ṇ**	ai.
	any	also	benefit	not	to be-PRS.3SG

Ais	**mulk**	**dā**	**āpnā**	**qānūn**	ai,
it-OBL	country	of	own	law	to be-PRS.3SG

baṟ-ā	**piār-ā**		**qānūn**		ai,
very-M.SG	beautiful-M.SG		law		to be-PRS.3SG

baṟ-ī	**piār-ī**	opportunity	ai.
very-F.SG	beautiful-F.SG		to be-PRS.3SG

People have opportunities for everything. […] Where there's no law, you don't have any benefits at all there. This country has its own law, very nice law, and there are very good opportunities. […]

I: *Aithai* tension **kyūṇ kis ćiz dai,**
here why any-OBL thing of
step by step *ai sārā.* […]
to be-PRS.3SG whole

Merī problem-āṇ **merī** tension-āṇ **Pākistān par** ai.
I-POSS problem-PL I-POSS tension-PL on to be-PRS.3SG
Why worry, everything is step by step. […] My problems and my tensions are in Pakistan.

(3) [A and C are talking about the languages used in driving schools]

A: **Brāvā,** *uthai* **Yūrap** *tai nahi̯ṇ nā samajh ai!*
brother here Europe on not not to understand to be-PRS.3SG
Brother, here in Europe they don't understand (anything)!

C: **Aglai nai Jirman dī zabān rakhī** ai.
next A German of language to keep-PRF to be-PRS.3SG
So they have kept the German language.

A: **Ćāćājī,** French *jiṇ ai* country *ai* **Frāns.**
uncle which this to be-PRS.3SG France
Anāṇ **nai** countr-*iāṇ* oh select *kitiāṇ* **nai**
they A country-PL that-PL to do-PST.PTCP A
jiṇ **kam nai.**
which less A
Uncle, French is the language of the country (France). They have selected countries which are less in number.

As seen from the extracts above, the Urdu and English insertions within a Punjabi frame do not seem to have any specific function, and they clearly represent nonce borrowings which do not alter the morpho-syntactic frame of the main language of conversation, in this case Punjabi. Moreover, the choice of Urdu and English cannot be interpreted as an interactional strategy to fill in lexical gaps, since the items exist in Punjabi, and the speakers have access to them. The presence of these occurrences demonstrates that a new urban variety, used by younger generations, who are more educated and exposed to the official languages compared to their contemporaries who live in rural areas or do not have access to schooling, is rising, and it may eventually lead to a sort of 'mixed code' (Auer 1999).

2.3 Contact phenomena within the refugee centre

As mentioned before, CAS can accommodate a very high number of migrants within the same building. This makes immigrants communicate with a wide range of people having different languages and different backgrounds, and to make use of all the linguistic resources at their disposal through various strategies, sometimes alternating different languages with different speakers, sometimes mixing more languages within the same speech event. The examples provided below belong to the same corpus collected in the CAS where the migrants are settled.

When dealing with the analysis of the part of the corpus in which the Italian language is present, an explicative approach has been followed, as done before with Urdu and English. It can be seen that Italian is used insertionally in the urban variety of Punjabi when communicating with other Pakistani people, whereas it is used as sole means of communication when talking to other refugees and Italian-speaking people. As far as the grammatical analysis is concerned, the grammatical model proposed by Muysken (2000), which has already been used for the description of the new urban variety of Punjabi, has been applied to the data collected in the centre as well. As far as the socio-functional analysis is concerned, since it is not always possible to define the reasons behind particular choices with reference to previous models aimed at schematising certain behaviours, in this chapter I only focus on code alternation connected to interlocutors and situational event.

To schematise the linguistic panorama in which the Pakistani informants taken into account find themselves, a very complex triglossic situation could be drawn, exemplified in Table 2.1:

Table 2.1 Adaptation of the model proposed by Mioni (1988: 300) for African countries

H	Urdu	(Standard) Italian	(Standard) English
M	Punjabi	Pakistani English	
L	Minority languages of Pakistan	Dialect of Abruzzo	

The diglossic model (H language and L language), is further expanded with the addition of a M language that serves as *lingua franca*

Marginal spaces in small urban areas 23

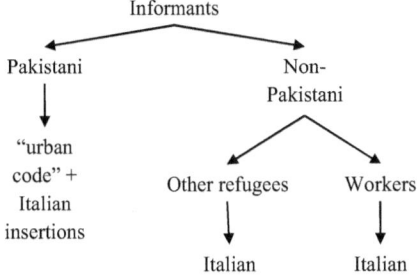

Figure 2.1 Language choices by the informants.

Of course, informants do not speak the dialect from the Italian village, because Italian people refrain from speaking it to them, except for some colloquial expression denoting ludic usage; further, as we have previously seen, speakers do not use the resources in their repertoire as if they were watertight compartments, but they make use of various communicative strategies, like the creation of the new urban Punjabi variety. Upon their arrival in Italy, the informants introduced the Italian language in their repertoire, especially by communicating with other people within and outside the centre, watching TV and doing some work with local farmers. These migrants have adopted the same strategies used in their country, specifically the insertion of Italian lexical items within the urban Punjabi frame, and the use of Italian as *lingua franca* with Italian workers in the centre and refugees coming from other countries. This is shown in Figure 2.1.

2.3.1 Code-mixing

Looking at the interaction data from a linguistic point of view, it is immediately clear that the Pakistani immigrants researched here are making use of the Italian language as they previously did with Urdu and English while in Pakistan, meaning that Italian is becoming part of their speech variety via insertions of single items or small fixed expressions. The following examples show this process:

(4) [two informants are talking about their job in Italy while filling in the questionnaire]

    C: ITALIA   *aithai*   LAVORO   *kar-nā?*
           Italy   here   job   to do-INF
           The job I do here in Italy?

    A: LAVORO   CAMPAGNA!
           Job   countryside
           I have got a job in the countryside.

C: CAMPAGNA *maiṇ* *kuć* *ćalāndā*!
countryside in carriage to drive-PRS-M.SG
I drive vans[19] in the countryside.

(5) [two informants are talking about a document that they have left somewhere]

D: CARTOLINA[20] *ćhaḍ* *diyā*!
paper / document to leave-STEM to do-PST.PTCP
We have forgotten the document!

C: Oh, CARTOLINA *kithai* *ćhaḍ* *diyā?*
paper / document where to leave-STEM to do-PST.PTCP
Oh, where did we leave the document?

As the above extracts show, the usage of Italian items mainly concerns words related to doing a job (e.g.: LAVORO, CAMPAGNA) and bureaucracy (e.g.: CARTOLINA), words that belong to specific semantic fields associated with domains in which migrants find themselves daily, both inside and outside the centre. This usage of Italian seems particularly interesting because speakers are well aware of their Punjabi counterparts (as they are when inserting Urdu and English items), but they still decide to use words in the new language as part of their repertoire.

2.3.2 Code alternation

From a socio-functional point of view, it is worth noting on the basis of the recorded data how Italian functions as *lingua franca*[21] within the centre, for Italian speakers (workers at the centre, social assistants, lawyers etc.) and for refugees (regardless of their origin and their linguistic background), even if many refugees from Africa share the English language with the informants of this research. The following example shows how the speakers choose the languages in their repertoire according to the speech event and the interlocutors, and it also shows their considerable fluency in the Italian language even without formal education within the centre. The lack of formal education in Italian and their acquisition of the language through daily activities are also confirmed by the questionnaire that they filled in.

(6) [two Pakistani informants are talking to O, an Italian worker from the centre]

O: TU VUOI CHIEDERE IL
you to want-PRS.2SG to ask-INF the
PERMESSO DI SOGGIORNO PERCHÉ POI
residence permit because then

VUOI　　　　　　　　CHIEDERE　　　IL　　　CONTRATTO.
to want-PRS.2SG　　to ask-INF　　　the　　contract
You want to obtain the residence permit in order to ask for a contract.

A: CONTRATTO　CON　　AZIENDA,　QUANDO
   Contract　　with　　firm　　　　when
   IO　　PRESO,　　　　　　　SUBITO　　ANDARE　　AZIENDA!
   I　　to take-PST.PTCP　　soon　　　to go-INF　　firm
   Contract with a firm, once I get it (*the permit*) I'll go immediately to the firm.

O: HAI　　　　　　　　TROVATO　　　　　　QUALCHE　　AZIENDA?
   to have-PRS.2SG　　to find-PST.PTCP　any　　　　　firm
   Have you found any firm (already)?

A: SÌ　ATESSA!
   yes
   Yes, in Atessa!

O: ANCHE　IO　VENIRE　　　　CON　　TE,　　DOVE?
   also　　I　　to come-INF　with　　you　　where
   I'm coming with you, where?

A: CINQUINA!
   Cinquina

O: CINQUINA　TRASPORTI²²?
   Cinquina　　transports

A: 50% COSÌ,　　ADESSO…　PARLARE,　　　TRATTAZIONE…
   like this　　now　　　　to talk-INF　　discussion
   50% like this, now they have to talk…

O: BUONO!　PER　　FARE　　　　CHE?
   good　　　for　　to do-INF　what
   Good! To do what?

A: PACCO!
   Package
   Packaging!

O: AH, IMBALLAGGI,　PREPARARE　　　　IMBALLAGGI.
   packaging　　　　to prepare-INF　　Packaging
   Ah, packaging, preparing packaging.

A: [talking to I]
   Tū　　kī　　kar　　　　　　rihā　　　　　　　　　　ō?
   you　　what　to do-STEM　　AUX.PROG-M.SG　　to be-PRS.2SG
   What are you doing?

I: **Maiṇ   kāfī   pī   rihā   āṇ!**
    I   coffee to drink-STEM   AUX.PROG-M.SG   to be-PRS.1SG
    I'm drinking coffee!

A: [talking to O]
   GUARDA!   GUARDA!   LUI!
   to look-IMP   to look-IMP   he-OBJ
   Look at him!

The extract above shows that the migrants in the CAS use the Italian language as a means of communication with people not belonging to their group or community. Despite the presence of English in their repertoire (which may as well function as *lingua franca* with English-speaking African refugees, or as an additional strategy if the Italian word is unknown), it is never used when speaking to people from other countries, and Italian becomes the high language to be used in all the domains in which people with different mother tongues happen to be together.

2.4 Conclusion

The analysis of the linguistic repertoire of a sample of Pakistani migrants, living in a CAS in Abruzzo, has shown the high complexity of their repertoire. It is originally resourced in the basis of at least three languages (Punjabi, Urdu and English), to which Italian is added upon arrival. The analyses showed how Pakistani informants use an urban variety of Punjabi amongst each other, made up of Punjabi as the base language, and insertions from Urdu and English. This variety is widely used in big cities of Punjab. It is suggested that, over time, this situation may eventually contribute to the creation of a 'mixed code', as described by Auer (1999). The analysis of the data has also shown how this new urban variety of Punjabi (which is different from the standardised variety of the language, and of course from Urdu and English as well) is the sole unmarked choice for the Pakistani speakers, as it is always used for intracommunity communication.

Looking at the interaction and questionnaire data, it can be argued that the migrants do not speak the Abruzzese dialect, which is considered a 'we-code' (Gumperz 1982) of the local Italian people. On the other hand, they have learnt spoken Italian quite well, and the language has become a very important resource in their repertoire, as evidenced by the fact that they make use of it through two strategies. From a socio-functional point of view, Italian serves as a lingua franca for interethnic communication, even with speakers who can express themselves in English. From a grammatical point of view, and in the same way that Urdu and English are utilised in the new urban variety emerging in Pakistan, Italian has become part of the 'medium' (Gafaranga 2007) of conversation among fellow countrymen, through insertions of single items or short expressions, often referring to a specific semantic domain.

It follows that these contact phenomena, encountered within the conversations of the migrants settled in extraordinary refugee centres, define how these newcomers make use of all the resources available, both in terms of mixing and in terms of alternation. They do so not only as a response to their situation of mobility, but also to demonstrate their willingness to integrate into the new society and positively contribute to it, even though they come from a different background. The contact phenomena analysed before can also be seen as part of a recurring linguistic process within CAS, where multiculturalism and multilingualism are the norm.

However, further research has to be carried out in order to understand better the possible evolution of these language contact phenomena in refugee centres, like the ones presented in this contribution, and to underline how even in small urban areas there is a wide range of phenomena which contribute to the evolution of the new globalised society.

2.5 Acknowledgements

I wish to express my deep gratitude to Prof. Carmela Perta, my supervisor, for supporting me and giving me constructive and inspirational advice throughout my PhD studies. I am extremely grateful to Prof. Joseph Gafaranga, for he devoted his time to helping me during my visiting programme at the University of Edinburgh. Of course, I also owe an immense debt of gratitude to the editors of this volume, my informants, my family, my precious helpers Somia and Sidra, and my friends.

Notes

1 For further information on the new 113/2018 legislative decree proposed by Salvini, please refer to www.gazzettaufficiale.it/eli/id/2018/10/04/18G00140/sg.
2 According to the Italian constitutional law, a legislative decree is a normative act, issued by the Government (executive power) through authorisation by the Parliament, which produces legal effects.
3 Further information is available on www.openpolis.it/parole/che-cosa-sono-i-cas-lo-sprar-e-gli-hotspot/ and https://openmigration.org/glossary-term/centri-di-accoglienza-straordinaria-cas/ .
4 According to the UNHCR regulation (mentioned in Gentileschi 2009: 48), migrants can request the status of asylum seekers, refugees, or beneficiaries of humanitarian protection.
5 For example, *Consorzio Matrix Cooperativa Sociale*.
6 Tender procedures (in Italian *gara di appalto*) refer to the processes whereby the government chooses the best company or business to fulfil a job, among several businesses which offer bids.
7 Authorisation was asked to the informants and the heads of the organisation managing the centre before the beginning of the study, through a General Data Protection Regulation specifically created for this purpose.
8 *Comune*, in this specific case of Torino di Sangro translatable as 'village', is the basic administrative division in Italy.

9 ISTAT 2018.
10 The recorder was switched on by a third party, not included in the conversation, or by the researcher before leaving the place.
11 Here and elsewhere, all translations from Italian are my own.
12 For the aim of this research, we consider national language the language "associated with a particular country where it is recognised as a symbol of national identity" (Swann et al. 2004: 219), whereas the official language as the language "used for political, legal and administrative communications within a given political territory" (Swann et al. 2004: 227).
13 Here generally defined as 'a language which is spoken by a numerical minority or by a politically subordinate group' (Swann et al. 2004: 206).
14 It is also the mother tongue of 48% of the whole population of Pakistan.
15 For a definition of 'core vocabulary' refer to Yorkston et al. 1988.
16 Matthews, 2014.
17 Here defined as items which have not come to be integrated into the other language, as in Poplack et al. 1988.
18 Henceforth, Punjabi will be written in cursive, Urdu in bold, English in normal font, words belonging to both Punjabi and Urdu in bold cursive, and Italian in capital letters.
19 The speaker probably refers to a tractor or some sort of van.
20 The literal translation for the word '*cartolina*' would be 'postcard', but it is here interpreted as a folder, a document, because the word '*cartellina*' in Italian means 'binder, folder', so it might be a mispronunciation of this word.
21 Here interpreted as 'any form of language serving as a means of communication between speakers of different languages' (Swann et al. 2004: 184).
22 *Cinquina Trasporti* is the name of the company.

References

Auer, Peter (1999) From code-switching via language mixing to fused lects: towards a dynamic typology of bilingual speech. *International Journal of Bilingualism*, 3 (4), pp. 309–332.

Baumgardner, Robert (1993) *The English Language in Pakistan*. Karachi: Oxford University Press.

Berruto, Gaetano (1987) *Sociolinguistica dell'italiano contemporaneo*. Roma: La Nuova Italia Scientifica.

Berruto, Gaetano (1990) Italiano regionale, commutazione di codice e enunciati mistilingue. In: *L'italiano regionale, Atti del XVIII Congresso Internazionale di Studi della Società di Linguistica Italiana*. Michele Cortellazzo and Alberto Mioni (eds.), pp. 105–130.

Bourdieu, Pierre (1991) *Language and Symbolic Power*. Harvard: Harvard University Press.

Dal Negro, Silvia and Guerini, Federica (2007) *Contatto. Dinamiche ed esiti del plurilinguismo*. Roma: Aracne.

Eberhard, David, Simons, Gary and Fennig, Charles (eds.) (2019) *Ethnologue. Languages of the World*. Dallas: SIL International.

Ferguson, Charles Albert (1959) Diglossia. *Word*, 15, pp. 325–340.

Fishman, Joshua (1972) Domains and the relationship between micro- and macro-sociolinguistics. In *Directions in Sociolinguistics*. John Gumperz and Dell Hymes (eds.), pp. 435–453. Oxford: Blackwell.
Gafaranga, Joseph (2007) *Talk in Two Languages*. Basingstoke: Palgrave Macmillan.
Gentileschi, Maria Luisa (2009) *Geografia delle migrazioni*. Roma: Carocci.
Gumperz, John (1982) *Discourse Strategies*. Cambridge: Cambridge University Press.
ISTAT (2018). Annuario Statistico Italiano 2018. Roma: ISTAT.
Mansoor, Sabiha (2004). The status and role of regional languages in higher education in Pakistan. *Journal of Multilingual and Multicultural Development*, 25(4), 333–353.
Matthews, Peter (ed.) (2014) *The Concise Oxford Dictionary of Linguistics*. Oxford: Oxford University Press.
Mioni, Alberto (1988). Standardisation processes and linguistic repertoires in Africa and Europe: some comparative remarks. In *Variation and Convergence: Studies in Social Dialectology*. Auer, Peter and Di Luzio, Aldo (eds.), pp. 293–320. Berlin: De Gruyter,
Mirza, Faisal Mehmood, Jaffri, Atif Ali and Hashmi, Muhammad Saim (2014) *An Assessment of Industrial Employment Skill Gaps among University Graduates in the Gujrat – Sialkot – Gujranwala Industrial Cluster, Pakistan*. Washington D.C.: International Food Policy Research Institute.
Muysken, Pieter (2000) *Bilingual Speech. A Typology of Code-mixing*. Cambridge: Cambridge University Press.
Myers-Scotton, Carol (1993) *Social Motivations for Codeswitching. Evidence from Africa*. Oxford: Clarendon Press.
Phillipson, Robert (1992) *Linguistic Imperialism*. Oxford: Oxford University Press.
Poplack, Shana, Sankoff, David and Miller, Christopher (1988) The social correlates and linguistic processes of lexical borrowing and assimilation. *Linguistics*, 26, pp. 47–104.
Rahman, Tariq (1997) Language and ethnicity in Pakistan. *Asian Survey*, 37(9), pp. 833–839.
Rahman, Tariq (2006) Language policy, multilingualism and language vitality in Pakistan. *Trends in Linguistics Studies and Monographs*, 175.
Swann, Joan, Deumert, Ana, Lillis, Theresa and Mesthrie, Rajend (2004) *A Dictionary of Sociolinguistics*. Edinburgh: Edinburgh University Press.
Yorkston, Kathryn, Dowden, Patricia, Honsinger, Melissa, Marriner, Nola and Smith, Kathleen (1988) A comparison of standard and user vocabulary lists. *Augmentative and Alternative Communication*, 4, pp. 189–210.

3 Urban language practices online?
Multilingualism among German-Namibians in computer-mediated communication

H. Radke

3.1 Introduction

Urban areas are an interesting starting point for research on multilingualism since they constitute 'sociolinguistic systems in their own right' (Smakman and Heinrich 2017, 1). Smakman and Heinrich conclude that '[t]he city is more diverse than mainstream sociolinguistic theories have portrayed it to be (ibid., 2015, 186).' Recent research reflects the potential of contemporary urban settings for the understanding of multilingual practices. To give an example, studies on the urban variety of *Kiezdeutsch* have shown the sociolinguistic interplay between migrant languages and older German varieties in cities such as Berlin (Freywald et al. 2011; Wiese 2012; Wiese et al. 2014). They allow for a comparison with other recent and historic vernaculars in urban (youth) culture such as *Straattaal* in the Netherlands. Observations on such multilingual practices in urban settings are reflected in the notion of metrolingualism which 'posits the contemporary city as a key site of creative and "fluid" language practices' (Androutsopoulos 2015: 186). However, multilingual practices are not exclusively limited to urban settings and can be found in rural areas, as well. Two examples from Europe: the majority of individuals who live in the rural Dutch province of Friesland are bilingual speakers of Frisian and Dutch (Breuker 2001; Bosma et al. 2017: 3). Some rural areas within the German federal states of Brandenburg and Saxony are bilingual and provide spaces for individuals to use both the Sorbian and the German language in their daily life. In fact, rural multilingualism is a global phenomenon and should therefore also be approached by novel perspectives on linguistic in-group speech. In many postcolonial African countries, rural multilingualism is a rule rather than an exception. However, Di Carlo, Good and Ojong Diba (2017: 1) note that 'sociolinguistic research on this topic has concentrated mostly on urbanised areas, even though [...] rural multilingualism is clearly of much older provenance than its urban counterpart'.

This chapter strives to extend the focus on urban multilingual practices by applying them to rural multilingualism. It argues that urban and rural areas are not necessarily isolated phenomena. In many cases, they are interconnected

DOI: 10.4324/9780429348037-4

through what I call *Networks of Exchange (NoE)*. This term is usually used in the context of trade history and focusses on the 'the rich networks of people, goods, and ideas that were exchanged' across continents and oceans throughout history (Galavan 2019: 90). In some cases, these exchanges led to the evolution of new, multilingual societies, especially during the colonial era. The German-speaking minority in Namibia is just one of many examples of such a community. Within this context, the term NoE receives a special connotation: it emphasises the *interactional processes* between dyads and triads in social contexts and, therefore, focusses on in-group interaction. The size and focus of a NoE is highly individual. It often includes family, friends, colleagues and others. Sometimes, NoE are locally limited. In other cases, they extend across rural areas, towns and cities. They can unfold various forms of face-to-face communication, as well as forms of computer-mediated communication (CMC). This chapter focusses on NoE, in which multilingual individuals of both urban and rural backgrounds meet. It addresses the following questions:

- What are the similarities and the differences between rural and urban language practices in multilingual societies when they meet virtually in CMC?
- Is there a sharp dichotomy between the city and the countryside in CMC-based NoE?
- How do multilingual individuals of both urban and rural backgrounds negotiate their linguistic practices in CMC environments?

These questions serve as the core focus of the current chapter. It therefore draws on Speech Act Theory by Austin (1975) and Searle (1976, 1979) to unveil the role and function of multilingual patterns in both urban and rural CMC. Today, speech acts are increasingly performed in CMC due to the rise in use of social media.

German-speaking Namibians are a particularly interesting case, enabling us to study different forms of multilingualism, since their NoE connect both (smaller) urban and rural areas between and within Namibia[1] and Germany, as many (younger) German-Namibians go to study or work abroad. Zimmer notes that German-Namibians deploy 'more or less stable sociolinguistic variation' (in press: 14) among all age categories, including 'a cross-generational use of Namibia-specific loan words'(in press, 22). Due to the relatively small size of about 20,000 individuals, their NoE are particularly well developed (Wiese et al. 2014: 20; see Pütz 1991). According to Zappen-Thomson, they extend across rural areas, towns and cities. It is likely that only a small percentage of (mainly elderly) German-speaking individuals have (almost) no contact to other German-speaking Namibians in either urban or rural areas.[2] With such regional, transnational and trans-urban NoE all intertwined, CMC becomes an important means of communication as it is, by definition, not located in a geographical place.

For these reasons, this study uses CMC as an empirical source to analyse German-Namibian speech acts (see Section 3.4.2). Qadir and Riloff

(2011: 749) note that there is 'relatively little work on applying Speech Act Theory to written text genres, and most of the previous work has focused on email classification.' This study contributes to bridging this gap. It uses the broad term *multilingual language practices* to indicate a wide range of contact phenomena, including inter- and intrasentential code-switching, borrowing and the Namibia-specific variety of *Namdeutsch,* which is 'eine durch Sprachkontakt entstandene Nonstandardvarietät der deutschen Sprache in Namibia, die durch zahlreiche Entlehnungen von sprachlichen Einheiten und Strukturen aus dem Englischen und Afrikaans gekennzeichnet ist' (a non-standard contact variety of the German language in Namibia shaped by various borrowings of linguistic units and structures from Afrikaans and English) (Kellermeier-Rehbein 2016: 228). In other words, Namdeutsch reflects the ongoing contact situation in which urban and rural individuals of German background find themselves.

3.2 Individuals from urban and rural areas in Namibia

Bhattacharya (2010: 45) notes that there are 'no universal criteria applicable for determining urbanhood', which makes it rather challenging for scientists to compare urban settings in different world regions or even among neighbouring countries.[3] Hence, it is necessary to define the two notions of *urbanhood* and *rurality* within the Namibian context for the purpose of this research.

The Republic of Namibia is essentially rural in nature. With about 2.3 million inhabitants populating an area of 823,988 km², it has 'the second-lowest population density in the world after Mongolia' (Gray 2016: 147). The capital of Windhoek is the administrative, political and cultural centre of Namibia. The latest sociodemographic data for Windhoek date back to 2011, when the city (incl. its peri-urban environment) had a population of about 340,000 inhabitants and an annual growth rate of 5% (Pendleton, Crush and Nickanor 2014: 193). If growth remained the same, Windhoek is projected to reach 500,000 inhabitants by 2020 (ibid., 2014, 193). On a global scale, it may therefore be considered a city of a smaller size. In the Namibian context, it is by far the largest urban hub of the entire region. The nearest cities, which outnumber the population size of Windhoek, are the city of Menongue in Angola (880 km to the north of Windhoek[4]) and the city of Cape Town in South Africa (1,271 km to the south[5]). Windhoek can therefore be considered the largest urban area on a north–south axis of about 2,000 km. The nearest bigger city to the east is Bulawayo in Zimbabwe with a distance of about 1,220 km.[6]

Windhoek itself is home to many languages.[7] Notwithstanding English being the sole official language of the country, Afrikaans has maintained a strong position as a lingua franca in Windhoek and Southern Namibia. In 1971, about 18% of Windhoek's population spoke German at home.[8] However, this number has dropped significantly and is currently about 3%.[9] Furthermore, the coastal town of Swakopmund is also home to a considerable number of German speakers. With its 44,000 inhabitants (Pendleton, Crush and Nickanor 2014: 193), Swakopmund is the second largest urban area in Namibia with a significant German-speaking minority. It is situated 30 km to the north of Walvis Bay. Together, they form a common *high-growth agglomeration* (OECD and AfDB 2007: 417) of more than 100,000 inhabitants (Pendleton, Crush and Nickanor 2014: 193). In the following, it is therefore listed as a separate category alongside Windhoek and the category of smaller urban and rural areas (see Tables 3.1, 3.3 and 3.4).

In this study, four individuals are part of a micro-analysis of urban and rural language practices (see Section 3.4). All individuals have a biographical link to Germany, as they have migrated there for study or work. Hence, they are no longer in day-to-day contact with the multilingual settings of Namibia but are rather exposed to regional linguistic settings within Germany. With limited exposure to English and the absence of Afrikaans in daily life, (multi-)linguistic settings in Germany differ considerably from Namibian settings. All individuals in this study use CMC, which serve as the empirical basis of this study.

3.3 Dataset

The data analysed in this study were collected from social media, and automatically extracted and exported to a spread sheet using the add-on programme *Web Scraper*.[10] The resulting corpus contains both the original linguistic output as well as sociodemographic data, such as place of origin and place of living. Subsequently, they were ranked, categorised and counted. Correlation analyses between metadata and linguistic output served to reveal socio-linguistic patterns from both a quantitative and qualitative perspective to analyse multilingual utterances and their pragmatic functions within CMC discourse. The structure of the analysis is twofold: a qualitative description of four selected participants and their linguistic behaviour leads to a quantitative analysis of the linguistic behaviour of the group as a whole. The four participants were chosen because they have an active history of participation in German-Namibian CMC and come from areas with different degrees of urbanisation. All data were published in Facebook groups within a period of seven years ranging from 2011 to 2018. These Facebook groups centre around the Namibian diaspora in Germany. The overwhelming majority of active members are indeed German-speaking Namibians living in Germany. A minority of members is of a similar background: Namibians who once lived in Germany and have returned to Namibia, Namibians who have always lived in Namibia, and Germans with a link to Namibia. This study focusses on individuals of Namibian background who live in Germany.

3.3.1 Discourse on Facebook

Comments are perhaps the most important units to structure discourse on Facebook. They are highlighted as separate fields with written information posted by a user in reaction to a piece of content. They indicate the name of the author as well as the time and date of publication. This makes them an

Table 3.1 Distribution of place of origin among users and their comments

Place	Users		Comments		Comment per user on average
Swakopmund	63	23%	514	24%	8.2
Windhoek	158	58%	1,423	65%	9.0
Other areas	52	19%	241	11%	4.6
Total	**273**	**100%**	**2,178**	**100%**	**8.0**

important unit to measure and quantify interaction on Facebook. Depending on its content and structure, a comment can contain one or several speech acts at the same time. For this reason, Section 3.4.2 also focusses on the relationship between comments and speech acts in CMC. The corpus used in the context of this study consists of 2,178 comments of which 1,451 comments (67%) where exclusively published in Standard German (SG). 727 comments (33%) include Namibia-specific language practices on the orthographic, lexical or morphosyntactic level. Comments posted by German speakers from Europe were not included in the corpus. Table 3.1 shows the distribution of comments and users with respect to their place of origin. As Windhoek and Swakopmund are the largest urbanised areas in Namibia, being home to a significant German-speaking minority, they are listed as separate categories in the context of this study.

Users from Windhoek are the majority and the most active group within the corpus: they published 65% of the comments, although they only account for 58% of all users. With an average of 9 comments per user, they clearly surpass the overall average of 8.0 comments. The second largest group comes from Swakopmund and represents 23% of all users. With an average of 8.2 comments per user, the group deploys an activity rate that almost meets the overall average of 8.0. Users from other (smaller urban and rural) areas represent 19% of the participants and account for 11% of the linguistic output in the corpus. Their activity rate is below average. Hence, the German-Namibian CMC used in the context of this study can be described as primarily urban. At the same time, it includes linguistic output from rural users.

3.4 Results of the analysis

3.4.1 Intra-individual language choices displayed in CMC

This section focusses on four Namibian users who express intra-individual language variation to different degrees. Their sociodemographic background is a cross-section of the entire group: one male individual from the city of Windhoek, one female individual from the town of Otjiwarongo and two individuals (one male and one female) from rural environments. Table 3.2 provides an overview of the sociodemographic data and mono- and multilingual practices within CMC. It shows that two participants use comments in

Table 3.2 The four participants

Sociodemographic data				Comments		
Name[11]	Gender	Grew up in	Lives in	total	German-only	
Alex	M	Windhoek	Germany	149	97	65.1%
Laura	F	Otjiwarongo	Germany	107	95	88.8%
Mark	M	Farm	Germany	108	73	67.6%
Marie	F	Farm	Germany	11	5	45.5%

Standard German (SG-only comments) to a similar degree (65.1% and 67.6%) whereas the practice of the other two participants deviates on both ends of the spectrum (88.8% and 45.5%). Comments were countered as *German-only* when the entire comment did not contain any Namibia-specific language practice on any linguistic level. The remaining comments did include at least one Namibia-specific language practice.[12]

Alex lives in the German state of Saxony and grew up in the capital Windhoek, by far the largest urban environment in Namibia. The degree to which Alex uses Namibian language practices in CMC differs greatly, as can be seen in (1) – (4). Namibia-specific language practices are underlined.

Alex from Windhoek:

(1) Hab Fahrrad fahren auch nicht verlernt
    I haven't forgotten how to ride a bike.

(2) Komm net Donnerstag dann Sitz ich nicht alleine
    Come around on Thursday then I won't be sitting around alone.

(3) Daarsy boys
    There you are, boys!

(4) Bra da war dicker fock op… bin ja Straight von Namsa nach Bulgarien geflogen da hab ich dann alle Bilder auf mein bru sei laptop gecooied das ich plek hab um da fotos zu machen…toe mein bru mir n Brief schickt mit usb drin kommt der Brief aufgeschnitten und leer an
    Dude, it was a big mess… I flew straight from Namsa to Bulgaria. There, I downloaded all photos on my brother's laptop. Then I had space to take pictures. When my brother sent me a letter with the flash drive, the letter arrived opened and empty.

3.4.1.1 *Utterance acts: Lexical and syntactic implications*

(1)–(4) show that the degree to which Alex uses Namibia-specific language practices differs remarkably: it ranges from comments in Standard German only

(SG-only) in (1) to comments with well-established Namibian loanwords like *net* (only) in (2) and comments displaying a variety of Namibia-specific language practices. Some of them affect the syntactic structure of a phrase, as can be seen in the syntagmatic construction *mein bru sei laptop* (4).[13] Here, the possessor (*mein bru*) precedes the head noun (*laptop*), which is in the reverse order of the corresponding SG phrase.

(5) Original   **mein bru** sei laptop
     German (Genitive case)   der Laptop **meines Bruders**
     German (Dative case)   der Laptop **von meinem Bruder**

Both examples,[14] the genitivus possesivus and its dative substitute consisting of a *von*-PP (Eng.: *of*-PP) require the head noun to be followed by its possessor in SG (*head first*).[15] Hence, they show the reverse order of the *head second* construction in the original phrase. However, *head second* is also subject to non-standard language use in German, as well as to standard possessive constructions in Afrikaans, as can been seen (6).

(6) Original   **mein bru** sei laptop
     Non-Standard German   **mein Bruder** sein Laptop
     Standard Afrikaans   **my broer** se laptop

3.4.1.2 Users of urban and rural backgrounds

(1)–(6) show the variability of intra-individual language choices ranging from SG-only to a high degree of Namibia-specific language practices. With 149 published comments, Alex is the most active user among the group. Laura and Mark come second with 107 and 108 comments, respectively. Although Marie is remarkably less active with only 11 published comments, the majority of her comments contain Namibian-typical speech deploying both ad-hoc and well-established borrowings. All four users know each other in person and sometimes directly interact with one another within the CMC group. (7) shows a comment from Mark on an advertisement for clothing. Alex reacts to it. In addition, they both indicate a positive attitude towards one another's comments by marking them with the *like* button. Namibia-typical language practices are underlined.

(7) Mark   <u>Bar</u>[16] bring welche nach <u>Namsa</u> will eine kaufen!
            Bro, bring some of them to Namsa. Want to buy one!
     Alex   Same

(7) shows how NoE are being maintained in CMC. It is a good example of how individuals from both urban and rural areas interact in a transnational space: Mark grew up on a Namibian farm and Alex was born and raised in Windhoek. They both live in Germany now. They plan to meet at Namsa, an annual event for Namibians held in Germany. How do such individual interactions shape the

Table 3.3 Standard German in German Namibian CMC (n = 2,178)

Total	Windhoek	Swakopmund	Other
67%	69%	65%	56%

general linguistic practices within German-Namibian CMC? The following section addresses this question.

3.4.1.3 Multilingual speech in comparison

Table 3.3 is based on 2,178 comments posted by 273 German Namibian users in CMC. It shows the frequency of SG-only comments and its distribution among Windhoek, Swakopmund and less urbanised areas.

There is a consistent tendency throughout all categories: users from rural areas tend to use SG-only comments less frequently than their counterparts from the urban areas of Windhoek and Swakopmund. This result is in line with the general impression among German-speaking Namibians, who often state that Namibia-specific language practices are more frequent in rural areas. Furthermore, it shows that multilingualism among German-speaking Namibians stretches from (sub)urban settings well into rural areas and vice versa. As a result, in-group speech between individuals of both backgrounds unfolds Namibia-typical patterns of multilingualism in CMC. A micro-analysis on the individual level seems to confirm this impression: the multilingual speech patterns of Mark (coming from a Namibian farm) and Laura (originally from Otjiwarongo) are as diverse as those of Alex from Windhoek. The patterns range from SG-only comments to comments with Namibia-typical phenomena on the lexical and syntactic level. However, it is important to note that individual language choices can differ from these macro-level tendencies. Laura, for example, has published a high number of English-only comments as a reaction to a prior comment that is almost entirely written in English. Otherwise, she rather sticks to SG and uses Namibia-typical language practices less frequently. To capture the different degrees of multilingual practices, this chapter includes a micro-perspective on individual language choices. The analysis entails a speech act classification of all four participants to unveil the pragmatic functions of Namibia-specific language practices. We will therefore turn back to (1).

3.4.2 Roles and functions of Namibia-specific language practices

(1) Hab Fahrrad fahren auch nicht verlernt
     I didn't forget how to write a bike.

(1) is a good example of a comment that entails a single speech act. In this case, it can be classified as a *Representative*, which 'commit[s] a speaker to the truth of an expressed proposition' such as in 'asserting, stating, concluding (…)'

(Hidayah 2019, 3). This category was first described by Searle (1976), who built on Austin's Speech Act Theory (1975). Searle (1976) developed five main categories of speech acts. In addition to *Representatives*, he introduced *Commissives*, which 'commit a speaker to some future action', such as in 'promising, pledging, threatening' (Hidayah 2019: 3). The third category is *Directives*, which a speaker uses in an attempt to get the addressee 'to carry out an action'. This can be done by 'advising, commanding, challenging' (Hidayah 2019: 3). The fourth category is *Declarations*, which affect an immediate change of affairs, such as in 'declaring, resigning, arresting' (Hidayah 2019: 3). The fifth category is *Expressives*, which express a psychological state, such as in greeting, thanking or congratulating (Searle 1976: 355–7; Hidayah 2019: 3). By applying Speech Act Theory to the data gathered, the roles and functions of Namibia-specific language practices in CMC become obvious. I will therefore turn back to the examples (1)–(4). Subsequently, I will clarify whether users of both urban and rural backgrounds use Namibia-specific language practices with similar pragmatic effects when communicating in CMC.

3.4.2.1 German-Namibian speech acts in CMC: Users of urban backgrounds

The representative speech act in (1) exclusively entails language practices that are identical to European German, whereas the directive speech act in (2) and the expressive speech act in (3) also contain Namibia-specific language practices. In (2), the borrowed item *net* emphasises the inviting character of the speech act as a whole to strengthen its perlocutionary effect, that is to convince Alex's chat partner to join him. This invitation gains additional strength by the use of the Afrikaans-based loanword *net* and turns it into a friendly yet demanding request. In (3), the Afrikaans-based borrowing *daarsy* (originally from Afrikaans *daar is hy* = there he is)[17] stresses Alex's agreement with a previous comment and serves to positively reassure social bonds with his chat partner. Since it is published in a CMC group, it also invites other users to leave comments with a similar high degree of consensus. (4) is not only longer than the previous examples; it also bears a narrative character, making it different to the short comments in (1)–(3). It contains a single Representative and proves that Namibia-specific language choices also occur in this sort of speech acts (*da hab ich dann alle Bilder auf mein bru sei laptop gecooied*). Therefore, (1)–(4) show that Alex uses a wide range of speech acts. He deploys pragmatic variation and flexibility in SG-only speech acts as well as in multilingual speech acts. His linguistic behaviour is in line with the general trend of the group coming from Windhoek: in this group, Representatives, Commissives, Directives and Expressives can be found for all of the three languages and a combination thereof. An exception to this finding are declarative speech acts, which do not occur in the corpus at all. This observation is in line with the findings of Qadir and Riloff (2011: 780), who subsequently omitted Declarations from their study on digital message board posts 'because we virtually never saw declarative speech acts in our data set.'. The absence of this category may be due to the nature of many CMC groups, in which users rarely communicate to 'affect an immediate change of affairs' (Hidayah 2019: 3). Paradigm cases that prompt Declarations include resigning, firing or hiring, for which CMC groups are usually not a suitable medium. Therefore, Declarations will not be further discussed in this chapter.

3.4.2.2 German-Namibian speech acts in CMC: Users of smaller urban and rural backgrounds

Even though Laura uses Namibia-specific speech less frequently than Alex does, her multilingual choices still cover various speech acts covering Representatives, Commissives and Expressives, as can be seen in (8)–(10). Contrary to Alex, Laura frequently uses Namibia-specific speech to express politeness.

(8) Representative München ist leider <u>bietjie</u> weit weg
Munich is a bit far, unfortunately.

(9) Expressive <u>Plesier</u>!:) Da hab ich meine Wohnung auch gefunden.:)
You're welcome. That's where I've found my apartment, too.

(10) Commissive <u>Awesome</u>!!: D wir checken definitiv!
Awesome! We will definitely check it out.

In (8), Laura states that the city of Munich is too far to go visit. She also uses the Afrikaans downtoner *bietjie* (a bit) to soften her statement. By using a representative speech act, she rejects the offer of her chat partner and chooses Namibia-specific language to make her rejection sound friendlier. Another politeness marker is the Afrikaans-based borrowing *plesier* (lit. *pleasure* for *you're welcome*), which is followed by an exclamation mark in (9). As a typically Namibian (and South African) response to acknowledgements, *plesier* stresses the common identity and local background among the chat partners, especially when used within a SG-only conversation. It can be classified as an Expressive, indicating sympathy, and is followed by a Representative to convey further information. Both speech acts are part of the same comment. They indicate how users can convey multiple pragmatic purposes within a single CMC-based comment. The same strategy applies to (10), which also consists of two speech acts within a single comment. Here, the Commissive entails the Namibia-typical, intransitive use of the verb *checken* ('wir checken definitiv'), which can only be used as a transitive verb in SG (e.g.: wir checken <u>das</u> definitiv). This Commissive is preceded by an Expressive for which Laura uses the English borrowing *awesome* to value and positively reinforce the prior comment of her chat partner. Laura's Namibia-typical language practices thus include strategies of politeness to establish bonds with other users. Coming from the small town of Otjiwarongo, she contributes to the cohesion of the CMC-based NoE by using Namibia-specific speech acts.

Unlike Laura, Mark and Marie come from a rural environment. However, they are part of the same NoE and deploy a wide range of multilingual practices, too:

(11) Mark Was ist <u>net</u> los mit den <u>namboys</u>
Just what is going on with the namboys?

(12) Mark du musst <u>recht kommen</u> check in deinem kopferraum [sic]
You'll have to manage. Check your boot.

(13) Marie <u>Kak ou</u>…du hast die [den] ganzen abend getragen
Shit, man. You've been carrying it for the whole night.

(14) Marie Denke dein <u>bru</u> hat die von dir und dann war se <u>gone</u>
[I] guess your brother got it from you and then it was gone.

In (11), Mark uses Namibia-specific language to emphasise the expressive nature of his speech act. Here, the Afrikaans-based borrowing *net* serves as an intensifier (German: nur; English: only). In combination with the neologism *namboys*, both loanwords are used as a vocative to address the ingroup (for more information on the interplay between vocatives and in groups see Radke (2021b; in press)). (12) shows how Mark utilises Namibia-specific language as a Directive in an attempt to get the addressee 'to carry out an action' (Hidayah 2019: 3). Therefore, he advises the addressee to finally manage the situation, which he expresses through the loan translation *recht kommen* (Afrikaans: regkom; SG: hinbekommen, sich zurechtfinden). Marie shows a similar range of pragmatic variation in (13) and (14). Both comments are extracted from a discourse in which she is looking for her Namibian flag that has disappeared. Her initial question about the whereabouts of the flag remains unanswered since the addressee cannot help her. She then reacts by using the Afrikaans-based swear word *kak* (13) to emphasise the expressive nature of her speech act. Subsequently, she turns her comments into a more directive speech to prompt the addressee to provide her with more information (du hast die [den] ganzen abend getragen). In (14), she revises this strategy and uses a Representative by referring to the addressee's brother as *bru*. She then uses the ad-hoc borrowing *gone* (SG: weg, verwunden) to indicate her disappointment with the disappearance of her flag. The informality of the speech act is further emphasised by the personal pronoun *se*, an informal variant of *sie* (English: she), which also exists in European German varieties.

An analysis of all users coming from smaller urban and rural areas in Namibia unveils the pragmatic variation of rural multilingual practices among this group. Like urban users, they make wide use of the four speech act classes. The only difference to the urban subgroup are Commissives in Afrikaans-only utterances, which do not occur in the corpus. A possible explanation for the missing evidence is probably the size of the data set, which may simply be too small. Since Afrikaans is an important source language amongst the smaller urban and rural subgroup, it seems plausible that a larger corpus would capture Commissives in Afrikaans-only utterances. In the current data set, users of rural backgrounds draw on Afrikaans quite extensively in their multilingual comments, as can be seen in (15).

(15)   Eish.kla gevat / Tah wie ein Jakkals / Malles ding
       Outch, it's done / Well, like a jackal / crazy you

Therefore, it does not seem unlikely that a larger corpus of German-Namibian CMC would also cover Afrikaans-only Commissives. But even with this type of speech act missing in Afrikaans-only comments, it indicates the high degree of pragmatic variation in Namibia-specific language practices amongst the smaller urban and rural subgroup. Hence, their multilingual speech acts cover a broad pragmatic paradigm and are thus similar to the utterances of individuals coming from urban environments.

3.5 Urban, rural or CMC practices?

The analysis raises the question as to how these multilingual practices can be classified. Are there separate urban and rural practices that are digitally transmitted? The frequency analysis in Table 3.3 suggests that there is at least a quantitative difference in Namibia-specific language practices between users of urban backgrounds with a more frequent use of SG-only comments and users of rural backgrounds with a less frequent use of SG-only comments, even though the pragmatic range of their multilingual behaviour is similar. This observation raised the question as to whether there is a correlation between the population size of a given area and the frequency by which German speakers from that area use Namibian-specific language practices. To answer this question, I performed a logistic regression.[18] The null hypothesis predicts that the two variables (population size and frequency of SG or Namibia-specific comments) are independent and not associated. The alternative hypothesis claims that the linguistic behaviour of their German-speaking inhabitants is the dependent variable, which is technically predicted by the population size of Namibian areas the speakers live in. In that case, the null hypothesis is to be rejected. Table 3.4 contains the data that were used to perform the logistic regression:

The results are shown in appendix I. The p-value equals 0.0001 and shows that the result is statistically significant; there is a statistically significant correlation between the population size of an area German-Namibian speakers originate from and the frequency rates of Namibia-specific language practices among these speakers in CMC: individuals originating from larger urban areas

Table 3.4 Population size and frequency of Namibia-specific comments

	logarithmic population size[19]	Namibia-specific comments	SG-only comments
Windhoek	5,70	442	981
Swakopmund	4,78	178	336
Other areas	3,00	107	134

tend to use Namibia-specific language practices less frequently than individuals from smaller urban or rural areas. In other words, there is an inverse association between the size of population and the frequency by which German-speakers use Namibia-specific language practices in CMC. The chance that non-city dwellers will use Namibia-specific utterances is 1.75 times bigger (Odds Ratio) than for inhabitants of Windhoek. This result is in line with the general perception of many German-Namibians which is reflected in the frequently used advice: 'If you want to hear more *Namdeutsch*, you should pay a visit to the farms.'[20]

Although the size of population proves to be a statistically significant independent variable, one has to ask which causal relation there may exist, which finds its expression in this correlation. Population size reflects social and economic structures, which in turn affect the use of non-standard language practices among minority groups. Areas with a higher population size usually provide tighter networks of institutions such as schools, churches or associations for minorities. These institutions often provide spaces in which the use of standard-near registers is encouraged while counteracting non-standard language practices. For that reason, the size of population may just reflect the degree of institutional effects on linguistic choices.

The association between population size and linguistic behaviour is further supported by the fact that all data are taken from the same type of source: CMC. Therefore, a bias based on different language modes can be excluded, as all data consistently represent digital language practices. From that perspective, CMC is not only a medium but also a stable stratification that affects linguistic practices. These effects are well-discussed in literature, pointing out the emergence of written speech, a hybrid form of oral and written language styles (Weininger 2001: 89). Hence, CMC is likely to be a defining factor, for which Androutsopoulos (2015) introduced the notion of *networked multilingualism*. This term 'encompasses everything language users do with the entire range of linguistic resources within three sets of constraints: mediation of written language by digital technologies, access to network resources, and orientation to networked audiences' (Androutsopoulos 2015: 185). Furthermore, CMC can trigger Namibia-specific language use, when a given social media group is labelled as such. Are the language practices investigated in this chapter predominantly CMC-influenced? This assumption was supported by the reactions of the German-Namibian audience during a 2018 public evening lecture in Windhoek.[21] When presented with selected material from CMC, the German-Namibian audience stated that not all but at least some of the multilingual language practices seemed somewhat 'exaggerated' due to a high frequency of borrowed expressions: 'Die Wortwahl und das viele *Namdeutsch* scheinen etwas übertrieben zu sein' (The choice of words and the highly frequent use of *Namdeutsch* seem to be a bit exaggerated). Since the investigated CMC groups have as many as 1,200 members each, it seems likely that this potential reach affects the user's linguistic behaviour and occasionally prompts a stylised language use amongst participants. Therefore, the CMC setup is an influential and defining factor for triggering Namibia-specific language practices.

This stance still leaves out an important fact: social media brings together individuals from both urban and rural areas and creates a geographically independent space for communication. In this perspective, isolated urban language practices do not exist, as the city itself is not only interconnected with its surrounding countryside but is also digitally linked to any group of individuals through digital media. Hence, CMC creates an environment for a hybrid form of German-Namibian language practices melting together influences from their personal linguistic settings in urban or rural areas as well as influences from digital media, which result in the emergence of German-Namibian written speech. This perspective emphasises both the influence of CMC as a genre and the sociodemographic background of the individual user (e.g. their place of origin). In case of the German-Namibian community with multilingual practices being part of their daily life in both urban and rural areas, CMC serves to further connect the multilingual networks between the city and the countryside. Even when Namibians from rural areas migrate to Windhoek, Munich or any other city, they are likely to stay connected with their friends through social media. Hence, a comprehensive view on postmodern individuals in urban settings should go beyond the administrative borders of the city. It should therefore take into account the individual NoE, which are likely to combine rural and urban linguistic practices.

3.6 Summary and outlook

This chapter shows how closely intertwined urban and rural multilingual practices can be. Especially in CMC, in which geographical distances and boundaries vanish. CMC is an online-performing type of NoE with an increasing importance for the German-Namibian community (cf. Radke 2021a). It can be divided into different subtypes, such as peer and family networks, networks of common interests or a hybrid form thereof. However, some of those networks do not exclusively communicate online but also meet face-to-face. They have the potential to serve as a link between urban and rural environments. In doing so, they affect exchange and multilingual communication in real life. In an online interview, Prof. Marianne Zappen-Thomson[22] describes the case of a German-speaking female, who lives in a rural area south of Windhoek. In her day-to-day life, she almost exclusively uses Afrikaans. However, whenever she visits her family in the city of Windhoek, she is not only exposed to German but also engages in conversations using *Namdeutsch*. This example shows how NoE not only connect urban and rural settings but also stimulate the use of different varieties within their networks.

Furthermore, I have analysed CMC-based NoE in correlation to the individual's place of origin. This chapter has shown that multilingualism among German-Namibians is a trans-urban phenomenon fulfilling a wide range of pragmatic purposes: Representatives, Commissives, Directives and Expressives can be found in speech originating from individuals of both urban and rural origin. There are two exceptions: Afrikaans-only Commissives could be found among urban users but were absent among rural users. This lack may be due to the size of the corpus. Since Afrikaans is an important source language for Namibia-specific language practices among German-speaking Namibians, it seems likely that Afrikaans-only Commissives are also used by rural individuals. The second exception, the complete lack of Declaratives throughout all categories, is likely due to the inherent feature of social media providing a rather non-declarative mode for communication. It became clear that urban and rural multilingualism in German-Namibian CMC seem similar from a pragmatic point of view. However, further research is necessary to zoom in on the full range of pragmatic purposes, e.g. by a fine-grained analysis of politeness strategies. Moreover, the current data only account for CMC-based speech. There are clear signs that the speech used in CMC is (partially) stylised, since CMC serves as a publication tool to reach a greater audience. It remains to be clarified whether pragmatic speech patterns in private CMC and in face-to-face communication show similar patterns in (trans-)urban and rural areas.

3.7 Acknowledgements

This chapter is a result of my PhD research on multilingualism and mixed-mode communication among the German-Namibian diaspora. I want to thank my supervisors Arjen Versloot and Horst Simon for providing me with valuable feedback as well as Gergely Szabó and Sofiya Mitsova for their input. I also owe many thanks to the editors of this volume, Dick Smakman, Kapitolina Fedorova and Jiří Nekvapil, for their careful reading of the manuscript and thoughtful comments.

Notes

1 According to the 2011 census by the Namibia Statistics Agency, Namibia had a population of 2,113,077 (p. 8). 43% lived in urban areas (ibid.) and 1,6% of the urban population had German as their first language (p. 172). Hence, the following calculation applies: 2,113,077★0.43★0.016 = 14,538 German-speakers in urban areas. 57% of Namibia's population lived in rural areas (p. 8). 0.3% of the rural population is German-speaking (p. 172). Hence, the following calculation applies: 2,113,077★0.57★0.003 = 3,613 German-speakers in rural areas.
2 Extracted from an online interview with Prof. Marianne Zappen-Thomson, German Section at the University of Namibia, 27–29 August 2019.
3 Bhattacharya calls the lack of universal criteria 'rather annoying' (p. 45) which is certainly an unambiguous way to describe the situation.
4 www.distance.to/Windhoek/Menongue,Cuando-Cubango,AGO [27 August 2019].

5 See www.distance.to/Windhoek/Cape-Town,Western-Cape,ZAF [27 August 2019].
6 See www.distance.to/Windhoek/Bulawayo,ZWE [27 August 2019].
7 Languages of European descent include Afrikaans and English. Indigenous languages include Oshiwambo, Khoekhoegowab and Otjiherero, amongst others (cf. Stell 2016: 331).
8 Based on the numbers published by the Reading Eagle on 18 July 1971, p. 61: '[...] in Windhoek there are 26,000 whites to 24,000 blacks. The 9,000 Germans among the whites give Windhoek a thoroughly Teutonic atmosphere.' https://news.google.com/newspapers?nid=1955&dat=19710718&id=9gorAAAAIBAJ&sjid=YJoFAAAAIBAJ&pg=2800,3519162 [31 August 2019].
9 German is the first language of about 20,000 Namibians in Namibia or 0.9% of the total population with the Khomas region having the second highest proportion of German speakers (2.6%, Namibia Statistics Agency 2011, 172). Since Windhoek is part of Khomas and accounts for 95% of its inhabitants (Namibia Statistics Agency 2011, 14), an estimated 3% of Windhoek's population have German as their first language.
10 https://chrome.google.com/webstore/detail/web-scraper-free-web-scra/jnhgnonknehpejjnehehllkliplmbmhn [6 February 2021].
11 All names were changed.
12 A small number of comments was written in English or Afrikaans only. They were part of multilingual discourses. As code-switching between languages is a typical feature of Namibian multilingualism, such comments were also counted as Namibia-specific language practices.
13 For more examples of this sort, see Shah (2007: 28) and Wiese et al. (2017: 4).
14 Both are frequent constructions in SG with the dative case generally considered to be slightly more informal than the genitive case.
15 The alternative *meines Bruders Laptop* is considered to be archaic in European SG varieties. While it can be found in (contemporary) poetry, it would be highly marked as part of a CMC comment.
16 Most likely meant to be *bra*.
17 See https://afrikaans.livejournal.com/4027.html#/4027.html [4 November 2019].
18 For the analysis I used https://statpages.info/logistic.html [1 September 2020]. I owe many thanks to my supervisor Prof. Arjen Versloot for his advice.
19 To harmonize the different population sizes from Zipfian to linear, I applied a logarithmic transformation of population size with base 10. The following calculations apply: Windhoek: $\log_{10}(500,000) = 5.7$; Swakopmund: $\log_{10}(60,000) = 4.78$; smaller urban and rural areas: $\log_{10}(1,000) = 3.0$. The population size of 1,000 is an estimated number to indicate that the local networks of German speakers in smaller urban and rural areas are smaller than in Windhoek and Swakopmund.
20 Often heard during fieldwork in Namibia, April–May 2018.
21 The evening lecture entitled *Die deutsche Sprache in Namibia und das Internet* took place at Namibia Scientific Society on 17 April 2018. I owe many thanks to Prof. Julia Augart from the University of Namibia for organizing this event.
22 Extracted from an online interview with Prof. Marianne Zappen-Thomson, German Section at the University of Namibia, 27–29 August 2019.

References

Androutsopoulos, Jannis. 2015. 'Networked Multilingualism: Some Language Practices on Facebook and Their Implications'. *International Journal of Bilingualism* 19 (2): 185–205.

Austin, John L. 1975. *How to Do Things with Words: Second Edition*. Edited by J. O. Urmson and Marina Sbisà. 2nd edition. Cambridge, MA: Harvard University Press.

Bhattacharya, Bhargab B. 2010. *Urbanization, Urban Sustainability and the Future of Cities*. New Delhi: Concept Publishing Company.

Bosma, Evelyn, Eric Hoekstra, Arjen Versloot, and Elma Blom. 2017. 'The Minimal and Short-Lived Effects of Minority Language Exposure on the Executive Functions of Frisian-Dutch Bilingual Children'. *Frontiers in Psychology* 8. https://doi.org/10.3389/fpsyg.2017.01453.

Breuker, Pieter. 2001. 'West Frisian in Language Contact'. In *Handbook of Frisian Studies*, edited by Horst Haider Munske, Nils Århammar, Volker F. Faltings, Jarich F. Hoekstra, Oebele Vries, Alastair G. H. Walker, and Ommo Wilts, 121–129. Thübingen: Max Niemeyer.

Di Carlo, Pierpaolo, Jeff Good, and Rachel Diba. 2017. 'Multilingualism in Rural Africa', June. www.researchgate.net/publication/313556469_Multilingualism_in_Rural_Africa.

Freywald, Ulrike, Katharina Mayr, Tiner Özçelik, and Heike Wiese. 2011. 'Kiezdeutsch as a Multiethnolect'. In *Ethnic Styles of Speaking in European Metropolitan Areas*, 45–73. Amsterdam: John Benjamins Publishing Company.

Galavan, Susan. 2019. 'Transoceanic Networks of Exchange: New Brunswick Lumber, Merchant Trade, and the Building of Victorian Britain'. *Acadiensis: Journal of the History of the Atlantic Region / Revue d'histoire de La Region Atlantique* 48 (2): 90–116. https://doi.org/10.1353/aca.2019.0011.

Gray, Mel. 2016. *The Handbook of Social Work and Social Development in Africa*. London, New York: Taylor & Francis.

Hidayah, Arini. 2019. 'An Analysis of Directives Speech Acts in Film Script of Iron Man 2 (2010)'. *Surakarta English and Literature Journal* 2 (1): 1–8.

Kellermeier-Rehbein, Birte. 2016. 'Sprache in postkolonialen Kontexten II. Varietäten der deutschen Sprache in Namibia'. In *Sprache und Kolonialismus: Eine interdisziplinäre Einführung zu Sprache und Kommunikation in kolonialen Kontexten*, edited by Thomas Stolz, Ingo H. Warnke, and Daniel Schmidt-Brücken, 213–234. Berlin / Boston: Walter de Gruyter.

Namibia Statistics Agency. 2011. 'Census 2011. Population & Housing Census Main Report'. https://cms.my.na/assets/documents/p19dmlj9sm1rs138h7vb5c2aa91.pdf.

OECD, and AfDB. 2007. *African Economic Outlook 2007*. OECD Publishing.

Pendleton, Wade, Jonathan Crush, and Ndeyapo Nickanor. 2014. 'Migrant Windhoek: Rural–Urban Migration and Food Security in Namibia'. *Urban Forum* 25 (2): 191–205. https://doi.org/10.1007/s12132-014-9220-x.

Pütz, Martin. 1991. '"Südwesterdeutsch" in Namibia: Sprachpolitik, Sprachplanung und Spracherhalt'. *Linguistische Berichte* 136: 455–476.

Qadir, Ashequl, and Ellen Riloff. 2011. 'Classifying sentences as speech acts in message board posts'. In *Proceedings of the 2011 Conference on Empirical Methods in Natural Language Processing*, 748–758. Association for Computational Linguistics.

Radke, Henning. 2021a. 'Die Rolle computervermittelter Kommunikation und vernetzter Mehrsprachigkeit für die deutsch-namibische Diaspora.' In

Kontaktvarietäten des Deutschen im Ausland, edited by Csaba Földes, 461–478. Beiträge zur interkulturellen Germanistik (BIG). www.researchgate.net/publication/ 348541511_Die_Rolle_computervermittelter_Kommunikation_und_vernetzter_ Mehrsprachigkeit_fur_die_deutsch-namibische_Diaspora

Radke, Henning. 2021b. 'Language contact and mixed-mode communication: On ingroup construction through multilingualism among the German-Namibian diaspora'. In *German(ic) in Language Contact Grammatical and Sociolinguistic Dynamics*, edited by Christian Zimmer, 127–158. Language Variation 5. Berlin: Language Science Press.

Radke, Henning, and Arjen Versloot. In press. 'Referential multimodality, multilingualism and gender. How German Namibians use Afrikaans and English brocatives in their CMC'. In *Multilingualism from Manuscript to 3D. Intersections of Modalities from Medieval to Modern Times*, edited by Matylda Włodarczyk, Elżbieta Adamczyk and Jukka Tyrkkö. Routledge Studies in Multimodality. New York; London: Routledge.

Searle, John R. 1976. 'A Classification of Illocutionary Acts'. *Language in Society* 5 (1): 1–23.

Searle, John R. 1979. *Expression and Meaning: Studies in the Theory of Speech Acts*. Cambridge: Cambridge University Press. www.pdcnet.org/pdc/bvdb.nsf/ purchase?openform&fp=phr&id=phr_1982_0091_0003_0488_0493.

Shah, Sheena. 2007. 'German in a Contact Situation: The Case of Namibian German'. *EDUSA* 2 (2): 20–45.

Smakman, Dick, and Patrick Heinrich. 2017. *Urban Sociolinguistics: The City as a Linguistic Process and Experience*. Milton: Routledge.

Stell, Gerald. 2016. 'Trends in Linguistic Diversity in Post-Independence Windhoek: A Qualitative Appraisal'. *Language Matters* 47 (3): 326–348.

Weininger, Markus J. 2001. 'Orality in MOO: Rehearsing Speech in Text. A Preliminary Study.' In *C.A.L.L. – the Challenge of Change: Research and Practice*, edited by Keith Cameron, 89–96. Loughborough: Elm Bank Publications.

Wiese, Heike. 2012. *Kiezdeutsch: Ein neuer Dialekt entsteht*. Vol. 6034. München: Beck.

Wiese, Heike, Horst Simon, Marianne Zappen-Thomson, and Kathleen Schumann. 2014. 'Deutsch im mehrsprachigen Kontext: Beobachtungen zu lexikalisch-grammatischen Entwicklungen im Namdeutschen und im Kiezdeutschen'. *Zeitschrift für Dialektologie und Linguistik* 81 (3): 274–307.

Wiese, Heike, Horst Simon, Christian Zimmer, and Kathleen Schumann. 2017. 'German in Namibia: A Vital Speech Community and Its Multilingual Dynamics'. www.academia.edu/34564624/German_in_Namibia_A_vital_speech_community_and_its_ multilingual_dynamics_1 (2.12.2017).

Zimmer, Christian. In press. 'Linguistic Variation and Age of Speakers in Namibian German: Loan Word Usage in "Wenker Sentences"'. In *German Abroad: Comparative Perspectives on Language Contact*, edited by Hans C. Boas. Leiden: Brill.

Appendix 3.1

Results of the logistic regression described in Section 3.5

Inhabitants		Nam-specific	SG		SG
5,70	1,00	442	981	1423	69%
4,78	0,66	178	336	514	65%
3,00	0,00	107	134	241	56%
		727	1451	2178	

Descriptives

727 cases have Y=0; 1451 cases have Y=1.

Variable	Avg	SD
1	51.841	0.8604

Overall Model Fit

Chi Square	163.408
df	1
p	0.0001

OR from 3.00 to 5.7

1,754964

Coefficients, Standard Errors, Odds Ratios, and 95% Confidence Limits

Variable	Coeff.	StdErr	p	O.R.	Low–High	
1	0.2083	0.0511	0.0000	12.316	11.141	13.614

Intercept   −0.3840   0.2669   0.1502

4 Motorcycle taxi drivers in Ngaoundéré, Cameroon

Communication in a diffuse multilingual setting

K. Beyer

4.1 Introduction

In this chapter, I look at recurrent communicative challenges of individual speakers in a highly heterogeneous multilingual context which, in various respects, may serve as an example of urban postmodern settings in the Global South. Postmodern settings are described in Drzewiecka and Nakayama (1998: 20): 'As multinational interactions and interconnections multiply and accelerate, it is no longer possible to maintain a modernist imagery of distinct cultural identities nested within a fixed configuration of culture, nation, and space.' Although previously attributed to Global North settings, it is clear that identity constructions based on fixed space and culture configurations also play a role in the Global South. Those were often instigated by the colonial powers and continued in post-colonial times. The current growth of urban space and concomitant debates on autochthony, belongings and identities are in many ways comparable to Global North discussions (Lamola 2017) in general. The study presented in this chapter focuses on a group highly exposed to such a postmodern setting, namely motorcycle taxi drivers (MTD) in the city of Ngaoundéré, the capital of the Adamawa province in Northern Cameroon.

The northern territory of Cameroon is one of the linguistically most diverse areas worldwide (cp. Eberhard, Simons and Fennig 2020). This diversity is intensified by recently growing influxes of foreigners from other parts of Cameroon and neighbouring countries.[1] This multilingual situation is mirrored by the linguistic situation of Ngaoundéré where, besides French as the official language, the Atlantic language Fulfulde is spoken in a local variety as the lingua franca of the region (Mohammadou 1978). This local Fulfulde displays a range of variable features that are partly contact-induced and/or due to the use of the language by L2 speakers. The values and frequencies of these features are far from stable. They not only differ between social groups but also vary between speakers of one group or even between utterances of one single speaker. Moreover, many indigenous languages of different families (mainly Adamawa and Chadic) are spoken, and other major African languages (e.g., Hausa, Kanuri, Shuwa Arabic) are also present in the city. Mbum, from the Adamawa family, and

DOI: 10.4324/9780429348037-5

Adamawa-Fulfulde are considered to be the local languages in Ngaoundéré, but again, a codified standard is not defined for either of them. Apart from Fulfulde (in its most prestigious variety called *Diamaré*, usually attributed to the extreme North of Cameroon), no standard orthography or a generally acknowledged reference grammar exists for these languages. Apart from French, none of the multiple languages is used in a coherent way in education or the mass media.

As there is also no single outstanding group whose language may serve as kernel for a focused system, a great variety of multilingual repertoires on the individual and communal level prevails. Thus, today in Ngaoundéré many groups and many languages are accessible parts of the daily communicative praxis, and 'language' can be considered generally a more diffuse phenomenon (Le Page 1992: 78, 79). Nothing comparable to the highly focused European language situation (Tabouret-Keller 1992: 181) can be established for Ngaoundéré; the urban language situation under scrutiny here can thus be regarded as representative for many contemporary urban Global South contexts.

Against the backdrop of this multilingual setting, mutual linguistic influences play out in daily encounters among speakers, who are constantly challenged by what has been labelled 'simple' or 'on-line management' of communication by Nekvapil and Sherman (2015: 6, 7). This management of obstacles between the communicative partners is governed by a range of interrelated factors such as individual social network structures, speech group prestige, level of linguistic norm developments, and economic and political importance of the involved varieties. As it is not possible to cover all those different factors in one single chapter (if at all), I focus on variation observable in the use of the lingua franca Fulfulde by some MTDs in their communication with clients. I correlate these with their individual ethno-linguistic backgrounds and characteristics of their personal social networks and derive some general insights from this.

To this end, the following part of the chapter describes the linguistic background in more detail with emphasis on the local Fulfulde variety. Here, I also lay out some methodological and theoretical problems related to such diffuse linguistic settings. Subsequently, I present a variety of social and linguistic data related to the group of MTDs. After a more general appraisal of the overall make-up of the group, I look at correlations between individual MTD's social attributes and features of their Ego-Centred-Networks (ECN) on the one hand and linguistic variation they display on the other. I thus throw light on some of the governing principles for the actual management of the communicative tasks at hand. The concluding part, then, sums up those findings from the communicative challenges in a typically postmodern Global South setting and tries to relate them to postmodern urban communicative settings in general.

4.2 The linguistic background, theory and method

The spectrum of Fulfulde[2] spoken in northern Cameroon reaches from the highly prestigious variety of Diamaré, mainly found around the city of Maroua in the far North, to an L2-variety widely used all over N-Cameroon and earlier glossed as 'pidgin' Fulfulde (Noss 1979: 183, 184). The two varieties, Diamaré Fulfulde and the L2 lingua franca version, can be regarded as the opposite poles of a continuum of socially valued speech forms. The values attributed to these forms recently seem to change, as Diamaré is nowadays often seen as an old-fashioned and somehow backward and rural variety (p.c. R. Kramer). However, speakers who exclusively use linguistic features associated with either particular variety are rare. Rather, language use of Fulfulde speakers oscillates between the two poles comprising a broad range of linguistic variation showing the speakers' proficiency in several dialectal or sociolectal registers (Kramer 2017: 29, 30).

Being part of that continuum, the Fulfulde of Ngaoundéré also does not exhibit a defined linguistic standard with clear-cut features on any linguistic level. Accordingly, it is difficult to measure deviation and variation when there is nothing that serves as *tertium comparationis*. One way to handle this methodological problem is to define a linguistic norm that prevails in a group of actors which is related to the speakers under scrutiny. As has been shown by the Milroys (1985) and others (e.g. Eckert 2000; Gal 1979), in tight-knit social networks speech norms tend to stay conservative and do not display great dynamics and fluidity. The linguistic behaviour in a social network (preferably tight-knit) of personally acquainted actors could thus be used as a proxy for comparison. This method was applied also in Ngaoundéré, where Kramer (2017, 2018: 8, 9) showed that, under certain conditions, i.e. extreme degrees of network-centralisation, connectedness and compactness, a group norm develops among the mechanics of open road-side garages.

The research on MTDs is different as members of this group are extremely mobile during their workday and often live far out of town in cheaper peripheral or even rural areas. I therefore chose an adapted approach and started to investigate MTD's Ego-Centred-Networks (ECN). 'An ego-centred, or local, network consists of a focal person or respondent (ego), a set of alters who have ties to ego, and measurements on the ties from ego to alters and on the ties between alters' (Wasserman and Faust 1994: 53). Accordingly, one focuses on one ego at a time, questioning him (MTDs are all men) for his most important relation in socially relevant fields like friendship, work relations, spare time activities and household members. Moreover, an ego not only reveals his relations to others (alteri) but also judges the relations between those. Hence, the resulting ECN is an individually biased subjective view of these relations and does not allow for certain analyses that are possible with complete networks; e.g., to differentiate between in- and outgoing ties of actors. The idea behind the ECN approach is to cover a vast or dispersed group via random sampling and derive probabilistic evidence from statistical analysis for the entire group. Although some specific SNA-measures are not possible with ECNs, more general measures (e.g., degree, density, multiplicity) are comparable with SN-data from closed groups and can thus be used for comparative purposes.

The linguistic side of the research is also challenging. The researcher was keen to get 'naturalistic' data, which are quite difficult to gather, especially when one wants to grasp linguistic accommodation strategies between customers and service providers (see below). A further aspect of the linguistic data gathering is the question of comparability and frequency. This was tackled by asking all MTD egos to recount two picture stories (dog story 1 + 2, developed by R. Kramer and designed by M. Bastian) in their idiosyncratic Fulfulde. On the one hand, this sort of data gathering is not as artificial as, for example, a simple word list or a reading test, but, on the other hand, keeps the amount of variation manageable as the respondents stick to the story description. These data yielded variables from all linguistic levels that are used to determine specific group norms (cp. Beyer 2020a: 660, 661; Kramer 2017: 41, 42). I will be discussing only the subset of variables that was used to evidence the Fulfulde variation by MTDs of different social and ethnolinguistic backgrounds.

The first variable, [DOG], is the lexical item used for 'dog'. It is inspired by a shibboleth known all over Northern Cameron which is also captured in a popular saying. The saying states that people from Maroua use the word *rawaandu* to express the notion 'dog' while in Garoua (a major city between Maroua and Ngaoundéré) *boosaaru* is used, and in Ngaoundéré *goyru*.[3] The second variable, [AGR], reflects variation in noun-class agreement morphology. The values of the variable range from full use of agreement marking on targets like object markers, adjectives, definite articles, etc. to a mere reflection of number and/ or animacy on the agreement targets. The [PL.CL]-variable considers whether plural nouns are marked using the inherited Fulfulde gender pairing or any other device, like a generalised plural suffix or a numeral (Kramer 2017: 40–3). Table 4.1 shows the variables arranged along a scale from the more reduced L2

Table 4.1 Linguistic variables and their values as used in the Ngaoundéré study (adapted from Kramer 2018)

Variable	linguistic level	L2 ------- continuum ------- L1 (Diamaré)	
[DOG]	Lexeme used for the concept DOG	*goyru*	*boosaaru* *rawaandu*
[AGR]	Agreement classes or number/ animacy distinction	Number distinction: *o do naŋga* **mo** 'he is catching it (the dog)' animacy distinction: *o do naŋga* **ŋga** 'he is catching it (the dog)'	Agreement classes: *o do naŋga* **ndu** 'he is catching it (the dog)'
[PL.CL]	Number distinction marked by paired noun form classes or plural marker	Use of a fixed plural marker or numeral *ɓoggo ɓoggolji* 'rope/ropes' *pade-padeeji* 'shoe/shoes' *hooseere - hooseereʔen* 'mountain/ mountains' *debbo-debbo didi* 'woman, two women'	Use of paired noun form classes marked by suffixes: *ɓoggol - ɓoggi* 'rope/ropes' *fado - pade* 'shoe/shoes' *hooseere - kooseeje* 'mountain/ mountains' *debbo - rewɓe dido* 'woman/two women'

version to the high status Diamaré variety, but, as already remarked, these elements are rarely found in a clear-cut one-to-one correspondence.

A second set of data comes from recordings which selected MTDs made while actually riding their bikes and transporting passengers. These language data reflect the audible aspects of language use in actual customer-MTD relations. The main body of this data was collected in March 2019 and is not yet fully transcribed and analysed. For the purpose of this chapter, I give a first impressionistic account of those speakers' usage of construction types, the variety of discourse markers, and of their linguistic versatility in general.

4.3 Motor taxi drivers in Ngaoundéré and linguistic variation

The MTDs of Ngaoundéré are an extremely heterogeneous group of people. The only unifying features are their sex (all male) and the fact that they are mostly between their early twenties and mid-thirties. The age of the MTDs in this study displays a normal distribution with the largest group from 26 to 30 years old (Table 4.2). Apart from these two attributes, MTDs differ widely in their individual social backgrounds. For instance, the educational level among MTDs ranges from students financing their university years to drivers who have not received any formal education at all. Some MTDs are only in town for some months while others were born there and stayed ever since, others again only do the job on a part-time basis, switching between taxi driving and a range of other occupations.

This heterogeneity is also reflected by the distribution of ethnic and concomitant linguistic backgrounds (hence, ethno-linguistic background[4] (ELB)). While there is a natural dominance of local ethno-linguistic groups like Adamawa-Ful and Mbum, the distribution of all other groups again reflects the highly heterogeneous make-up of the MTD community (Table 4.3).

It thus appears that the fifty-one MTDs analysed so far cannot be classified as a social group as such but are only unified by their common occupation as taxi drivers. The question now is, whether there are any attributes that govern the use of linguistic variation within this occupational group. Therefore, I firstly

Table 4.2 Age groups among the MTDs of Ngaoundéré

age of MTDs	number	Percent
< 20	3	5.9
21–25	11	21.6
26–30	22	43.1
31–35	7	13.7
36–40	6	11.8
41 >	2	3.9
Total	51	100

Table 4.3 Distribution of ethno-linguistic background among MTDs

Ethno-linguistic background	Number	Percent	Code nr. in ECN Figures (below)
Adamawa-Ful	14	27,4	1
Mbum	10	19,6	3
Diamaré-Ful	6	11,8	2
Shuwa Arab	5	9,8	10
Biu-Mandara	4	7,8	12
Northern Cameroon	3	5,9	8
Ngambay	3	5,9	5
Southern Cameroon	2	3,9	6
Kanuri/Kole	2	3,9	11
Hausa	1	2	7
Gbaya (Ubangi)	1	2	4
Total	51	100	

look at the correlation between linguistic variable use and the classical attributes; for example: age, education and duration in town. Secondly, I try to uncover relations between ECN measures and variable uses.

A first approximation to adaption processes can be made via the relation between the time an actor has spent in the linguistic environment of Ngaoundéré and the value of the linguistic variables he uses. Correlating actors' length of stay in the city with the three linguistic variables may give some first hints as to their proneness to adaption. While [DOG] and [PL.CL] do not show any kind of effect, the [AGR] variable displays a slight positive tendency (cor. = 0.27 and p = 0.053) towards the use of agreement marking on a reduced set of dependant categories, namely adjectives, numerals and class pronouns. Apparently, agreement marking is sensitive to duration in the Fulfulde-as-lingua franca environment of Ngaoundéré whereas the shibboleth value of [DOG] is much less affected by this (cp. below). The same sort of correlation test also reveals that neither the attribute 'age' nor 'education level' correlates with either of the linguistic variables. The fact that the lexical variable is much less affected by a given actor's length of stay in the city is further corroborated by the Kendall's tau correlation test (for nominal variables like ELB) showing that the ethno-linguistic background determines the [DOG] variable with a probability above 70%. As for the [PL.CL] variable, no correlation could be detected. It generally looks like the speakers mostly apply a division along human/non-human-reference and are gradually giving up the noun-class related plural marking system.

Turning to ECN measures, some first general observations are in order. The average net size (degree) of an MTD displays about 8 contacts. Within such an average ECN, the average density is at 0.626, which means that of all possible connections 63% are realised on average. However, the extreme values of both measures are widespread, between 4 and 15 contacts per ECN and between

17% and 100% for density. Comparing these figures with whole networks, we see that the average degree and density is much higher among MTDs than among the workers of the ten roadside motorcycle garages researched by Kramer (2018). These latter groups show average degrees around 2.7 (1.6 < 2.7 > 3.5) and densities of about 38% (28% < 38% > 50%). This comparison of network measures seems to indicate, again, the outstanding heterogeneity of the MTDs and, at the same time, the high relevance of their personal networks. Given their highly mobile work, my informed guess would be that they feel a general need for extended and well entertained ego networks, at least compared to the locally more stable workers at the garages.

Looking at MTD's ECN-measures and variable use, some interesting correlations also show up. There is a negative correlation (cor.= −0.33, p = 0.01) between density and the use of the lexical variable [DOG]. That is, dense ECNs show more variation than those that are more loosely connected and centred around an ego. Another interesting correlation tells us something about the general setups of the ECNs: The ei-index (Krackhardt and Stern 1988) is a measure that looks at homogeneity within a single ECN in calculating whether the contacts of a given ego are in a different (**e**xternal) or a same (**i**nternal) attribute category. The ELB_ei index thus indicates the proportion of contacts with an ego's own or other ethno-linguistic groups (oscillating between +1 (heterogeneity) and −1 (homogeneity)). Among the MTDs, this index displays a negative correlation (cor. = −0.38, p = 0.005) with ECN-density. This translates to the fact that the denser an ECN is, the more contacts within its own ethno-linguistic group it contains.

So, actors from the MTD group have the tendency to build their networks mainly along ethnolinguistic ties but seem to blur the lexical shibboleth at the same time. The flip side of this are actors with low density networks who do not have much contact to their own ELB-group but stick more to their appropriate lexical identification word. Keeping the above displayed general observations in mind, we now look at some individual MTD's and try to make sense of their linguistic behaviour.

4.3.1 Actor Ego1

The first individual (Ego1) is a student at the University of Ngaoundéré and originally from the Republic of Chad. He has been in town for six years and just recently started to work as MTD. It is only through taxi driving that he began to speak Fulfulde because French is the dominant language at the university. He therefore counts as a learner who is still struggling to express himself clearly in this language.

The ei-index of Ego1 (Figure 4.1) shows maximal heterogeneity (+1), which is explained by the fact that none of his contacts is from the same ELB as he himself and is further signalled by the ethnic labels and the colours reflecting ELB-codes. So, he has no contacts with actors from his own group (*Ngambay*)

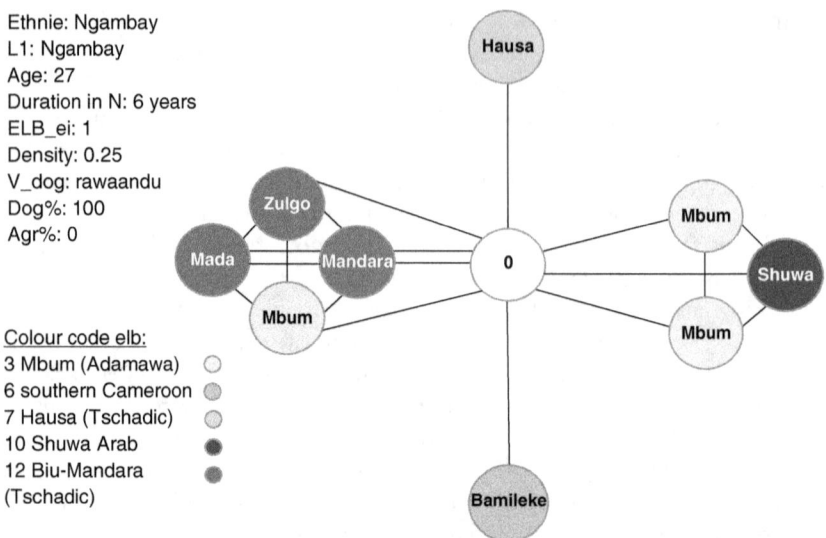

Figure 4.1 ECN of Ego1 (University student originally from Chad).

and his alteri are from many other different ethnic groups. For him, the notion for [DOG] is just the one he has learned first and no one in his heterogeneous and not very dense network imposes another one. His status as language learner is most clearly displayed by the non-existence of agreement marking.

The graphic representations in this study are produced with a built-in option of the R-package 'EgoR' for analysing ECN (Krenz 2017). In the figures, ego is always represented by (0). On the left side figure the discussed attributes (ego's ethnic label, L1= ELB of his up-bringing, age, duration in Ngaoundéré), the relevant ECN-measures (ELB_ei = homogeneity (−1)/heterogeneity (+1), density) and the values for the linguistic variables (V_dog = *rawaandu/boosaaru/ goyru*, Dog% = percentage of value frequencies (the ego of Figure 4.1 uses *rawaandu* as value for [DOG] in 100% of the occurrences), Agr% = percentage of use of agreement markers). The colours of the vertices represent the ELB of the alteri (for code numbers cp. Table 4.3 above) while the labels display the concrete ethnic names.

Looking at the discourse data of Ego1 with a taxi customer, we see him using Fulfulde but – as is to be expected – with quite a low level of grammatical complexity. That is, he employs verbs either in infinitive forms or in the only non-finite form he seems to know, i.e. a copular construction where a *be*-verb is combined with the usual imperfective ending *[-a]* in active voice yielding a progressive reading. A sentence like (1), where Ego1 asks the client what she is waiting for, is immediately corrected by her (with a somewhat funny answer) employing the correct verb form, which exceptionally is *[-i]* in the case of the verb *reenugo* 'to wait' (cp. Noyé 1974: 58).

(1) Ego1

    | a | ɗo | reen-a | ɗume? |
    | 2SG | COP | wait-IPFV | what?[5] |

    'What are you waiting for?'

(2) Client

    | mi | ɗo | reen-i | jawmu | geɗal |
    | 1SG | COP | wait-IPFV | chef | destiny |

    'I am awaiting (my) master of destiny'

Throughout the transcript, no other finite verb than the imperfective *[-a]* for active voice in combination with the *ɗo*-copular is used, even when it is incompatible with the verb semantics or with the actual state of affairs that normally would not licence a progressive form. What is more, Ego1 is not using any object pronoun or other anaphoric means. He very consistently sticks to an S-V-structure, occasionally adding some object-like elements as a kind of afterthought or relating basic sentences by some sort of multipurpose connector:

(3) Ego1

    | geɗal | ɗume | je | ɓang-ugo | na? |
    | Destiny | what | CNJ | mary-INF | INT |

    What destiny, for the marriage (to marry)?

All of his grammatical structure is really basic and close to pidgin style. However, the customer doesn't seem to be bothered. She is very open-minded, laughs with him and accepts his way of speaking. She is, however, not adapting her level to his as she uses many more noun-class related agreement markers on pronouns and adjectives.

4.3.2 Actor Ego2

The next individual (Figure 4.2) represents a somehow opposite case. He is a native from Ngaoundéré and was raised in the local Fulfulde community. His ei-index signals a quite homogenous make-up of his ECN, which is corroborated by the ethnic labels of his contacts. The density of his ECN is close to the overall average (cp. above). The shibboleth variable reflects the Ngaoundéré version *goynu* with occasional incursions from the Garoua variety. His value for noun-class agreement (Agr% = 79) is among the highest in my data, reflecting his high Adamawa-Fulfulde competence.

The discourse data from his taxi recording were taken while a rain shower just started. In the conversation, the client reflects on the fact that all of a sudden the usually ubiquitous MTDs have disappeared and Ego2 explains why that is

Ethnie: Pullo (Adamawa)
L1: Adamawa Fulfulde
Age: 29
Duration in N: 29 years
ELB_ei: 0.454
Density: 0.563
V_dog: goyru/boosaaru
Dog%: 93
Agr%: 79

Colour code elb:
3 Mbum (Adamawa) ○
1 Adamawa-Ful   ○
6 southern Cameroon ●
11 Kanuri, Kolé   ●

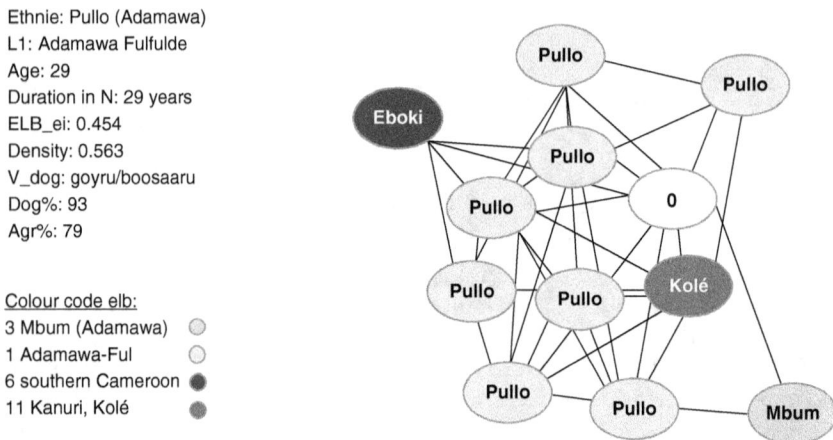

Figure 4.2 ECN of Ego2, native Fulfulde speaker of Ngaoundéré.

so. This short extract exemplarily shows his versatility in Fulfulde as different TAM-forms and a great variety of discourse markers appear:

(4) Ego2

Ahh,	to	ɓe	jood-an	banni	kam,
INTERJ	if	they	sit-FUT	like.this	EMPH

iyende	do	helt-ataa	banni	kam
Rain	be	stop-NEG	like.this	EMPH

Jonta	kam	na	sey	jango.
Now	EMPH	and	until	tomorrow

'Ahh, if they (the MTDs) sit like this (and) the rain will just not stop until tomorrow…'

(5) Ego2

Moto	darataa;	on	ndee	saft-i
MTD	stand-NEG	2PL.EMPH	then	be.enough-PFV

Moy	fuh	naast-i	jood-i	kayum,	too.
INT	all	enter-PFV	rest-PFV	just.like	right!

'…moto taxis don't stay, they then have enough, (who) all go home (and), stay just like this, right?!'

Without going into detail, one can already see the richness and the more complicated structures Ego2 is employing while doing his work. His use of TAM-constructions and discourse particles reflects the usual level of complexity of Adamawa-Fulfulde as heard in the city. It is simply the fact that – as depicted in Figure 4.2 – the actor is a native Fulfulde speaker from Ngaoundéré and exploits the whole range of his L1. His customer seems to be of the same general background as there is no great linguistic discrepancy or any misunderstandings between her and him.

4.3.3 Actor Ego3

The third close-up actor is somehow an in-between case. The family of Ego3 (Figure 4.3) is originally Kolé-speaking, a dialect of Kanuri from the northern border area with Nigeria and Chad. He himself was born in Garoua and has been living in Ngaoundéré for ten years, where he has been working as taxi driver for six years. His ECN displays a very high density but at the same time a less homogeneous structure than the overall correlation (cp. above) would predict. In this case, the heterogeneity in terms of ELB- contacts also explains the fact that no clear shibboleth use is observable. The actor switches quite freely between *rawaandu* and *ɓoosaaru* but doesn't employ the Ngaoundéré typical *goyru*. Noun-class agreement [AGR% = 63] is in the middle range reflecting his non-nativity but comparatively long stay in Ngaoundéré. The extreme density and slight heterogeneity of the ECN explains the fact that no specific speech norm (in terms of the variables tested) seems to develop here.

His data from the taxi ride reveal that he is well acquainted with the language. There is no real difference to Ego2 (the native speaker from Ngaoundéré). Ego3 also uses a variety of TAM constructions, conjunctions and emphatic discourse markers. His use of subject and object pronouns displays a certain familiarity

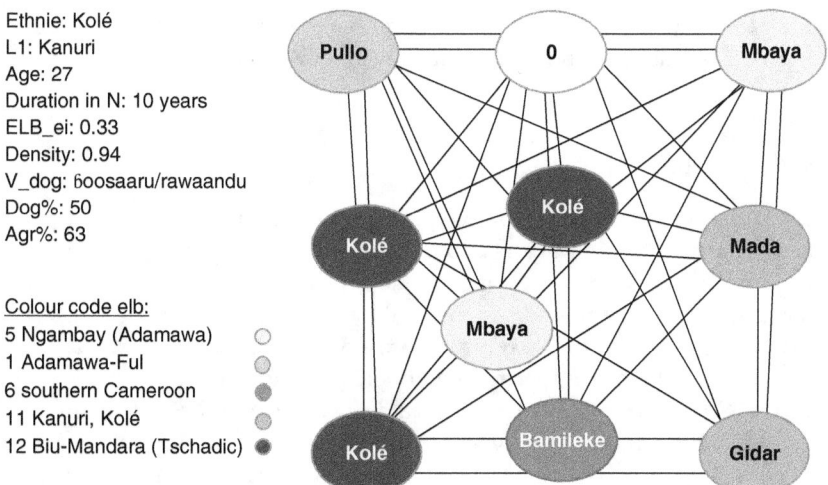

Figure 4.3 ECN of Ego3, a Kolé-speaker from the northern borderland of Cameroon, Chad and Nigeria.

with the 1PL inclusive/exclusive differentiation albeit using the exclusive form in an unusual way (6).

The excerpt is a reaction to the customer's demand to have a stopover at a money-transfer point. His concern is that it will take very long while he is bound to wait without extra money.

(6) Ego3

    Too annd-a   kadi   min   kam   daam-aay-am
    Ok   know-IPFV EMPH 1PL.EXCL EMPH bother-NEG-1SG.OBJ
    'Ok, you know, we, I am not bothered …'

(7) Ego3

    To   a   annd-i   en   neeɓ-ataa   ko   Ni
    CNJ.CAUS 2SG know-PFV 1PL.INCL take.long-NEG CNJ.TEMP EMPH
    '…if you know we don't take long…'

(8) Ego3

    En   yah-u   ammaa to   en   Annd-i   neeɓan…
    1PL.INCL go-IMP CNJ   CNJ.CAUS 1.PL.INCL know-PFV take.long-FUT
    '…we go, but if we understand (it) will take long… .'

All in all, his Fulfulde seems well adapted to the Ngaoundéré environment and he makes his point pretty clear. There are no unclear propositions and the customer understands Ego3's propositions well.

As far as I can see up to now, this speaker reflects the general level of lingua franca use in the city quite closely. He is quite familiar with the verbal system and TAM markings and shows some mastering of the pronoun and agreement marking.

4.4 Conclusion

This chapter intends to show some typical communicative challenges of post-modern individuals in an urban Global South context. Such an environment poses problems on various levels and warrants specific adapted approaches, both in terms of data gathering and analysis. Above all, the fact that the languages involved in the communicative setting are not standardised in the European sense of the word requires specific methodologies and heuristics.

In the Ngaoundéré case, I derive a kind of ad-hoc standard from language behaviour that is observed in a given group at a given time. Within the group of MTDs, this sort of comparative base relies on the statistically defined average linguistic behaviour observed in a random sample of MTDs. The appraisal of those actors' social attributes combined with measures of their social bonds, as captured by the analysis of their ego-centred network, throw some light on the features that play a major role in the overall communicative behaviour among this group of actors.

Thus, actors who display ECNs that are not well connected in terms of density and show a rather heterogeneous setup find themselves at the lower end of the language performance scale. They often stick to idiosyncratic forms of the Lingua Franca and do not converge easily to the mainstream in terms of lexicon (shibboleth) and grammatical structure (agreement). Actors who have a denser and more homogenous ECN, seem to be the ones who come closest to some sort of underlying standard. The most interesting case appears to be the ECN, where high density couples with heterogeneity. The example of Actor Ego3 shows that his heterogeneous but dense network doesn't support a lexical shibboleth but gets him close to a native speaker from Ngaoundéré in terms of grammatical structure.

The communicative problem at hand, namely to communicate successfully with customers, seems to be solved by any one of these actors. Be they somewhat marginal newcomers to town or part of the so-called autochthonous speaker group, when it comes to customer talk it seems that everybody involved accepts even the most rudimentary language use. One has the impression that the fact that everybody is aware of the unfocused and multi-layered language situation in Ngaoundéré leads to a quite liberal standpoint concerning language use, at least in an occupational field like taxi service.[6]

On the linguistic side, one interesting question to ask is whether and how these language behaviours shape the overall make-up of Adamawa-Fulfulde in Ngaoundéré. As far as can be judged from the analysis of the MTDs and from the garage networks (Kramer 2018), an urban variety exists that is difficult to pinpoint for a single speaker, but that displays some general characteristics that may serve as a generally accepted basis for local users. This variety is characterised by a restricted set of agreement targets, a reduced set of anaphoric pronouns that often operate along an animacy-hierarchy and some specific lexical items. It is mainly spoken by native people from Ngaoundéré and non-natives who stayed long enough and developed extended social networks. Even those speakers who are from a traditionally Fulfulde background who may be able to speak a closer-to-prestige variety seem to converge to this Ngaoundéré variety, which, however, is still to be defined more precisely, and that also seems to be constantly in flux.

Translating these findings to postmodern urban settings in general, one might infer something along the following lines: To the extent that urban language settings become more diffuse and less focused (which can be observed in urban capitals worldwide), actors with dense but at the same time heterogeneous networks seem to adapt more easily to communicative tasks than actors who stick to homogenous ethnic backgrounds and/or centralised groups. It is not ruled out that such developments add to the shape of a given dominant language in such a way that it diverges gradually from a predefined standard in developing even more diffuse and simplified structures.

As daring as such a prediction based on the extremely small data base and evidence presented in this chapter is, it mirrors mechanisms of simplification and reduction in other urban linguistic settings worldwide and also seems to correlate with common sense.

Notes

1 This is mainly due to a multitude of currently ongoing regional crises and concomitant migration: the interior tensions (bordering on a civil war) between English-speaking and French-speaking provinces of Cameroon, the Boko Haram problem in the Nigerian borderland, the warlord problem in the Central African Republic on the Eastern border, and the enduring economic and ecological crisis in the northern neighbour country Chad.
2 Fulfulde (Atlantic family, Niger-Congo phylum) or Fula is the language of the Fulani or, in the French tradition, of the Peul (derived from the singular of the ethnonym, i.e. *pullo* (sg.), *fulɓe* (pl.)).
3 This saying inspired the two picture stories (dog story 1 + 2) that were used for linguistic data gathering. They feature dogs in various situations (stealing meat from a butcher, gathering under a tree, being with their masters, etc.).
4 The ELB-labels are a mixture of individual language and ethnic names (e.g., Kanuri, Hausa), classificatory terms of language groups, where the individual languages are very small and/or closely related (e.g., Biu-Mandara) or just lump categories for speakers from not clearly defined or locally unknown groups (e.g., southern Cameroon).
5 Abbreviations used in the interlinearisation: CAUS = causative; CNJ = conjunction; COP = copula; EMPH = emphatic; EXCL = exclusive; FUT = future; IMP = imperative; INCL = inclusive; INF = infinitive; INT = interrogative; INTERJ = interjection; IPFV = imperfective; NEG = negation; IPFV = imperfective; OBJ = object; PL = plural; PFV = perfective; SG = singular; TEMP = temporal.
6 A comparable conclusion, namely that in an unfocused language situation with many more or less non-standardised languages involved, speakers tend to stretch their willingness to communicate even beyond the actual understanding has also been reached in the analysis of a rural communicative situation in Africa (Beyer 2020b).

References

Beyer, Klaus (2020a), Contact among African Languages. In: *Handbook of Language Contact* (second edition). Raymond Hickey (ed.), 649–668. London: Wiley-Blackwell.
Beyer, Klaus (2020b), Input limitations in a diffuse linguistic setting: Observations from a West-African contact zone. In: *Limited Input. International Journal of Bilingualism (Special Issue)*. Ad Backus and Helena Halmari (eds.). London: Sage Publishing (https://doi.org/10.1177/1367006920937785).
Drzewiecka, Jolanta A. and Thomas K. Nakayama (1998), City sites: Postmodern urban space and the communication of identity, *Southern Communication Journal*, 64:1, 20–31.
Eberhard, David M., Gary F. Simons and Charles D. Fennig (eds.), 2020. *Ethnologue: Languages of the World*. (23rd edition), Dallas, Texas: SIL International. (www.ethnologue.com/country/CM accessed 5.10.2020)
Eckert, Penelope (2000), *Linguistic Variation as Social Practice*. Oxford: Blackwell.

Gal, Susan (1979), *Language Shift: Social Determinants of Linguistic Change in Bilingual Austria*. New York: Academic Press.

Krackhardt, David and Robert N. Stern (1988), Informal networks and organizational crises: An experimental simulation, *Social Psychology Quarterly*, 51:2, 123–140.

Kramer, Raija L. (2017), On canines, classes and concordances: Linguistic variation and norm development in Fulfulde varieties of Ngaoundéré (Northern Cameroon). In: *Language contact and change under multilingual conditions. Case studies from Africa. FAB 24–2012*. Beyer, Klaus and Raija Kramer L. (eds.), 29–50, Cologne: Rüdiger Köppe.

Kramer, Raija L. (2018), The role of central actors in distribution processes of linguistic variants: A multiple group analysis of motorcycle garages in Ngaoundéré (Cameroon). Paper held at *WOCAL 9*, 25–28 August 2018, Rabat, Morocco.

Krenz, Till (2017), *EgoR. R-package to import and analyse Ego-Centred Network Data*. Online: https://github.com/tilltnet/egor.

Lamola, M. John (2017), African Postmodernism: Its Moment, Nature and Content. *International Journal of African Renaissance Studies – Multi-, Inter- and Transdisciplinarity*, 12:2, 110–123.

Le Page, Robert B. (1992), 'You can never tell where a word comes from': Language contact in a diffuse setting. In: *Language Contact: Theoretical and Empirical Studies*. Ernst Håkon Jahr (ed.), 71–101, Berlin, New York: Mouton de Gruyter.

Milroy, James and Leslie Milroy (1985), Linguistic Change, Social Network and Speaker Innovation. *Journal of Linguistics* 21, 339–384.

Mohammadou, Eldridge (1978), *Les royaumes foulbé du plateau de l'Adamaoua au XIXe siècle: Tibati, Tignère, Banyo, Ngaoundéré*. Tokyo: Institute for the Study of Languages and Cultures of Asia and Africa.

Nekvapil, Jiří and Tamah Sherman (2015), An Introduction: Language Management Theory in Language Policy and Planning. In: *The Language Management Approach: Perspectives on the Interplay of Bottom-up and Top-down*. [Special Issue]. *International Journal of the Sociology of Language* 232: 1–12.

Noss, Phillip A. (1979), Fula: A language of change. In: *Readings in Creole Studies*. Hancock, Ian F. (ed.), 173–188, Gent: E. Story-Scientia.

Noyé, Dominique (1974), *Cours de Foulfouldé. Dialecte Peul du Diamaré, Nord-Cameroun*. Paris: Librairie Orientaliste.

Tabouret-Keller, Andrée (1992), Language contact in focused situations. In: *Language Contact: Theoretical and Empirical Studies*. Ernst Håkon Jahr (ed.), 179–194. Berlin, New York: Mouton de Gruyter.

Wassermann, Stanley and Katherine Faust (1994), *Social Network Analysis: Methods and Applications*. Cambridge: Cambridge University Press.

Part II
Competing identities

ns in Japan

5 Language choices and language identities of Finns in Japan

Liisa-Maria Lehto

5.1 Introduction

5.1.1 Identity

Sociolinguistic changes influence the language identities of growing numbers of highly mobile people (Blommaert and Dong 2007; Dong 2012) who are moving around the globe and living in transcultural contexts (De Fina and Perrino 2013). Multilingual situations are growing in number and they are even more diverse than they used to be. Despite this fact, multilingualism is often seen through the lens of monolingualism, which is or at least has been considered as the norm (e.g. Lilja, Luukka and Latomaa 2017). People living in multilingual and multicultural situations encounter conflicts in their linguistic choices (Pavlenko and Blackledge 2004). There are different options at their disposal, but at the same time, social context creates restrictions and contradictions. Language choices and language identities of migrants are influenced by contradictions between practice and ideology: whether the speaker chooses the majority language to communicate and take part in society or chooses the language of one's heritage and feelings (Rampton 2005; Blackledge and Creese 2008). Immigrants' language situations change, and language issues play a crucial part in everyday life.

Language and communication are important in the production of identities (Kroskrity 2001: 106), and identities are constructed in linguistic interaction in relation to other people and groups (Pavlenko and Blackledge 2004). This chapter concentrates on language identities of Finns in Japan, and identities are considered rather as collective entities, not just as a property of individuals (see e.g. Bucholtz and Hall 2005; Block 2006). Language does not only reflect existing identities, but it actively takes part in the construction, reproduction and transformation of such identities (Rosa and Burdick 2017). Because identities are not essential in nature but are social and cultural products which are constantly in motion, they are processes of becoming something rather than being something (Block 2006). Identities are constructed in language when speakers take identity positions and assign different or similar identities to other parties in social interactions. This is a process called negotiation of identities

DOI: 10.4324/9780429348037-7

(Blackledge and Pavlenko 2001). As is the case with other types of identities, language identities can change during one's lifetime (Block 2006). In the same way that identities are created, ideologies are constructed in society. In particular, collective identities are ideological and an important part of identity negotiations. Ideologies are social in nature; therefore, it follows that identities are influenced by different ideologies about languages and language users, as well as the everyday situations in which languages are used (on ideologies, see e.g. Silverstein 1979; Irvine 1989; Blackledge and Creese 2010).

Globalisation has affected the link between language and identity. The non-essential, fragmented and contested nature of identities is emphasised in the lives of multilingual migrants (Blommaert 2003; Vertovec 2009; Jørgensen 2010), who may find their identities to be hybrid and ambivalent (Benwell and Stokoe 2006). Questions arise as to which languages or variants should be used with whom and in what context (Pavlenko and Blackledge 2004), as the traditional connection between language and nationality – as a building block of language identities – breaks down (e.g. Blackledge and Creese 2010). Language choices and attitudes cannot be separated from people's views of their own and others' identities (Pavlenko and Blackledge 2004). Hence, national and transnational identities are complex constructions in a globalised world (Wodak 2012), and the negotiation of identities is present in the everyday life of multilinguals (Pavlenko and Blackledge 2004), such as Finns in Japan.

5.1.2 Finns in Japan

In this chapter, the analysis concentrates on the language identities which were formed in discourses of urban immigrants, using the example of Finns in Japan. They were studied from interviews and pair conversations to show how language choices and language identities were expressed. There are approximately 800 Finnish citizens in Japan, and about half of them reside in Tokyo metropolitan area (see https://finlandabroad.fi/web/jpn/finland-in-japan1). Finns in Japan form a heterogeneous group: they are Finnish born but have moved to Japan for multiple reasons in different stages of their lives. These Finns represent facets of today's diverse global migration, transnationalism and multilingual lives (see e.g. Vertovec 2007): they should be seen as transnational individuals and have not formed actual communities. Finns in Japan can be considered elite migrants who have moved to Japan of their own accord, compared to migrants who have been forced to leave their home countries (e.g. refugees) (Dong 2009, 2012).

5.1.3 Research questions

This chapter aims to find out: (1) what everyday language choices reveal about the identities of Finns in Japan and (2) how languages and language speakers are constructed in the discourses. The aim is to determine how identity positions are formed in the ways Finns in Japan talk about their multilingual everyday life. Critical discourse analysis (CDA) (e.g. Fairclough 1989) is used to analyze language identities via language choices and certain language features in the use of speech amongst Finns in Japan. For example, choice of a pronoun can be a meaningful feature. It can reveal discourses and identities: how self and the other are seen and constructed by language use.

5.2 Data and method

5.2.1 Informants

The informants of this study, Finns in Japan, were multilingual speakers who lived in Japanese metropolitan areas[1] during the interviews. They were first generation migrants, born in Finland, who moved to Japan as adults. There were eight informants in total, aged 20 to 60. Two were women and six were men. The mother tongue of all the informants was Finnish, and according to informants' own evaluation, most could speak both Japanese and English fluently. The informants are referred to with pseudonyms. The data of this study consists of eight recorded one-on-one interviews and four recorded pair conversations; all collected during a field trip to Japan in the autumn of 2014. Each informant first participated in an interview, and then the same informants were divided into pairs for pair conversations. Two pairs were strangers to each other before the interview, one pair were acquaintances (Lauri and Krista) and one pair were friends (Veijo and Niko), but it seemed that the familiarity or the lack of it between the interviewees did not affect the effortlessness of the flow of conversation. Both the interviews and the pair conversations were conducted in Finnish (translations to English by the author) and following the scheme of a semi-structured interview (Tiittula and Ruusuvuori 2005). There is approximately 13 hours of recorded data used for this study: nine hours of interview data and four and half hours of pair conversation data. The recordings were transcribed, and the Finnish excerpts were later translated into English. The data was a part of a larger study of fourteen interviews and seven pair conversations (see Lehto 2018). In this chapter, only the data from informants who lived in urban settings has been included. The informants had moved to Japan for various reasons and lived there for different lengths of time; some of the younger ones only for a few years, others for over a decade. As a trend, the younger Finns first came to Japan to study and stayed on to work. Several informants also found spouses while in Japan. Younger informants have attended Japanese language courses before moving to Japan, but amongst the older Finns in Japan this is often not the case.

5.2.2 Technique used: CDA

The data was analyzed using critical discourse analysis (CDA), which is widely used in the field of multilingualism, identity and ideology (e.g. Fairclough 1989, 1992; Milani and Johnson 2008; Wodak 2012; Wodak and Meyer 2016).

Critical discourse analysis studies language in relation to society. It concentrates on ideologies and power that are enacted in language and the social practices of people. Language is understood to be determined by social structure. At the same time, language constantly reshapes and consolidates social structures in society (Fairclough 1992; Wodak and Meyer 2016). Discourses were here considered as a social form of language use, socially shared ways of constructing the world: in terms of shared ways of thinking, shared meanings and ideologies (see, e.g. Gee 1999; Wodak 2012). Language does not merely reflect identities of individuals and groups, but identities are constructed, reproduced and transformed in language (Rosa and Burdick 2017). CDA is suitable for analyzing identities in a multilingual situation, because it takes into consideration two facets of identity construction. First, it concentrates on language's connection to society and language as a social phenomenon (see, e.g. Fairclough 1992; Wodak and Meyer 2016). Additionally, it acknowledges the importance of language features; that is, meaningful choices in language use, in which identities are materialised (Fairclough 1989). Connecting linguistic features to the macro-level social theory of society (Pietikäinen and Mäntynen 2009) makes CDA a powerful tool to study identities.

Language identities can be detected in language discourses; in other words, in the ways people talk about languages and speakers. In language discourses, roles and meanings reveal identities taken on by the speaker or given to someone else (Buckholz and Hall 2005; Wodak 2012). Identities are shaped in communication and in relation to other people: groupings and positionings are seen in linguistic features. Divisions between the self and others, 'we' and 'they', can be detected in linguistic data. Language identities are reflected, constructed and challenged in language (Pavlenko and Blackledge 2004). Consequently, they can be found by using critical discourse analysis. Language choices and language features were scrutinised in the data to investigate how language identities were constructed by a certain urban immigrant group, that is, Finns in Japan. First, it was determined which languages the informants reported they used in different situations in their daily lives in Japan. These language choices revealed identities that are bound to domains, which reveal the importance of the social context when choosing a language. Next, Fairclough's (1989) model on critical discourse analysis was used, concentrating on certain language features that the informants chose during the interviews and pair conversations. The focus was on different names and functions that the informants used when speaking about different languages and speakers, as well as evaluations given to different languages. These features were markers of different in-groups and out-groups, which informants positioned themselves in.

5.3 Language choices as acts of identity

Contexts define values of different languages and determine how functional the language users' repertoires are (Karjalainen 2012; Blommaert and Backus 2011). As for Finns in Japan, situations in which English could be spoken were rare – not to mention the almost non-existent situations where they were able to use Finnish. Their identities were influenced in two ways. First off, their language choices were, at least partially, conditioned at the macro level by the surrounding society, which, in this case, was mostly monolingual Japanese (e.g. Siddle 2011). Additionally, in many cases English was neither a visible language in Japanese society nor a useful language resource (about language resources, see, e.g. Blommaert 2010). However, the situation of these individuals at a micro level was inherently multilingual, including their family situations, and there were multiple languages in use in the lives of the informants. During the interviews, the informants were asked which languages they use in certain situations, also called domains (Fishman 1991), and with whom. Their answers were grouped in five different domains of language use, which stem from the interview questions. The domains of language use (Fishman 1991) do not cover all aspects of the language situations in which multilingual migrants live today. However, these domains were considered as language choices and hence regarded as relevant indicators of identities (Pavlenko and Blackledge 2004). Furthermore, the informants did not seem to question the existence of different domains, and sometimes domains came up in their speech even without asking. The language domains found in the data were: (1) relatives and friends in Finland, (2) home, (3) society, (4) work and/or study and (5) friends and contacts in Japan. When considering the usage of different languages on an everyday basis, there was a great deal of variation among the Finns residing in Japan.

It was obvious from the data that the language used with relatives and friends in Finland would be Finnish, and this was the case with all eight informants. English was the language at home for three out of eight informants. In these homes, English was used alongside Japanese in two cases and had a role as a lingua franca between spouses. For one informant, remarkably, it was the only language used with the spouse. The majority of the informants, six out of eight, used Japanese at home; hence the main language at home was typically Japanese. However, two of the informants used Finnish as a second language with their children. Interestingly, except for these two informants, all the other informants only used Finnish in the domain of relatives and friends who reside in Finland or occasionally with other Finns living in Japan. Modern-day methods of communication and networks have created opportunities to keep in touch with people around the world more easily than in the past (De Fina and Perrino 2013). Because of technological advances like the Internet, Finns in Japan now had the possibility to use Finnish, even daily, if they wished to do so. Despite this, as the informants themselves described the situation, their use of the Finnish language was sparse. When Finnish was used, it was mostly done about once a month with relatives or during special occasions in Japan; for instance, at festivals of Finnish associations. In Weckström's (2011) study on people with a Finnish background in Sweden, it is shown that Finnish language use was restricted inside home. For some of the Finns in Japan the situation is similar: Finnish is typically used with children. However, when their children grow up, the language of the surrounding society may become more central in the children's lives through school and hobbies (see also Lehto 2018). Hence, it is fairly realistic to assume that at least for the Finns who have children, the role of the Finnish language in the lives of the informants might change in the future.

In the informants' everyday life, Japanese dominated almost all the domains of language use, leaving not only Finnish, but also English behind. Monolingualism could be seen as a norm (see, e.g. Lilja, Luukka and Latomaa 2017) in Japanese society and, excluding English, other foreign languages are fairly invisible. This was especially noticeable when speaking about the language of society, as Japanese was the only language the informants mentioned. Here, communication-based perception of language, which considers languages merely as resources (Blommaert 2003), became emphasised when the surrounding society required the use of a certain language. The language used for work and study had more variation even though this domain mostly demanded the use of the Japanese language. Three out of eight informants regularly used English at work or in their studies and, in addition, two needed English at least occasionally. However, when out in society – in shops, public places, or with officials – all the informants used only Japanese. To conclude, in certain urban settings, even a commonly recognised lingua franca, such as English, could become an almost completely useless resource in communication (Blommaert 2003). In a way, English could be seen as a lingua franca in Japan, but it was not a lingua franca as we usually understand it: a language between all people who do not share the same mother tongue. Instead, it was seen as the language of *foreigners* in Japan and, especially, as the common language among foreigners. English might be used at home with a Japanese spouse or more generally between spouses who do not share the same native language, but in many cases, it was replaced by Japanese. This usually happened once the informants became fluent in Japanese. In most cases, English was restricted to one domain, because it was used only with foreign friends and contacts.

5.4 Finns, Japanese and foreigners: Self-positioning and identity

The preceding sections discussed language choices as markers of identities. In the following section, examples of transcribed data were used to illuminate identity negotiations in the data sets. In these sections, specific notations were utilised. When quoting the informants in the body text, simple quotation marks (") were used. Double parentheses were used to indicate remarks or additions made by the researcher, and dashes were used to mean one (-) or more (- -) words left out of the original text.

Throughout the interviews and pair conversations, the informants negotiated their identities (on identity negotiations, see, e.g. Buckholz and Hall 2005) as they talked about their linguistic situations. They took social positions (Davies and Harré 1990) by giving different labels to languages and language users, themselves included. They also gave varying evaluations to languages, the speakers of those languages and their skills in different languages, and, thus, they took a stand on such questions as authenticity and the degree of nativeness of a speaker. They created memberships in different categories, as well as in-groups and out-groups denoting 'we' and 'they'. Behind these groupings and identity positions, there were language ideologies (e.g. Irvine 1989; Rosa and Burdick 2017), which played a role in the formation of boundaries between different language groups (e.g. Blommaert and Verschueren 1998; Dahingen 2012).

Most informants self-identified with a common grouping: they belonged to the group of 'Finns', but, surprisingly, probably because of the surrounding society, not as tightly and clearly as they belonged to the group of 'foreigners' or 'other foreigners'. Japanese was the language informants had mastered well enough to participate in society. Finnish was the language for special occasions and was used with other members of the group of 'Finns'; however, this group did not seem to be an important group to identify with when staying in Japan. Four informants implicated that they had become distanced from Finnish friends, and life in Finland. One of them, Niko, reported that other aspects of life, other than keeping in touch with Finns, had grown more important. In his opinion, other foreigners have become closer to him than Finns:

(1)   Niko: In Japan I have gotten to know foreigners who have moved away (from their country of origin) - they are closer to that what I do nowadays.

When positioning themselves in an in-group, language, and especially skills in English, determined belonging. Speaking English meant being a foreigner in Japan, and skills in English, rather than lack of skills in Japanese, was a marker of this identity position. This contrast between in-group and out-group meant that the informants considered a lack of English skills as a characteristic of the Japanese. As one of the informants, Tatu, said: 'the English spoken by Japanese people is pretty poor of course'. The informant evaluated the typical English skills of the Japanese and gave the impression that he himself is different from them as a 'foreigner and Finn'. According to the informants, the Japanese people were a group who do not speak English, which they contrast to the self-evident fact that English was a commonly known language among Finns in Japan. It was not said out loud, but rather implicated, and also taken for granted, that Finns and foreigners speak English. In this way, the Japanese represented an out-group to the informants when compared to 'other foreigners' who shared a language with them. Tatu reported: 'almost every weekend - - we met - - with other exchange students and then of course - - all day was in English'. The Japanese were constructed as an out-group that rarely speaks English. Tatu evaluated this trait as common among Japanese people and describes how, in the Japanese high school he attended as an exchange student, 'even the English teachers did not know the ((English)) language properly'.

It seemed that a crucial language that determines identities and belonging could be something other than the language of the local society or the mother tongue. According to the informants, the English-speaking in-group included 'foreigners' or 'other foreigners' or those who were categorised by their nationality ('Russian'; 'Singaporean'), and the informants were a part of this group. As for the Japanese, they were regarded as English learners rather than speakers, and the informants described situations where they wanted to use the Japanese language, but the Japanese wanted to practice English:

(2) Joonas: - - there were all kinds of international events at the university, and in them the situation was one in which the Japanese would have wanted to practice speaking English, but I was not interested in attending those events at all, because I wanted to practice Japanese instead.

5.5 The identity of multicultural children and heritage language speaker parents

Questions about language choices inside the family become relevant when migrants have children (e.g. Karjalainen 2012) and a changed situation is often followed by negotiations on family language policies (King, Fogle and Logan-Terry 2008). Family language policy (FLP) is used when discussing language planning in the family (Curdt-Christiansen, 2009), and it can be implicit or explicit, consisting of family members' linguistic ideologies, practices and management (Curdt-Christainsen, 2009; King, Fogle and Logan-Terry, 2008). Here, the analysis concentrated on the way the Finns residing in Japan talked about their children's linguistic upbringing. Which languages were chosen to be used in multicultural families tells not only of different family language policies but also of the ideologies and practices behind those choices and the uses of different languages. The speakers' chosen languages also indicated their language identities. The assumption was that the Finns' distinctive situation in a geographically distant place from their origin and being part of a different culture was reflected in their discourses. For example, the importance of their mother tongue versus other languages may vary under these circumstances.

During the interviews, informants were given the chance to ponder family language policies together with other Finns. The informants created a picture of language choices conditioned not only by their own opinions, desires and hopes concerning their children but also the expectations of their spouses and society and possible limitations they set to the upbringing. There seemed to be a constant balancing between their heritage language that is connected to their national identity, and the local language of communication and Japanese society (compare Rampton 2005; Bucholtz and Hall 2005). Their multicultural and multilingual situation led not only to a reconsideration of the informants' own identity, but they also reflected upon their children's possible identities as Finns, Japanese or both. Ambivalence between the heritage language and the language of communication could be seen primarily in the nationality labels given to the children and secondarily in the evaluations given to different languages as well as their children as speakers of certain languages.

Language identities are co-existent with other social identities, such as ethnic and national identities (Block 2006). The Finns residing in Japan constructed language identities in which nations and languages seemed tightly connected. This connection was evident in the data despite the fact that in everyday lives of Finns in Japan, the Finnish language didn't play a central role. Especially in the case of the children of Finns in Japan, identities were not easy to define. Finns in Japan described their children's multifaceted identities in many ways. The aspect of nationality and origin could be seen in the given labels: 'half Japanese, half Finn'; 'half foreigner' and 'another homeland'. Additionally, they referred to their children's multilingualism as: 'two languages'; '((my child)) wants to speak Finnish still'. A father of two children born in Japan, Joonas, evaluated his children's skills in Finnish, and before these evaluations he used the term 'bicultural' when he referred to his children. Then he evaluated his children's language skills by saying that his children:

(3) Joonas:- - understand ((Finnish)) - - really well - - surprisingly well.

Example 3 indicates that no matter how highly Joonas evaluated his children's ability to understand Finnish, he at the same time implied that they do not actually speak Finnish or at least left that unsaid for one reason or another. There was another important point that example 3 showed, which related to identity positions and forming in-groups and out-groups. Even though Joonas said his children are bicultural, he commented on his children's Finnish in a way that one would comment on second-language speakers or on the language of a non-native Finn. Self-evident facts are revealing in CDA, and people can reconstruct certain discourses and ideologies without being aware of them (Mäntynen et al. 2012). The example here showed how it might not be necessary to comment on the language of a native speaker or the Finnish spoken by a Finn. Instead, as the father here pointed out, his children's foreignness is something to be mentioned, in this case by evaluating their skills in Finnish. There were hints of a tight connection between language, ethnicity and nationality in these kinds of evaluations and positioning in the discourses. He unconsciously implied that his child belonged either to a Japanese or Finnish group, but not both at the same time. Here a picture of one essential and whole identity is constructed (about identities see e.g. Hall 1999).

Language identities, alongside nationalities, can be defined through language skills, at least when language and nation are seen in tight connection. This kind of evaluating could be detected in the discourses: who was a language speaker and hence a member of a certain language group. In Joonas' and Tatu's conversation, there were many occasions when they constructed this kind of grouping based on language skills. As mentioned above, Joonas referred to his children as 'bicultural' and saw language as a part of his identity when he described how he wanted to teach his language to his children and, in doing so, 'provide foundations for life'. Later in the pair conversation, Joonas again described how his children are 'very native Japanese, of course'. He justified this with the fact that the mother of the children is Japanese. He stated that his children understood Finnish well, but example 4 shows that his children's Finnish language identity seemed to be some kind of side product of everyday language life, enacted only in certain situations. As for Krista (example 5), she presumed that her future child's language identity would be Japanese, since her and her husband's current place of residence is Japan. Finnish language identity was seen as quite distant at the time of the interview.

(4) Joonas: - - personally, it is still really important, the Finnish language. But how would I keep my children's language at least at that sort of level, even if it is hidden, so that if we go to Finland at some point in the future it would be easier to activate the language then.

(5) Krista: - - maybe at first Japanese would be the everyday language used in conversations. Since we live in Japan it would be the base ((for the languages)), - -. but then, when ((the child)) would grow up, it would be English or even Finnish then, later on.

In examples 4 and 5, the Finnish language and Finnish language identity were placed in a different time and space. They were situated in some undefined time in the future and in Finland. The Finnish language was not something that was present in their current everyday life in Japan. On the contrary, it was presented as distant from daily life and one's identity. According to the data, Finns in Japan constructed the identity of a Finnish speaker and Finn by contrasting themselves with these children and the identity of these children. For themselves, Finnish appeared as a de facto native language and the language of their home country. When they compared themselves to their children, the positioning was different: the children had another culture, language and home country, and they were perhaps not seen as Finns at all.

5.6 Successful and non-successful linguistic upbringing

When the informants spoke about raising children linguistically, different opinions, hopes and fears were mentioned, together with identities. The informants explained how they considered skills in the language of the surrounding society important to learn. On the other hand, keeping the Finnish language alive in Japan was essential from a heritage-language point of view, and important to being able to keep in touch with relatives in Finland (Weckström 2011). Deciding between practical use of language and ideologies was an everyday reality for multilinguals. However, even though the parents did their best when raising their children, the Finnish language was not always successfully transmitted to the next generation, as children will make their own language and identity choices at some point. Example 6 reveals the fact that even though Joonas chose the strategy to speak only Finnish with his children, his children made their own choices. He describes the situation at home:

(6) Joonas: – if I ask something like, so did you put that shirt in the washing machine, then comes, ((in Japanese:)) yes, I did.

Joonas also explained how he had insisted on speaking Finnish with his children and pretended not to speak Japanese. However, the children started questioning their fathers' lack of Japanese skills:

(7) Joonas: – – if they speak in Japanese, – I say that, you must speak Finnish to daddy, because daddy doesn't understand Japanese. – – my oldest son has now started to say that, but you understand Japanese spoken by mother and you understand Japanese spoken by all the other Japanese people – –

Joonas positioned himself as a Finnish-speaking parent, but implied that his children have another kind of language identity. By quoting his son, Joonas included the children in the 'other' group, who he 'doesn't understand'; that is, native Japanese speakers. It was clear in the pair conversations that there were contrasts between different group memberships, and thus the identity positions were intertwined with parenthood (see, e.g. Karjalainen 2012). The informants positioned themselves as parents (e.g. by saying 'daddy, dad') who spoke another language from the rest of the family or the surrounding society. Veijo explained, in general, how the children learned the language of the society, not for example Finnish. Niko described his own situation: because of work, he was not able to actively be present at home and speak Finnish to the child. However, he wanted to give a child access to Finnish by showing, for example, TV programmes:

(8) Veijo: – – it happens in many cases, that they ((the children)) do not learn their dad's or, foreign parent's ((language))

(9) Niko: – – so ((the child)) could hear some other languages than just Japanese.

It was seen in examples 8 and 9 that the Finns residing in Japan did not consider Finnish to be present in the lives of their children and considered children's everyday life and surroundings to be 'just Japanese'. This appeared to be mostly because of the monolingual surroundings and lack of Finnish contact. The informants also constructed a picture of a situation in which teaching one's heritage language to their children appeared, no matter how important, to be a difficult task to perform successfully. In the pair conversations, many stories of successes and failures were shared, and in these stories, there seemed to be a connection to identity (see also Karjalainen 2012; Weckström 2011).

The language discourses of Finns in Japan built in-groups and out-groups, and membership in these was based on the fact that some families had succeeded in raising their children multilingually and some had not. Stories about these situations were shared knowledge, as three out of eight of the informants had children. However, many of the experiences of other foreigners raising children in Japan or in other countries were told and reflected upon. Regardless of whether they have children or not, it seemed that being successful in raising children in the heritage language – or at least doing one's best – was the preferred situation. The in-group consisted of those who have succeeded or tried hard to succeed in their task. The out-group included parents who were not perceived as doing their job of sharing a culture, language and identity properly. In the data, the children of these people aroused pity in the informants. They also wondered whether the children who had not acquired the heritage language of their migrant parents felt neglected in this respect. Firstly, parents said things such as: 'damn - - I also should have taught more of ((my native language)) to the children'. Secondly, they spoke on behalf of multilingual children who regretted not being taught the native language of the parent.

(10)   Joonas ((speaking hypothetically as a child)): I wish my dad would have taught ((me Finnish)), or mother would have taught ((me Finnish)). I would have always wanted. - -
Tatu: I also think that these are tragic stories.

(11)   Tatu: I've - - met many of such - - those Finns who live here - - unfortunately often it has occurred that they have tried to ((use Finnish with the children)) but at some stage it just gradually ceased - - later they ((the children)) do sometimes regret it.

In examples 10 and 11, Joonas and Tatu brought the voice of the multilingual children into the conversation, and the informants shared the opinion that these kinds of cases were failures. The informants positioned themselves as if they were looking at the situation from outside, probably because they did not wish to include themselves in the group of parents in these stories. They built a picture of responsible parenthood by using warning examples of failures and pitied the children.

5.7 Conclusions

The negotiation of identities takes place in everyday situations in multilingual contexts when different ideologies of language and identity come into conflict (Pavlenko and Blackledge 2004). This is the case especially when considering the language situations of multilingual migrants in urban settings.[2] In this chapter, the identities of Finns residing in Japan were examined from the perspective of the language choices they made and how they chose to describe languages and language speakers. There were contradictions between the usage the language of daily communication and the native or heritage language. This was seen in the way Finns in Japan pursued individual use of multiple languages, but their multilingualism was quite unseen at the societal level. Japanese was used on a daily basis, but the use of other languages, and especially of the Finnish language, were restricted to special occasions or the family domain. These findings illustrate how research on the language choices and identities of small, scattered groups increases the understanding of a wider phenomenon concerning the complex language situations of mobile multilingual individuals at large.

In their identity negotiations (e.g. Pavlenko and Blackledge 2004), Finns in Japan took into account not only their identity as native Finnish speakers but also as a speaker of a foreign language, Japanese, and usually also re-evaluated the meaning of English as a part of their language identities (see Blommaert 2003 about re-evaluation). Balancing between at least three languages had an influence on their personal lives, especially inside multicultural families. Japanese had an important role as a language of communication in these Finns' lives. Japanese was the language of the local society they live in, and in many cases, it was also the language of the multicultural family. On the other hand, Finnish was important from the perspective of preserving contact with relatives, country of origin and one's identity. The study revealed that even though these two languages were essential to Finns in Japan, there was also one other language that was a marker of identity: English. English indicated a certain kind of belonging, but it was important in quite a different way from the other two languages. It seemed that being a foreigner was more essential than being a Finn, and English language, as well as having English-language skills, connected the Finns to the in-group of foreigners. Japanese people's skills in English were evaluated by the informants in this study as low, and hence they were excluded from this in-group based on language. It was interesting how, in certain multilingual urban settings, assumed roles and meanings of languages changed. Because English was not widely used in the Japanese context, it was not necessarily a lingua franca. On the other hand, being a foreigner in Japan was not necessarily associated with a lack of skills in the language of the local society, Japanese, but mastering another language, English, was.

The informants chose to give different names and labels to themselves and others, and by doing so, created groups based on language, language skills and nationality. Informants included themselves as members of an English-speaking in-group of 'foreigners' in contrast to Japanese people. They also commented on their children's identities by naming them for example 'half Finns' or 'half foreigners' and evaluating their language skills. These names and evaluations were essential, especially in their conversations concentrating on the linguistic upbringing of multilingual children in a complicated society. The children discussed by the informants in this study were seen as multicultural and multilingual but based on the evaluations of the children's language skills, they were not seen as equals compared to their parents and other Finns. They were rather considered Japanese or Japanese speakers. In the pair conversations, Finns in Japan agreed that transmitting their heritage language to their children was valuable. The informants shared stories about successes and failures of themselves and others in performing this task. At the same time, they constructed a picture of an in-group: parents who tried to do their best to complete their task. According to informants, the out-group was those who were considered 'non-dutiful parents' and their children, who were pitied by the informants, because they did not have the opportunity to acquire the heritage language and the identity that comes with it.

As the case of Finns in Japan has demonstrated, identities are fluid in changing communicative and social situations and influenced by imagined boundaries between languages and speakers. The surrounding society may determine language choice and, consequently, language and identity are not necessarily free identity choices of individuals, but rather necessary tools for communication conditioned by circumstances. This study showed how linguistic choices and decisions inside families, at the micro level of society, are ideological and influence identities. In the broader picture, family language policies and language identities are parts of today's urban and multicultural societies, in which membership and involvement in a society raise topical questions: What and whose language should be the language of communication in these societies? What is the relation between heritage languages and family language policies? Alongside language politics, the phenomena studied in micro-level sociolinguistics can have far-reaching impacts on complicated societies at large. Therefore, the identities and ideologies of multicultural migrants and their families should be a constant point of interest in sociolinguistics.

Notes

1 The informants' exact places of residence, areas or cities, are not mentioned to protect anonymity.
2 The findings of the study could have been different if other areas than metropolitan areas had been taken into consideration. However, according to Lehto (2018) the place of residence in Japan didn't have much influence for example on the daily use of Finnish language amongst Finns in Japan.

References

Benwell, Bethan and Stokoe, Elisabeth (2006): *Discourse and Identity*. Edinburgh: Edinburgh University Press.

Blackledge, Adrian and Creese, Angela (2008) Contesting 'Language' as 'Heritage': Negotiation of Identities in Late Modernity. *Applied Linguistics* 29 (4): 533–554.

Blackledge, Adrian and Creese, Angela (2010) *Multilingualism. A Critical Perspective*. London: Continuum International Publishing Group.

Blackledge, Adrian and Pavlenko, Aneta (2001) Negotiation of Identities in Multilingual Contexts. *The International Journal of Multilingualism* 5(3): 243–257.

Block, David (2006) *Multilingual Identities in a Global City*. Houndmills: Palgrave Macmillan.

Blommaert, Jan (2003) Commentary. A Sociolinguistics of Globalization. *Journal of Sociolinguistics* 7(4): 607–623.

Blommaert, Jan (2010) *The Sociolinguistics of Globalization*. Cambridge Approaches to Language Contact. Cambridge: Cambridge University Press.

Blommaert, Jan and Backus, Ad (2011) Repertoires Revisited. 'Knowing Language' in Superdiversity. *Working Papers in Urban Language & Literacies* 67. www.klc.ac.uk/lcd.

Blommaert, Jan and Dong, Jie Kathy (2007) *Language and Movement in Space*. Working Papers in Language Diversity.

Blommaert, Jan and Verschueren, Jeff (1998) *Debating Diversity: Analysing the Discourse of Tolerance*. London: Routledge.

Buckholtz, Mary and Hall, Kira (2005) Identity and Interaction: A Sociocultural Linguistic Approach. *Discourse Studies* 7(4–5): 585–614.

Curd-Christiansen, Xiao Lan (2009) Invisible and Visible Language Planning: Ideological Factors in the Family Language Policy of Chinese Immigrant Families in Quebec. *Language Policy* 8, 351–375.

Dahinden, Janine (2012) Rethinking Migrant Integration? In M. Messer et al. (eds), *Migrations: Interdisciplinary perspectives*, 117–128. Wien: Springer.

Davies, B. and Harré, R. (1990) Positioning: The discursive production of selves. *Journal for the theory of Social Behaviour* 20 (1), 43–63.

De Fina, Anna and Perrino, Sabina (2013) 'Transnational identities'. *Applied Linguistics* 34 (5), 509–515.

Dong, Jie (2009) 'Isn't it Enough to be a Chinese Speaker'. Language Ideology and Migrant Identity Construction in a Public Primary School in Beijing. *Language and Communication* 29, 115–126.

Dong, Jie (2012) Mobility, Voice, and Symbolic Restratification. An Ethnography of 'Elite Migrants' in Urban China. *Diversities* 14(2): 35–48.

Fairclough, Norman (1989) *Language and Power*. London: Longman.

Fairclough, Norman (1992) *Language and Social Change*. Cambridge: Polity Press.

Fishman, Joshua A. (1991) *Reversing Language Shift. Theoretical and Empirical Foundations of Assistance to Threatened Languages*. Clevedon: Multilingual Matters.

Gee, James Paul (1999) *An Introduction to Discourse Analysis. Theory and Method*. London: Routledge.

Hall, Stuart (1999) *Identiteetti*. Tampere: Vastapaino.

Irvine, Judith T. (1989) When Talk Isn't Cheap. Language and Political Economy. *American Ethnolinguist* 16: 248–267.

Jørgensen, Jens N. (2010) *Languaging. Nine Years of Poly-lingual Development of Young Turkish-Danish Grade School Students Vol I–II*. Copenhagen: University of Copenhagen.

Karjalainen, Anu (2012) *Liikkuva ja muuttuva suomi. Diskursiivis-etnografinen tutkimus amerikansuomalaisten kielielämäkerroista* [The Finnish Language in Motion. An Ethnographic and Discourse Analytic Study of Finnish-American Language Biographies]. Jyväskylä: Jyväskylän yliopisto.

King, Kendall A., Fogle, Lyn and Logan-Terry, Aubrey (2008) Family Language Policy. *Language and Linguistics Compass* 2(5): 907–922.

Kroskrity, Paul V. (2001) Identity. In: Key Terms in Language and Culture. Alessandro Duranti (ed.), 106–109. Oxford: Blackwell.

Lehto, Liisa-Maria (2018) *Korpusavusteinen diskurssianalyysi japaninsuomalaisten kielipuheesta* [Japan Finns' ways of talking about languages – corpus assisted discourse analysis]. Acta Universitatis Ouluensis B Humaniora 162. Kielten ja kirjallisuuden tutkimusyksikkö. Oulun yliopisto.

Lilja, Niina, Luukka, Emilia and Latomaa, Sirkku (2017) Kielitietoisuus eriarvoistumisekehitystä jarruttamassa [Language awareness as a factor, that mitigates increasing equality]. In: *Kielitietoisuus eriarvoistuvassa yhteiskunnassa* [Language Awareness *in an increasingly unequal society]. AFinLAn vuosikirja 2017.* Latomaa, S., Luukka, E., and Lilja, N. (eds), 11–29. Jyväskylä: Suomen soveltavan kielitieteen yhdistys.

Milani, Tommaso M. and Johnson, Sally (2008) CDA and Language Ideology –Towards a Reflective Approach to Discourse Data. In: *Methoden der Diskurslinguistik: Sprachwissenschaftliche Zugänge zur transtextuellen Ebene.* Jürgen Spitzmuller and Ingo H. Warnke (eds), 361–384. Berlin: Walter de Gruyter.

Mäntynen, Anne, Halonen, Mia, Pietikäinen, Sari and Solin, Anna (2012) Kieli-ideologioiden teoriaa ja käytäntöä. [Theory and Practice of Language Ideologies] – *Virittäjä* 116: 325–346.

Pavlenko, Aneta and Blackledge, Adrian (2004) Introduction: New Theoretical Approaches to the Study of Negotiation of Identities in Multilingual Contexts. In: *Negotiation of Identities in Multilingual Contexts.* Aneta Pavlenko and Adrian Blackledge (eds), 1–33. Clevedon: Multilingual Matters.

Pietikäinen, Sari and Mäntynen, Anne (2009) *Kurssi kohti diskurssia* [Course Towards Discourse]. Tampere: Vastapaino.

Rampton, Ben (2005) Crossing. Language and Ethnicity among Adolescents. Manchester: St. Jerome Publishing.

Rosa, Jonathan and Burdick, Christa (2017) Language Ideologies. In: *The Oxford Handbook of Language and Society.* Ofelia García, Nelson Flores and Massimiliano Spotti (eds), 103–123. Oxford: Oxford University Press.

Siddle, Richard (2011) Race, Ethnicity and Minorities in Modern Japan. In: *Routledge Handbook of Japanese Culture and Society.* Victoria Lyon Bestor, Theodore C. Bestor and Akiko Yamagata (eds), 150–162. Oxon: Routledge.

Silverstein, M. (1979) Language Structure and Linguistic Ideology. In: Paul R. Clyne, William F. Hanks and Carol L. Hofbauer (eds), The Elements, 193–248. Chicago: Chicago Linguistic Society.

Tiittula, Liisa – Ruusuvuori, Johanna 2005: Johdanto [an introduction]. – Liisa Tiittula and Johanna Ruusuvuori (toim.), *Haastattelu. Tutkimus, tilanteet ja vuorovaikutus* [Interview. Research, situations and interaction], 9–21. Tampere: Vastapaino.

The Embassy of Finland in Japan's webpage. https://finlandabroad.fi/web/jpn/finland-in-japan1. Cited 4.11.2020.

Vertovec, Steven (2007) Super-Diversity and Its Implications. *Ethnic and Racial Studies* 30(6): 1024–1054.

Vertovec, Steven (2009) *Transnationalism. Key Ideas.* Oxon: Routledge.

Weckström, Lotta (2011) *Representations of Finnishness in Sweden.* Studia Fennica Linguistica 16. Helsinki: Suomalaisen Kirjallisuuden Seura.

Wodak, Ruth (2012) Language, Power and Identity. *Language Teaching* 45(2), 215–233.

Wodak, Ruth and Michael Meyer (2016)[2001] Critical Discourse Studies: History, Agenda, Theory and Methodology. In: *Methods of Critical discourse Studies.* Ruth Wodak and Michael Meyer (eds), 1–22. London: Sage Publications.

6 PC goes East-Central Europe

Enregistering politically correct language in Budapest university dormitories

Csanád Bodó, R. K. Turai and G. Szabó

6.1 Introduction

Controversies of political correctness embody debates around (post-)modernity. Political correctness might be understood as a modernist project that endeavours to liberate individuals from the traces of oppressive linguistic norms of the past. Postmodernism contests the logic of this modernist endeavour. As Calinescu (1987: 276) puts it: 'postmodernism has entered into a lively reconstructive dialogue with the old and the past'. Apparently, old and unquestionable categories, such as gender, ethnicity or nation, cannot constitute grand narratives anymore in their conventional sense due to the 'postmodern turn'. Cameron (2005) underlines the significance of local contexts discussing this postmodern turn in sociolinguistic research. She suggests to 'look locally' when analysing the diverse linguistic practices of seemingly universal concepts such as masculinity and femininity. In the present chapter, we aim to unfold the local meanings and categories of political correctness in a contemporary East-Central European context: among university students in Budapest, Hungary.

The recent emergence of the concept of political correctness in East-Central Europe cannot be adequately approached without addressing the ways 'Western' concepts circulate globally. Solid scholarship examines the travelling political and media discourses in the buffer zone of Western and Eastern Europe (Koobak and Marling 2014, Chojnicka 2015, Gal 2018). Instead of focusing on the public sphere, we analyse individual understandings of political correctness in the region. Everyday conversations between university students in Budapest, the capital city of Hungary, provide data on the notion of 'political correctness' (PC). Individuals perceive it as a constraint originated from an external (mainly Western) authority, and they constantly negotiate this expected speech mode in their spontaneous interactions. This negotiation might be framed as a reconstructive dialogue between 'new' and 'old', between 'ours' and 'theirs' (for East-Central Europe, see Bakić-Hayden 1995, Melegh 2006). At the same time, stances to political correctness serve as a means to construct individual and collective selves. The desire for a politically correct language can be understood as a modernist re-imagination of social hierarchies through practices of 'verbal hygiene' (Cameron 1995). The local critiques of this language, as we will discuss in the context of Hungary, strengthens the 'indeterminacy' and the 'undecidability' of postmodernism (Calinescu 1987: 298).

Political correctness is a phenomenon which has both global and local meanings. From a pro-PC stance, global understanding of politically correct language embraces the imaginary of respect and non-discrimination toward vulnerable groups like women, LGBTQ people, racial and ethnic minorities, and people with disabilities. In contrast, this definition has less in common with how local critiques of political correctness define the concept itself. Both approaches share the view that political correctness is about an attempt to change linguistic representations; the desire for the change is defended or attacked on universalist grounds. This universalist concept is based on a normative theory of language, which revolves around the aspect of correctness from either perspective. Nevertheless, this putative universalism of a politically (in)correct language has been rarely addressed empirically in local contexts. Most studies are limited in scope to the 'Western' world, and they have shown that political correctness has been ambivalent since its inception as an umbrella term for a prescriptivist movement, which never existed (Cameron 1995) and which is isolated from efforts towards a more general social inclusivity (Fairclough 2003). It is also ambivalent as both 'a criticism of unspoken cultural norms' (Granath and Ullén 2019: 265) and a positive means, among others, 'to perform considerate and respectful personae, to project a more desirable state of discourse, to do playfully affiliative interpersonal bonding, and to serve as a vehicle for irony' (Wikström 2016: 169). Moreover, its local understandings can vary to such a degree that in Sweden and Denmark, two countries geographically and culturally close to each other, there is an overarching difference between the politically 'correct' or 'incorrect' language about disability, respectively (Kulick and Rydström 2015).

In Section 6.2, we discuss the historical and geopolitical background of post-socialist Hungary and its discourses on global relations including political correctness. Then, to provide an understanding of our theoretical framework, we introduce the concept of voice and enregisterment (Agha 2005). Section 6.3 gives a brief summary on our empirical research and the corpus we used for this analysis. After a discussion of our empirical findings on the metadiscourses of politically correct language among Hungarian students, the chapter concludes that this language is assigned to the Other. When individuals express their critique towards PC, that contributes to constructing selves who are questioning Western modernist projects.

6.2 Questioning modernity and political correctness in post-socialist Budapest

For an East-Central European country like Hungary, the question of the position of the country in relation to countries understood as Western has been central to political, economic and cultural discourses (Gal 1991). Regional discourses are framed in a constant comparison, labelling not only countries but also domestic groups as Western or Eastern, according to the logic of nested orientalism (Bakić-Hayden 1995). The 'East-West slope', as Melegh (2006: 191) calls this framework of hierarchical difference, functions 'as a complex way of creating identities based on differences and exclusions of the local 'non-enlightened' society'. Language use, including hate speech and political correctness (cf. Barát 2011a, 2011b), becomes part of East-Central European identity constructions in relation to notions of cultural backwardness. In Hungarian domestic discourses, reactions to the relatively inferior position vis-à-vis the West take on two extremes. These extremes became even more polarised as political discourses underwent a significant transformation in the past decade over the right-wing nationalist government emblematised by its prime minister, Viktor Orbán, which has been gaining increasing influence into all spheres of Hungarian society (Gal 2018). The current dominant political rhetoric rests on a polarised distinction between Hungary and the West, mostly embodied by the European Union. In this distinction, politically correct language figures as part of unwanted Western influence. The government's rhetoric and policies rest on an idea of national superiority resistant to the expectation of Western foreign powers, including their linguistic norms. Orbán, in a speech after Donald Trump's election, named political correctness a 'global intellectual oppression' with its European and American 'pillars', from which the latter is already 'knocked out'.[1] In contrast, the shrinking political opposition sees allies and protectors in Western institutions, and tends to embrace ideas of catching up (Böröcz 2006; Gille 2010).

In East-Central Europe, the concept of political correctness includes the idea that it originates in Western core countries. Its presence in the region is therefore seen as the consequence of the general influence of the West. The expectation of politically correct language is therefore tied to a Western identification, since it is often the EU or other international organisations that promote it. Consequently, many welcome this language use as the index of progressivity, even if they might not label it as politically correct. At the same time, those, including the nationalist right-wing, who are against the impact of the West in the region, also criticise this form of respect for vulnerable groups understood as external imposition (Kováts 2017: 7, 66).

In the region, it is usually questions of racism and ethnicity (especially about the Roma) as well as sexism and gender around which discourses about the West as either role model or imperialist imposer emerge (Woodcock 2011; Gal 2018). We are examining interactions in which the representations of the West display through metadiscourses on political correctness. In our data, questions of gender and sexuality are far the most discussed topic among dormitory students related to political correctness, compared to the topics of race/ethnicity, disability and religious minorities. As an illustration to the approach that political correctness is a constraint by the West, first we cite a conversation which explicitly targets 'liberalism imported from Germany and the USA', in the context of a less frequent topic of political correctness, namely ethnicity. It is from one of our focus group interviews which was made with three young male students sharing a dormitory room. After talking about the term Gypsy ('*cigány*') as politically incorrect ('*politikailag nem korrekt*') and Roma ('*roma*') as politically correct ('*píszí*'), one man notes:

> Excerpt 1 (transcription conventions are given at the end of the chapter)
>
> *Mer ott tartunk, hogy ez Németországban, ott zajlik ez a liberalizmus, ami-Amerikából importáltak, és ők meg az Entschuldigungukban tartanak még mindig, mert nem lehet rámondani arrafele, hogy cigány, mer akkor meg 'holokauszt', és akkor 'úristen', és 'megint ott fogunk tartani'. Ez bullshit, ez nem igaz.*
>
> Because we've got to the point that this liberalism is happening in Germany, which was imported from America, and they are still in their *Entschuldigung* [apology], because there one cannot be labelled a Gypsy, because then 'Holocaust' and 'Oh my God' and 'we're gonna get there again'. This is bullshit, this isn't true.

In Excerpt 1, a student is defending the Hungarian use of the world 'Gypsy', arguing that Western demands to use the politically correct 'Roma' exaggerate the danger of words. Hungarian discourses around politically correct language like the ones we are analysing in students' conversations do not only reflect on but also reproduce ideas of the East–West slope (Melegh 2006) and Hungary's position in it. In contrast to the specific meanings of political correctness, however, 'political incorrectness' has less specific connotations. If politically correct language is something imported from the West, then logically it would follow that 'political incorrectness' is more Hungarian, more genuine and more honest. As we show, it is more a default position; something unmarked, natural or normal, something which speakers assume themselves to be. Ironically, while expressing critique towards foreign anti-racist discourses, the student employs both German (*Entschuldigung*) and English (*bullshit*) resources, thereby marking himself as eloquent, well-educated and knowledgeable in foreign languages.

6.3 Voice and enregisterment

The differentiation between the local and Western worlds inextricably involves the sociolinguistic distinction of different speech forms that are linked to these social worlds. The connection does not rely on a universalist ideology of associating 'languages', such as those of political correctness, with static cultural typifications of social life, in our case with the Western world. Instead, according to Agha (2003, 2005), it is more useful to imagine the link between speech forms and speaker types as specific and divergent cultural models of speech. Each model is limited to heterogeneous social domains, i.e. groups of persons, ranging from an accidental encounter between two people to the largest possible audience on a mass-media platform. The models emerge in these domains and move across them, from event to event, until they are recognised as 'common sense' knowledge in some domains, but not in others (Mortimer and Wortham 2015). The metapragmatically driven emergence and spread of a model is what Agha calls 'enregisterment', that is, 'processes whereby distinct forms of speech come to be socially recognised (or enregistered) as indexical of speaker attributes by a population of language users' (2005: 38). Enregisterment works through indexical processes and it results in a widely known and conventionalised register which is, as a rule, a distinct set of speech forms linked with and constitutive of speaker types and their attributes (Dong 2010; Johnstone 2016).

Not every model is enregistered, however. A cultural model of speech, by and large, is confined to a specific domain where the participants connect contrasting speech forms and contrasting types of speakers which are recognisable by that group of persons who constitute that very domain (Agha 2005; Wortham 2005). These types of persona or 'characterological figures' (Agha 2003: 243) can range from 'racist' and 'cosmopolitan' Delhiites (Singh 2019) to 'bear gays' (Barrett 2017) and 'fierce queens' (Calder 2019), just to mention a few recent examples. Speaker types are recognised by their discrete voices; in the Bakhtinian sense, a voice is not the attribute of a speaking person, but the entextualised construction of a social persona, that is, '[a] figure performed through speech' (Agha 2005: 39). Put another way, the concept of voice 'addresses the question 'Who is speaking?' in any stretch of discourse' (Keane 2000: 271). It means that any social event is populated with many figures, either speaking from the position of a present person or giving voice to 'someone else's' speech (Bakhtin 1981: 293). According to Agha (2005), there are three types of voices; the first two of them are what Bakhtin called individual voices. These are 'unnamed voices' with no biographical reference to the speaking person, on the one hand, and the voices of 'named individuals', who can be identified as biographical persons through the use of personal deixis, on the other hand. The third type is that of social voices. They can be twofold: depending on the social domain where they are recognised as speech forms typical of a social group, they are enregistered or not. If the social domain is not restricted to a unique encounter between a group of interactants, a social voice is on its way to be enregistered.

PC in Hungary is a social voice that has been enregistered. But as Gal (2018) points out, it is not enough to identify processes of enregisterment; we also need to scrutinise how and with what effects it happens. Moreover, preoccupations with 'successful' enregisterment divert attention from the cultural models of speech that are not so widespread. It remains to be seen that these latter models are the background against which any other model is enregistered and that such background processes are critical to understand how contrasts between the different social or individual voices emerge in everyday interactions. As both voicing effects and enregisterment are a function of contrasts between characterological figures of speech, the study of political correctness is inseparable from the discourses in which it is subject to metapragmatic processes of negative evaluation, referring to PC as a hindrance to making 'individual' voices be heard. In the analytical section of this chapter, we focus on the way in which enregisterment of political correctness is mobilised in order to link a mode of speech with a 'liberal' characterological figure in an effort to resolve a tension between authenticity and Western-type modernisation. We will show that the two poles of politically correct and incorrect language are represented differently in the interactions. While the former has become a socially recognised and confirmed voice of a characterological figure who is oriented towards 'Western' values of liberal democracies, utterances which count as politically incorrect are mostly heard as individual voices without indexing characterological figures of personhood.

In the interview that we quoted in Excerpt 1, voices enregistered as PC are evoked. The phrases of '*Entschuldigung*', 'Holocaust', 'Oh my God' and 'we're gonna get there again' are all quoted in the interviewee's speech as belonging to a figure whom he cannot agree with. This figure is characteristically Western (German or American); however, the topic of the whole conversation was the Roma in Hungary. Politically correct voice is thus enregistered as something foreign which is gaining ground in Hungary as well. In contrast to this social voice, an unnamed voice in the excerpt is that of a Hungarian who would label someone a 'Gypsy'. The interviewee identifies a process, with Hungary undergoing a transformation towards a Western type of discourse (see Gal 2018), which he dislikes. A German or Hungarian liberal is the one who might evoke the Holocaust, exaggerating the significance of ethnic labels. The East–West distinction is clear in the comment about 'there you cannot label someone a Gypsy', i.e., in contrast to Hungary where, he assumes, Gypsy is not considered a slur. Political correctness is therefore understood as typically Western. At the same time, the speaker's own (apparently authentic) position is not enregistered as a local social voice. Indeed, to affirm his opinion as the truth, he uses an English-origin term from American popular culture, 'bullshit', as his own voice.

6.4 Data and methodology: The Budapest University Dormitory Corpus

To study enregistered speech modes in spontaneous conversations, we used a corpus from the research project Budapest University Dormitory Corpus ('*Budapesti Egyetemi Kollégiumi Korpusz*'). The corpus offers 20 hours of everyday conversations transcribed, annotated and pseudonymised. These interactions were recorded between 2015 and 2017 in dormitory rooms by the participants themselves, who were university students staying in Budapest, but originally coming from the countryside. Social stratification among university students is apparent in their housing situation: children of wealthier families tend to rent rooms or flats in university cities, which is extremely costly in Budapest. Nevertheless, most students still dwell in significantly cheaper but crowded dormitories, where they face limited access to privacy. Most rooms are shared by 3 or 4 students of the same gender. Roommates might not even know each other when they move in but they will have to spend most of their nights together in their rooms.

The data collection occurred as follows. Peer researchers (students taking sociolinguistic courses) recruited participants from a wide range of dormitories. The principle was to record everyday conversations in their dormitory rooms without the presence of the fieldworker. The inhabitants of each room were asked to sign a written consent, in which they accepted to inform everyone who enters the room that a recording was taken place. They used their mobile devices for this purpose. This way we gathered at least 3 hours of audio recordings from each (mostly same-gender) groups of 2–4 students. The total number of participants (aged between 19 and 24) was 56, from which 34 participants were women and 22 were men. We received material from 16 rooms of various dormitories, from which we chose one to one and a half hours of each to constitute the final corpus (for further description, see Bodó et al. 2019).

After the recording period, the peer researchers also conducted structured focus group interviews with the students. In these interviews, the participants were asked to speak about their dormitory life and language practices, and to discuss some short texts dealing with recent Hungarian hot cases connected to sexual abuse, Budapest Pride Marches, and anti-Roma racism. In these focus group discussions, especially in line with the latter topic, the interviewees enregistered 'politically correct' speech mode as an external expectation. In the following section, we will illustrate how these expectations are subject to continuous discursive negotiations in students' everyday conversations.

6.5 Analyses: From silence to voicing correctness

Using politically incorrect language, similar to any obscenity, can function in various ways. In the conversations recorded by the students themselves, it seemed to index in-group solidarity (especially as a male bond). The use of politically incorrect language manifests confrontational rudeness, which is typically viewed as the sign of being uneducated underclass, but also as masculine. Students did reprimand each other for not being politically correct. Much more often, however, they ignore or even appraise others' overtly derogatory comments on vulnerable groups. In this section, we show quotes that illustrate the whole scale of positive and negative reactions from silence to voicing and enregistering political correctness. Excerpt 2 provides an illustration of that lack of referencing political correctness. The two interlocutors, Olívia and János, are a straight couple who were allowed to share a room, which was a rare privilege among dormitory inhabitants. Olívia facilitates János recalling his past trip during a private conversation about their memories.

Excerpt 2
OLÍVIA: *Horvátország. Szerbia.*
JÁNOS: *Jaj!*
OLÍVIA: *Koszovónak mentetek?*

JÁNOS: De jó, most megálltunk benzinkúton Szerbiába, ahol a cigánykurvák jöttek kéregetni.
OLÍVIA: Tök mindegy, ott voltál. Több órát töltöttél ott.
JÁNOS: Jaj, nem volt wifi sehol se.
OLÍVIA: Koszovóba volt- Koszovón keresztül mentetek?
[…]
JÁNOS: De valami izével, valami buzival táncoltam, nem? Vagy hogyan volt?
OLÍVIA: Nem a csajjal?
JÁNOS: Fú, ja nem, aki ig- de, de, de, a buzit kellett odébb löknöm, és azzal a- a zsírdisznóval kellett (.) izélnem, táncolnom.
OLÍVIA: Áh tudom, együnk sütit!

OLÍVIA: Croatia. Serbia.
JÁNOS: Ouch!
OLÍVIA: Were you going to Kosovo?
JÁNOS: Good, this time we stopped at a petrol station in Serbia, where the gypsy whores came and begged.
OLÍVIA: Whatever, you were there. You spent a couple of hours there.
JÁNOS: Ah, there wasn't any wifi anywhere.
OLÍVIA: Was it in Kosovo- were you going through Kosovo?
[…]
JÁNOS: But I was dancing with some thing, with some fag, wasn't I? Or how was that?
OLÍVIA: Not with the girl?
JÁNOS: Woa, but no, then one who- yes, yes, yes, I had to push the fag away, and I had to (.) what, dance with that- that greasy pig.
OLÍVIA: Ah, I know, let's eat some cookies!

This excerpt includes utterances often enregistered as voices of anti-Roma racism ('Gypsy whores'), homophobia ('fag'), sexism ('Gypsy whores'), and fat talk ('greasy pig'). The stereotypes intersect, as the 'greasy pig' clearly denotes a woman ('the girl' Olívia just mentioned). These are derogatory expressions that János would have not allowed himself using in a more formal setting. Furthermore, he used all these expressions in the context of a trip to the Balkans, which stereotypically represents a backward East compared to Hungary (cf. Todorova 1997). The Balkans appear in this dialogue as a dangerous and adventurous place where all these characters appear, presented as disgusting, which provides material for funny story-telling. Moreover, these characters serve as the Other; a background against which János presents himself as masculine and heteronormative. The disrespectful way he treats them (both in the past and in his talk) contributes to his gendered identity construction. Displays of ethnonationalism and aggressivity coded as masculine reinforce each other here. Yet, the story here does not unfold; probably, it was told already between the couple and they seem to be bored of it. Olívia leaves János' final sentence without any comment, and changes the topic. The politically incorrect voice does not get enregistered; it quickly passes by and does not become explicit as a metalinguistic category.

In the analysis of the following excerpts, we will show the different ways in which enregisterment of politically correct language happens in our corpus. Excerpt 3 illustrates how the actual fulfilment of this semiotic process functions as a source of humour. The context of the conversation is that the wireless connection was not working in the dormitory currently, and the three men who share a room were making jokes about what they should do with the system administrator referred to with his surname, Kovács.

Excerpt 3

SZABI: *Ez van srácok, szóval lehet Kovács- menjél le és* (laughing) *törd be Kovács ajtaját, hogy csinálja már meg, a kurva anyját, az teljesen jó lesz./*
ÁDÁM: /*Hát ennyi.*
SZABI: *Nézd.* (.) *Szolidan és píszín ordítsuk azt, hogy 'csinálj magadnak kistestvért'!*
ÁDÁM: (nevet) *Mm:*
GÁBRIS: *Vat?*
SZABI: (laughing) *De mégse kiabálhatod, hogy 'baszd meg a kurva anyádat'.*
ÁDÁM: (laughing) *Na ugye.*
GÁBRIS: *Ez van.*
ÁDÁM: (laughing) *Hát ugye.*

SZABI: That's it guys, so Kovács might- go down and (*laughing*) break in Kovács's door saying, motherfucker, do it; that will be completely fine./
ÁDÁM: /That's it.
SZABI: Look. (.) Decently and PC, let's shout, 'make a little sibling for yourself!'
ÁDÁM: (*laughs*) Mm:
GÁBRIS: What?
SZABI: (*laughing*) But you can't just shout, 'you motherfucker'.
ÁDÁM: (*laughing*) See.
GÁBRIS: That's it.
ÁDÁM: (*laughing*) Well, see.

In the first line, Szabi envisions a ludic threatening of Kovács in order to make him fix the problems with their internet connection, and this includes a quotation of a common obscenity ('motherfucker'). Then Szabi continues with an unconventional way of shouting at somebody ('make a little sibling for yourself'). He offers an interpretation of this voice as 'decent' and 'PC'. Ádám bursts into laughter, but this utterance remains unintelligible for Gábris, who does not recognise the social figure voiced by Szabi. After that, Szabi clarifies that his convoluted wordplay translates into the simple swearing 'motherfucker'. In this excerpt, political correctness is not about marginalised social groups (as we will see in Excerpt 4). It is rather about another type of social taboo, i.e., anger against someone expressed by obscenities, which is also identified as something 'you can't' do. The register of political correctness and the meanings in connection with it are discursively negotiated by the interactants, and the newly proposed enregisterment voiced by Szabi is accepted by the last utterances of the others.

Excerpt 4 illustrates the effects of audience design (Bell 1984), that is, how speakers adjust their speech to different audience groups, or, to use Agha's term, social domains. At a late night hour, the participants discuss a viral pornographic video gag, titled 'Black Salami', where the performer is a black male with an exceptionally long penis. Andor, who brings up the subject, recommends that they all watch the video together, even if his roommates had both expressed their intent on going to bed in an earlier phase of the interaction.

Excerpt 4

ANDOR: *Ismeritek azt a videót, hogy Black Salami?*
BALÁZS: (laughing) *Nem, de nagyon jól hangzik.*
ANDOR: *Elmesélhetem vagy megmutathatom holnap.*
BALÁZS: *Inkább mutasd meg!*
ANDOR: *Biztos?*
BALÁZS: *A:- biztos. Bár- bá- bár- bár nem tudom. Valahogy azér kulcsszavakat emelj ki belőle!*
ANDOR: *Ne:m, szeretném, hogy meglepetés legyen, szóval döntsd el, hogy elmondjam az egészet vagy inkább megmutassam holnap.*
VINCE: *Hö.*
BALÁZS: *Ez olyan dolog, ami miatt törölni kéne az egész idáig- eddigi felvételt?*
ANDOR: *Nem, dehogyis, semmi miatt nem kell, itt szókimondás van, én nem vagyok hajlandó cenzúrában részt venni.*
BALÁZS: *Mhm, akkor inkább mondd el, én félek.*
[...] (they speak about a person who has not woken up yet)
ANDOR: *Szóval én ne- én nem vagyok hajlandó részt venni, ha akarják, majd ki- kivágják, de én nem fogok- a pofámat befogni azér, érted.*
BALÁZS: *Ne, nem kell. Mo- mondd mi az a black szalámi,* (laughing) *most már érdekel.*
ANDOR: *Tényleg elmondjam? A: csávó- vagy figyelj, itt van a net, beírom és megmutatom./*
BALÁZS: */Te tudod mit, holnap mutasd meg, most/*
VINCZE: */Hallod, inkább meséld el, és holnap megnézzük.*
BALÁZS: *Most már alváshoz ide nem/*
ANDOR: */De ha elmesélem, nem biztos, hogy lesz kedvetek megnézni.*
BALÁZS: *Sőt, ebben egészen biztos vagyok, [azért mondtam].*
ANDOR: *[Na mindegy], elmondom, oké? Az a lényege/*
BALÁZS: */Ah:.*
ANDOR: *Egy nigger csávó természetesen, de: nincs semmi bajom a niggerekkel,* (laughing) *nehogy ez így jöjjön le. És akkor ilyen tudósok ott nézik, hogy*

ott tudod, ott benn van, ahogy szokták a tudósok ilyen üvegszobából vagy miből nézni, vagy nem tudom, csak ilyen vicc a felvétel, tudo d.

ANDOR: Do you know that video called the Black Salami?
BALÁZS: (laughing) No, but it sounds great.
ANDOR: I can tell it now or I can show it tomorrow.
BALÁZS: Show it, rather!
ANDOR: Sure?
BALÁZS: Uhm:- sure. Although- though- though- though I don't know. Just take some keywords from it somehow!
ANDOR: No:, I want it to be a surprise, so please decide if I shall tell you the whole or rather show it to you tomorrow.
VINCE: Hah.
BALÁZS: Is this something because of which the whole recording this far- so far should be deleted?
ANDOR: No, not at all, it shouldn't be because of anything, there is outspokenness here, and I'm not willing to take part in censorship.
BALÁZS: Mm, then rather just tell it, I'm scared.
[…] *(they speak about a person who has not woken up yet)*
ANDOR: So I'm no, I'm not willing to take part, if they want, they will cut it out- out, but I won't- I won't shut my mouth just because, you see.
BALÁZS: No, you don't have to. Tell- tell us what black salami is, (*laughing*) now I'm interested.
ANDOR: Shall I really tell? The: guy- or look, here is the net, I'll write it in and show it./
BALÁZS: /You know what, show it tomorrow, now/
VINCZE: /Hey, rather tell it, and we'll watch it tomorrow.
BALÁZS: Now just before sleeping, not/
ANDOR: /But if I tell it, you may not want to watch it.
BALÁZS: Indeed, I'm pretty sure about it, [that's why I said so].
ANDOR: [Whatever], I'll tell it, all right? The gist of it is/
BALÁZS: /Ah:.
ANDOR: A negro[2] guy of course, but: I have nothing against negroes, (*laughing*) it shouldn't be taken as such. And then these scientists are watching him, you know, as he is inside, the way scientists usually watch from this glass room or what, or I dunno, the recording is just a joke, you now.

During the negotiation of whether to watch the video without Andor's account of its story, Balázs interprets the offer of telling them the story as something that can damage the success of recording their speech and delivering the audio recording to the researchers. Andor heavily opposes this interpretation, which would hinder his proposed performance, by stating that not telling the story of the video is a restriction on freedom of speech. He confines the statement to the social domain of the actual interactants by using the deictic word 'here'. Andor represents his group's relation to sensitive or embarrassing topics as 'outspoken'; the reference to this speech form brings along with it a characterological figure who, according to Andor's intent, should be positively recognised by the participants. Andor relies on the authority of a social voice, which, however, is not enregistered. In other words, he cannot be sure that all of his interactants recognise this figure as an authority. Therefore, he goes on to take a stand against censoring his words, by blaming censorship to be a restraint on making his individual voice be heard ('I won't shut my mouth'). This implication is often mentioned in the critique of political correctness (Alan and Burridge 2006: 101; Granath and Ullén 2019: 269). Furthermore, in the post-socialist world this critique is associated with the impression that within the EU 'far from valorising authenticity, one has to pretend to be someone else in order to be accepted as a legitimate participant' (Gille 2010: 23).

When expressing his own commitment to plain speech, Andor links the opposite mode of speech with a characterological figure of the researcher, a typically 'progressive', politically correct speaker with a 'Western' orientation. This figure speaks in an enregistered social voice that is incompatible with Andor's individual voice, the authenticity of which is discursively constructed by using the above mentioned 'slangish' expression *befogni a pofámat* ('shut my mouth'). After the others agree with his objection to the 'censoring' figure, Andor proceeds to tell them the story and introduces it by labelling the performer as a 'negro'. He then laughingly avails himself of the rhetorical device which starts with 'I have nothing against' and ends with a name of a marginalised social group (cf. Chiang 2010), as a means of distancing his own voice from the social voice, of the racist in this case. This stance on political incorrectness is also there when Andor sketches out the scene; a racist dehumanisation of the performer, intersecting with sexual objectification, and he interprets all this as a 'joke'. Through sexual and racist obscenities attached to the idea of political incorrectness, masculinity can also be reinforced in these conversations, mostly recorded among men (see Bodó et al. 2019). Just like in the earlier extracts, there is no dissent from his stance. In this interaction, driven by a shift in orientation to the audience, reference to political correctness is used to make a distinction between the individual voice of the speaker and the enregistered social voice of the opposed other. By contrasting the two voices, the speaker can put emphasis on the voice he represents as his own authentic one.

The context of the utterances in Excerpt 5 and the activity the interactants are doing in between is not entirely clear, but they are certainly checking a Middle Eastern girl's social media profile. Ádám and Gábris warn Szabi of his politically incorrect utterances, and Szabi later makes a distinction between political and mathematical correctness.

Excerpt 5

ÁDÁM: *De szerintem ez nem píszí, hogy* (laughing) *csak azér me jordániai és tizenöt éves, akkor má gyereke van, bazmeg.*

SZABI: *Nem, azt tudjuk, hogy* (laughing) *jordániai, és gyereke van. Ebből gondolom, hogy tizenhat éves, mer csak egy van neki.*
GÁBRIS: *A: biztos, tiszta píszí.*
ÁDÁM: (laughing) *Szerintem ez se píszí.*
SZABI: (laughing) *Ez mé-, de matematikailag helyes.*

ÁDÁM: But I think this isn't PC that (*laughing*) just because she is Jordanian and 15 years old, then she must have a child, fuck you.
SZABI: No, what we know is that (*laughing*) she is Jordanian and has a child. This makes me think she is 16 years old, because she has only one.
GÁBRIS: Ah: sure, completely PC.
ÁDÁM: (*laughing*) I don't think this is PC, either.
SZABI: (*laughing*) This m-, but mathematically correct.

In the first quoted line, Ádám starts a debate on Szabi's statements about the mentioned Jordanian and supposedly teenage girl who had a child. Szabi then clarifies his assumption: he argues that the girl must be a teenager, because she is Jordanian and has only one child. In this reasoning, judgements about age, race and gender intersect. While Gábris's reaction is unequivocally ironic, Ádám explicitly misses the political correctness in Szabi's message. In contrast with our previous excerpt, in this conversation enregistering PC language use and accepting it as a legitimate speech mode also seem to be an internal need. Nevertheless, Ádám does not argue against what he feels is disrespectful (sexist, ageist, and/or racist) in Szabi's comment. This might suggest that referring to political correctness primarily aims at representing a social voice, more than expressing a substantial worldview against social inequalities. Some of these utterances are followed by laughter, which may also refer to their agreement with the logic of Szabi's thoughts. The laughter and his last line together create a differentiation between political and mathematical correctness voicing a critique of PC. In this encounter, political correctness is thus understood as a register that obscures real, mathematically intelligible correctness. As Jonsson, Franzén and Milani (2020: 3) put it, humour can be 'a discursive tool with which to impose the social order' inter alia. In this sense, enregistering and evaluating political correctness function as a platform to (re)construct gender identities and power relations.

6.6 Conclusions

In our chapter, we discussed how politically correct language is enregistered and evaluated in an East-Central European context. Drawing on our data from dormitory room conversations in Hungary's capital, Budapest, we argued that political correctness as a socially recognised voice indexes a 'Western' and progressive characterological figure, while this persona is often accused of insincerity. Our data demonstrated a wide range of possible assessments on pejorative speech about vulnerable groups, mostly about women and gays, and less often about others such as the Roma and people of colour. In some cases, expressions usually labelled as racist, sexist and homophobic are not commented on at all by neither of the interactants (Excerpt 2), while elsewhere the speaker feels obliged to state that he has no prejudice against the group of people which he addresses by their undesired name (Excerpt 4). Political correctness is frequently negotiated in these conversations: for example, an unconventionally obscene utterance is enregistered as PC because of its euphemism (Excerpt 3); at another instance, they discuss the correctness of an observation taken on an adolescent Jordanian girl applying the opposing category of mathematical (and thus, rational) correctness (Excerpt 5).

Taking everything in account, we found that participants of these everyday conversations do not lean on a shared definition of political correctness, albeit they reflect on ideas of globally circulating Western norms. The students in our study seem to be aware of the norms of politically correct language. However, they mostly reject these norms, but even if they question the rejection, they do not engage in a substantial critique of social inequalities when talking to each other. We therefore argued that negotiations around political correctness in East-Central European private interactions primarily function to express a supportive or critical relation towards social voices identified as Western and modernist. With their non-affirmative stance towards PC, young individuals in Budapest construct their selves through giving voice to resistant, non-Western, heteronormative and masculine figures. Politically correct language is thus enregistered as others' social voice. Consequently, we suggest, PC language is not well integrated into East-Central European students' individual voice and does not become their personal political project.

The principles and values of modernity seem unsteady and alterable from a postmodernist point of view. As we showed, the desire for a language which does not address marginalised groups with derogatory expressions is part of a 'Western' and liberal conceptualisation of modernity. The postmodern turn in sociolinguistics emphasises the need for describing local interpretations of globally dispersing concepts. Our data demonstrated that in the Hungarian context political correctness can often be translated as a constraint coming from an external force. Politically correct language in this very locus is a Janus-faced phenomenon in the sense that applying this speech mode is a way of voicing an enlightened figure, while the voice itself is enregistered as a form of silencing reality.

6.7 Transcription conventions

- (.)   a pause shorter than 0.5 second
- [ ]   overlapping speech
- /   no discernible silence between the speakers' turns
- :   stretching of the preceding vowel
- -   a cut-off or self-interruption

(*word*)   the transcriber's description of events, e.g. (*laughing*)
[…]   omitted 'side-talk'

6.8 Acknowledgements

This chapter is a result of the research project 'Constructions of gender, sexuality and ethnicity in everyday conversations', funded by the Eötvös Loránd University between 2015 and 2017. We thank Henning Radke, Dick Smakman, and Anna Szlávi for their valuable comments on our text.

Notes

1 The original text is available on the government site: www.kormany.hu/hu/a-miniszterelnok/beszedek-publikaciok-interjuk/orban-viktor-beszede-a-magyar-diaszpora-tanacs-vi-ulesen (last retrieved 5 February 2020). For a summary in English, see Hungarian Spectrum (2016).
2 We translated the English-origin Hungarian word *nigger* into 'negro'. Although this is not a fully adequate translation either, it seems to be the most appropriate for the derogatory Hungarian term which is not used publicly. It is far less offensive and racist than its English etymological equivalent.

References

Agha, Asif (2003) The Social Life of Cultural Value. *Language & Communication* 23(3–4): 231–273.
Agha, Asif (2005) Voice, Footing, Enregisterment. *Journal of Linguistic Anthropology* 15(1): 38–59.
Allan, Keith and Kate Burridge (2006) *Forbidden Words: Taboo and the Censoring of Language*. Cambridge: Cambridge University Press.
Bakhtin, Mikhail (1981) *The Dialogic Imagination*. Austin: University of Texas Press.
Bakić-Hayden, Milica (1995) Nesting Orientalisms: The Case of Former Yugoslavia. *Slavic Review* 54(4): 917–931.
Barát, Erzsébet (2011a) Queer in Hungary: Hate Speech Regulation and the Queering of the Conduct/Speech Binary. In: *Queer in Europe: Contemporary Case Studies*. Downing, Lisa and Robert Gillet (eds.), 85–98. London: Ashgate.
Barát, Erzsébet (2011b) Cynical References to Political Correctness in Hungarian Media in the 2000s. *Hungarian Cultural Studies* 4: 58–69.
Barrett, Rusty (2017) *From Drag Queens to Leathermen: Language, Gender, and Gay Male Subcultures*. Oxford: Oxford University Press.
Bell, Allan (1984) Language Style as Audience Design. *Journal of Sociolinguistics* 13(2): 145–204.
Bodó, Csanád, Gergely Szabó and Ráhel Katalin Turai (2019) Voices of Masculinity: Men's Talk in Hungarian University Dormitories. *Discourse & Society* 30(4): 339–358.
Böröcz, József (2006) Goodness is Elsewhere: The Rule of European Difference. *Comparative Studies in Society and History* 48(1): 110–138.
Calder, Jeremy (2019) From *Sissy* to *Sickening*: The Indexical Landscape of /s/ in SoMa, San Francisco. *Journal of Linguistic Anthropology* 29(3): 332–358.

Calinescu, Matej (1987) *Five Faces of Modernity*. Durham: Duke University Press.
Cameron, Deborah (1995) *Verbal Hygiene*. London: Routledge.
Cameron, Deborah (2005) Language, Gender, and Sexuality: Current Issues and New Directions. *Applied Linguistics* 26(4): 482–502.
Chiang, Shiao-Yun (2010) 'Well, I'm a lot of Things, but I'm Sure not a Bigot': Positive Self-Presentation in Confrontational Discourse on Racism. *Discourse & Society* 21(3): 273–294.
Chojnicka, Joanna (2015) Homophobic Speech in Post-socialist Media: A Preliminary Typology of Homophobic Manipulative Discourse. *Journal of Language and Sexuality* 4(1): 138–173.
Dong, Jie (2010) The Enregisterment of Putonghua in Practice. *Language & Communication* 30(4): 265–275.
Fairclough, Norman (2003) 'Political Correctness': The Politics of Culture and Language. *Discourse & Society* 14(1): 17–28.
Gal, Susan (1991) Bartók's Funeral: Representations of Europe in Hungarian Political Rhetoric. *American Ethnologist* 18(3): 440–458.
Gal, Susan (2018) Registers in Circulation: The Social Organization of Interdiscursivity. *Signs and Society* 6(1): 1–24.
Gille, Zsuzsa (2010) Is there a Global Postsocialist Condition? *Global Society* 24(1): 9–30.
Granath, Solveig and Magnus Ullén (2019) 'The Elevation of Sensitivity over Truth': Political Correctness and Related Phrases in the Time Magazine Corpus. *Applied Linguistics* 40(2): 265–287.
Hungarian Spectrum (2016) Trump and Orbán on political correctness. https://hungarianspectrum.org/2016/12/02/trump-and-orban-on-political-correctness/ (Last retrieved 4 February 2020)
Johnstone, Barbara (2016) Enregisterment: How Linguistic Items Become Linked with Ways of Speaking. *Language & Linguistics Compass* 10(11): 632–643.
Jonsson, Rickard, Anna Gradin Franzén and Tommaso M. Milani (2020) Making the Threatening Other Laughable: Ambiguous Performances of Urban Vernaculars in Swedish Media. *Language and Communication* 71: 1–15.
Keane, Webb (2000) Voice. *Journal of Linguistic Anthropology* 9(1–2): 271–273.
Koobak, Redi and Raili Marling (2014) The Decolonial Challenge: Framing Postsocialist Central and Eastern Europe within Transnational Feminist Studies. *European Journal of Women's Studies* 21(4): 330–343.
Kováts, Eszter (ed.) (2017) *The Future of the European Union. Feminist Perspectives from East-Central Europe*. Budapest: Friedrich-Ebert-Stiftung.
Kulick, Don and Jens Rydström (2015) *Loneliness and its Opposite: Sex, Disability and the Ethics of Engagement*. Durham & London: Duke University Press.
Melegh, Attila (2006) *On the East/West Slope. Globalization, Nationalism, Racism and Discourses on Central and Eastern Europe*. New York & Budapest: CEU Press.
Mortimer, Katherine S. and Stanton Wortham (2015) Analyzing Language Policy and Social Identification across Heterogeneous Scales. *Annual Review of Applied Linguistics* 35: 160–172.
Singh, Jaspal Naveel (2019) Loudness Registers: Normalizing Cosmopolitan Identities in a Narrative of Ethnic Othering. *Journal of Sociolinguistics* 24(2): 209–227.
Todorova, Maria Nikolaeva (1997) *Imagining the Balkans*. New York: Oxford University Press.

Wikström, Peter (2016) 'No One is Politically Correct': Positive Construals of *Political Correctness* in Twitter Conversations. *Nordic Journal of English Studies* 15(2): 159–170.

Woodcock, Shannon (2011) A Short History of the Queer Time of 'Post-Socialist' Romania, or Are We there yet? Let's Ask Madonna!' In: *De-centring Western Sexualities: Central and Eastern European Perspectives*. Kulpa, Robert and Joanna Mizielińska (eds.), 63–84. Farnham: Ashgate.

Wortham, Stanton (2005) Socialization beyond the Speech Event. *Journal of Linguistic Anthropology* 15(1): 95–112.

7 The Haarlem legend

The unpredictable formation of a national language norm

D. Smakman

7.1 Haarlem and the language norm

The Netherlands is a North-West European nation state that borders on the North Sea and lies north of Belgium and France, and borders on Germany in the east. The Dutch city of Haarlem is located in the western urban area of the Netherlands. This city of 162,902 inhabitants is the 12th largest city in the Netherlands (Haarlem 2019). It is the official administrative city of the province of North Holland. In the same province lies Amsterdam, the capital city of the country. Figure 7.1 shows Haarlem and its location within the Netherlands.

This chapter will explain how Haarlem is popularly associated with 'good' Dutch. This language norm is popularly referred to as *ABN*, *Algemeen Beschaafd Nederlands*, 'Standard Civilised Dutch'. Linguists in the Netherlands tend to refer to this language variety as *Standaardnederlands*, 'Standard Dutch', so as to frame it as part of a broader standard-language paradigm which exists in (mostly European) nation states with national and official standard languages. The Dutch standard language fits in the broader standardisation model – as initially laid out by Haugen (1966) – as in the past few hundred years it has gone through the stages of selection, acceptance, codification and elaboration.

An illustration of the popular image of Haarlem can be found on YouTube; a group of friends (Jansen et al. 2015), who were possibly from the city of Haarlem, posted a parody of a well-known Dutch song, *Praat Nederlands met me*, 'Speak Dutch with me', renaming it *Praat Haarlems met me*, 'Speak Haarlemmish with me'. The singer sings: '*Praat Haarlems met me. Even ABN met me*', 'Speak Haarlemmish with me. Just some General Civilised Dutch'. There is also empirical evidence. Smakman (2006) found that more than one in four of his Dutch respondents associated Haarlem with Standard Dutch, while none chose Amsterdam (cities and areas were presented as response categories). The western urban area, the 'Randstad' (introduced below) in the Netherlands was chosen by almost four out of ten respondents. It can be concluded that the western Netherlands urban conurbation as a whole, and Haarlem in particular, were associated with the national language norm by these respondents (who were from all over the country).

DOI: 10.4324/9780429348037-9

The Haarlem legend: The unpredictable formation 101

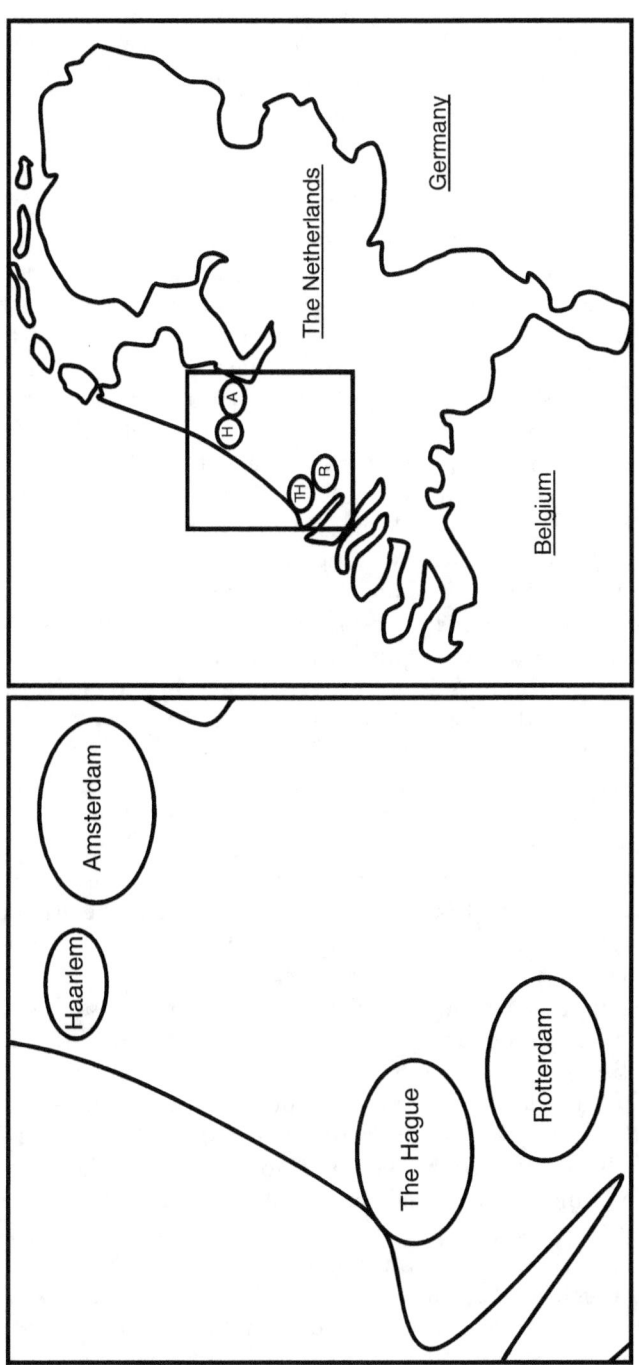

Figure 7.1 Location of the city of Haarlem.

The above findings confirm a commonly heard association between this city and a language norm. This chapter will describe how this association possibly came to existence and why it keeps going strong. Focussing on Haarlem, it discusses the difference between actual active language norms and symbolical ones, which may or may not coincide or overlap.

7.2 The *Randstad* area

As indicated above, Haarlem is part of an urban conurbation; this area has been nicknamed *Randstad*. The area holds a string of cities that together symbolise an urban way of life, both to its inhabitants and to Dutchmen not living there, although much nature can still be found within the area. The name '*Randstad*', as Cornips, De Rooij and Smakman (2018) explained, translates as 'Ring City', which refers to the C-shapedness of the region. The area is commonly referred to as an entity in the media and in general discourse within the country.

The *Randstad* region incorporates the cities of Amsterdam, Utrecht, Rotterdam and The Hague, amongst others, all of which are relatively close to each other. The *Randstad* megalopolis housed around 8.2 million inhabitants in 2020 (CBS 2020), which in that year represented roughly 47% of the total population of the Netherlands. The population number of the Netherlands in 2020 was 17.4 million (CBS 2020). The largest distance between cities within the area is 77 kilometres (between Amsterdam and Rotterdam).

The area lies in the deltas of several Dutch rivers flowing into the North Sea. Warf (2010) referred to the area as a 'Delta Metropole'. Formerly consisting of stretches of separated marshlands and large lakes, the area gradually transformed through large-scale land reclamation and water management, enabling cities in the region to expand. Nowadays, several of them physically almost connect. Mobility between the various urbanised centres gradually developed in the twentieth century. A major motorway system connects the largest towns and cities. Rotterdam and Amsterdam each have an airport. Within the major cities, there are well-functioning tram and/or bus systems, and in Amsterdam and Rotterdam a metro system is in operation. An extensive bicycle-lane and long-distance cycling route system, in combination with a mostly flat surface, makes cycling a practical means of transport within and even between cities. Electric bikes are increasingly often used to travel between and inside cities.

Due to the independent histories of the cities, the *Randstad* has no central authority, and there is no obvious city centre in the middle. All cities actually lie around a relatively green area. Inhabitants tend to identify with the city where they live or are from. Inhabitants of Amsterdam, Rotterdam and The Hague in particular have been known to feel pride when it comes to their place of residence. A certain rivalry in fact exists between the cities, perhaps expressed most overtly through football-club allegiance. The cities in the *Randstad* all have well-known local dialects. For all kinds of historical reasons, the area is nevertheless seen as an entity and as the centre of the Netherlands, despite its peripheral and stretched-out location. It is the area where the Netherlands as a nation state was founded and shaped. It attracts most immigrants, tourists, and students; the largest companies are there, and important national institutions in the Netherlands are often situated in this region. The feeling of unity may come from the fact that these institutions are scattered across the region and not located in one of the cities. Several of the cities in the region hold important official and symbolical (often national) functions (explained below).

7.3 The *Randstad* region and the norm

The *Randstad* quite obviously receives most of the media attention in the Netherlands, largely due to this region having a large and dense population and housing the nation's most important political and administrative institutions as well as the largest companies. Most national radio and television broadcasting is from the region and to many people from outside the region the language used during much of Dutch broadcasting has a distinctive *Randstad* ring to it. *Randstad* inhabitants stereotypically possess a certain self-assurance and pride, and this is said to show in their evaluation of language too. Daan and Blok (1969), for instance, said that the idea that dialects are uncivilised is most common in the minds of people from the *Randstad* region, while Kloeke (1937) talked about '*Hollanders*' (7) not being able to recognise their own deviations from the standard language. Similar comment were made by Van Bree (1981), who added that many westerners will simply feel that they speak the standard language.

7.4 Cities as a norm space

The special status of the *Randstad* region underscores the fact that in the Netherlands urban areas are associated with the language norm. Indeed, cities are typically the places where linguistic innovations are negotiated and performed the most. Speakers with different backgrounds tend to come together and challenge each other's language norms, with linguistically influential speakers placing themselves at the forefront of change and innovation by speaking, developing, and spreading their prestige sociolect. This way, an urban sociolect may eventually gain the status of a broader language norm. Massey (2005) described cities as 'peculiarly large, intense and heterogeneous constellations of trajectories, demanding of complex negotiation' (154). The resultant intense communication amongst people with various experiences and intentions leads to efforts to understand each other better (through levelling) but also efforts to distinguish oneself from others (for identity-related motivations).

Cities seem to have a double image when it comes to the norm. On the one hand, they are the places where the language norm arises and is maintained and developed into a conservative broader (national) norm. At the same time, cities are the places where the norm is challenged through more modern, trendy, and even local urban speech. It is true that cities are not only hubs of linguistic diversity but also the places where norm development seems particularly active. Trudgill (1974) suggested that innovative language is spread from large population centres, bypassing less populated areas. This mechanism is referred to as the Gravity Model. According to this model, cities influence each other first, and the rural areas in between come next in adopting linguistic innovations, once these innovations have become accepted in urban circles.

Capital cities in particular are often associated with language norms (Smakman 2012, 2018; Bassiouney and Muehlhaeusler 2017). There are many exceptions, and the Netherlands is one of them. In the United States, too, the capital city of Washington is not a main focus of national language norms, and instead an area (the 'Midwest') in the North West of the country carries this association. In England, the South West of the country is traditionally associated with the standard language, not necessarily or explicitly the capital city of London.

It should also be noted that a common trend in urban contexts described here is the blurring of the distinction between the national language norm and the norm within the city. In many cases, the original dialect of a specific city may in fact be associated particularly strongly with a national norm. Tzitzilis (2001) explained how local idioms and general language use in the diverse cities of Thessaloniki and Athens (Greece) are blending with the standard language. Another illustration of this blurring is the language norm in Egypt; the media broadcast almost exclusively in Cairene Arabic, making this city's local/regional dialect more or less synonymous with the national norm language. Cairene Arabic, in fact, is associated with Egyptian identity. Pedersen (2003) observed a similar trend in Denmark. In the Danish capital city of Copenhagen, features typically employed by the educated middle classes were by younger ambitious speakers not exclusively associated with standard speech. Instead, this group associated features typical of the more local type of Copenhagen speech with a broader language norm. In Beijing, too, younger speakers attach prestige to local features, even if these features deviate from the traditional standard style (Hu and Smakman, this volume). In England and the Netherlands, as for two final examples, the speech that is typical of London and Amsterdam has high prestige amongst young and ambitious people, including educated ones (Coggle 1993; Stroop 1998), and the qualification 'standard' often seems to be subconsciously associated with either a London or Amsterdam ring (i.e., pronunciation).

City norms and the mechanisms in accordance with which they develop and spread seem to be changing. While in the mid-1960s one could walk into a New York City department store and have reasonable assumptions as to the language use of staff (Labov 1963), nowadays the people in such department stores are, first of all, more diverse. Secondly, these same people are nowadays more likely to be in the constant process of developing their own, custom-made language norms rather than following the norms as spread through the media and education (Blommaert and Rampton 2011; Pennycook 2018). It is a safe assumption that this trend is a broad, global trend, in a world that is globalising.

7.5 Reasons in favour of the Haarlem Legend

So, it has been established that urban areas in particular play a strong role in the coming to existence of language norms. It has also been established that within the Randstad urban area in the Netherlands, the city of Haarlem is overtly associated with this role even more than nearby Amsterdam or any other city in the region. Let's look at reasons why the city of Haarlem would deserve the special image it has and reasons why it would not. Below are eight reasons that support the distinctive linguistic status of this city.

7.5.1 Special role in the history of printing

According to lore, a famous Haarlemmer, Laurens Janszoon Coster (c. 1370–1440), can be connected to the language norm in the Netherlands. Coster is said to have introduced printing in the Netherlands. He was an important Haarlemmer and lived and worked in this city for most of his life. Coster is also suggested to have invented the printing press. This is in the literature referred to as *de Costerlegende*, 'the Coster Legend', which was passed down orally. Research (Robbe 2010) has shown that the earliest mention of this figure is in the 17th volume of a series of books, called *Batavia*, by the Haarlem resident Hadrianus Junius (1652). This was noticed, amongst others, by Van Meurs (1870), who challenged the existence of Coster and established that there may have been some confusion of names of people called Coster. Despite the lack of clarity surrounding Coster, it is true that Haarlem played an important role in the development of printing. During the Dutch Golden Age (roughly the seventeenth century), Haarlem was one of the main places where documents were printed that spread the stereotypically Dutch ideology of religious and political freedom. This city possibly held more of a pioneering spirit than other cities. The special position of printing in Haarlem is illustrated by the existence of the *Haarlems Dagblad*, 'Haarlem Daily', newspaper, which claims to be the newspaper with the longest publication history (HCB 2019) in the world. The origins of this newspaper can be traced back to 1656 (Oldest.org 2019). The Coster legend and these claims have likely contributed to Haarlem's status as central place of printing, and, as a consequence, its association with a language norm.

7.5.2 First train connection

On 20 September 1839, the first train in the Netherlands made its maiden voyage, between Amsterdam and Haarlem. For the first time in history, train connections allowed common people to regularly hear Dutch as it was spoken in a nearby city. It is not unlikely that some kind of levelling, or regional standardisation, took place through this mutual exposure, and that the Haarlem–Amsterdam nexus was at the centre of this development.

7.5.3 Johan Winkler's publication

In 1874, Johan Winkler published a linguistic description of about 200 dialects of Dutch (Winkler 1874). Winkler was born in the north of the Netherlands but studied medicine in Haarlem. After inheriting a large sum of money, he settled in Haarlem in 1875 and from then on devoted his time to the study of the Dutch language. He wrote: 'undoubtedly of all Holland and Dutch vernaculars [...] the spoken language in Haarlem is closest to the Dutch written language' (p. 77). He called the Amsterdam dialect 'disgusting, roaring' (p. 145), and about the Leiden dialect he said: 'without a doubt the ugliest, most unpleasant, and broad-sounding in all of Holland' (pp. 109–110, Part II). He went on to explain the special status of the local Haarlem speech: 'During the time of the church reformations, and later too, many strangers settled in Haarlem [...], from Flanders, Brabant, and from the area around the Lower Rhine. These new citizens [...] exerted a great influence on the Haarlem tongue. This way, the typical Haarlem tongue came to existence.' It seems like Winkler was talking about a levelling process that was taking place in Haarlem in particular and which led to some kind of unmarked way of speaking Dutch; the avoidance of language (phrases, words, pronunciation) that may have been perceived as local or unclear by other speakers (dialect and regional differences were considerable in those days). Winkler's comments and his explanation are often said to be at the basis of the current Haarlem Legend (Smakman 2003, 2006), which assigns a special normative role to the way Dutch is spoken in this city.

7.5.4 Measured dialect distance

Research (Hoppenbrouwers and Hoppenbrouwers 2001, Nerbonne and Heeringa 1997, Heeringa 2004) has shown that of all the local ways of pronouncing Dutch, the way Haarlemmers pronounce this language is most similar to Standard Dutch. The number of phonetic steps necessary were measured to calculate the phonetic difference between local dialects and standard Dutch, and Haarlem speech required the least number of steps.

7.5.5 Administrative position of Haarlem

Haarlem is the official administrative city of the province of North Holland. Nearby Amsterdam is the country's capital city but does not have a leading role in provincial affairs.

7.5.6 Stereotypical image of Haarlem

The perceived social atmosphere of the city of Haarlem is another possible reason why the language of this city is managing to maintain its special status. Although the difference between Amsterdam and Haarlem speech is relatively unknown, Haarlem Dutch may be seen as the more stylised and educated version of Amsterdam speech. In a YouTube clip (Nuijt 2009), a reporter is seen going to Haarlem and asking people what they think of the city. In the first minute, the following quotes are given by random interviewees: 'It is both a city and a village', 'beautiful', 'full of atmosphere, cosy', 'authentic', 'Mini-Amsterdam, but more posh', 'civilised, neat, bourgeois, quiet, provincial, conservative', 'culture, shopping, restaurants, enjoying life', 'X-factor that Alkmaar doesn't have' (Alkmaar is another city in the North Holland province), and, for instance, 'trendy'. These answers sum up the stereotypical image of Haarlem; it is a city that is culturally rich and is in fact quite beautiful, and it is associated with well-to-do inhabitants. In the same clip, the reporter runs into a famous Dutch lawyer, Bénédicte Ficq, who summarises Haarlem as 'a game reserve for spoiled people'. So, the image of Haarlem is not that of an ordinary city. One might say that it is a 'good' city. In good cities, people speak good language.

7.5.7 Popular residence of MYSFs

Related to the previous issue is the image of Haarlem as being the residence of prototypical speakers of the standard language. Trudgill (1986) invented the acronym 'NORM' to denote the 'Non-mobile Older Rural Male', the stereotypical speaker of non-urban dialects. This speaker lives in a secluded village, away from the city, and doesn't indulge in travel and meeting people other than the ones close to him and like him. The assumption was that males who live this way and are not so mobile are likely to speak a 'pure' form of the rural dialect, i.e. the opposite of standard. As a reaction to the NORM concept, the Dutchman Goeman (2000) put forward its urban equivalent, the 'MYSF' ('Mobile Younger Suburban Female'). Geographically and socially mobile female speakers in urban contexts in the Netherlands are stereotypically more likely to be attracted to the norm language, so Goeman hypothesised. Although (again prototypically) MYSFs are more likely to work in Amsterdam than in Haarlem, they may occasionally choose to live in Haarlem, as part of an idealised less hectic private lifestyle – Haarlem is like Amsterdam, but its popular image does not include the many city issues associated with Amsterdam, such as drug abuse, prostitution, crime, poverty and extreme tourism. The conviction that successful speakers of the norm language (and their equally successful partners) live in the quiet and conservative city of Haarlem may contribute to the continuation of the special linguistic status of Haarlem.

7.5.8 Haarlem's anonymity

Related to the previous argument is the relative anonymity of the city of Haarlem. National and international tourists are not likely to visit Haarlem if they have already been to Amsterdam. Even Dutchmen usually do not go to Haarlem as a day out, as Amsterdam has many more points of attraction.

7.6 Arguments against the Haarlem legend

It is now clear that there are reasons to believe that Haarlem can be considered to play an important role in the spreading and 'maintenance' of a national language norm. However, Haarlem is different from other large cities in the *Randstad* area, as it seems to lack certain important functions and images. In many cases, other cities are more likely to qualify as places where a broader, national language norm may develop. Let's look at nine reasons that suggest this lack of specialness of Haarlem.

7.6.1 Not the political centre

Haarlem is not the political centre of the Netherlands. The city of The Hague holds the seat of parliament. Politicians are interviewed on a daily basis while they are near or in the Dutch Houses of Parliament, so the city of the Hague and politicians based in it are more likely to appear on TV news. Because politicians are associated with Standard Dutch (Smakman 2006), this may create a link between The Hague and the Dutch language norm in the Dutchmen's minds. The Hague is a major international centre of peace and justice, and is home to the International Criminal Court, the International Court of Justice, and the Permanent Court of Arbitration. Haarlem does not have this or a related national function.

7.6.2 No royal residence

The Hague is most strongly associated with the royal family, as the royal head of state traditional has their official residence there. *Het Koninklijk Paleis*, 'The Royal Palace', is situated in the very heart of Amsterdam, the famous Dam square. Haarlem is not the place of residence of the most well-known members of the royal family. No well-known royals are currently known to live in Haarlem.

7.6.3 Not the capital city

The official capital city of the Netherlands is Amsterdam. Capital cities in particular are known to be places where the standard language is not only more or less constructed but from there language norms are also spread (Bassiouney 2015).

7.6.4 No national/international cultural hub

Amsterdam is not only the capital city of the Netherlands, it is also the cultural hub of the country (Cornips, De Rooij and Smakman 2018). Of all the Dutch cities, it is believed to be a place where cultures come together but also where Dutchmen come together. The city hosts the most important music concerts, it has strong associations with art and museums, and Dutchmen flock to this city *en masse* to celebrate the king's birthday every year. International tourists often visit only Amsterdam, and Dutchmen often go on daytrips to this city. Haarlem does not carry this type of attraction. It sports one of the most impressive and beautiful shopping centres in the country, but its geographical closeness to Amsterdam makes it an unlikely place for Dutch people to visit. Amsterdam attracts people from all over the country, while Haarlem mainly attracts people from surrounding towns.

7.6.5 Not amongst the largest cities

According to (CBS 2020), the four largest cities on 1 January 2019 in the Netherlands are Amsterdam (872,757 inhabitants), Rotterdam (651,157 inhabitants), Utrecht (357,597 inhabitants), and The Hague (537,988 inhabitants). The city of Haarlem has 162,902 inhabitants (Haarlem 2019). Haarlem, in fact, is relatively small. Outside the *Randstad* region, several cities have a similar or higher number of inhabitants than Haarlem. The provincial cities of Groningen, Tilburg and Eindhoven all have over 200,000 inhabitants (CBS 2020).

7.6.6 Geographically peripheral

Haarlem lies close to the sea and is geographically not a central city, neither in the Netherlands nor the *Randstad*. The city of Utrecht is generally considered the geographical centre of the country. Utrecht is also known to be the city with the largest train station, being connected to many other centres across the country.

7.6.7 Not an academic centre

Haarlem does not have a university. The three oldest universities in the Netherlands are Leiden University (est. 1575), Groningen University (est. 1614), and Utrecht University (est. 1636). These and other academic institutes enjoy a high status and are the alma maters of Dutch politicians and other leading figures and of royals. Haarlem is not associated with academia in any way.

7.6.8 No centre of broadcasting

Media, such as radio and television, have traditionally been regarded as important sources of language-norm formation (Livingstone and Lunt 2014; Inoue 2011; Shioda 2011; Bell 1983, 1991). According to Bell (1991), broadcast media are important providers of language in society and language norms. Bell (1984) indicated that a shift towards national norms is most likely to be active in programmes aimed at a national audience. The idea that media speech (from radio and/or television) is close to a (national) linguistic norm in the Netherlands is supported by remarks hereon in the literature; for instance, Goudsblom (1964), Lotzmann (1974), Bell (2013), and Van de Velde (1996). The idea is that media speakers adjust their language so as to be understood correctly by the whole population. The first Dutch radio channels started broadcasting in the 1920s, and television channels came to existence in the 1950s. The Dutch standardised spoken language took a leap in the 1950s and 1960s, and this was largely due to the spoken media, which Vandeputte, Vincent and Hermans (1997) considered a tool towards the standardisation of Dutch. Much of national broadcasting takes place from the north-eastern periphery of the *Randstad* area, particularly in the town of Hilversum, which is about 50 kilometres away from Haarlem. Amsterdam lies between Haarlem and Hilversum. Haarlem is not in any serious way associated with broadcasting.

7.6.9 No economic centre

The economic centres in the Netherlands are Amsterdam and Rotterdam. Rotterdam has the largest port and Amsterdam has the fourth largest port in Europe. Amsterdam in particular is associated with international business, and attracts many national and international companies. The so-called *Zuidas*, 'South Axis', is an area in Amsterdam that attracts companies and employees from all over the country. Haarlem does not have a port, nor is it known to be economically important nationally or internationally. It qualifies as an average mid-sized city in this respect, with a residential rather than a business image.

7.7 Conclusion

So, the question now is how this Haarlem legend stays in place and keeps being passed on to future generations of Dutchmen, despite considerable counter-evidence. An explanation is that once the legend was created, it was not refuted. People are often aware of the counter-evidence but do not act or communicate accordingly. Some of the reasons mentioned in favour of the legend are more convincing than others, but they may act in formation to confirm or maintain a certain image of the city in question and its special linguistic status.

Within societies, beliefs may persist and take on the shape of myths. Well-known ones are that women and men in Japan speak wholly different languages (Heinrich 2015) and that all languages in India are derived from Sanskrit. Two other examples of famous assumptions about language were put forward by Bloomfield (1944), namely that Hungarians and Finns can understand each other's language, and that in certain remote places in England original sixteenth-century Elizabethan English is still spoken. Language myths of another kind were discussed in Bauer and Trudgill (1998), like the bad influence of the media on language proficiency and the deterioration of language standards. This type of myth concerns the workings of language in society and in people's brains. The detrimental effect of speaking more than one language is another well-known belief. Niedzielski and Preston (2000) summarised a number of such general beliefs. First of all, there is the belief in the minds of many non-linguists that some languages are primitive, while others are richer and more intricate systems of expression. Dialects in particular are often considered to be simplified forms of the norm language. Another common belief is that speaking 'correctly' is the fruit of 'good efforts' made by the speaker, while any deviant kind of speech is the fruit of 'sloppiness' or 'laziness'. Furthermore, languages are often thought to reflect the ethnic/racial background of speakers, and mother-tongue speakers are authorities (and there is therefore no necessity for a science of language). Language, finally, is often said to be deteriorating; change and variation are generally regarded as detrimental.

The Haarlem legend is merely another item in this long list of language myths that laymen tend to hold on to. There is no tenable set of reasons for defending this myth. The very uncritical way in which the myth is not questioned and is simply passed on, despite its lack of evident logic, shows a need that is felt across generations that certain norms should not be questioned. It is particularly striking that in a time when information on all the above-mentioned reasons is more accessible than before, the solidity of the myth seems untouched. In a time when diversity is 'super', such norms may function as a symbolical beacon to the individual trying to find their way in a forest of linguistic choices and blurring norms.

References

Bassiouney, Reem. 2015. *Language and Identity in Modern Egypt*. Edinburgh: Edinburgh University Press.

Bassiouney, Reem, and Mark Muehlhaeusler. 2017. 'Cairo: The linguistic dynamics of a multilingual city.' In *Urban Sociolinguistics around the World: The City as a Linguistic Process and Experience*, edited by Dick Smakman and Patrick Heinrich, 27–44. London: Routledge.

Bauer, Laurie, and Peter Trudgill, eds. 1998. *Language Myths*. London: Penguin Books Ltd

Bell, Allan. 1983. 'Broadcast news as a language standard.' *International Journal of the Sociology of Language* (40): 29–40.

Bell, Allan. 1984. 'Language style as audience design.' *Language in Society* 13: 145–204.

Bell, Allan. 1991. *The Language of News Media*. Cambridge, MA: Blackwell.

Bell, Allan. 2013. *The Guidebook to Sociolinguistics*. Malden & Oxford: Wiley-Blackwell.

Blommaert, Jan, and Ben Rampton. 2011. 'Language and superdiversity.' *Diversities* 13 (2): 1–21.

Bloomfield, Leonard F. 1944. 'Secondary and tertiary responses to language.' *Language* 20: 45–55.

CBS. 2020. 'Statline.' CBS, accessed 30 December 2020. https://opendata.cbs.nl/statline/#/CBS/nl/dataset/37296ned/table?ts=1609330171652.

Coggle, Paul. 1993. *Do You Speak Estuary?* London: Bloomsbury.

Cornips, Leonie, Vincent A. De Rooij and Dick Smakman. 2018. 'The Randstad area in the Netherlands. Emergent and fluid identity-locality production through language use.' In *Urban Sociolinguistics. The City as a Linguistic Process and Experience*, edited by Dick Smakman and Patrick Heinrich, 162–180. London: Routledge.

Daan, J., and D. Blok. 1969. 'Van Randstad tot landrand.' Bijdragen en Mededelingen der Dialectcommissie van de KNAW XXXVI, Amsterdam.

Goeman, Ton. 2000. 'Naast NORMs ook MYSFs in het veranderende dialectlandschap en het regiolect [Besides NORMs also MYSFs in the changing dialect landscape and the regiolect].' *Taal en Tongval* 52 (1): 87–100.

Goudsblom, J. 1964. 'Het Algemeen Beschaafd Nederlands.' *Sociolinguïstische Gids* 11: 106–124.

Haarlem. 2019. 'Gemeente Haarlem. Feiten en Cijfers.' accessed 12 September 2020. www.haarlem.nl/feiten-en-cijfers/.

Haugen, Einar. 1966. 'Dialect, language, nation.' *American Anthropologist* 68: 922–935.

HCB. 2019. 'Haarlem.' *Haarlem Marketing*, accessed 25 August 2019. www.visithaarlem.com/nl.

Heeringa, Wilbert Jan. 2004. *Measuring Dialect Pronunciation Differences Using Levenshtein Distance*. Groningen: Groningen University Library

Heinrich, Patrick. 2015. 'The study of politeness and women's language in Japan.' In *Globalising Sociolinguistics. Challenging and Expanding Theory*, edited by Dick Smakman and Patrick Heinrich, 178–193. London: Routledge.

Hoppenbrouwers, C., and G. Hoppenbrouwers. 2001. *De indeling van de Nederlandse streektalen*. Assen: Koninklijke Van Gorcum BV.

Inoue, Fumio. 2011. 'Standardization and de-standardization processes in spoken Japanese.' In *Language Life in Japan. Transformations and Prospects*, edited by Patrick Heinrich and Christian Galan, 109–123. London / New York: Routledge.

Jansen, Joost, Adaja Boersma, Rick Uilenbroek and Michael Baatje. 2015. 'Praat Haarlems met me (Speak Haarlemmish with me).' www.youtube.com/watch?v=d6WSuhfC6c0.

Junius, Adrianus. 1652. *Hadriani Junii Batavia In Qua præter gentis & insulæ antiquitatem, originem, decora, mores, aliáque ad eam historiam pertinentia, declaratur, quæ fuerit vetus Batavia, quæ Plinio, Tacito, & Ptolomæo cognita: quæ item genuina inclytæ Francorum nationis fuerit sedes*. Dordrecht: Vincent Caimax & Jacob Braat.

Kloeke, G. G. 1937. *Voordracht van den voorzitter Dr. Kloeke over beschaafd Nederlands*. Leiden: Maatschappij der Nederlandsche Letterkunde.

Labov, William. 1963. 'The social motivation of sound change.' *Word* 19: 273–309.

Livingstone, Sonia, and Peter Lunt. 2014. 'Mediatization. An emerging paradigm for media and communication research?' In *Mediatization of Communication*, edited by K. Lundby, 703–723. Berlin: De Gruyter Mouton.

Lotzmann, G. 1974. 'Sprechwissenschaftliche Aspekte zur Aussprachenormierung des Deutschen.' In *Sprach- und Sprechnormen*, edited by G. Lotzmann, 65–83. Heidelberg.

Massey, Doreen B. 2005. *For Space*. London: Sage.

Nerbonne, John, and Wilbert Jan Heeringa. 1997. 'Measuring dialect distance phonetically.' Third Meeting of the ACL Special Interest Group in Computational Phonology, Madrid.

Niedzielski, Nancy A., and Dennis R. Preston. 2000. *Folk Linguistics*. Vol. 22, *Trends in Linguistics. Studies and Monographs*. Berlin/New York: Mouton de Gruyter.

Nuijt, Jasper. 2009. 'Wat is het imago van Haarlem?'. www.youtube.com/watch?v=kNLSDJrieco.

Oldest.org. 2019. '10 Oldest Newspapers in The World.' www.oldest.org/artliterature/newspapers/.

Pedersen, Inge Lise. 2003. 'Traditional dialects of Danish and the de-dialectalization 1900–2000.' *International Journal of the Sociology of Language* 159: 9–28.

Pennycook, Alastair. 2018. *Posthumanist Applied Linguistics*. Abingdon/New York: Routledge.

Robbe, J. 2010. 'De literaire aspecten van de Costerlegende: Mythologie in de vorm van een klassieke pleitrede.' *Internationale Neerlandistiek* 48 (3): 17–29.

Shioda, Takehiro. 2011. 'Constraints on language use in public broadcasting.' In *Language Life in Japan. Transformations and Prospects*, edited by Patrick Heinrich and Christian Galan, 124–139. London / New York: Routledge.

Smakman, Dick. 2003. 'Algemeen Beschaafd Haarlems. Gebruikskenmerken van het Standaardnederlands [General Civilised Haarlem Dutch. User characteristics of Standard Dutch].' In *Waar gaat het Nederlands naartoe? Panorama van een Taal*, edited by Jan Stroop, 120–130. Amsterdam: Bert Bakker.

Smakman, Dick. 2006. 'Standard Dutch in the Netherlands. A Sociolinguistic and Phonetic Description.' PhD, Landelijke Onderzoekschool Taalwetenschap (LOT).

Smakman, Dick. 2012. 'The definition of the standard language: A survey in seven countries.' *International Journal of the Sociology of Language* 218: 25–85.

Smakman, Dick. 2018. *Discovering Sociolinguistics. From Theory to Practice*. London: Palgrave Macmillan.

Stroop, Jan. 1998. *Poldernederlands. Waardoor het ABN Verdwijnt [Polder Dutch. Due to which Standard Dutch is disappearing]*. Amsterdam: Bert Bakker.

Trudgill, Peter. 1974. 'Linguistic change and diffusion: Description and explanation in sociolinguistic dialect geography.' *Language in Society* 3: 215–246.

Trudgill, Peter. 1986. *Sociolinguistics*. 2nd ed. Harmondsworth: Penguin.

Tzitzilis, Christos. 2001. 'Modern Greek dialects and modern Greek dialectology.' In *Encyclopaedic Guide for the Language*, edited by Anastassios Christidis, 168–174. Thessaloniki: Center of Greek Language.

Van Bree, C. 1981. *Hebben-constructies en datiefconstructies binnen het Nederlandse taalgebied: een taalgeografisch onderzoek*. Leiden: Leiden University Press.

Van de Velde, Hans. 1996. *Variatie en Verandering in het Standaard-Nederlands (1935–1993) [Variation and change in Standard Dutch (1935–1993)]*. Utrecht: Landelijke Onderzoeksschool Taalwetenschap (LOT).

Van Meurs, Peter. 1870. *De Keulsche Kroniek en de Costerlegende van Dr. A. van der Linde te zamen getoetst*. Haarlem: A. C. Kruseman.

Vandeputte, O., P. Vincent, and T. Hermans. 1997. *Dutch – the Language of Twenty Million Dutch and Flemish People*. Renkum: Stichting Ons Erfdeel.

Warf, Barney, ed. 2010. *Encyclopedia of Human Geography*. Edited by Barney Warf. Vol. 1. Los Angeles: Sage.

Winkler, Johan. 1874. *Algemeen Nederduitsch en Friesch Dialecticon*. The Hague: Nijhoff.

8 The sociolinguistic situation in Hradec Králové, the best researched town in the Czech Republic[1]

J. Nekvapil

8.1 Introduction

Hradec Králové (HK) is a regional centre situated about 100 km northeast of the Czech Republic's capital, Prague. With approximately 100,000 inhabitants, it is the eighth most populous municipality in the country. As such, it is perceived as a large town or city in the Czech context. More or less by coincidence, it may be the best researched town in the Czech Republic in terms of its sociolinguistic situation. This body of research arising since the 1960s can be divided into several areas: (1) studies in language variation carried out in the framework of urban speech which emerged in connection with the work on the Czech Linguistic Atlas, (2) studies in onomastics, (3) studies in various kinds of social interaction such as asking for directions to the railway station, service encounters in a kiosk or the management of communication in religious proselyting. Currently, the present author deals with the use of multiple languages in the town (its multilingualism), particularly the linguistic landscape, which represents the fourth research area.

This chapter provides an overview of the research done in the above areas, draws attention to the research paradigms involved, and, most importantly, seeks to present it as a coherent whole. It addresses the question of the extent to which it is possible to provide such a coherent picture. On a more general level, the chapter aims to outline the degree to which the agenda of present-day sociolinguistics is compatible with or even can profit from the sociolinguistic agenda of the past.

The development of research areas, disciplines and sub-disciplines is hard to map; thus, researchers can often choose to what extent they want to represent it – either via the rhetoric of continuity or revolution. The revolutionary rhetoric is marked by the denial of the previous approaches to the analysis of social happenings since it presents these happenings as being fundamentally different from the present ones – following this logic, fundamentally different social happenings call for fundamentally different theoretical-methodological approaches, which in sociolinguistics goes currently hand in hand with applying the novel concept of superdiversity, with its transformation potential in the

DOI: 10.4324/9780429348037-10

social sciences in general and in sociolinguistics in particular.[2] This chapter, on the other hand, subscribes to the rhetoric of continuity – this rhetoric is, of course, not quite as ostentatious as the rhetoric of revolution; it does not draw as much attention. Nevertheless, even the rhetoric of continuity has been recently gaining momentum (e.g., see Coulmas 2018, especially p. 19). What is also worth mentioning is that the need to found a 'new sociolinguistics' was recently called into question by Fox and Sharma (2018); authors who, paradoxically, conducted their research in the cradle of superdiversity in London (Fox and Sharma 2018: 127).

In this chapter, I will map the sociolinguistic situation in one town situated in the northern part of the Czech Republic. Many readers may read about this town for the first time in this chapter; moreover, it may be assumed that not all readers are equally familiar with the wider research context which underlies the sociolinguistic research performed in this town. These circumstances, on the other hand, offer indisputable advantages – the example of Hradec Králové can help us to illuminate the rigmarole sociolinguistics has been going through; what it means for the discipline to have 'Anglo-Western bias' and what all the factors are that sociolinguists should absorb and/or take into account if sociolinguistics is to gradually gain global relevance as Smakman and Heinrich (2015, 2018) systematically call for.

8.2 Research into urban speech in the Czech Republic and in Hradec Králové (HK)

The research into urban speech in the Czech Republic was being done since the 1960s in connection with the work on the Czech Linguistic Atlas. An important impulse in this respect was a programmatic paper by a prominent Czech dialectologist, Jaromír Bělič, in which he discusses the specificity of urban speech research (see Bělič 1962). Bělič calls for a multifaceted approach to urban speech, i.e. not just research into the phonological and morphological level, as it used to be common in traditional, rurally oriented dialectology, but also the syntactic and lexical level(s); and when it comes to the linguistic research targeted on towns, he anticipated changes in research methodology. Similarly to Labov (1966), Bělič deemed it crucial for the urban speech of a particular town to be characterised from the perspective of 'social and stylistic stratification' (Bělič 1962: 572). In this respect, we can recall Labov's own later comment that his influential book published in 1966 with the title *The Social Stratification of English in New York City* 'might have been more accurately called *The Stylistic and Social Stratification of English in New York City*' (Labov 2006: 397). The article by Bělič inspired a number of research studies mapping the linguistic situation in both smaller and bigger Czech towns; ironically, most of these projects still only focussed on phonological and morphological phenomena. It should be also noted that – rather than being inspired by Labov – these studies were largely following the Czech theoretical-methodological design typical of the functional-structuralist approach of the Prague school. Nevertheless, since

Labov's monograph was available in the Czech Republic soon after its publication and Czech specialists also could have learned about it from an extensive review by Utěšený (1968), it does not come as a surprise that in some respects they followed Labov's or other variationist studies.

One of the most active Czech urban speech researchers was Bohumír Dejmek. His first empirical study, conducted between 1962 and 1971, culminated with a comprehensive monograph on Přelouč, a town of six thousand inhabitants. He cooperated closely with leading dialectologists from Prague who were, at that time, working on the Czech Linguistic Atlas (see Dejmek 1976: 1), and his project was coordinated by Jaromír Bělič, the above-mentioned scholar. Even though Dejmek was systematically using quantitative research methods in his project (in contrast with traditional dialectology and linguistic geography), the relatively small number of his key informants prevented him from obtaining reliable data pertinent to the analysis of the influence of social variables on the extent of using phonological and morphological variants. Interestingly, this prompted him to comment on the linguistic behaviour of individual informants, as illustrated by the following comment: 'Informant nr. 8, nurse, vivacious, energetic, speaks both with patients and physicians equally and naturally, "as she pleases"' (Dejmek 1976: 195).

In 1974, Dejmek started to explore phonological and morphological variation in the urban speech of HK (see Dejmek 1986: 109) and published two monographs on it (Dejmek 1981 and 1987). The most general goal of Dejmek's research was to point out the ongoing changes in the Czech language through the analysis of the development of urban speech in HK, as an illustrative example. Dejmek joined a number of researchers, who were trying to show that such development is partly socially conditioned; herein lies his interest in correlating linguistic and social variables and in sociolinguistic methodology. Especially when it comes to methodology, he quotes studies by Labov (see Dejmek 1980: 55; Dejmek 1981: 16, 18; Dejmek 1987: 13). The first of the above-mentioned books on HK by Dejmek took the following social factors into account: gender, regional origin (having been born in the old town, i.e. former city centre vs. in the suburbs), social status (manual worker, attendant, small sole trader, public service, homemaker), education (elementary, lower secondary, higher secondary, tertiary). It is worth noting that social variables did not include 'class'; during that era, i.e. in communist Czechoslovakia, this notion had a specific meaning derived from the then common Marxist-Leninist doctrine, and was hence hard to operationalise for purposes of empirical research.[3] Furthermore, 'class' was a problematic variable even with Labov and other variationists. As far as the correlation of social and linguistic variables is concerned, Dejmek's most convincing and statistically significant finding was that varying a number of language features correlates with the level of education: 'the higher the education level, the lower the tendency to employ regional and dialectal elements' (Dejmek 1981: 111). Having explored the representatives of the oldest generation in 1978, Dejmek proceeded to explore the youngest generation, i.e. elementary and high school students (Dejmek 1987). Social factors that were taken into account in this project concerned the pupils'/ students' mother(s) and father(s) including: their gender, social status (this time with two categories only: blue-collar and white-collar), regional origin, and education. One of the typical regional language variants (i.e. the identity of forms in nominative and accusative plural masculine animate nouns, such as *-i* in the Czech sentence *má dva* **kluci**/'she has two lads') proved to strongly correlate with the factor of education and social status (higher incidence in speakers with a lower educational, or more precisely blue-collar background). Another two locally typical variants (dative/locative singular masculine animate nouns *-oj* such as in the Czech form *bratroj*/'to the brother' and instrumental singular feminine soft nouns *-ej* such as in the Czech form *ulicej*/'along the street') illustrated a rather weak link with social factors (more on this below).

It would be a mistake though to treat Dejmek's two monographs separately since they represent essentially *one synchronically-oriented research*, albeit one conducted over the course of more than ten years. What follows is that Dejmek's monographs as a whole also provide the social variable of age. Dejmek compared linguistic variation between the oldest and youngest generation looking at fourteen language variables. Based on this, he concluded that we are witnessing an even larger shift towards non-standard equalised Czech (the so-called 'Common Czech') than was signalled by the research of the oldest generation; also, he concluded that a marked retreat of regional and dialectal variants is taking place (Dejmek 1987: 66, 67).

We shall now come back to the three above-mentioned morphological variants, for Dejmek gives them special attention (Dejmek 1987: 68 and 82). It is apparent that in the communicative behaviour of the citizens of HK he ascribes them an indexical value. While – in line with what was mentioned above – the accusative form –i (see *kluci*) marks the speaker pejoratively as an uneducated person, the instrumental form –ej (see *ulicej*) and to a smaller degree also the dative and local form –oj (see *bratroj*) have an identity-forming potential, i.e. they mark an affiliation with the town; hence, it is not surprising that their usage does not vary much across generations.

Many years later, Dejmek (1998) published the ethnography-inspired brochure *The Old Town of Hradec Králové Tells Its Stories* (*Starý Hradec vypravuje*), in which he published longer fragments of narratives he elicited in the 1970s from the representatives of the oldest generation (this is also reminiscent of the original activities of Labov, who – inspired by the interesting nature of the sociolinguistic data gathered from his respondents – was already studying oral narratives in the 1960s). These narrative fragments are presented with local phonological and morphological features, and are accompanied by period photographs. The selection of texts is motivated by the effort to form the city identity. In this context, what should be mentioned is the account of Dejmek's respondents when it comes to the usage of the word *votrok*, which became a colloquial denomination for a citizen of HK (a part of this account was even placed on the cover of Dejmek 1981). The word *votrok* contains a prothetic *v–* at the beginning, which is a colloquial feature typical for Common Czech, frequently used in HK. The standard form of this word is *otrok*/'slave' – the systematic insertion of *v*– has contributed to the establishment and fixation of a new meaning characteristic of the urban speech in HK.

The monograph *The History and Present of Hradec Králové in Street Names* (*Historie a současnost Hradce Králové ve jménech ulic*) (Dejmek 1993) provides material for the historical sociolinguistics of the town. Street names are classified according to their semantic motivations, which are, in turn, correlated with the historical stages of the town's development (Dejmek 1993: 31). A comprehensive historical overview of all street names (incl. more than 500 objects) makes it possible for us to analyse the impact of social revolutions on this semiotic area. The fall of the communist regime in 1989 was a good impetus when it comes to the analysis of changes in street names; surprisingly, such changes did not orient to employing iconic signs (according to this strategy, e.g. a long street would be labelled *Dlouhá*/'Long street') as much as to using ideologically motivated names (*Lenin* street or *Lenin* square, for example, become *Masaryk* street or *Masaryk* square[4]) (see Nekvapil 2000: 168).

What follows from the above is that, similarly to Labovian variationism, the basis of urban speech research in Czech conditions was monolingualism; in other words, the orientation towards the study of the usage of *one single* language dominant in that particular society. In Czech society, this was re-enforced by the fact that in Central Europe, languages were assigned a nation-forming function – a 'national language' therefore became the prime research object drawing the attention of the key national research institutions. This, however, does not entail that Dejmek never mentions other languages in his works; for example, he comments on the influence of German on street nomenclature during the German occupation 1939–1945 (Dejmek 1993: 16, 35) or he quotes his oldest respondents, who pointed out to him that German was still spoken in HK after WWI (Dejmek 1998: 88, 91); or he observes that some parents of his youngest respondents come from Slovakia, which influences the Czech spoken by those particular family members (Dejmek 1987: 72). Because Dejmek was chiefly an institutional lecturer in Czech studies, multilingualism in the city remained, however, rather marginal to his professional interests. It is also characteristic that – apart from Czech – not just Dejmek, but also no other researchers focussed on the use of other languages in HK. In the ambitious project devoted to the language situation in HK, which was to be conducted ten years prior to Dejmek's research, Uličný (1966) did include the variable of nationality, but again, it was a marginal factor, and – even more importantly – the project never came to fruition. The absence of sociolinguistically oriented research into urban multilingualism was essentially characteristic for the whole of the Czech territory.[5]

The question remains whether this approach was merely the result of the mainstream research paradigm or was caused by the actual absence of multilingualism in HK after WWII. Even though HK was a distinctively Czech town, members of other national minorities lived there as well; some of them were monitored thanks to the regular census or other statistical surveys. These sources indicate that apart from ethnic Czechs, also Slovaks, Ukrainians, Ruthenians, Russians, Poles, Hungarians, Germans and Roma (Gypsies) lived here. We can only speculate about the linguistic behaviour of these ethnic groups; the nationwide census conducted between 1970–1991 did not even survey the respondents' mother tongue. Speakers of other languages were, however, not just representatives of the above-mentioned national minorities with Czech citizenship. The author of this chapter has lived in HK since the 1960s and he himself has witnessed the multitude of languages being utilised there. Based on various sources such as those given above and personal experience, we can retrace and schematically model certain aspects of the multilingualism in HK (i.e. the repertoire of languages used and the profile of their speakers) of that time as follows:

- Polish (residents, tourists, temporary workers, academic contacts)
- English (English teaching programme at the Faculty of Medicine, foreign students)
- Slovak (residents, students, tourists)
- Romani (residents, migrants from Slovakia)
- Russian (groups of tourists, residents, Soviet soldiers)
- German (residents, tourists, exchange of pupils and students)
- Vietnamese (guest workers)
- Hungarian (residents, migrants from Slovakia)

This schema essentially depicts the situation in the last two decades of the existence of communist Czechoslovakia, i.e. roughly between 1968 and 1989, and completely leaves out the issue of foreign language teaching (for more on this, see Neustupný and Nekvapil 2003 – this study, however, maps the situation in the country as a whole). It also, of course, fails to capture the fact that these languages were also spoken to varying degrees by native speakers of Czech and that the speakers of these languages also spoke some level of Czech.

8.3 From the variationist approach to interactional studies (since the 1990s)

After the political turn in 1989, research approaches coming from the West started to gain ground more forcefully.[6] Following especially the tradition of conversation analysis (CA), new studies focussing on various aspects of interactions taking place in HK were devised. In terms of genres, these interactions can be characterised as:

> asking for directions to the railway station (see Zeman 1999), service encounters in a kiosk (see Nekvapil 1997), and the management of communication in religious proselyting (Sherman 2007).

8.4 Asking for directions to the railway station

A collection of minor studies edited by Zeman (1999), see also Nekvapil and Zeman (2000), concentrated on the CA problem of how to 'give directions' in an ordinary daily interaction (Schegloff 1972 was a quoted authority in this collection). An example of one of these interactions follows:

> A: dobrý den, prosim vas, já hledám nádraží. / 'good morning, could you tell me the way to the railway station.'
>
> B: no tak to můžete takhle touletou ulicej, (.) ... / 'well you can go this way, along this street,'
>
> (Zeman 1999:45; abbreviated)

Even though the research goals of the authors were inspired by the tenets of CA, they also noticed that 'the collected material is also suitable for the study of language varieties used among strangers, one of whom is a "foreigner" and the other one a "local" – we can see from the transcripts that apart from Common Czech features, linguistic features used in HK can also include explicitly regional traces, even among the younger generation: see *touhle ulicej*' (Nekvapil and Zeman 2000: 31).

The claim that *ulicej* / 'along this street' is a regional feature is supported by Nekvapil and Zeman referring to Dejmek (1981) and (1987), thus basically confirming his conclusion of a cross-generational usage of this particular inflectional form (for more see above).

The authors also, in a way, follow Dejmek's work in that they explain why the study's informants – when they give directions – fairly rarely use street names. Dejmek (1993) documented extensive changes of street names in HK, including the re-introduction of ideologically motivated names after 1989, which made the effective usage of street names in daily communication difficult (Nekvapil and Zeman 2000: 34).

8.5 Service encounters in a kiosk

My own study (Nekvapil 1997) deals with data recorded in one small shop in HK; more specifically, it features interactions between a shop assistant and his customers. It is a comparative analysis of pre-sequences, especially pre-requests and pre-announcements (referring to authorities such as S. C. Levinson and again E. A. Schegloff, among others). The conclusions of the study enumerate the similarities and differences in the composition of American and Czech pre-sequences. The data used in the study are introduced as follows: '[e]mpirically, my research is based on the analysis of service encounters recorded in a small Czech shop in autumn 1995.' (Nekvapil 1997: 444). Note that this research is presented in the paper as the study of Czech conversation, not of conversation as practised in HK.

At this point we stumble upon an interesting theoretical-methodological question which was already covertly present in Dejmek's monographs: are his findings regarding urban speech in some way only specific to HK? Or, rather, to what extent are they specific? Dejmek (1978) proposed distinguishing between what is specific (a) to every town (as contrasted with rural areas), and (b) what is specific to individual towns. Characteristic features of the speech of individual Czech towns are given – among other factors – by their different geographical location on the dialectal map of Czech. This applies to phonological and morphological features, but what about more complex linguistic levels, and conversational structures? Dejmek signals that his studies are locally bound already in the very titles of his five monographs: the first one contains the town name of 'Přelouč', the other four always include 'Hradec (Králové)'.

Interestingly, 'Hradec Králové' is also included in the title of a collection of studies on direction-giving, even though it was possible to assume that the findings were not valid locally only, i.e. valid for Czech in general, or Czech culture.[7] One possible explanation for this is that direction-giving is based on elements specific to the town such as names of buildings (supermarkets, institutions) or streets (see above), i.e. local common-sense geography. Such a connection is obviously missing when it comes to formulating pre-sequences. Nonetheless, even pre-sequences found in the published material bear traces characteristic of urban speech in HK – local names and Common Czech.

I will illustrate this with one example quoted from Nekvapil (1997). B is a jovial shop assistant, A is a customer:

'T1 B: You know what they said on TV. You don't? (3s) What they said on TV. (1s) About that (.) about this shop.
T2 A: I don't know.
T3 B: At Střelák round the corner there is a shop with cottage cheese. (2s) ((Cz. Na Střeláku za rohem máme konzum s tvarohem))
T4 A: ((laughter)) I haven't heard that[8]'. (Nekvapil 1997: 444–445)

This excerpt contains the local name *Střelák* used in its Common Czech form; the Standard Czech form is *Střelnice* (the whole name is the *Kulturní dům Střelnice* /'Culture centre Střelnice').

The analysed data is thus locally anchored. Nevertheless, when compared with all the other studies discussed above, I point this characteristic out only now. In my paper from 1997, due to a different research focus, this characteristic was not 'in the spotlight'. This illustrates that new research agendas can reveal an interesting aspect of previous research. What is important in this respect is that current research can successfully draw on previous studies.[9]

8.6 Management of communication in religious proselyting

Focussing on various communication aspects of religious proselyting, Sherman (2007, 2010, 2015) works with data obtained in HK similarly to Nekvapil

(1997). She takes interactions between missionaries and local residents recorded in this town as typical of all of the Czech Republic, referring to it as 'the Czech case' (Sherman 2015). Her approach, however, goes beyond a mere presentation up-scaling since she integrated it in her research design, in which the choice of HK was justified by the effort to explore religious proselyting in an 'average Czech city' (Sherman 2007: 59). Although her research agenda is chiefly rooted in ethnomethodology (conversation analysis, membership categorisation analysis), her research has also contributed to our understanding of which varieties of Czech are spoken by American missionaries and local residents; moreover, since her data include English sequences, her research also illuminates post-communist multilingualism in HK, i.e. multilingualism brought about by the global phenomenon of religious proselyting. We will now provide one example documenting a missionary activity of addressing people in public. M is an American missionary; C is a local Czech speaker.

(from Sherman 2010: 1005f.)
1. M: uh prosím vás mohli bychom mluvit s vámi?
2. C: já spěchám
3. M: ((fast)) no my taky spěcháme jenom my jsme tady jako
4.   dobrovolníci misionáři ze církve ježiše krista, a tady my nabízíme několik uhm
5.   služeb, například my tady učíme zdarma angličtinu nevím jestli umíte
6.   anglicky náhodou nebo jestli
7.   znáte někoho
8. C: umím trochu ((laughs))
9. M: yeah? domluvíte se?
10. C: domluvím
11. M: yeah? ((slowly)) what is your name?
12. C: my name is ladislava
13. M: d- well nice to meet you.

Translation of the example (Sherman 2010: 988f).
1. M: uh excuse me could we speak with you?
2. C: I'm in a hurry
3. M: ((fast)) well we're in a hurry too we're just here as
4.   volunteers missionaries from the church of jesus
5.   christ, and we offer several uhm services here,
6.   for example we teach free english I don't know if you
7.   happen to know english or if you know someone
8. C: I know a little ((laughs))
9. M: ((English)) yeah? ((Czech)) are you able to speak?
10. C: ((Czech)) I am
11. M: ((English)) yeah? ((slowly, English)) what is your name?
12. C: ((English)) my name is ladislava
13. M: ((English)) d- well nice to meet you.

When it comes to Czech used in the interviews, American missionaries tend to use Standard Czech, thus following the guidelines of their sending organisation (Sherman 2010: 987). Apart from standard features, however, they often use elements typical of Common Czech; nonetheless, these features are not of a prototypically regional identity-forming nature as pointed out by Dejmek (1987), and later by Nekvapil and Zeman (2000). As far as Czech spoken by native speakers of Czech is concerned, they were found to markedly accommodate to the forms of Czech used by the missionaries, which means they too avoided strong regional features. In the extensive appendix of transcribed data accompanying Sherman's (2007: 272–352) doctoral dissertation, not even one occurrence of these (regional) forms was documented.

8.7 Intermezzo: city identity

Before presenting my own research on multilingualism in HK, it is beneficial to review the nature of the research projects discussed thus far. On the whole, their scope and volume is remarkable and from a sociolinguistic perspective HK may truly appear as the 'most thoroughly researched town in the Czech Republic'. Though I would like to insist on this statement, it is still vital to realise that in the above projects HK is presented in two different senses: 1. as a unique place with a specific identity, 2. as an example illustrative of any other town; in other words, as a token of the type 'town'. Accordingly, the studies I analysed above can be divided into the following:

- Research studies displaying a strong orientation to the town identity (works by Dejmek)
- Research studies displaying a weak orientation to the town identity (Zeman 1999)
- Research studies with no orientation to the town identity (even hiding a particular town identity) (esp. studies by Sherman)

Two comments are essential to clarify the above; first, disguising the town identity is often motivated not only by the social construction of research, but also by the effort to anonymise data. Second, to express identity, some linguistic and communication phenomena are more suitable than others. As we have observed, the most commonly used ones are phonological and morphological features, which were the focus of Dejmek's studies.

Nevertheless, apart from language and communication, the residents of HK naturally have other means of asserting their town identity. The majority of HK residents, for example, associate the town identity with its architecture, which is illustrated, for example, by a popular slogan 'Hradec Králové – the salon of the republic', i.e. a town unique and remarkable for its urban architecture. This component of the city identity is supported even institutionally (the municipality, for example, promotes publishing promotional materials on HK's architecture in various languages).

8.8 Current research into multilingualism in HK

I started to systematically review the use of different languages (including Czech) in HK in November of 2018; most of my data stem from the subsequent year, i.e. before the coronavirus outbreak. The data was compiled as a result of a continuous participatory observation of interactions taking place in various shops, restaurants, and cafés; these observations were subsequently recorded as field notes. This also applies to short conversations which I conducted with different interlocutors in these facilities. During these conversations, or more precisely, interviews, I never took on the role of a researcher – in the majority of cases, my engagement could be rather characterised as that of a 'curious customer'. On occasion, I also noted down interactions that took place on the street and in parks. The second major source of my data were records of linguistic landscape of HK, mostly photographs (over 600 of them). Both data sets are often linked – typically, a combination of an interview with either the shop owner or his/her staff, and a photograph of the shop sign.

To accurately interpret the collected data, it is essential to consider the given context. Context can be conceptualised differently and always selectively. Apart from what has been given so far above, for this study, it is appropriate to supply a statistical overview of foreigners living in the district of Hradec Králové. Note that we do not focus on the *town* of HK, but the whole *district* of HK. The structured statistics pertinent to the number of foreigners living in the town of HK is dated, but the data available for the whole district seem to be more or less representative of the town itself; nevertheless, the difference in the number of residents in the district and in the town is not insignificant – the district of HK: 164,283 residents, town HK: 92,939 residents. In total, as of February 2020, i.e. closely before the coronavirus outbreak in the Czech Republic, 6,235 foreign nationals lived in the whole district of HK, which represents 3.8% of all residents of the district (Ukrainian nationals are the most numerous group, accounting for 2.5%).[10]

Table 8.1 provides an overview of the most numerous groups of foreign nationals in HK according to their citizenship; only groups of 100 and more residents (i.e. 0.1% of all residents of the district of HK) have been included.

Further relevant macro-data come from the regular census (see also above); their validity is, however, compromised due to several factors: the newest data, available from 2011, is, of course, dated. The data include the total number of Czech residents according to their nationality and their mother tongue; about one quarter of all respondents, however, did not provide the information on nationality in the survey. Therefore, below, in Table 8.2, I only provide numbers pertinent to the mother tongue(s); nevertheless, the accuracy of these numbers is not to be overestimated either.

When trying to elucidate multilingualism in HK, another aspect is highly relevant, namely that out of roughly 10,000 university students studying in HK over 1,000 (10.5%) are foreign students (numbers as of the end of 2019). There are seven faculties belonging to three universities in HK; hence, another

Table 8.1 Foreign nationals, February 2020, Hradec Králové district

Country of origin	Temporary residents	Permanent residents	Total
Ukraine	1,063	1,242	2,305
Slovakia	513	555	1,068
Vietnam	90	424	514
Poland	57	132	189
Mongolia	73	112	185
Hungary	147	7	154
Russia	66	76	142
Rumania	117	14	131
Germany	70	36	106
Other			1441
Total	3086	3149	6235

Source: Czech Statistical Office.

Table 8.2 Residents of Hradec Králové district according to their mother tongue (as of March 2011)

Total no. of residents	162,661	100.0%
Czech	149,870	92.14%
Slovak	1,828	1.12%
Ukrainian	748	0.46%
Vietnamese	288	0.18%
Russian	218	0.13%
Polish	186	0.11%
Hungarian	126	less than 0.1%
German	97	
Romani	74	
Moravian	13	
Sign language	45	

Source: Czech Statistical Office.

city identity, which is commonly shared and promoted by the municipality, is 'Hradec Králové – the student town'.

8.9 The perception scale of the representation of individual languages in the linguistic landscape of HK

The linguistic landscape of a town can be approached from various perspectives. One of them is the perspective of the town's visitor who comes here for the first time and wanders around, for example, from the railway station to the city centre and further into the historical heart of town observing the local street arrangement and house architecture; in doing so, the visitor's attention is inevitably drawn to different shops and restaurants including their semiotic appearance (or perhaps precisely because of it). She perceives the local architecture and the linguistic landscape more or less in a synchronic view, i.e. without knowing the motives of either the builders and architects or the shop keepers; she notices which elements (either architectonic styles or languages) prevail. Based on such wanderings (often with a camera in hand), or more precisely based on repeated walks, the author of this study put together a perception scale of the representation of individual languages in HK. The ranking on this scale is given first by the frequency of occurrence of these languages in city signs; second, by where these signs are located (centre – suburbs); and finally, their flashiness (i.e. their size, design, colour etc.). Such an initial probe into the city linguistic landscape only 'scratches the surface', but represents a good analytical start which can be followed by subsequent phases, for example, thicker ethnographic descriptions.

The visibility of individual languages in HK

- Very dominant language: (Standard) Czech
- First foreign language, fairly frequent: English
- Less frequently used languages: German, Italian, French, Spanish, Russian, Vietnamese, Turkish
- Rare languages: Chinese, Latin, Arabic, Slovak, Slovenian, Japanese
- Absent: Polish, Ukrainian etc.

In total, I detected 15 languages in the linguistic landscape of HK. Within the limited confines of this chapter, I will tease apart the most interesting selected aspects of this scale. Perhaps rather surprisingly, I will start with languages that were labelled as 'absent'. Clearly, thousands of languages are absent from the linguistic landscape of HK; what I have in mind is the absence that is conspicuous and thus deserves an explanation.[11]

The presence of Polish could be expected for a number of reasons: the wider district of HK neighbours directly with Poland and HK itself is only 50 kilometres away from the Czech-Polish border. Promotional materials on HK distributed in the tourist information office are offered – among other language versions – in Polish, which, as a minimum, indicates some presence of Polish tourists, or is an attempt to promote such presence. The municipality even supports the publication of a Polish version of the local magazine called *Salon republiki. Hradec Králové, magazyn wolnego czasu* / 'Salon of the Republic. Hradec Králové, A Guide to Leisure Time Activities'. A rather small group (nevertheless, the fourth most numerous group among the recorded foreign nationals; see Table 8.1) of Poles live in HK or in its vicinity. What we also have to take into account is a small group of residents reporting Polish nationality or Polish as their mother tongue (these residents are listed in Table 8.2). Roughly the same number of them have lived here for decades; this group classifies as a traditional national minority. The absence of Polish is thus not easily explained; it may be related to the low appeal of the town – both for business (goods and services offered) or tourist purposes – for Polish visitors; to some extent, it could also be related to the structural closeness of Czech and Polish which enables, especially in spoken interactions, receptive bilingualism.[12]

The absence of Ukrainian in the linguistic landscape of HK is conspicuous due to rather different reasons. Ukrainians are the most numerous group of foreign nationals in HK (see Table 8.1) and similarly to the Poles they form a small, yet traditional national minority (see also above). The absence of Ukrainian in the linguistic landscape of HK can probably be attributed to two factors: first, many Ukrainians communicate on a daily basis in Russian; second, due to the fact that Ukrainian nationals often have low-paid jobs, Ukrainian has low social prestige. There are no promotional materials on HK in Ukrainian (even materials in Russian are rather scarce).

Slovak is another language worth mentioning in this context; its next to negligible representation (but not total absence) could perhaps also be considered conspicuous (I found one single sign – a memorial plaque commemorating activities of the Slovak revivalist Ľudovít Štúr in HK in 1840). Slovaks are the second most numerous group of foreign nationals in the district of HK, and a traditional minority, but both Slovaks and Czechs still stick to the communication patterns established in communist Czechoslovakia – what it essentially means is that owing to the structural closeness of Czech and Slovak, speakers of these two languages easily understand one other (i.e. they are receptively bilingual); hence, Slovak signs in the linguistic landscape of the Czech Republic (the same goes for Czech signs in the linguistic landscape of Slovakia) are redundant (see also Sloboda 2021). No promotion materials on HK in Slovak are published.

Some signs constitute a more or less permanent, stable component of the linguistic landscape of HK; other signs appear only temporarily. The extent of the stability of these signs corresponds to a certain degree with their different functions. Permanent signs typically display names of shops, businesses, cafés, or restaurants and thus are often used for their identification; both in official, as well as in everyday communication. Often, we come across either foreign brands, e.g. *Body Basics*, *Keim Farben*, *Bianco e Nero*, or brands that wish to be perceived as foreign or international. Apart from Slovak, this identification function is fulfilled by all languages included on that scale. Other than Czech and English, all these languages mostly index the country which the particular product or service is from, or which they are commonly associated with, whereby the service provider/shop keeper actually needn't necessarily come from that country at all (*Casa del Prosecco,* for example, is not run by Italians, but by Czechs). It is rather exceptional for permanent foreign language signs to point to the presence of a particular ethnicity in HK (one example are Vietnamese restaurants); conversely, quite a few languages that are spoken in HK are absent from the town's linguistic landscape; young Armenians, for example, who communicate amongst themselves in Armenian (in external communication they speak Czech, Russian and sometimes English) have been running a kebab bistro in HK city centre since 2020 called monolingually as *Armenian Kebab*. A number of languages appear in bilingual signs, mostly combined either with Czech or English (for example,

La femme dámský obchůdek,[13] *Asian Bistro* 祝胃口好[14]). It is not uncommon for elements of two languages to be mixed (e.g. *the Le nail bar*).

The identification of these facilities by means of foreign language signs can be avoided in daily interactions (this may be due to the lack of knowledge of these languages, the fear of mispronouncing them, or due to their incompatibility with the Czech declension system[15]); instead, they are identified differently; for example, by referring to what they sell, which street they are on, etc. Hence, traits of multilingualism in everyday communication are exemplified by a rather different language function, namely the operational one. When compared with signs with the identification function, signs that have the operational function are often temporary: either they are associated with a particular event ('event-related signs'), or created ad hoc ('ad-hoc signs' – both terms according to Blommaert 2013). Such signs inform us, for example, about a temporary change of working hours, a shop being newly opened or closed, instructions on payment, and the like. One example of this is a hand-written bilingual Czech-English sign placed on the door of an Indian restaurant: *Zvonek / Ring the bell for pick-up*.[16] Importantly, of the fifteen languages used in the linguistic landscape of HK, only two are used in the operational function: English and Czech.

Czech (Standard Czech for that matter) – both in its identification and operational function – clearly dominates in the linguistic landscape of HK. Nonetheless, even in the case of Czech, we witness a certain degree of variation, both social and functional. Variation caused by a limited language competence, i.e. unintentional variation, is typically found in temporary signs created by foreign nationals (e.g. the Nepalese announcing the change of the working hours of their restaurant during the last week of the year: *31.12. – otevřeno od 11:00–18:00)*.[17]

Intentional variation chosen for stylistic effects is, on the other hand, typically found in signs created by native speakers of Czech. Variation of this latter type taps into the long tradition of using Standard Czech in public space. The influence of this tradition is remarkably strong: there is, for example, no structural reason not to use the Common Czech form *riflový*, and *levný* in the signs: *Riflové zboží* (English: Jeanswear) or *Levné knihy* (English: Cheap books), and thus to create hypothetical shop signs *Riflový zboží* or *Levný knihy*. In the hundreds (perhaps even thousands) of Czech signs that I came across in the linguistic landscape of HK, though, I only found two signs that diverge from this tradition.

The first one is *Rychlý kafe* (English: A quick coffee), which is the name of a small café in the city centre that refers to their main customer article – coffee to-go (see Figure 8.2). Linguistic foregrounding – commonly characteristic of poetic language – is achieved by the Common Czech form *rychlý* (the standard form is *rychlé*) and the Common Czech or colloquial expression *kafe* (the standard form is *káva*). The creation of an unusual Czech shop name goes hand in hand with other exponents of linguistic creativity of the shop owner such as novel names for drinks and desserts that are advertised both on

INDICKÁ NEPÁISKA RESTAURACE
TANDOOR

24.12 - zavřeno

25.12 - zavřeno

26.12 - zavřeno

27. 12 otevřeno

28. 12 otevřeno

29. 12 otevřeno

30.12 zavřeno

31.12 - otevřeno od 11:00 - 18:00

Nový rok otevřeno od 13:00 -19:00

Figure 8.1 A door sign of the Indian-Nepalese restaurant *Tandoor* (*zavřeno* English: closed; *otevřeno* English: open). December 2018.

notice boards inside the café and on the sidewalk sign in front of the café. The most remarkable contribution of this café to the linguistic landscape of this street, however, is through a blackboard placed next to the shop window; every few weeks, the owner posts new chalk-written sayings, pieces of wisdom, and

Figure 8.2 Rychlý kafe (A quick coffee). June 2020.

quotations on the blackboard; for example, one in English *I will start working when my coffee does* (see Figure 8.3). From the point of view of multilingualism in HK, it is important to highlight that this playful language function is only fulfilled by signs written in Czech and English. When being asked if customers understand these English signs, the owner (in his thirties) explained: 'They are here because many of our customers are foreigners. And, also to educate since English is really important these days.' The playfulness is then motivated also by

The sociolinguistic situation in Hradec Králové 131

Figure 8.3 A blackboard on the wall of *Rychlý kafe*. January 2019.

(reported) educational motives. To clarify, this particular café has been open for three years and targets younger clients, many of which are students, hence, also foreigners (see above).

The second sign that resisted the pressure towards using standard language is exemplified by the name of the travel agency *Votrok* (see Figure 8.4). We have already come across this expression when discussing Dejmek's book *The Old*

132   J. Nekvapil

Figure 8.4 A shop window of the travel agency *Votrok*. June 2020.

Town of Hradec Králové Tells Its Stories. This local non-standard expression (the standard form is *otrok*) has become one of the identity-forming features of HK. *Votrok* is the inhabitant of HK (see my comment above). By using this name, the travel agency *Votrok*, which has been doing business in HK for 17 years, clearly signals its affiliation with the town.

Within the Czech linguistic landscape of HK, both the name *Rychlý kafe* and *Votrok* are exceptions that only confirm the rule of using Standard Czech in public space. They may be breaching the normative pressure of Standard Czech to a point, but not too much; this is further evidenced by their use of Standard Czech on their website and Facebook profile.

8.10 Conclusion

The sociolinguistic situation in HK is a complex matter and the studies discussed above elucidate only certain aspects of it. Any sociolinguistic situation is in a constant flux and so are the theoretical-methodological approaches underlying research studies. In this chapter, I have tried to sketch the dynamics of such development as one fairly coherent whole which is shaped by the linguistic reality, the borders of which are marked by the city identity, the shared knowledge of this reality and, of course, by researchers themselves; the role of researchers cannot be underestimated as they always have their own agenda, reflecting research paradigms of the time, and they reject or respectfully follow their predecessors. Hence, the presented coherent whole is not a mere social construct – its formation can essentially be studied 'turn-by-turn', similarly to a CA specialist studying individual turns in an ongoing interaction or in a dialogical network (Nekvapil and Leudar 2006). This approach has revealed that a number of findings are relevant across different research paradigms – variation studies may be deemed interesting for interactional studies and those, in turn, can bring relevant insight(s) into language variation. Linguistic variation is observable also in the linguistic landscape; thus, variation research proves to be relevant for linguistic landscape studies,[18] i.e. one of the newest branches of sociolinguistics. Variation research projects may be essential when it comes to studying the formation of city identity, which in itself is a complex matter and requires an interdisciplinary approach. My chapter has supplied evidence that the demand to form a city identity is high (moreover, reflexively – city identity is the very premise of this chapter).

Reviewing the key findings regarding the linguistic landscape of HK, this chapter provides further evidence of increasing sensitivity towards linguistic, communication and socio-cultural diversity in the Czech Republic (see Sloboda 2016). As far as the socio-cultural dimension is concerned, diversification in HK is most visible when it comes to the opening of new 'ethnic' restaurants, bistros, kiosks and/or bars, and shops specialising in offering foreign goods or services. This socio-cultural diversification is chiefly the result of social and economic changes after the collapse of the communist regime in 1989, and in HK, it has become especially visible in the last 15 years, i.e. after the Czech Republic joined the EU. The facilities, restaurants and shops in question also have their communication and linguistic dimension. The fifteen languages that I detected in the linguistic landscape of HK can be seen as one of the indices of the linguistic (super)diversity of this town. The relevance of this index, however, has to be qualified with respect to the fact that the languages found in the linguistic landscape of HK each carry a different, i.e. a higher or lower functional load. This study has shown that the only polyfunctional languages are Czech and English; even German, for example, which was still considered an international language in the Czech Republic in the 1990s and was more widely taught than English, is hard to imagine to be used today in operational and playful functions. On a more general level, we can thus conclude that signs found in the linguistic landscape have to be analysed also from the point of view of their function(s). In HK, specifically, a fairly rich linguistic diversity is limited to the identification function (i.e. to the names of restaurants, shops and similar facilities).

Finally, I found that the linguistic landscape of HK is dominated by Standard Czech. Both native speakers and non-native users of Czech (foreigners) identify themselves with the ideology of the standard language. As a result, the diversification of Czech in the linguistic landscape of HK is negligible.

Notes

1 The first versions of this chapter were presented on different occasions at Leiden University, University of Hradec Králové, Charles University, Prague, and Sophia

University, Tokyo. I would like to thank for all the feedback and inspiration I received in the follow-up discussions. Thanks are also due to Marián Sloboda and Veronika Quinn Novotná for critical reading and suggestions. This research was supported by the Charles University project Progres 4 – Language in the Shifting of Time, Space, and Culture. A revised Czech version appeared in *Jazykovedný časopis* [*Journal of Linguistics*] 71 (2), 2020.

2 For more on the tenets and the interdisciplinary scope of this concept, see Creese and Blackledge (2018). For details on its application to the situation in the Czech Republic, see Sloboda (2016).

3 See a quote from a period brochure (Putrin 1982: 11): 'In a mature socialist society, which is based on *public ownership* of the means of production, the social structure consists of the working class as the leading force in society and its allies – the collective-farm *peasantry*, the people's *intelligensia*, and office employees and professional workers' (italics in the original).

4 V. I. Lenin (1870–1924) was a communist revolutionary; T. G. Masaryk (1850–1937) was the first president of Czechoslovakia – the communist ideologists considered him a 'bourgeois thinker' and his name was made taboo in the public space.

5 One research project published in the early 1990s is exceptional in this regard; it focussed on the communication within large companies in the urban agglomeration of Ostrava (see Davidová, Bogoczová and Jandová 1991).

6 To what extent this was taking place remains an under-researched question. It is unclear not just to what extent Western approaches were gathering momentum, but also – parallel to that – to what extent the influence coming from the then Soviet Union and other affiliated states was declining. A good indicator in this respect could be, for example, the reception of classical works on urban speech by the Russian linguist B. A. Larin (1928a, 1928b), who is referenced also by Dejmek (1980: 55; 1981: 15; 1986: 122). Substantial information regarding the research focus of linguistic institutions and individual researchers in HK can be found in a monograph on the local subsidiary of the Linguistic Association (Zeman 2015).

7 Schegloff (1972) approaches this issue even more generally, i. e. he is primarily interested in 'formal structures'; he would admit only exceptionally that his conclusions could be specific to American society and/or Western culture. Also, his data can be localized only partially and rather generally (the most specific geographical localisations of his data include 'a mid-western city' and 'a western city' – implicitly in the USA; p. 118).

8 The joke in line T3 is not humorous because of its propositional content put forth by speaker B, but rather due to the fact that the response rhymes – see Czech original in double parentheses. The English translation cannot capture this nuance.

9 Within the variationist paradigm, this can be documented also by Chromý (2017) who – for the purpose of his recent research – 're-counts' relevant data from Dejmek's studies (Chromý 2017: 81–83). Dejmek's studies (1981, 1987) offer themselves to such 're-use'; even though his primary focus was on correlating linguistic and *social* categories, Dejmek included complete data sets pertinent to each individual informant.

10 When we look at the total number of foreign nationals living in HK (or more precisely in the district of HK), the numbers are lower than the statewide average; as of February 29, 2020, the total number of inhabitants of the Czech Republic was 10,694,448, of which 602,616 were foreign nationals, i. e. 5.6%.

11 This is inspired by ethnomethodological conversation analysis, in which a conspicuous, or more specifically a 'significant absence' is a term clarifying, for example, the functioning of pair sequences. Expecting the presence of a language in a particular linguistic landscape, of course, depends on the extent of the individual's knowledge (including the researcher him-/herself) about the given sociolinguistic situation.
12 When it comes to orthography, which is relevant for the analysis of linguistic landscape, on the other hand, Czech and Polish are fairly dissimilar (see Heeringa et al. 2013).
13 *Dámský obchůdek* means in English 'a little shop for ladies'.
14 As it is obvious from this and the previous sign, foreign language components in signs needn't have the same meaning – the Chinese expression 祝胃口好 (zhu weikou hao) means 'enjoy your meal/bon appetite'.
15 The above-mentioned shop sign *Body Basics* can create all of these communication and language problems for Czech people from different social strata.
16 Czech *zvonek* means 'the bell'.
17 The correct standard spelling is *otevřeno*. Note that in the whole sign which provides the working hours for each day of the last working week in December we can precisely quantify the variation of this particular grapheme – put formally, the variable (e) appeared next to *ř-* and *–n* nine times – of which *e* was used five times and *é* four times. See Figure 8.1.
18 From a different perspective, this is also documented by Soukup (2020).

References

Bělič, J. (1962) Ke zkoumání městské mluvy [Researching urban speech]. *Acta Universitatis Carolinae – Philologica. Slavica Pragensia* IV, 569–575.
Blommaert, J. (2013) *Ethnography, Superdiversity and Linguistic Landscapes: Chronicles of Complexity*. Bristol, Buffalo, Toronto: Multilingual Matters.
Chromý, J. (2017) *Protetické v- v češtině* [The prothetic *v-* in Czech]. Praha: Filozofická fakulta Univerzity Karlovy.
Coulmas, F. (2018) Urbanisation and linguistic multitude. In D. Smakman, and P. Heinrich (eds.), *Urban Sociolinguistics: The City as a Linguistic Process and Experience*. London, New York: Routledge, 12–24.
Creese, A. and Blackledge, A. (eds.) (2018) *The Routledge Handbook of Language and Superdiversity. An Interdisciplinary Perspective*. London, New York: Routledge, Taylor & Francis Group.
Davidová, D., Bogoczová, I. and Jandová, E. (1991) *Využití jazyka při řízení pracovních kolektivů v ostravské průmyslové aglomeraci se zaměřením na zkoumání česko-slovensko-polské jazykové interference* [Effective application and use of language in overseeing working groups in large factories of the Ostrava conurbation, from the perspective of interference between Czech, Slovak and Polish]. Praha: Státní pedagogické nakladatelství.
Dejmek, B. (1976) *Běžně mluvený jazyk (městská mluva) města Přelouče* [Everyday language (urban speech) in the town of Přelouč]. Hradec Králové: Pedagogická fakulta.
Dejmek, B. (1978) Postavení městské mluvy v současné jazykové situaci [Position of urban speech in the contemporary language situation]. *Naše řeč* 61 (4), 183–192.
Dejmek, B. (1980) Městská mluva – problematika sociolingvistická [Urban speech: The sociolinguistic perspective]. *Sborník Pedagogické fakulty v Hradci Králové* XXXIV. *Jazyk – Literatura – Metodika*, 47–57.

Dejmek, B. (1981) *Mluva nejstarší generace Hradce Králové se zaměřením na diferenční jevy hláskové a morfologické* [Speech of the oldest generation of Hradec Králové: Phonemic and morphemic variation]. Hradec Králové: Pedagogická fakulta.

Dejmek, B. (1986) Sociolinguistic aspects of research into urban speech. In J. Chloupek and J. Nekvapil (eds.), *Reader in Czech Sociolinguistics*. Prague, Amsterdam, Philadelphia: Academia, John Benjamins, 106–122.

Dejmek, B. (1987) *Běžně mluvený jazyk nejmladší generace Hradce Králové* [Everyday language of the youngest generation of Hradec Králové]. Hradec Králové: Pedagogická fakulta.

Dejmek, B. (1993) *Historie a současnost Hradce Králové ve jménech ulic* [The history and present of Hradec Králové in street names]. Hradec Králové: Gaudeamus.

Dejmek. B. (1998) *Starý Hradec vypravuje* [The old town of Hradec Králové tells its stories]. Hradec Králové: Garamond.

Fox, S. and Sharma, D. (2018) The language of London and Londoners. In D. Smakman, and P. Heinrich (eds.), *Urban Sociolinguistics: The City as a Linguistic Process and Experience*. London, New York: Routledge, 115–129.

Heeringa, W., Golubovic, J., Gooskens, C., Schüppert, A., Swarte, F. and Voigt, S. (2013) Lexical and orthographic distances between Germanic, Romance and Slavic languages and their relationship to geographic distance. In C. Gooskens, and R. van Bezooijen (eds.), *Phonetics in Europe: Perception and Production*. Frankfurt am Main: Peter Lang, 99–137.

Labov, W. (1966) *The Social Stratification of English in New York City*. Washington: Center for Applied Linguistics.

Labov, W. (2006) *The Social Stratification of English in New York City*. 2nd Edition. Cambridge: Cambridge University Press.

Larin, B. A. [Ларин, Б. А.] (1928a) О лингвистическом изучении города [The linguistic investigation of the city]. Л. В. Щерба (ред.), *Русская речь: сборник статей*. Вып. 3. Ленинград: ACADEMIA, 61–75.

Larin, B. A. [Ларин, Б. А.] (1928b) К лингвистической характеристике города (несколько предпосылок) [The linguistic features of the city (some preliminaries)]. *Известия Ленинградского государственного педагогического института им. А.И. Герцена*. Вып. 1, 175–184.

Nekvapil, J. (1997) Some remarks on item orderings in Czech conversation: The issue of pre-sequences. In B. Palek (ed.), *Typology: Prototypes, Item Orderings and Universals*. Prague: Charles University Press, 444–450.

Nekvapil, J. (2000) Language management in a changing society. In B. Panzer (ed.), *Die sprachliche Situation in der Slavia zehn Jahre nach der Wende*. Frankfurt am Main: Peter Lang, 165–177.

Nekvapil, J. and Zeman, J. (2000) K verbální strukturaci Hradce Králové v každodenních rozhovorech [On verbal structuration of Hradec Králové in everyday conversation]. *Cahiers du CEFRES* 18, 19–37.

Nekvapil, J. and Leudar, I. (2006) Sequencing in media dialogical networks. *Ethnographic Studies* 8, 30–43.

Neustupný, J. V. and Nekvapil, J. (2003) Language management in the Czech Republic. *Current Issues in Language Planning* 4 (3&4), 181–366. [Reprinted in R. B. Baldauf and R. B. Kaplan (eds.) (2006), *Language Planning and Policy in Europe*, Vol. 2: *The Czech Republic, The European Union and Northern Ireland*. Clevedon, Buffalo, Toronto: Multilingual Matters, 16–201.]

Putrin, B. (1982) *Political Terms. A Short Guide*. Moscow: Novosti Press Agency Publishing House.

Schegloff, E. A. (1972) Notes on a conversational practice: Formulating place. In D. Sudnow (ed.), *Studies in Social Interaction*. New York: Free Press, 75–119.

Sherman, T. (2007) *'Obracení na víru' jako komunikační problém: situace prvního kontaktu / Proselyting in first-contact situations*. Praha: Univerzita Karlova v Praze, Filozofická fakulta (unpublished dissertation).

Sherman, T. (2010) Proselyting in first-contact situations as an instructed action. *Sociologický časopis / Czech Sociological Review* 46 (6), 977–1009.

Sherman, T. (2015) Behaving toward language in the Mormon mission: The Czech case. *International Journal of the Sociology of Language* 232, 33–57.

Sloboda, M. (2016) Transition to super-diversity in the Czech Republic: Its emergence and resistance. In M. Sloboda, P. Laihonen and A. Zabrodskaja (eds.), *Sociolinguistic Transition in Former Eastern Bloc Countries. Two Decades after the Regime Change*. Frankfurt am Main: Peter Lang, 141–183.

Sloboda, M. (2021) Demarcating the space for multilingualism: On the workings of ethnic interests in a 'civic nation'. In R. Blackwood and D. A. Dunlevy (eds.), *Multilingualism in Public Spaces*. London, New York: Bloomsbury, 31–58.

Smakman, D. and Heinrich, P. (eds.) (2015) *Globalising Sociolinguistics: Challenging and Expanding Theory*. London, New York: Routledge.

Smakman, D. and Heinrich, P. (eds.) (2018) *Urban Sociolinguistics: The City as a Linguistic Process and Experience*. London, New York: Routledge.

Soukup, B. (2020) Survey area selection in Variationist Linguistic Landscape Study (VaLLS). A report from Vienna, Austria. *Linguistic Landscape* 6 (1), 52–79.

Uličný, O. (1966) Ke koncepci výzkumu běžně mluveného jazyka městského (městské mluvy) v Čechách [An approach to the research on urban speech in Czechia]. *Sborník Pedagogické fakulty v Hradci Králové* III, 155–170 [reprinted in *Slavica Pragensia* XXXVIII, 2003, pp. 72–81].

Utěšený, S. (1968) Americká práce o variabilitě a stratifikaci mluvy velkoměsta [An American study on variation and stratification of the speech of a large city]. *Slovo a slovesnost* 29(2), 197–203.

Zeman, J. (ed.) (1999) *Strukturace města ve verbální komunikaci: Poznámky z výzkumu Hradce Králové* [Structuration of the town in verbal interaction: Notes on the research on Hradec Králové]. Hradec Králové: Gaudeamus (supplement of *Češtinář* 9).

Zeman, J. (2015) *Padesát let pobočky Jazykovědného sdružení v Hradci Králové (1965–2015)* [Fifty years of the Linguistic Association of the Czech Republic branch in Hradec Králové (1965–2015)]. Ústí nad Orlicí: Oftis.

Part III
Multilingual strategies

9 The social linguistic soundscape and its influence on language choice in Stornoway

I. Birnie

9.1 Introduction

Gaelic has been categorised as 'definitely endangered in the UNESCO Atlas of the World's Languages in Danger' (Moseley 2010) as a result of what MacKinnon (2011) has referred to as 'runaway language shift'. The last national census, conducted in 2011, indicated that there were only 57,375 individuals remaining in Scotland who reported to be able to speak Gaelic, 1.1% of the population (National Records of Scotland 2015). This represents a 77.5% decrease in absolute speaker numbers since 1891, the first time the census systematically collected information pertaining to the language and when 254,415 individuals, 6.3% of the population of Scotland, were recorded as Gaelic speakers (Thomas 1998).

The increasing fragility of the language – which not only saw a reduction in the speaker number but also in the levels of intergenerational transmission, influencing language use patterns in the home, the family but also the wider community – across all Gaelic communities (see, for example, Duwe 2005; MacKinnon 1977; The Scottish Council for Research in Education 1961) went largely unnoticed by the authorities throughout the twentieth century, despite increasing pressures from communities to provide support for the language (Durkacz 1983). This started to change in the late 1970s and early 1980s, when the authorities recognised that the rapid decline in speaker numbers might result in the language disappearing, and that strengthening the position of the language might also support the fragile socio-economic position of the Gàidhealtachd, the traditional stronghold region of the language in the northwest of Scotland (the area covered by the three local authorities of Argyll and Bute, Highland Council and Comhairle nan Eilean Siar today). This marked the start of what McLeod (2010) has termed the 'era of professionalisation and institutionalisation', away from community based, local initiatives and towards an increasing centralisation and national approach towards language revitalisations, cumulating, in 2005 with the Gaelic Language (Scotland) Act. This Act of the Scottish Parliament (which is often referred to as the Gaelic Act) established Gaelic as 'an official language in Scotland, commanding equal respect to the English language' (Gaelic Language (Scotland) Act 2005). Dunbar

(2010) and McLeod (2010) have described this Gaelic Act as enabling legislation as the formal recognition for the language has not created any rights for Gaelic speakers to use the language with the authorities.

The Gaelic Act established *Bòrd na Gàidhlig* (the Gaelic language board) as a statutory agency to promote the use and understanding of the Gaelic language at a national level, through the creation and enactment of a national plan for Gaelic. A further function of Bòrd na Gàidhlig is to request, and oversee, the preparation of Gaelic language plans by public authorities based in Scotland in which the organisations are required to set out their strategy for the promotion of Gaelic through its service provision. The increasing provision of goods and services in the language is expected to result in a greater perception of usefulness and stimulate both the motivation to use and learn the language (Strubell 2005) in order to fulfil the official aim, as articulated by Bòrd na Gàidhlig (2018), to increase the use of Gaelic, by more people and in a wider range of situations. Oliver (2010) has suggested that there has been an explicit expectation on the part of the public authorities that 'the public domain can reverse what it arguably precipitated – language shift' (p. 77). The most obvious indication of this official support and promotion of the language is the inclusion of Gaelic in the public linguistic landscape of public authorities, with Landry and Bourhis (1997) suggesting that this inclusion of a language in the public linguistic landscape can be used as an indicator that 'the language in question can be used to communicate and obtain services within public and private establishments' (p. 25).

This increased visibility of Gaelic in the public linguistic landscape has come at a time when analysis of the census data has indicated that intergenerational transmission of Gaelic has all but ended (National Records of Scotland 2015). This absence of intergenerational transmission, the *sine qua non* of language revitalisation according to Fishman (1991), has had a significant impact on the extent to which Gaelic is used, not only in the home, but also within the family, with younger generations typically not speaking the language with their elders (Birnie 2018; Smith-Christmas 2016a). These changing linguistic practices have also affected the use of the language in the community, with NicAoidh (2010) identifying that English was used in community interactions, even in circumstances where all participants in the conversation recognised that Gaelic could have been used. These findings were supported by Munro, Mac an Tàilleir and Armstrong (2011), who found that English is used in 'virtually every social setting in the community' as a result of 'uni-directional bilingualism' where 'only Gaelic speakers are expected to be bilingual; they expect and are expected to use the dominant language of the majority, English' (p. 9) in their interactions. The language used in interactions in the different social and public settings of a community creates a social linguistic soundscape. This concept, first described by Birnie (2018), is similar to the notion of the linguistic landscape, but whereas the linguistic landscape is defined as the 'visibility and salience of languages on public and commercial signs in a given territory or region' (Landry and Bourhis 1997: 23), the social linguistic soundscape refers to the language used in spoken interaction in a public space. These spoken interactions are an important indicator of the vitality of a language as they are characterised by spontaneous improvisation and are often based on a 'reflex action rather than a result of reflection' (Altuna and Basurto 2013: 28). Whereas the inclusion of Gaelic in the public linguistic landscape can be managed and coordinated by an organisation, often as part of their language management programme, the use of Gaelic for spoken interactions is not be as easily managed; it depends on a number of factors, including the linguistic competences and confidence of the participants in the conversation.

The dichotomy between the traditional L (low) domain use of Gaelic and the language management initiatives promoting its use in public domain interactions is most obviously played out in Stornoway, the location of this study. Stornoway is the largest town in Comhairle nan Eilean Siar, the most north-westerly of Scotland's 32 local authorities and the only region where a majority of the population, 52.2%, have reported to be able to speak Gaelic (Mac an Tàilleir 2013). Stornoway, as the only settlement with any 'urban characteristics' (Comhairle nan Eilean Siar 2018), acts as the *de facto* capital and administrative and economic centre of CnES, and although it might be considered the 'least Gaelic' of all the parishes in the CnES, with 43.4% of the population self-reporting to be able to speak the language in 2011 (National Records of Scotland 2013), the language makes a significant contribution to the social, economic and cultural life of the town. Stornoway is home to a number of Gaelic-sector organisations, mainly associated with education, the media and language development, as well as public organisations, including the headquarters of the local authority, with Gaelic language plans produced as a result of the Gaelic Act. This raises the question whether these language management initiatives in the public domain in Stornoway can, as Oliver (2010) suggested, 'reverse what it arguably precipitated – language shift' (p. 77), or whether, in fact, these initiatives have resulted in what Smith-Christmas and Ó hIfearnáin (2015) have termed 'reverse diglossia', with Gaelic speakers in the town using the language in H (High) language functions (education, the workplace and in interactions with the authorities), but with no or limited use in L domain functions, such as the home, the family and the community.

9.2 Methodology

A question pertaining to Gaelic has been included in the national decennial census since the late nineteenth century, and this has created the impression that there is a clear understanding about the sociolinguistic position of Gaelic. Although the census data can be used to provide an indication of the trajectory of Gaelic in terms of speaker numbers and density, this data is based on self-reporting and personal interpretation of the question which asks whether respondents can speak Gaelic, but without providing a definition or minimum level of proficiency. Munro (2011) has therefore concluded that without any data about relative ability and domains of frequency of language use it is 'impossible to know how, and even if, those who self-report to have Gaelic are actually using Gaelic' (p. 165).

Information about the frequency and domains of use of Gaelic have been based on a limited number of studies. These studies have all followed a similar approach with participants, speakers, and non-speakers of Gaelic being asked to fill in pre-coded scaled responses to indicate the use of Gaelic in different social situations and settings, which typically ranged from 'never' to 'all the time', but without providing further quantification on what this might mean in practice. Bourhis and Sachdev (1984) have suggested that, in the case of a minority language, the political and social circumstances as well as personal ideology might influence how speakers report their use of, in this case, Gaelic, which can result in either an over- or under-estimate of the extent to which the language is really used. A further factor which might influence how the use of Gaelic is reported on in these studies is what Hill (2008) has referred to as 'reporting bias', also known as the 'phenomenon of misplaced scale' (Urla 2013). This reporting bias suggests that the occurrence of a word or phrase in a minority language might be enough for this to be reported as an interaction in that language (Hill 2008). These studies have, therefore, been very valuable in tracing the perceptions of how the use of Gaelic has changed in the community (see, for example, MacKinnon 1977; Munro, Armstrong and Mac an Tàilleir 2011; NicAoidh 2006) based on retrospection, where participants' recall can lead to aggregate response, with a particular focus on the more recent experiences, rather than giving weight to each instance (Bolger, Davis and Rafaeli 2003).

The research method used in this study was adapted from the *Kale Neurkata* (Street Surveys of Basque Language use), conducted once every five years across the different communities of the Basque Country (Altuna and Basurto 2013). During the *Kale Neurkata* data collection period, researchers visit neighbourhoods and, over a period of two hours for each session, record (using a standardised observation form) the language(s) of each conversation they observe, together with the demographic profile of the participants in the conversation (age profile and gender). The quantitative data gathered has been used as a 'kind of barometer of the efficacy that language promotion and education policies are having in … making Basque a 'public' language' (Urla 2013, 18), mirroring the aims of the Gaelic language management initiatives in Scotland.

This study used the same principles as have been adopted in the *Kale Neurkata*; systematically recording all observed conversations in a given space over a defined period of time. As with the Basque study, the unit of measurement was taken to be a conversation, defined as a face-to-face interaction involving two or more individuals in which information was exchanged beyond an initial greeting – as previous research by Birnie (2018) has indicated that the language used in a greeting need not be a reliable indicator of the language used in the remainder of the interaction. Conversations were delineated by a change in participants, a change in language or a change in purpose. Similar to the *Kale Neurkata* study, the researcher would position themselves in a particular public space for a defined period of time to collect information on the demographic profile (age-profile, gender) as well as the designation of the participants (member of the public or a member of staff), the language of the interaction and its purpose (private or business), noting the information on the observation form. Whereas in the Basque Country, where these observational surveys have been conducted since the 1980s and where there is longitudinal record of how the public use of Basque has evolved over time, this was the first time that a study of this kind has been conducted in the context of Gaelic to assess the extent to which Gaelic is used.

The lack of longitudinal data on the effect of language planning initiatives meant that for this study it was decided to compare public spaces with Gaelic language plans, as per the provisions of the Gaelic Language (Scotland) Act, and public places without these. In both types of locations (with and without a Gaelic language plan), the participant demographic and designation, as well as the purpose of the interaction was observed and analysed. Eight locations were selected, all in the centre of Stornoway, four in organisations with a Gaelic language plan (GLP) and four in locations without any language management initiatives. These locations were selected to represent publicly accessible open spaces with a single service point for interactions between members of staff and members of the public and all were surveyed multiple times by the researcher; at different times of the day and different days of the week, to capture, as far as possible, a representative cross-section of the users of these spaces. A total of 2,000 conversations were collected over the duration of the study; 1020 in locations with a GLP and 980 in locations without formal support mechanisms for the language (see Table 9.1).

This data was analysed according to the mathematical model developed by Yurramendi and Altuna (2009) for the *Kale Neurkata*, which considers the size of the data set, the number of participants in each interaction and the presumed level of bilingualism in the community in order to determine the validity and reliability of the sample size. Applying this model to the dataset gave a confidence level of 99.0% with a margin of error of ± 2.85%, suggesting that the results obtained can be confidently assumed to be an approximation of the statistically expected results for this community.

Table 9.1 Language use survey locations and observation results

Location	Gaelic plan	No. of observations	% English conversations	% Gaelic conversations
CnES public reception area	Yes	440	82.3%	12.7%
Sport Centre reception area	Yes	200	98.5%	1.5%
Library	Yes	240	89.6%	10.4%
Ferry waiting room	Yes	140	82.2%	7.8%
Arts and Creative centre	No	480	95.0%	5.0%
Café	No	240	95.9%	4.1%
Restaurant	No	160	99.4%	0.6%
Public house	No	100	65.0%	35.0%

In all of the eight locations, at the end of the OLUS (observational language use surveys) data collection period, the results were discussed with the main gate-keepers of the locations in which the surveys had taken place to discuss the findings and collect information about the linguistic competences of the members of staff in public-facing roles and the position of Gaelic within the organisation, including, where present, the conceptualisation of the GLP in the daily practices.

9.3 Results and discussion

9.3.1 Social linguistic soundscape

The results of the OLUS show that English is the dominant language across the public spaces surveyed, and as a representative sample across Stornoway as a whole. English was used in 90.9% of all the interactions recorded in the OLUS. These findings are not surprising; 42.4% of the population self-reported to be able to speak Gaelic, well below the threshold proposed by O Giollagain, Mac Donnacha, Ni Chualain, Ni Sheaghdha and O' Brien (2007) of 67% of active speakers required for the use of a language to be sustainable in a community. Without any clear linguistic or social markers to identify Gaelic speakers in the community, the question, therefore, should not be whether Gaelic only makes a small contribution (9.1%) to the social linguistic soundscape of Stornoway, but precisely how Gaelic is negotiated as a linguistic norm in those instances where the language is used.

One of the main indicators that was presumed to be a contributing factor to the use of Gaelic in a particular space was the inclusion of the language in the linguistic landscape of a location. The overt inclusion of Gaelic in permanent signage of a location was directly linked to the existence of an organisational GLP and thus the presumed promotion of the language in the goods and service provision of the organisation. Analysis of the OLUS data shows that the average use of Gaelic across locations with and without a GLP was the same, 9.1%, suggesting, in the first instance, that the presence of language promotion initiatives does not result in a greater use of spoken Gaelic in these locations. Further analysis shows, however, that this situation is more complex than the overall numbers would suggest, and this is evident when the designation of the participants in the conversations was analysed.

Across the study, there was, on average, no statistical difference in the extent to which Gaelic was used in conversations involving only members of the public (14.1% in locations with a GLP and 14.9% in locations without language management initiatives). It may be assumed that in the majority of these interactions the individuals involved were already acquainted with each other and had established a set of linguistic norms based on the language competences and ideologies of the various participants in the conversation. Spolsky and Cooper (1991) have suggested that once a particular language is established as the unmarked code-choice between a group of individuals, this will, in almost all instances, be the language that continues to be used, regardless of the situation or circumstances in which the conversation takes place, the so-called 'inertia condition of language choice' (p. 146). This would, therefore, suggest that the language that members of the public use to interact with each other in public spaces is also likely to be the language they use in private domains, and this data can, therefore, be used as an important indication of the extent to which Gaelic is used in *Gemeinschaft* domains.

Whereas there was a consistent level of Gaelic language use in conversations involving only members of the public across the two types of locations (with and without a GLP), this was not the case for conversations involving members of staff. In locations with a GLP, members of staff used Gaelic in 14.7% of their interactions with other members of staff, compared to no Gaelic conversations between members of staff in locations without a GLP. This could have been due to language competence of the members of staff; recruitment processes for customer interfacing roles in organisations are likely to have favoured Gaelic speakers. Organisations with a GLP might also have expressed an expectation towards members of staff to act as agents of the language policy (Nahir 1998), with organisations without a GLP not having these same expectations even in circumstances where members of staff are able to speak the language. It is important to note that in these circumstances 'no policy is also a policy' – if members of staff are not explicitly given encouragement to use Gaelic, or if the implicit expectation is that the only unmarked code-choice of the organisation is English, this will be the language that members of staff will use. It is interesting to note that the same GLP was in place in three locations included in the OLUS; the main CnES reception area, the sports centre and the library, but that the extent to which Gaelic was used by members of staff varied significantly across these three locations. In both the CnES reception area and the library, Gaelic was used regularly in interactions between staff whereas in the sports centre the language was not used at all by this group despite being subject to the same staff recruitment and language promotional initiatives. In the library and the CnES reception area, Gaelic had been the long-established linguistic norm between colleagues, even before the implementation of the GLP. In the leisure centre, the established linguistic norm between members of staff was English, despite a number of the individuals working in this location being recorded on the organisation's system as Gaelic speakers, resulting in an 'English-only' social linguistic soundscape.

This would suggest that the policy and the encouragement by the organisation to use Gaelic alone are not enough but that personal ideologies, as well as the aforementioned inertia condition of language choice, also contribute to the use of Gaelic:

> The real language policy of a community is more likely to be found in its practices than in management. Unless management is consistent with the language practices and beliefs, and with the other contextual forces that are at play, the explicit policy written in the constitution and laws is likely to

have no more effect on how people speak than the activities of generations of schoolteachers vainly urging the choice of the correct language.

(Spolsky 2004: 222)

The importance of the extent to which members of staff used Gaelic in interactions with each other, and thus the overt inclusion in the social linguistic soundscape of the organisation, can be seen when analysing the language of the interactions between members of staff and members of the public. There was a direct correlation between the extent to which Gaelic was used in interactions involving members of staff and in interactions involving both members of staff and members of the public (mixed participant interactions). In locations, both with and without a GLP, where members of staff did not use Gaelic to speak to other members of staff, the language was also not used by members of the public to access goods and services in the language. The exception to this was the public house, where there was only one member of staff on duty at the time of the OLUS and where, therefore, no staff-to-staff interactions could take place.

The use of Gaelic by members of staff can be considered to serve two different, but interlinked purposes in terms of signalling that Gaelic is an unmarked code-choice (Myers-Scotton 1998). In a community such as Stornoway, where the default language is English, the 'etiquette of accommodation' (McEwan-Fujita 2010) means that individuals will only use the language(s) they consider to be the unmarked language. The use of Gaelic by members of staff indicates, in the first place, that Gaelic is one of the unmarked code-choices in that particular space, and is the equivalent to an implicit 'active offer' to members of the public (Heller 1983). Equally important, the inclusion of Gaelic by members of staff in the social linguistic soundscape served a second purpose; it allowed members of the public to explicitly identify, in the absence of other linguistic markers, those members of staff who were willing and able to speak the language in a particular location, thus removing the need to actively negotiate Gaelic as a linguistic norm.

9.3.2 Changing language use patterns

The OLUS did not only provide an indication of the extent to which Gaelic was included in the social linguistic soundscape of the public spaces in Stornoway, they can also be used to provide an insight into the changing linguistic practices of Gaelic speakers themselves, especially when comparing the use of language by members of the public and by members of staff according to the age-profile of the speakers. This analysis shows that the use of Gaelic was not equally distributed across the age-groups: participants aged 60 and over involved in 65.0% of the Gaelic interactions between members of the public, compared to young adults (aged 18 to 30), who were only involved in 8.3% of these interactions. This clear delineation in language use by age group is significant and supports the findings of other studies, NicAoidh (2010), Munro,

Armstrong et al. (2011) and MacKinnon (2011), for example, as well as evidence from the census, in providing a clear indicator that language shift is still ongoing and that 'Gaelic has ceased being the language used with the greatest facility and frequency' in young people (Dunbar 2011: 153). Young adult Gaelic speakers are most likely to be 'new speakers' (see McLeod and O'Rourke 2015), having acquired the language in the education system rather than through intergenerational transmission. Will (2012) has suggested that the absence of opportunities to use the language in a social setting, with both the social settings of the education environment and the home dominated by English, has resulted in this group of speakers not considering Gaelic as a language for social interactions. Smith-Christmas (2016b) has suggested that the formalised setting of the classroom for language acquisition might have resulted in an association between Gaelic and 'authority'. This association also has resulted in Gaelic being considered a skill to be acquired, and one that can be commodified and commercialised. This notion is, incidentally, further promoted by Bòrd na Gàidhlig (n.d.) in its 'information for parents', which promotes the acquisition of Gaelic as offering 'many career opportunities' through the opportunities that Gaelic Medium Education provides for young people to become bilingual, rather than encouraging the acquisition of the language as a communicative tool to be used in social interactions. The evidence of the commodification of the language is also clear from the results of the OLUS; whereas young adults were only involved in 8.3% of the Gaelic interactions between members of the public, this age-group was involved in 24.3% of the Gaelic interactions between members of staff, almost three times more frequently than as members of the public.

9.4 Conclusion

The OLUS study was the first of its kind in Scotland and allowed for the creation of a unique perspective on where Gaelic is spoken in Stornoway and by whom. The results, in the first instance, have provided an indication of the contribution of Gaelic to the social linguistic soundscape of the town, which indicated that although Gaelic was a minority language, it was audible, to a greater or smaller extent, in all locations surveyed. This would indicate that although the use of Gaelic is changing, the language is still being used as a means of communication, both in *Gemeinschaft* domains as well as the new domains of the language – public services. The data from the OLUS would appear to indicate, however, that language shift is still ongoing, with Gaelic generally more frequently used in the older age groups than in young adults in interactions between members of the public, which can be considered a reflection of the linguistic soundscape in the *Gemeinschaft* domains.

The post-modern era has seen the professionalisation and institutionalisation of Gaelic management initiatives, and this has created new opportunities for Gaelic to be used in formal, H domain interactions. The influence of these initiatives on linguistic practices not only influences who will use the language but also the extent to which Gaelic is used in the public domain, creating the conditions for 'reverse diglossia' (Smith-Christmas and Ó hIfearnáin 2015) through the language shifting from use in the private to the public domains. Rather than strengthening the language, this might in fact have created a competition between all domains (Romaine 2006), which might eventually result in further language loss, especially as the results of the OLUS study indicate that the presence of a GLP, often most evidently present in the public spaces of an organisation through the inclusion of Gaelic in the linguistic landscape, did not, of itself, increase the overall spoken use of Gaelic in these locations.

In a social linguistic soundscape that is dominated by English, it will be English that is the general 'norm', especially if the participants do not know each other in advance of the conversations, as is likely in interactions between members of the public and members of staff, especially in the more formal context of public organisations. This English as the unmarked code-choice can be replaced by the less categorical 'Gaelic is possible' when the language was overtly included in the public social linguistic soundscape of an organisation. Gaelic was more likely to be used by members of staff in locations with a GLP where there was a clear organisational expectation coupled with staff competence and ideology: the 'capacity, opportunity, and desire' model proposed by Grin (2009) and further developed by Lo Bianco and Peyton (2013). This, in turn, resulted in an implicit active offer to members of the public that Gaelic could be used in the particular locations with the particular members of staff present there, and therefore resulted in a greater use of the language in interactions between members of the public and members of staff.

References

Altuna, O., and Basurto, A. (2013). *Survey Methods. A Guide to Language Use Observation* (Vol. 1). Donostia: Eusko Jaurlarizaren Argitalpen Zerbitzu Nagusia.

Birnie, I. (2018). *'Gàidhlig ga bruidhinn an seo?' – Linguistic practices and Gaelic language management initiatives in Stornoway, the Western Isles of Scotland*. (PhD). University of Aberdeen, Aberdeen. Retrieved from https://digitool.abdn.ac.uk/webclient/StreamGate?folder_id=0&dvs=1598212799955~85

Bolger, N., Davis, A., and Rafaeli, E. (2003). Diary methods: capturing life as it is lived. *Annual Review of Psychology*, 54, 579–616. doi:10.1146/annurev.psych.54.101601.145030

Bord na Gàidhlig. (n.d.). Why should children learn Gaelic? Retrieved from https://fdp.gaidhlig.scot/en/welcome/why-should-children-learn-gaelic/

Bòrd na Gàidhlig. (2018). *National Gaelic Language Plan 2018–2023*. Retrieved from www.gaidhlig.scot/wp-content/uploads/2018/03/BnG-NGLP-18-23-1.pdf

Bourhis, R., and Sachdev, I. (1984). Vitality perceptions and language attitudes: Some Canadian data. *Journal of Language and Social Psychology*, 3(2), 97–126.

Comhairle nan Eilean Siar. (2018). Outer Hebrides Factfile – Population (overview). Retrieved from www.cne-siar.gov.uk/strategy-performance-and-research/outer-hebrides-factfile/population/overview/

Dunbar, R. (2010). A research stategy to support Gaelic Language Policy in Scotland. In G. Munro and I. Mac an Tàilleir (eds.), *Coimhearsnachd na Gàidhlig an-diugh / Gaelic communities today* (1st ed., pp. 139–161). Edinburgh: Dunedin Academic Press.

Dunbar, R. (2011). Bilingualism: Conceptual difficulties and practical challenges. In J. M. Kirk and D. P. O Baoill (eds.), *Strategies for Minority Languages: Northern Ireland, The Republic of Ireland and Scotland* (pp. 150–163). Belfast: Cló Ollscoil na Banríona.

Durkacz, V. E. (1983). *The Decline of the Celtic Languages* (1st ed.). Edinburgh: John Donald Publishers Ltd.

Duwe, K. C. (2005). *Gàidhlig (Scottish Gaelic) Local Studies: Vol. 02 Eilean Barraigh (Isle of Barra)*. Retrieved from www.linguae-celticae.org/dateien/Gaidhlig_Local_Studies_Vol_02_Barraigh_Ed_II.pdf

Fishman, J. (1991). *Reversing Language Shift – Theoretical and Empirical Foundations of Assistance to Threatened Languages* (1st ed.). Clevedon: Multilingual Matters Ltd.

Grin, F. (2009). Promoting language through the economy: Competing paradigms. In J. M. Kirk and D. P. O. Baoill (eds.), *Language and Economic Development: Northern Ireland, the Republic of Ireland, and Scotland* (1st ed., pp. 1–12). Belfast: Clo Ollscoil na Bionriona.

Heller, M. (1983). Negotiations of language choice in Montreal. In J. Gumperz (ed.), *Language and Social Identity* (pp. 108–118). Cambridge: Cambridge University Press.

Hill, J. H. (2008). *The Everyday Language of White Racism*. Oxford: Wiley-Blackwell.

Landry, R., and Bourhis, R. (1997). Linguistic Landscape and Ethnolinguistic Vitality - an Empirical Study. *Journal of Language and Social Psychology, 16*(23), 23–49.

Lo Bianco, J., and Peyton, J. K. (2013). Introduction: Vitality of heritage languages in the United States: The role of capacity, opportunity, and desire. *Heritage Language Journal, 10*(3), i–vii.

Mac an Tàilleir, I. (2013). *Cunntas-sluaigh na h-Alba 2011 - Clàran mun Ghàidhlig* (The 2011 Census – tables about Gaelic). Sabhal Mòr Ostaig.

MacKinnon, K. (1977). *Language, Education and Social Processes in a Gaelic Community*. London: Routledge.

MacKinnon, K. (2011). Runaway language shift: Gaelic usage in home, community and media in the Isle of Skye and Western Isles, 1986/8, 1994/5 and 2004/5 – any prospects for reversal? In R. Cox and T. Armstrong (eds.), *A' cleachdadh na Gàidhlig: slatan-tomhain ann an dìon cànain sa choimhearsnachd* (pp. 201–226). Slèite: Clò Ostaig.

McEwan-Fujita, E. (2010). Ideology, affect, and socialization in language shift and revitalization: The experiences of adults learning Gaelic in the Western Isles of Scotland. *Language in Society, 39*(1), 27–64. doi:10.1017/s0047404509990649

McLeod, W. (2010). Poileasaidh Leasachaidh na Gàidhlig: Paradaim Ùr (Gaelic development policy: a new paradigm). In G. Munro and I. Mac an Tàilleir (eds.), *Coimhearsnachd na Gàidhlig an-diugh / Gaelic Communities Today* (1 ed., pp. 1–18). Edinburgh: Dunedin Academic Press.

McLeod, W., and O'Rourke, B. (2015). 'New speakers' of Gaelic: perceptions of linguistic authenticity and appropriateness. *Applied Linguistics Review, 6*(2). doi:10.1515/applirev-2015-0008

Moseley, C. (2010). *Atlas of the World's Languages in Danger*. 3rd ed. Paris: UNESCO.

Munro, G. (2011). The Barail agus Comas Cànain survey of community language use, ability and attitudes: Some general observations regarding future Gaelic language policy planning in Scotland. In J. M. Kirk and D. P. O. Baoill (eds.), *Strategies for*

Minority Languages: Northern Ireland, The Republic of Ireland and Scotland (1st ed., pp. 163–171). Belfast: Clo Ollscoil na Banriona.

Munro, G., Mac an Tàilleir, I. and Armstrong, T. (2011). *The State of Gaelic in Shawbost*. Teangue: Sabhal Mòr Ostaig.

Myers-Scotton, C. (1998). A theoretical introduction to the markedness model. In C. Myers-Scotton (ed.), *Codes and Consequences – Choosing Linguistic Varieties* (pp. 18–40). Oxford: Oxford University Press.

Nahir, M. (1998). Micro language planning and the revival of Hebrew: A schematic framework. *Language in Society, 27*(3), 335–357.

National Records of Scotland. (2013). Table QS211SC Gaelic Language Skills. Edinburgh: HMSO.

National Records of Scotland. (2015). *Scotland's Census 2011: Gaelic report (part 1)*. Retrieved from www.scotlandscensus.gov.uk/media/cqoji4qx/report_part_1.pdf

NicAoidh, M. (2006). Pròseact Plana Cànain nan Eilean Siar: a' chiad ìre - rannsachadh air suidheachadh na Gàidhlig anns na h-Eilean Siar (The Gaelic Language Plan project in the Western Isles: first stage – research on the state of Gaelic in the Western Isles). In W. McLeod (ed.), *Revitalising Gaelic in Scotland*. Edinburgh: Dunedin Academic Press.

NicAoidh, M. (2010). Plana Cànain nan Eilean Siar (The Western Isles Gaelic Plan). In G. Munro and I. Mac an Tàilleir (eds.), *Coimhearsnachd na Gàidhlig an-diugh / Gaelic communities today* (pp. 49–60). Edinburgh: Dunedin.

O Giollagain, C., Mac Donnacha, S., Ni Chualain, F., Ni Sheaghdha, A. and O'Brien, M. (2007). *Comprehensive Linguistic Study of the Use of Irish in the Gaeltacht: Prinicpal Findings and Recommendations*. Dublin: Stationery Office.

Oliver, J. (2010). The predicament? Planning for culture, communities and identities. In G. Munro and I. Mac an Tàilleir (eds.), *Coimhearsnachd na Gàidhlig an-diugh / Gaelic Communities today* (1st ed., pp. 73–86). Edinburgh: Dunedin Academic Press.

Romaine, S. (2006). Planning for the survival of linguistic diversity. *Language Policy, 5*(4), 443–475. doi:10.1007/s10993-006-9034-3

Gaelic Language (Scotland) Act2005, Laws/Statutes (2005).

Smith-Christmas, C. (2016a). *Family Language Policy – Maintaining an Endangered Language in the Home*. London: Palgrave.

Smith-Christmas, C. (2016b). 'Is it really for talking?': The implications of associating a minority language with the school. *Language, Culture and Curriculum, 30*(1), 32–47. doi:10.1080/07908318.2016.1230619

Smith-Christmas, C., and Ó hIfearnáin, T. (2015). Gaelic in Scotland and Ireland – Issues of class and diglossia in an evolving social landscape. In D. Smakman and P. Heinrich (eds.), *Globalising Sociolinguistics: Challenging and Expanding Theory*. London: Routledge.

Spolsky, B. (2004). *Language Policy*. Cambridge: Cambridge University Press.

Spolsky, B., and Cooper, R. (1991). *The Languages of Jerusalem*. Oxford: Clarendon Press.

Strubell, M. (2005). Language proficiency and language use – interpersonal linguistic behaviour and language shift. Retrieved from www.euskara.euskadi.eus/r59-738/en/contenidos/informacion/artik3_1_strubell_05_10/en_10616/artik3_1_strubell_05_10.html

The Scottish Council for Research in Education. (1961). *Gaelic-speaking Children in Highland Schools*. London: University of London Press.

Thomas, F. (1998). *Gaelic in the census of population in Scotland 1881–1991*. Paper presented at the Colloquim on Minority Language – language population censuses and social surveys, Hatfield.

Urla, J. (2013). Preface. In O. Altuna and A. Basurto (eds.), *Survey Methods. A Guide to Language Use Observation* (pp. 111). Donostia: Survey Methods. A guide to language use observation.

Will, V. K. A. (2012). *Why Kenny can't can: The language socialization experiences of Gaelic-medium educated children in Scotland*. (PhD). University of Michigan,

Yurramendi, Y., and Altuna, O. (2009). Zuzeneko behaketaz hizkuntza-e-rabilera neurtzeko metodologiaren erendu matematikoa. Liginketa eta estimazioa. In S. Klusterra (ed.). Andaoin: Soziolinguistika Klusterra.

10 Bilingualism, ideology and identity
Change in the Finland-Swedish variety

J. A. E. Strandberg and C. Gooskens

10.1 Introduction

Finland has two national languages; Finnish and a variety of Swedish known as Finland-Swedish. Throughout most of the country's history, Swedish and Finnish were spoken side by side in largely distinct linguistic communities. Yet, with the urbanisation of southern Finland, which began in the late nineteenth century and continues to this day, regions that were historically monolingually Swedish are becoming majority Finnish-speaking. After the country's independence in 1917, Finnish was established as the main language of Finland, and over the course of the twentieth century the position of Swedish came to resemble that of a minority language, rather than a national language (Lindgren, Lindgren and Saari 2011). In 2018, only 5.2 percent of the Finnish population, i.e., fewer than 300,000 individuals, spoke Swedish as their first language (Statistikcentralen 2018).

As Finnish is the dominant language in the country, urbanisation and increased intergroup communication mean that bilingualism is increasingly demanded from Swedish native speakers in everyday social interactions. Linguistic exogamy (i.e., marriage occurring between speakers of different languages) has become progressively more common since the 1950s, with many individuals growing up in bilingual Finnish- and Swedish-speaking homes (see Finnäs 2015). In spite of this changing linguistic situation, relatively little research has been conducted on the extent of bilingualism within Finland or on the linguistic and social consequences of it. This chapter discusses the ideological and practical issues surrounding the two national languages of Finland, exploring how increasing bilingualism and frequent translanguaging in Finland-Swedish communities may lead to phonetic and lexical changes in the Finland-Swedish variety.

10.2 A brief history of Swedish in Finland

As early as AD 1000, speakers of Old East Norse, a language that later diverged into Swedish and Danish, established substantial settlements on the southern and western coast of Finland (Ivars and Huldén 2002). During the Swedish rule of Finland, from the twelfth until the nineteenth century, Swedish was the language of the state. It also continued to be used as the administrative language even after the 1809 annexation of Finland by Russia, until the country's independence in 1917 (Wide and Lyngfelt 2009). Standardised Finland-Swedish was generally the language of the upper class, while local Finnish as well as Swedish dialects were spoken by the lower social classes. Since Finnish was not used in high society or education, it remained unstandardised throughout most of the nineteenth century, and was seen as a social marker separating the Finnish-speaking lower classes from the Swedish-speaking elite (Saari 2012). In the late nineteenth century, the Finland-Swedish elite began promoting the use of the Finnish language through the *Fennomanian* movement. This National Romantic movement encouraged the use of Finnish in the higher social classes, simultaneously endorsing linguistic standardisation and education in Finnish. Many originally Swedish-speaking families began using Finnish at home and fennicised their surnames by translating or transliterating their name to Finnish; an example of this is how the Swedish surname Strengman was transliterated into the Finnish-sounding name Renkonen[1] (Di Luzio and Kotta 2012). By the 1900s, Finnish stopped being a social marker, as the language had conquered all domains in society, and internal migration and mass media continued to promote the standardisation of both written and spoken Finnish throughout the twentieth century (Saari 2012; McRae, Helander and Luoma 1997). Today, both Finnish and Swedish are official national languages in Finland, with the vast majority of Finnish nationals from all social circles speaking Finnish as their first language.

Finland-Swedish has only rarely been argued to be a separate language from the Swedish spoken in Sweden, but it is recognised as a separate variety with distinct features of pronunciation, lexicon, syntax and semantics. An example of a well-known distinction is that the majority of Swedish dialects spoken in Sweden make use of pitch accent, using the acute and grave accents to distinguish between homographs in speech; for instance, the acute accent is used in the word *anden* ($^{1'}$and-en, 'the duck'), while the grave accent is used in *anden* ($^{2'}$ande-n, 'the spirit') (Bailey 1988; Riad 2013). Finland-Swedish, on the other hand, does not use pitch accent, and thus such homographs are also homophones, with the words being distinguished only by the context. The pronunciation of some consonants also differs between the Swedish varieties spoken in Finland and in Sweden: for instance, the -*sj*- combination in *sju* ('seven') is pronounced as the voiceless palato-alveolar fricative [ʃ] in Finland-Swedish, but as the voiceless postalveolar-velar fricative [ɧ] in Sweden-Swedish. Similarly, while a Swedish individual would pronounce *keramik* ('ceramics') with initial [ɕ], a Finland-Swedish individual would likely use initial [k] (Reuter 2015).

Because of its geographical separation from the Swedish spoken in Sweden, Finland-Swedish has retained certain archaic features of pronunciation and vocabulary (Reuter 1977). Additionally, as a result of the long history of Finnish and Swedish being spoken side by side in Finland, the two languages have also influenced each other. In the last century in particular, an increasing number of

Finnish words and phrases have been borrowed into Finland-Swedish (Clyne, Norrby and Warren 2009; Jamrowska 1996). Finnish loanwords are common in everyday Finland-Swedish, and include nouns as well as adjectives and verbs; common examples include *juttu* ('thing, story'), *kiva* ('nice, fun'), and *håsa* ('to rush'). Loan-translations occur as single words or phrases, such as *med långa tänder*, a calque of Finnish *pitkin hampain* (lit. 'with long teeth'), which suggests doing something with aversion.

10.3 Language policy and identity

Finland-Swedish is only spoken by approximately 290,000 native speakers in Finland today, but still retains its position as one of the two national languages. In theory, the language rights of both linguistic communities are equal: in bilingual municipalities, all Finland-Swedish and Finnish individuals have the right to education and public services in their native tongue. However, in practice, in many regions it is challenging for Finland-Swedes to obtain healthcare or other official services in Swedish, and they often have to settle for services in Finnish. As the predominance of Finnish keeps growing steadily, it is becoming increasingly difficult to work or access services without Finnish, even in regions that until recently were Swedish-dominant (McRae et al. 1997).

Despite Swedish being a *de facto* minority language with relatively few native speakers in Finland, Finland-Swedes have traditionally upheld a strong linguistically anchored ethnic identity, and tend to be defined as a group mainly by their native tongue, *finlandssvenska*, 'Finland-Swedish' (af Hällström-Reijonen 2012; Skutnabb-Kangas 1999). While always claiming a Finnish national identity (Lojander 2008), Finland-Swedes often take great pains to distinguish themselves from Finnish-speaking Finns (frequently referred to as *finnar*, literally 'Finns'), by self-identifying as *finlandssvenskar* ('Finland-Swedish') or *finländare* ('Finnish'). While the terms *finlandssvensk* and *finne* are used to differentiate between Finland-Swedish and Finnish speakers, *finländare* can be used to refer to Finnish individuals of any language background. The relationship between Finland-Swedes and Finns can thus be compared to that of anglophones and francophones in Canada, where, according to Heller (1999 144) 'language is the principal characteristic differentiating between groups which clearly think of themselves as distinct.' The fact that language is the main inter-group distinction between Finns and Finland-Swedes means that occasional fennification of Finland-Swedish cultural heritage is often met with harsh criticism. For instance, films narrating the lives of historic figures such as composer Jean Sibelius or the painter Helene Schjerfbeck have been criticised by the public and by Finland-Swedish media for ignoring the Swedish-language heritage of the individuals, instead depicting them as Finnish-speaking.

Figure 10.1 Map of Finland highlighting bilingual municipalities with Finland-Swedish minority (light grey) or Finland-Swedish majority (dark grey), as well as monolingual Finland-Swedish municipalities on the Åland islands (black). Data source: Kuntaliitto 2017.

10.4 Urbanisation of southern Finland

The linguistic climate in Finland has been strongly influenced by considerable internal migration during the nineteenth and twentieth centuries. Due to the urbanisation of the capital city of Helsinki, located in southern Finland, Finnish native speakers have migrated in great numbers to traditionally Swedish-speaking regions on the southern coastline. As a result, the Greater Helsinki Area, and the southern coast of Finland in particular, have witnessed a rapid rise in bilingual speakers (Tandefelt 1996; Finnäs 2015).

Helsinki is located in the southern province of Uusimaa (Sw. *Nyland*), which hosts approximately 30 percent of the 5.5 million inhabitants of Finland, compared to 3.3 percent of the population in Ostrobothnia or 0.5 percent on Åland (Statistikcentralen 2018). As such, Uusimaa has the highest population density at 182 inhabitants per square kilometer. Due to urbanisation, the population in Uusimaa changed from being majority Swedish-speaking in 1880 to having only 11 percent of native Swedish-speakers in 1990 (Henning-Lindblom and Liebkind 2007). Similarly, coastal municipalities such as Porvoo, Kauniainen, Kirkkonummi and Hankoo[2] had a Swedish-speaking majority until the 1970s, when a vast number of Finnish-speakers moved from the inland to the southern coast (Finnäs 2012). As Figure 10.1 demonstrates, while the island of Åland is monolingually Swedish-speaking, there are no longer any monolingual Swedish-speaking municipalities on the Finnish mainland.

Although the majority of the Finland-Swedish population continues to live in southern Finland, today this area mainly consists of Finnish-majority bilingual municipalities,[3] where knowledge of Finnish is crucial. Meanwhile, in areas such as Ostrobothnia, on the western coast of Finland, Swedish is still the majority language in many places. In this region, many districts are still monolingually Swedish-speaking, and knowledge of Finnish may not be necessary for daily life. Research into the language use of Finland-Swedish university students in southern Finland and Ostrobothnia has revealed differences between the two regions: while 84 percent of Ostrobothnian students used mostly or only Swedish on a daily basis, only 60 percent of Swedish-speaking participants from southern Finland used Swedish as frequently as, or more often than, Finnish (Leinonen and Tandefelt 2007).

A natural consequence of the increase of bilingual municipalities, particularly in southern Finland, has been the rise of bilingual marriages. Linguistic exogamy has increased steadily in Finland since the 1950s due to growing urbanisation and the resulting language contact and bilingualism (McRae et al. 1997). Since the 1970s, the yearly number of marriages between a Swedish native speaker and a Finnish one has been higher than the number of marriages in which both parties are Swedish-speaking (Finnäs 2012). As the Finnish native speakers far outnumber the Swedish native speakers, linguistic exogamy influences the Finland-Swedish community as a whole a great deal more than the Finnish-speaking community (McRae et al. 1997). In 2012, in southern Finland, as many as three out of four marriages involving a Swedish-speaking individual were between a Finnish and a Swedish speaker. By contrast, in Ostrobothnia, less than one fifth of marriages involving a Swedish-speaking individual were bilingual (Finnäs 2012).

The Finnish state has documented the mother tongue of its citizens since 1865. Today, the linguistic affiliation of censused individuals is gathered in the Population Information System, which is handled by the Digital and Population Data Services Agency (DVV). Information about a child's full name, along with their registered native language, must be sent to the DVV within three months of the child's birth. Only one language can be entered as the individual's native language, but the person in question may change their preferred language at any time. Nevertheless, because it is currently only possible to report one language as an individual's mother tongue, data collection on bilingualism or multilingualism is difficult (Palviainen and Bergroth 2018).[4] In spite of the challenges of gathering precise data, the extent of native Finnish and Finland-Swedish bilingualism varies greatly across the country. It has been estimated that, out of all children born to a Finland-Swedish parent in the urban Greater Helsinki region between 2006 and 2011, 70 percent had another parent who was Finnish-speaking (Finnäs 2012). The corresponding numbers in relatively urbanised areas in western and eastern Uusimaa were between 50 and 60 percent. In comparison, fewer than one in five of the children born to a Finland-Swedish parent in the rural areas of Ostrobothnia and the Åland islands came from mixed-language backgrounds (Finnäs 2012).

10.5 Language ideology

Since it is only possible to report one native language per child in Finland, the concept of a single 'mother tongue' is socially enforced, and is often strongly connected to a person's experiences and identity (Palviainen and Bergroth 2018). In a study on the linguistic identities of parents in exogamous Finnish and Finland-Swedish families, Palviainen and Bergroth (2018) found that, whilst being effectively bi- or multilingual, most parents expressly identified themselves as either Finnish or Finland-Swedish. This shows that, while individuals are often functionally bilingual, the concept of language is a deeply ideological and political factor in Finland, as linguistic identities are performed and negotiated on the basis of language ideologies out of the socio-cultural context. Deciding which one of a bilingual child's two languages should be their official native language effectively requires their parents to take a political stance.

The conventions for choosing the mother tongue of the child within an exogamous marriage in Finland seem to have shifted over time. Until the 1980s, children from mixed Finnish and Swedish-speaking families were usually registered as Finnish-speaking. Conversely, according to demographic data, in 2012 as many as two-thirds of children from mixed Finnish and Finland-Swedish families were registered as Swedish-speaking (Finnäs 2012). In families where the mother is Swedish-speaking, her linguistic identity seems to be a deciding factor when choosing a child's registered native language; in 2011, more than 80 percent of families where the mother was Swedish-speaking registered their children as Swedish-speaking. The corresponding number for families in which the mother was Finnish-speaking was approximately 50 percent (Finnäs 2012).

Although the language of education may be determined by external factors, such as the proximity of schools in the desired language, the language of education of a child is usually the same as their official first language. A study by Lojander-Visapää (2008) indicated that the language in which bilingual children were educated had a large impact on their eventual language use, meaning that the language choice that the parents make for the child is also likely to determine the child's future linguistic identity. The study showed that bilingual children who went to Swedish-speaking schools also spoke Swedish regularly at home (Lojander-Visapää 2008). These students also used both Swedish and Finnish outside of the home, alternating between languages according to the communicative context. Bilingual children attending Finnish-language schools, on the other hand, were less likely to use Swedish at home and almost never used it elsewhere (Lojander-Visapää 2008). The choice concerning the official mother tongue and the language of education for a bilingual child may thus determine whether he or she becomes a *social bilingual*, using both the minority and majority languages in different social spheres, or a *private bilingual*, using the minority language only inside the home (Lojander-Visapää 2008).

10.6 Bilingualism in action

While the Swedish-speaking community in Finland is small in number, it is not always seen as an underprivileged minority, but rather often argued to be 'an indigenous ethnic group with a strong position in society' (Saarela and Finnäs 2014: 79). Unlike most minority groups, the language of the Finland-Swedes has – in theory – an equal standing to the Finnish language. Nevertheless, this is not always reflected in inter-group communication; although primary education in both Finnish and Swedish involves schooling in both national languages, far fewer native Finnish than Finland-Swedish speakers tend to be functionally bilingual. Although it is possible to exclusively use Swedish both in- and outside the home in certain communities (mainly in the regions of Ostrobothnia and on Åland; see Figure 10.1), Swedish monolingualism among individuals is limited to certain regions and certain jobs. Although proficiency in Swedish may be considered an advantage or even a requirement for certain (mainly government) jobs, due to the dominance of Finnish, many Finland-Swedish individuals use primarily Finnish in their professional life. Thus even an individual with a monolingual Swedish-speaking background may develop into what Lojander-Visapää (2008) refers to as a private bilingual, speaking Swedish only with family or friends.

For the Finland-Swedish bilingual, the choice between using Swedish or Finnish in a specific public setting may depend on a number of factors. Even for social bilinguals, one of the most important factors for language use is geographical location. For instance, a social bilingual Swedish native speaker is relatively likely to initiate a customer service interaction in Swedish in Porvoo, a formerly Swedish-majority coastal municipality which retains a high percentage of Swedish-speaking inhabitants to this day. On the other hand, they are less likely to try to use Swedish in Mikkeli, a monolingual Finnish municipality in central Finland. In general, it is notable that both social and private bilingual Finland-Swedes have a strong tendency to initiate interactions with strangers in the majority Finnish language, unless the area is well-known for having a large Swedish-speaking population.

Because it is often considered easier to initiate conversations in Finnish, rather than to try in Swedish and possibly have to switch to Finnish regardless, it may occasionally transpire halfway through an interaction that both parties are, in fact, native Swedish speakers. While the predisposition for bilingual Finland-Swedes to automatically switch to Finnish can be viewed as a direct result of the ongoing language shift in Finland, this behaviour is also often denounced for further weakening the position of Swedish. McRae et al. (1997) state that most Finland-Swedes are resigned to using Finnish in public spaces and adjusting to the dominant Finnish language. If a group of Finland-Swedes are having a conversation in Swedish, the language is likely to change to Finnish as soon as a single Finnish speaker joins the conversation. According to McRae et al. (1997), this behavioral mode may well lead to the eventual disappearance of Swedish in Finland, as 'among older [Finland-Swedish] informants there is occasionally wistful regret for a more comfortable past, while younger ones adjust more pragmatically to contemporary conditions' (1997; 432).

Whether or not the dominance of Finnish will eventually lead to the disappearance of Finland-Swedish remains unclear, but the increased influence of Finnish is evident in the high number of instances of translanguaging that take place in interactions of bilingual Finland-Swedish individuals. The concept of translanguaging relies on the idea of fluid use of linguistic resources, defining bilingualism not as a parallel use of two autonomous language systems, but rather as one linguistic repertoire (Pennycook 2017). The theory of translanguaging posits that it is not the prescribed and taught language of monolinguals that is the global norm, but rather the bilingual practice of strategically using features from a single repertoire in order to communicate effectively (García and Li Wei 2014). Translanguaging is often witnessed in interactions between Finland-Swedish individuals, in situations where both parties know each other to be bilingual speakers of Swedish and Finnish. The practice often occurs due to the ease and practicality of both speakers being fluent in the same languages, resulting in communication in which language features from either language are used regardless of the communication-related task or context. As such, translanguaging cannot be argued to be a result of a specific language being tied to a specific use. However, Henricson (2015) argues that shifting between Swedish and Finnish is often done to structure the conversation, for instance when changing topics or when indicating a change of speaker in the retelling of a story. Additionally, as translanguaging requires all parties in the conversation to share the same linguistic background, this type of language practice can be used to strengthen or maintain bi- or multilingual social networks and groups.

In spite of the frequent use of translanguaging among Finland-Swedish individuals, on a conscious level many speakers frown upon this type of communication. Translanguaging, as well as the use of borrowed Finnish words and phrases in Finland-Swedish, is considered incorrect use of language, and it is often argued to be a threat to the existence of the Finland-Swedish variety. Yet, the recent studies presented below suggest that, even when using only a single language in speech, bilinguals seem to be developing converging vowel systems for Finland-Swedish and Finnish.

10.7 Language contact and phonetic change

Phonetically, Finland-Swedish and Finnish are relatively similar, more so than Finnish and Sweden-Swedish. The only phoneme that is found in Finland-Swedish but not in Finnish is /ʉː/ (Kuronen 2000), although, overall, Finnish has fewer allophones than Swedish. For instance, both Swedish and Finnish make use of the phoneme [ø] for the grapheme <ö>, but in Swedish the phoneme usually has two allophones in complementary distribution, i.e., [ø] (as in *öga*, 'eye') and [œ] (as in *öra*, 'ear').

Some earlier scholars have suggested that the similarities of Finnish and Finland-Swedish are not a consequence of the geographical vicinity of the two languages, but of Finland-Swedish developing independently from Sweden-Swedish on the other side of the Baltic Sea (see Niemi 1981; Ahlbäck 1971). Niemi (1981) argues that the two linguistic groups have been culturally and linguistically separated throughout most of history, and that the existing changes are too small to suggest change due to language contact. However, Kuronen (2000) counters that it is precisely because the differences between the languages are small that we can presume that some adjustment towards Finnish has taken place in Finland-Swedish.

Kuronen (2000) also argues that phonetic changes are currently occurring in Finland-Swedish due to increased contact with the Finnish majority language. In a 2000 study, he compared vowel formant frequencies of four native and four childhood bilingual Finland-Swedish participants from Helsinki and Tampere, four monolingual Finnish participants from Tampere, and four monolingual Swedish participants from Sweden (Kuronen 2000). The participants were all males aged 17 to 18. Kuronen focused on the first formant (F_1), which relates to the height of the tongue in the mouth, and on the second formant (F_2), which relates to the frontness or backness of the tongue. Six out of eight bilingual Finland-Swedish participants in the study demonstrated use of largely the same vowel system for both Finnish and Swedish (Kuronen 2000). These bilingual participants did not break any norms of either Standard Finland-Swedish or Standard Finnish, but their Finnish did not include some dialectal phonetic features that were found in monolingual Finnish speakers (Kuronen 2000). For instance, the bilingual participants' Finnish pronunciation of [yː] had higher F_2 values than that of the monolingual Finnish-speakers from the same region, while their pronunciations of [eː] and [øː] had comparatively lower F_1 values (Kuronen 2000). According to Kuronen, this suggests that bilingual people who are fluent in both Finnish and Finland-Swedish may struggle to separate the qualitatively similar vowel systems, especially when using either vowel system is communicatively sufficient for both languages (2000: 60).

In a more recent apparent-time study on the vowel production of Finland-Swedes, Strandberg (2018, 2019) explored the influence of native or early childhood bilingualism on the pronunciation of the variable /ø/ in Finland-Swedish. In Swedish, the phoneme /ø/, indicated by the grapheme <ö>, occurs either as the close-mid front rounded vowel [ø], or as the open-mid front rounded vowel [œ] (Leinonen 2010; Riad 2002). The allophone [ø] occurs in most speech contexts, while [œ] only occurs before /r/ (compare öga [øːga], 'eye', and öra [œːra], 'ear'). As the open-mid front rounded vowel [œ] is notoriously difficult for Finnish native speakers to master, it is often replaced by the allophone [ø], leading to the latter being considered a linguistic marker for Finnish natives speaking Swedish as a second language. Due to evidence from previous studies such as that of Kuronen (2000), which suggests that bilingual Finnish and Finland-Swedish speakers may have converging vowel systems, Strandberg (2018, 2019) explored whether the increasing dominance of the Finnish language is affecting the pronunciation of [œ] in Finland-Swedish bilinguals. The hypothesis of the study was that, considering that [œ] rarely occurs and does not have phonemic status in Swedish, the increased influence from the Finnish majority language and increased use of translanguaging would cause [œ] to be pronounced more like [ø] (Strandberg 2019). The acoustic analysis consisted of examining differences in Hz values for the F_1 and F_2 formants of allophones [œ] and [ø] in fourteen speakers. In addition, the perception of the allophones and speakers' abilities to identify them in target words was explored in a nation-wide survey.

In order to collect the phonetic data, interviews with nine female and three male Finland-Swedish individuals between the ages of 5 and 84 with different levels of bilingualism were recorded. All speakers were from one extended family, which was expected to limit social or regional variation in their speech. However, the speakers differed when it came to fluency and age of acquisition of Finnish. The six participants from the two older generations of speakers, aged 51 to 84, had acquired Finnish as a second language in school, after the age of 10. On the other hand, three of the four third-generation speakers, aged 32 to 37, were mostly early childhood bilinguals, having been exposed to Finnish in kindergarten from the ages of 1;0 and 2;0 onwards. The fourth third-generation participant, aged 28, had acquired Finnish in kindergarten after the age of 5;0, thus being on the border between an early and late childhood bilingual. Finally, the four fourth-generation participants, aged 5 to 10 years old, were native bilinguals, having been exposed to both Finnish and Swedish from birth. Samples of speech of all participants were collected through *photo-elicited interviews* (PEIs), which involved asking participants to describe images involving target words. This elicitation method was chosen in order to sample target words in a similar fashion from both adult and child participants. The F_1 and F_2 formants produced by each participant for both the allophones [œ] and [ø] were then sampled in the acoustic analysis software Praat (Boersma and Weenink 2016).

The findings of the acoustic analysis indicated some differences in vowel production between older participants, who had learned Finnish in later childhood, and younger participants, who were early childhood or native bilinguals. Although no apparent-time generational change was evident for F_2, the F_1 measurements of [œ] and [ø] showed considerably more convergence for the seven participants aged 5 to 37 who were early or native bilinguals. The results suggest that age of acquisition of Finnish correlates with the discrimination of the allophones in relation to the height of the tongue, as native and early bilinguals were more likely to have converging F_1 values for [œ] and [ø]. On the other hand, the seven participants who acquired Finnish after the age of 5 produced significantly different mean values for the two formants (Strandberg 2019).

In addition to studying production, the study by Strandberg (2018, 2019) also explored the perception of the allophones [ø] and [œ] in Finland-Swedish. In a survey, 281 participants were asked to match target words containing either the [ø] or [œ] allophone to four other words containing the grapheme <ö>; for instance, the vowel in the target word *ö* ([øː], 'island') could be matched to the <ö>vowel in *öga* ([øːga], 'eye'), *öra* ([œːra], 'ear'), *smör* ([smœːr], 'butter'), or *bröd* ([brøːd], 'bread'). The participants could indicate that the target word vowel was the same as the vowel sound in one, two, or three of the other words, or that all the words contained the same vowel sound. Alternatively, the participants could indicate that the vowel in the target word did not match any of the other words. Overall, the participants were quite accurate in matching target words to other words containing the same allophone. When misidentification occurred, the errors were more likely to appear when identifying a target word containing the allophone [œ]. The data thus indicated that speakers are more likely to perceive an expected [œ] allophone in a word as [ø], rather than the other way around. This suggests that there is more variation in the production of /ø/ before /r/ than in any other context in Finland-Swedish. In spite of this, open-ended responses in the survey suggested that the use of [ø] in the place of [œ][5] was highly marked and stigmatised, since several survey participants remarked that the inability to pronounce [œ] is considered a native Finnish-speaking trait.[6] Interestingly, although the Finland-Swedish participants considered the replacement of the allophone [œ] by [ø] to be a stigmatised feature (often suggesting a Finnish second-language speaker of Swedish), the participants themselves only correctly identified <ö> as the allophone [œ] in words such as *öra* and *smör* between 64 and 77 percent of the times (Strandberg 2018).

A notable finding from the data was the difference between perception results of native monolingual and bilingual Finland-Swedish participants.

A Chi-squared test of independence found a highly significant difference (χ^2 (2) = 36.93, $p < .000$) when comparing the abilities of monolingual and bilingual speakers in matching allophones [œ] and [ø] to target words (Strandberg 2018). While monolingual Finland-Swedish speakers were able to match the target words containing [œ] to other words containing the same allophone 79.8 percent of the time, the corresponding accuracy for bilinguals was only 56.6 percent. Moreover, although bilingual speakers did perform better (at 80 percent accuracy) with allophone [ø] than with [œ], monolinguals still outperformed bilinguals with a mean percentage of identification accuracy of 92.1 percent (Strandberg 2018: 49). These findings support the production data, suggesting that highly proficient native or early bilinguals are less likely to clearly differentiate between the two allophones, both during perception and production of language (Strandberg 2018).

10.8 Loanwords, translanguaging and the Finland-Swedish identity

In addition to exploring phonetic change in Finland-Swedish as a result of increased language contact with Finnish, Strandberg et al. (2022) launched an investigation exploring the use of fennicisms in Finland-Swedish. The term *fennicism* refers to words, calques, or phrases originating in the Finnish language, such as the aforementioned *juttu* and *kiva*. A fennicism is a specific type of *finlandism*, a hypernym which denotes words, phrases, or structures that are either used exclusively in Finland-Swedish or with a different meaning than in Standard Swedish.[7] Due to the rise of bilingualism among Finland-Swedish speakers, new linguistic items labelled as fennicisms are constantly coined in the form of loan translations or semantic borrowings (Melin-Köpilä 1996). In the Strandberg et al. (2022) survey study, 126 participants were given examples of common fennicisms in the forms of loanwords, loan translations, or translated phrases. The participants were asked to indicate whether or not they had heard other people use these words or phrases, and whether or not they used them themselves. The participants were also asked to give examples of other fennicisms that they had used or heard others use. It should be noted that the words *finlandism* or *fennicism* were not explicitly used in the survey; instead, fennicisms were referred to according to their type (e.g., loanword, loan translation). This was done because, although the participants were expected to be familiar with the common umbrella term *finlandism*, the hyponym *fennicism* was considered a potential source for confusion.

The result of the survey by Strandberg et al. (2022) indicated that, for all types of Finnish borrowings that were investigated in the survey, the participants always reported a higher percentage of being exposed to fennicisms than for using the fennicisms themselves. However, due to the nature of the survey, it is difficult to assess whether people were accurate in self-reporting their use of *versus* their exposure to fennicisms. Based on the survey alone, it is unclear whether most people indeed are aware of and exposed to a much higher number of fennicisms than they themselves use, or if people under-report their own use of fennicisms due to the stigma related to using non-standard Swedish.

In addition to being asked which fennicisms they themselves used, the survey participants were presented with an open-ended question in which they were asked about their general thoughts regarding the use of Finnish loans or loan translations in Finland-Swedish. Four participants wished to make it clear that, although they were familiar with some or even all of the fennicism examples, they themselves avoided or never used fennicisms. One participant stated that it is 'a pity' that fennicisms are used in Finland-Swedish, and wondered if this was one of the reasons for 'the declining quality of Swedish in Finland' (authors' translation). On the other hand, several comments were also positive regarding the use of Finnish loanwords or calques in Finland-Swedish. Four participants stated that fennicisms may be fun and useful, particularly in situations where the Swedish equivalent is not as precise as the Finnish word. One participant also argued that finlandisms were part of the Finland-Swedish identity, stating:

'Tycker finlandismer är en del av vår 'språkidentitet', som gör att finlandssvenska skiljer sig från rikssvenska. Det finns dock någon, kanske diffus, gräns enligt mig, efter vilket språket blir 'dålig svenska'.' ['[I] think that finlandisms are a part of our 'language identity', resulting in Finland-Swedish differing from Sweden-Swedish. However, in my opinion, there is still some fuzzy line that can be crossed, resulting in 'poor Swedish'.']

(Authors' translation from Swedish)

Based on the above comment, it is clear that the participant considers words and phrases specific to Finland-Swedish part of his linguistic identity. Although the participant used the hypernym *finlandism*, the fact that the comment was encouraged by a survey on Finnish loanwords and calques suggests that the response refers at least partially, if not exclusively, to fennicisms. Similarly, another participant stated that, as long as the loanwords and phrases were used with 'correct Swedish conjugation, not incorrect Finnish conjugation' (authors' translation), it was acceptable to use them in Finland-Swedish.

Generally, although there were more positive comments about the diversity and uniqueness of using fennicisms than there were negative comments, most participants agreed that this type of language should only be used in informal circumstances, usually only in casual speech. Alongside the quantitative results, indicating a preference for reporting exposure to rather than use of fennicisms, qualitative responses suggest that there is a clear stigma attached to using fennicisms (and, by extension, finlandisms) in Finland-Swedish. The use of fennicisms and finlandisms seems to be persistently deemed incorrect, as even the participants who had positive attitudes towards fennicisms wished to point out that they were aware that these types of words are not considered appropriate Swedish.

10.9 Conclusion

To this day, languages are usually seen as autonomous systems, where multilingualism is only valued as the concept of parallel monolingual proficiency, and hybrid systems of communication are stigmatised (Heller 2006). Translanguaging of any kind, while usually effective in communication between bilingual individuals, is often perceived as detrimental to the standard variety. This is demonstrated in relation to Finland-Swedish by the attitudes of the participants in Strandberg (2018, 2019) and Strandberg et al. (2022), where both marked phonetic and lexical features from Finnish are denounced by speakers of Finland-Swedish. The use of the allophone [ø] in the place of [œ] is condemned on principle, as it is a marked feature of Finnish natives speaking Swedish as a second language. This is in spite of the fact that using [ø] instead of [œ] does not hamper comprehension, and many native Finland-Swedes struggle to match target words with [œ] to other words containing the same allophone. Similarly, in relation to lexical transfer, some individuals argue that the use of fennicisms in Finland-Swedish should be avoided altogether, and even speakers who generally demonstrate positive attitudes towards fennicisms believe that they should be avoided in 'proper' Swedish.

Many Finland-Swedes take pride in identifying as Finland-Swedish (rather than as Finnish or Swedish), and the distinctive features of the Finland-Swedish linguistic variety are often appreciated by its speakers. Nevertheless, Finland-Swedish is still broadly considered a deviant variety of Standard Swedish. Swedish-speaking children are taught in school that certain words and phrases are only acceptable in the Finland-Swedish narrative, not in 'proper' Swedish. Furthermore, since the single-language ideology is persistent in Finland, parents are compelled to choose an official linguistic identity for their child, regardless of the combination of languages actually used within the home. Finland-Swedes, like many other linguistic minorities, thus become doubly stigmatised; from the perspective of the state, they are second-language speakers of the majority language, and, additionally, their variety is considered inferior to the standard variety of that language (Gal 2006). For further reading on ideological standards and legitimacy in pluricentric languages, see, for instance, Ball and Marley (2017) for a comprehensive overview of the French-speaking world; the study by Hawkey and Mooney (2019) on new speakers and standardisation of Catalan and Occitan in France; and the discussion by Li Wei and Zhu Hua (2010) on linguistic standards and hierarchy in the Chinese diaspora.

It remains to be seen to which extent the increasing bilingualism within the Finland-Swedish community will affect the Swedish variety spoken inFinland. Studies by Kuronen (2000) and Strandberg (2018, 2019) suggest that phonetic change may already be occurring among bilingual Finland-Swedish speakers due to the dominance of the Finnish language. Whether the intake of Finnish loanwords and phrases will also increase as the Swedish-speaking population of Finland becomes more bilingual, remains to be explored in future research. However, it is evident that the borrowing of Finnish features into

Finland-Swedish is frowned upon, even though many individuals consider specifically Finland-Swedish linguistic features to be markers of their own ethnolinguistic identity as *finlandssvenskar*. The majority of Finland-Swedes partake in some level of translanguaging, a mode of interaction that mirrors the bilingual reality of most Finland-Swedish speakers in the twenty-first century and facilitates effective and meaningful everyday communication between bilingual individuals. Yet, such language use is often in direct contrast to what the speakers themselves regard as being appropriate or correct. More often than not, the combining of Finnish and Swedish linguistic features continues to be perceived as a threat to the integrity and continued existence of the Swedish variety in Finland.

Notes

1 The Swedish name Strengman [strɛŋman] has been transliterated to fit Finnish phonology and phonotactics by replacing the initial consonant cluster *str-* with *r-* to achieve Finnish CVC-structure, and substituting the voiced velar plosive [g] with voiceless [k]. The traditional Swedish ending *-man* has also been replaced with the Finnish diminutive ending *-nen*, thus resulting in the name Renkonen [reŋkonen].
2 The Finnish names of these municipalities are translations or transliterations of the original Swedish names, i.e., Borgå, Grankulla, Kyrkslätt and Hangö.
3 A monolingual municipality becomes automatically classed as bilingual if the number of individuals with the (local) minority language as their mother tongue rises to a minimum of 3,000 people or 8 percent of the municipality's population. A bilingual municipality remains bilingual until the number of individuals with the minority mother tongue falls below 3,000 or 6 percent of the municipality's population, at which point the municipality may become monolingual again. Additionally, a monolingual municipality can voluntarily apply for bilingual status without the required number of minority speakers (Kuntaliitto.fi, 2017). Bilingualism is immediately visible in the linguistic landscape of a municipality, in that official signs (e.g., street signs, signs of official institutions, traffic signs) are required to be in both Finnish and Swedish, with the dominant language in primary position. However, as Syrjälä (2017) points out, a Swedish majority in the municipality is generally required for Swedish to be visible alongside Finnish in the commercial sphere.
4 An investigation into introducing registration of several languages for individuals has been initiated by the Ministry of Justice in 2020 (Tammenmaa, 2020).
5 Participants sometimes referred to *öppet ö* (lit. 'open ö') when describing allophone [œ], or distinguished between the ö-sounds by using common words containing that allophone, e.g., *öra* ('ear') or *smör* ('butter').
6 None of the participants considered that a difficulty of pronouncing [œ] in Swedish could potentially suggest another language background except Finnish. However, the idea that pronunciation of [œ] as [ø] is a uniquely Finnish trait may reflect the fact that the vast majority of Swedish second-language speakers that Finland-Swedes encounter are native Finnish speakers.
7 Whether we as linguists choose to label fennicisms as loanwords or as translanguaging could be discussed at length, but instead we will here focus on the purpose of the investigation, which is to explore how these words and phrases are used and perceived by the Finland-Swedish community.

References

Ahlbäck, O. (1971). *Svenskan i Finland* [Swedish in Finland] (2nd ed.). Skrifter utgivna av Svenska språknämnden, 15.
Bailey, L. M. (1988). A non-linear analysis of pitch accent in Swedish. *Lingua, 75*(2–3), 103–124.
Ball, R. and Marley, D. (2017). *The French-Speaking World: A Practical Introduction to Sociolinguistic Issues* (2nd ed.). Routledge.
Boersma, P. and Weenink, D. (2016). Praat: Doing phonetics by computer. [computer program, version 6.0.19]. www.praat.org.
Clyne, M., Norrby, C., and Warren, J. (2009). *Language and Human Relations: Styles of Address in Contemporary Language*. Cambridge University Press.
Di Luzio, F. and Kotta, K. (2012). Suomalaiset etu- ja sukunimet: levinneisyys,tietoisuus ja tulkinnat [Finnish first and last names: Spread, awareness, and interpretation]. CIMO IV project. University of Jyväskylä.
Finnäs, F. (2012). *Finlandssvenskarna 2012: en statistisk rapport* [Finland-Swedes 2012: A statistic report]. Svenska Finlands folkting.
Finnäs, F. (2015). Tvåspråkiga familjer och deras betydelse för demokratin. In M. Tandefelt (ed.), *Gruppspråk, samspråk, två språk* [Group language, common language, two languages] (pp. 201–220). Svenska litteratursällskapet i Finland.
Gal, S. (2006). Contractions of standard language in Europe. *Social Anthropology, 14*(2), 163–181.
García, O. and Li Wei (2014). *Translanguaging: Language, Bilingualism, and Education*. Palgrave Macmillan.
Hawkey, J. and Mooney, D. (2019). The ideological construct of legitimacy for pluricentric standards: Occitan and Catalan in France. *Journal of Multilingual and Multicultural Development*, DOI: 10.1080/01434632.2019.1697275
Heller, M. (1999). Heated language in a cold climate. In J. Blommaert (ed.), *Language Ideological Debates* (pp. 143–170). Walter de Gruyter.
Heller, M. (2006). *Linguistic Minorities and Modernity: A Sociolinguistic Ethnography*. Continuum.
Henning-Lindblom, A. and Liebkind, K. (2007). *Objective Ethnolinguistic Vitality and Identity among Swedish-Speaking Youth*. Walter de Gruyter.
Henricson, S. (2015). Svenska och finska i samma samtal. In M. Tandefelt (ed.), *Gruppspråk, samspråk, två språk* [Group language, common language, two languages] (pp. 127–142). Svenska litteratursällskapet i Finland.
af Hällström-Reijonen, C. (2012). Finlandismer och språkvård från 1800-talet till idag [Finlandisms and language planning from the nineteenth century until today]. [Doctoral thesis, University of Helsinki]. *Nordica Helsingensia, 28*.
Ivars, A. M. and Huldén, L. (2002). *När kom svenskarna till Finland?* [When did the Swedish arrive in Finland?]. Skrifter utgivna av Svenska litteratursällskapet i Finland, 646. Svenska litteratursällskapet i Finland.
Jamrowska, J. (1996). Finskans inflytande på svenskan de senaste 20 åren [The influence of Finnish on the Swedish language in the last 20 years]. *Folia Scandinavica, 3*, 311–316.
Kuntaliitto.fi (2017). Svensk- och tvåspråkiga kommuner: Bakgrundsinformation 2008–2017 [Swedish-speaking and bilingual municipalities: Background information 2008–2017]. www.kommunforbundet.fi/sites/default/files/media/file/2017-02-svensk-och-tvasprakiga-kommuner.pdf.

Kuronen, M. (2000). Vokaluttalets akustik i sverigesvenska, finlandssvenska och finska [The acoustics of vowel pronunciation in Sweden-Swedish, Finland-Swedish, and Finnish]. [Doctoral thesis, University of Jyväskylä]. *Studia Philologica Jyväskylensia, 49*.

Leinonen, T. (2010). An acoustic analysis of vowel pronunciation in Swedishdialects. [Doctoral thesis, University of Groningen.]

Leinonen, T. and Tandefelt, M. (2007). Evidence of language loss in progress? Mother-tongue proficiency among students in Finland and Sweden. *International Journal of the Sociology of Language*, 187/188, 185–203.

Li Wei and Zhu Hua (2010). Voices from the diaspora: Changing hierarchies and dynamics of Chinese multilingualism. *International Journal of the Sociology of Language*, 205, 155–171. DOI: 10.1515/ijsl.2010.043

Lindgren, A.-R., Lindgren, K. and Saari, M. (2011). From Swedish toFinnish in the 19th century: A historical case of emancipatory languageshift. *International Journal of the Sociology of Language*, 209, 17–34.

Lojander-Visapää, C. (2008). New bilingualism in the bilingual Finnish context. *Europäisches Journal für Minderheitenfragen, 1*(2), 109–118.

McRae, K. D., Helander, M., and Luoma, S. (1997). *Conflict and Compromise in Multilingual Societies. Vol. 3, Finland*. Wilfrid Laurier University Press.

Melin-Köpilä, C. (1996). Om normer och normkonflikter i finlandssvenskan [Norms and conicts in Finland-Swedish]. [Doctoral thesis, University of Uppsala]. *Skrifter utgivna av Institutionen för nordiska språk vid Uppsala universitet, 41*.

Niemi, S. (1981). Sverigesvenskan, finlandssvenskan och finskan som kvalitets- och kvanitetsspråk [Sweden-Swedish, Finland-Swedish and Finnish as languages of quality and quantity]. *Folkmålsstudier, 27*, 61–72.

Palviainen, Å. and Bergroth, M. (2018). Parental discourses of language ideology and linguistic identity in multilingual Finland. *International Journal of Multilingualism, 15*(3), 262–275.

Pennycook, A. (2017). Translanguaging and semiotic assemblages. *International Journal of Multilingualism,* 14(3), 269–282.

Reuter, M. (1977). Finlandssvenskt uttal [Finland-Swedish pronunciation]. In B. Petterson and M. Reuter (eds.), *Språkbruk och språkvård* (pp. 19–45). Schildts.

Reuter, M. (2015). Finlandssvenskt uttal [Finland-Swedish pronunciation]. In M. Tandefelt (ed.), *Gruppspråk, samspråk, två språk* [Group language, common language, two languages] (pp. 19–34). Svenska litteratursällskapet i Finland.

Riad, T. (2002). *Artikulatorisk fonetik*. University of Stockholm.

Riad, T. (2013). *The Phonology of Swedish*. Oxford University Press.

Saarela, J. and Finnäs, F. (2014). Transitions within and from ethnolinguistically mixed and endogamous first unions in Finland.*Acta Sociologica, 57*(1),77–92.

Saari, M. (2012). The development of Finnish into a national language. In M. Hüning, U. Vogl, and O. Moliner (eds.), *Standard Languages and Multilingualism in European History* (pp. 179–204). John Benjamins Publishing Company.

Skutnabb-Kangas, T. (1999). Education of minorities. In J. Fishman (ed.), *The Handbook of Language and Ethnic Identity* (pp. 42–59). Oxford University Press.

Statistikcentralen (2018). Finland i siffror: Statistics Finland 2018 [Finland in numbers: Statistics Finland 2018]. www.stat.fi/tup/julkaisut/tiedostot/julkaisuluettelo/yyti_fis_201800_2018_19692_net.pdf

Strandberg, J. A. E. (2018). An acoustic analysis of generational change of the open-mid front rounded vowel [œ] in Finland-Swedish. [Master thesis, Leiden University].

Strandberg, J. A. E. (2019). Tvåspråkighet kan påverka vokaluttalet i finlandssvenskan [Bilingualism may affect vowel pronunciation in Finland-Swedish]. *Språkbruk*, 1/2019, 20–24.

Strandberg, J. A. E., Gooskens, C. and Schüppert, A. (2021). Errors or identity markers? A survey study on the use of and attitudes towards finlandisms and fennicisms in Finland-Swedish. *Nordic Journal of Liguistics*, 1–31. DOI: 10.1017/S0332586521000317.

Syrjälä, V. (2017). Naming businesses – in the context of bilingual Finnish cityscapes. In T. Ainiala and J.-O. Östman (eds.), *Socio-onomastics; The Pragmatics of Names* (pp. 183–202). John Benjamins Publishing Company. 10.1075/pbns.275.09syr

Tammenmaa, C. (2020). Usean kielen merkitseminen väestöjärjestelmään – selvitys. *Oikeusministeriön julkaisuja, Selvityksiä ja ohjeita* 2020:8. https://julkaisut.valtioneuvosto.fi/bitstream/handle/10024/162056/OM_2020_8.pdf

Tandefelt, M. (1996). På vinst och förlust: om tvåspråkighet och språkförlust i Helsingforsregionen [Loss and gain: Bilingualism and language attrition in the Greater Helsinki region]. *Forskningsrapporter, 35*. Svenska Handelshögskolan.

Wide, C. and Lyngfelt, B. (2009). Svenskan i Finland: Grammatiken och konstruktionerna [The Swedish language in Finland: Grammar and constructions]. In C. Wide and B. Lyngfelt (eds.), *Konstruktioner i finlandssvensk syntax. Skriftspråk, samtal och dialekter* (pp. 11–43). Svenska litteratursällskapet i Finland.

11 Trasyanka as a dying phenomenon of urban speech in the city of Minsk

I. Liskovets and K. Fedorova

11.1 Introduction

The linguistic composition of modern big cities tends to be complex and heterogeneous, bringing together, as a result of internal and external migration, languages very different both genetically and typologically, and thus creating 'extreme linguistic diversity' (Blommaert 2010: 7). However, in some cities, competing linguistic varieties can be closely related and differing very little from each other; moreover, there could be various hybrid forms resulting from the contacts between them; they would be clearly distinguishable for local citizens but less evident for outsiders.

Traditionally, contact varieties used to be treated as corrupted, less 'pure', and overall inferior forms of 'proper', i.e. socially more established, languages (see, e.g., Romaine 1988: 9–10; Todd 1990: 1–3). Standard language ideology (Coupland 2000; Milroy 2001) contributed even more to this tendency; in its terms, all linguistic forms are evaluated as more or less 'correct', i.e. close to certain norms. Such norms, being in fact superimposed and idealised standard forms, are, however, perceived by speakers as primary and natural: 'in the non-professional mind the idealised standard is the same thing as the language as a whole' (Milroy 2001: 539). Naturally, all deviations from these standards, be they regional or social dialects, jargons, special registers, or contact languages, could be seen as undesirable, and people using those 'imperfect' varieties would be marked as unwilling or unable to put enough efforts into achieving the standard.

Minsk, the capital of Belarus and a fast-growing city with a population of a little less than two million people, is an interesting example of the way in which rather specific urban communicative settings meet the challenges of further urbanisation and standard language ideology pressure.

The language situation in Minsk, and in Belarus as a whole, is usually described as stable bilingualism with overwhelming predominance of the Russian language over the Belarusian language. The fact that these two Slavic languages are closely related and very similar in both vocabulary and grammar makes their coexistence very interesting in terms of language contact studies. However, in fact, there are not two but three distinct language varieties used in the city – besides Standard Russian (with certain local features) and Standard Belarusian, there is also a non-standard vernacular usually placed somewhere in-between the two standardised languages. This vernacular is called 'Trasyanka' (the term means 'a mixture of hay and straw') and is often referred to by Belarusians as a 'rural' language. This variety, a very complex and non-homogenous one, is particularly interesting since it has arisen as the result of constant interaction of two very closely related languages, or rather two standardised languages and a number of dialects. Trasyanka's contact nature is recognised and reflected upon by the speakers; at the same time, its dubious status and the rather specific social meaning ascribed to it make its use an important social marker influencing the process of communication between urban dwellers. All that makes Trasyanka a fascinating object for analysis from the language ideology perspective we are trying to implement in this chapter.

Investigations (see, e.g., Zaprudsky 2008; Woolhiser 2011; Hentschel 2013, 2017; Liankevich 2014) tend to address the issues of Trasyanka's existence in Belarus more generally, treating it as a well-defined and stable variety, irrespective of particular conditions of its use. Meanwhile, one could argue that versions of Trasyanka used in Minsk, in other Belarusian cities, and in small towns and villages do not necessarily represent the very same phenomenon despite the fact it is labelled with the same term. In the present chapter, we will limit our discussion to the language situation in the city of Minskonly and we will try to reveal language attitudes and ideological constructs contributing to changes in urban linguistic practices.

11.2 Methods and data

The chapter is based on a 20-year-long (1999–2019) field study on language use in the city of Minsk. One of the authors, Irina Liskovets, originally from Minsk, made regular trips there and spent several weeks in the city every year making observations of and participating in everyday speech practices, and discussing language related matters with Minsk residents. Her position as both insider and outsider made it easier for her to approach people via personal networks and, at the same time, to ask them questions locals could find strange, confusing, or even embarrassing. Moreover, being able to keep her distance and compare her observations from different periods, she could trace changes both in the ways people communicate and in the ways they discuss their linguistic backgrounds and choices. As a result, the main corpus of the study is composed of field notes and recordings of spontaneous speech witnessed in the course of participant observation.

Alongside observational data, interviews data were obtained. In 2000–2002, Irina Liskovets interviewed 82 Minsk residents on the matters of their linguistic biographies, speech practices, and language attitudes. She made an attempt to include in her questioning people belonging to different social strata. Her interviews were taken in the farmer's market, in two workshops of a big industrial enterprise, in three shops, in a private company, in different private settings.

When recruiting respondents, several parameters were taken into account: age; educational level; the place of birth (Belarus city/town; Belarus village/small town; outside of Belarus); mother tongue; and the place of work. The main division, however, crucial for the respondents' language attitudes and linguistic identity, was based on the language they were using as dominant at the time of the study. We will distinguish, therefore, three types of speakers: Russian (R) speakers (62 persons), Belarusian (B) speakers (2 persons), and Trasyanka (T) speakers (18 persons). The extremely low number of Belarusian speakers in the sample is explained by the fact that in Minsk, Belarusian existed, at least at the time when the interviews were taken, predominately in official and public domains (and even there it was used only occasionally) while its use in everyday communication was practiced by very few individuals, mostly intellectuals perceived as belonging to nationalist circles. In fact, there was an unwritten taboo for using Belarusian, as S. Zaprudsky puts it (Zaprudsky 2008: 66). That is why Russian as the default language was chosen as the language for interviewing. Four of the respondents (three R-speakers and one B-speaker) were also re-interviewed in 2018 to trace the changes in their attitudes and behaviour. As an additional source of data, other methods were used including small-scale linguistic experiments (described below) and mass media analysis.

This approach, combining in-depth observation with a longitudinal perspective, has made it possible to assess the situation in dynamics, to trace subtle changes and discover new trends in language use and attitudes behind it. The chapter focuses on Trasyanka and aims at revealing the role this variety plays in the lives of Minsk citizens and the reasons for its decline. First, we will address structural features of Trasyanka and their origin; then we will turn to attitudes to Trasyanka typical for certain groups of speakers, both expressed overtly and reconstructed from behavioral patterns; finally, we will discuss the evidences for and the reasons of the language shift attested in the course of two decades of observations.

11.3 Trasyanka: Linguistic structure and patterns of usage

On the surface, Trasyanka can be seen as a linguistic compromise between two standard languages, Russian and Belarusian, and this compromise follows certain patterns. To illustrate these patterns, we will analyze several utterances (Table 11.1) recorded from everyday speech of Trasyanka-speakers (T-speakers hereinafter) and reflecting on its main linguistic features. The utterances are given in transcription, the stressed vowels are bold, Russian elements are underlined, Belarusian ones are wave-underlined. Unmarked elements are common for both languages .

These examples show that Trasyanka combines predominantly Russian stems (Russian 'rabot-' instead of Belarusian 'prac-'; 'cv'et-' instead of 'kv'et-', etc.) with Belarusian phonology. It should be noted that most differences between

Table 11.1 Utterances in Trasyanka

Trasyanka	Standard Belarusian	Standard Russian	English translation
J<u>o</u>n<u>rabo</u>taje na zavo<u>dz</u>'e	Jon prac**u**je na zav**o**dz'e	On rab**o**tajet na zav**o**d'i	He works at a plant
Jan<u>ataɣ</u>ujec'<u>cv'</u>atam'i	Janaɣandl'**u**je kv'**e**tkam'i	Ana targ**u**jet cv'**i**tam'i	She sells flowers
Na<u>s'l'eduščej astano</u>w<u>k'</u> <u>ev</u>yjsc'i<u>na</u>da	na nast**u**pnym prypynku vyjsc'i treba	na sl'eduš<u>č</u>'ej astan**o**vk'e vyjt'i nada	One should get off at the next stop
J<u>on pry</u>jdz'e<u>č</u>e<u>raz</u> try č<u>asy</u>	Jon pryjdz'e praz try ɣadz'iny	On pr'ijd'**ot** c'er'iz tr'i č'isa	He is to come in 3 hours

Russian and Belarusian lie on the phonological level; typically Belarusian features contrasting it to Russian phonology include:

- non-palatalised [č] instead of Russian palatalised [č'])
- non-palatalised [šč] instead of Russian palatalised [šč'])
- palatalised affricate [dź'] instead of Russian plosive [d'],
- palatalised affricate [c'] instead of Russian plosive [t']
- fricative [ɣ] instead of Russian plosive [g]
- bilabial [w] instead of Russian [v] after a vowel or [l] at the end of the word
- absence of palatalised [r'] (whereas Russian has two phonemes [r] and [r'] Belarusian has only one)
- ['a] in –post-stressed syllables after palatalised consonants, where the Russian norm requires [i].

A typical example of Trasyanka's deviation from both standards is the adverb [očen'] 'very' (Belarusian vel'm'i, Russian o*č'in'*); with non-palatalised Belarusian [č] and [e] in post-stressed syllable.

Prosodic features of Trasyanka are mostly Belarusian as well.

On the lexical level, three types of lexemes are found in Trasyanka: those with Russian stems, with Belarusian stems, and with stems identical in both languages. Words with Russian stems are mostly nouns related to work, social position, and urban lifestyle as well as terms and some of the most common words.

Words with Belarusian stems are mainly nouns associated with childhood and rural life as well as personal pronouns.

Another lexical phenomenon found in Trasyanka is its usage of inter-language paraphones, i.e. the words that underwent a semantic shift as a result of inter-language homonymy. For instance, the verb *rab'ic'* is used by T-speakers in the meaning of 'to work' (in BL – *pracavac'*; *rab'ic'* means 'to make smth') due to Russian *rabotat'* meaning 'to work'.

The morphology of Trasyanka is mixed: some elements are of Belarusian origin, for instance, Belarusian declensional endings in nouns and adjectives as

Table 11.2 Russian stems in Trasyanka

Trasyanka	Russian	Belarusian	Translation
Nouns			
da**wl'en'n'**e	davl'en'ije	c'isk	pressure
preds'ada**c**'el'	pr'ids'idat'il'	staršyn'**a**	chairman
astan**ow**ka	astan**o**vka	prypynak	(bus) stop
s'in**c'**a**bar**	s'int'**abr**'	v'eras'en'	September
dz'**en'**ɣ'i	d'**en'**g'i	ɣrošy	money
v**r**em'a	vr'**em**'a	Čas	time
uč**yc**'el'n'ica	uč'**itil**'n'ica	nastawn'ica	(female) teacher
Adjectives			
kha**ro**šy	kha**ro**šyj	d**o**bry	good
plakh'**i**	plakh**oj**	drenny	bad
Adverbs			
oč**en**'	**o**č'in'	v'el'm'i	very
Verbs			
izv'an'**ic**'	izv'in'**it**'	prabačyc'	to forgive
v'**idz**'ec'	v'**id**'it'	bačyc'	to see
smat**rec**'	smatr'**et**'	gl'adz'ec'	to watch, look
Participles			
s'l'**edušč**y	sl'**edušč**'ij	nastupny	next
Prepositions			
č**eraz**	č'er'iz	Praz or ceraz	through, in

Table 11.3 Belarusian stems in Trasyanka

Trasyanka	Russian	Belarusian	Translation
kh**a**ta	dom	khata	house, home
bac'ka	papa	bac'ka	dad
bul'ba	kartośka	bul'ba	potatoes
jon/jan**a**/jan**o**/jan**y**	on/an**a**/an**o**/an'**i**	jon/jan**a**/jan**o**/jan**y**	he/she/it/they

Table 11.4 Paraphones

Trasyanka	Russian	Belarusian	Translation
rab'**ic**'=to work	rab**o**tat'	pracavac'	to work
		rab'**ic**'	to do, to make
n'adz'**el**'a = week	n'id'**el**'a	t**y**dz'en'	week
		n'adz'**el**'a	Sunday

Table 11.5 Differences in syntax

Trasyanka	Russian	Belarusian	Translation
Pasmatry<u>c'i</u> <u>jos'c'</u> tam tvaj<u>o</u><u>maro</u>ž<u>a</u>naje j<u>o</u>n<u>v</u><u>umn'e</u>jza m'an'**e**	Pasmatr'**u**jest' **l'i** tam tvaj**o** marožynaje On umn**e**j m'in'**a**	Pagl'adzu<u>c'i</u> <u>jos'c'</u> tam tvaj**e** mar**o**z'iva Jon razumn'eiśy za m'an'**e.**	I'll check <u>if there is</u> (your) ice-cream there. He is smarter than I

well as personal endings in verbs, but some others are Russian, or common for both languages.

The syntaxes of Russian and Belarusian are very similar but in case of differences, T-speakers tend to favour Belarusian one. Thus, e.g., proposition 'za' + genitive is used for comparison, not Russian genitive without proposition.

However, the most important fact is a high level of variability in Trasyanka. Many words and even constructions may have different variants; therefore, in many cases a speaker can choose from two stems and two (or even more, due to dialectical variation) morphological forms. For instance, when speaking about money a person may choose either the Russian (*den'g'i*) or Belarusian (*γošy*) stem, and in case of choosing the Belarusian one he or she may also choose between three variants of genitive endings: (1) *γošei* (2) *γošau* (3) *γošai*. Other examples of this kind are:

slyša/čuje/čujec' (hears, RL=slyśyt, BL= *čuje*),
dz'arewn'a/dz'irewn'a/v'oska (village, RL – d'ir'**e**vn'a, BL - v'**o**ska),
kal'i/kaγda (when, RL – kagd**a**, BL – kal'**i**),
*mno*γ*a/ šmat (*much, many; RL – mn**o**ga, BL – śmat), etc.

Even more striking is that such variation can occur in one utterance produced by one speaker:

(1) Informant (female, rural-born, approx.70 yo, uncompleted secondary education, interview): *N'e / ja z dz'arewn'i/ b'arez'insk'i rajon v'oska M'ikul'i'čγ//*

(No, I am from the village (=dz'arewni), Berezinsky district, village (= v'oska) Mikulichi)

(2) Informant (female, rural-born, approx. 60 yo, uncompleted secondary education, interview): *Ya kal'i u v'osk'e tak pa b'ilarusku // kaγda u* γ*orad pryjekhala dyk na rusk'i p'erajšla//*

(When (= kal'i) I am in my village, I speak Belarusian, when (= **kaγda)** I moved to the city I started speaking Russian)

Speakers can also correct themselves, modifying their choice of forms, most probably taking into account their addressee or social settings:

(3) Informant (rural-born, approx. 70–80 yo, incompleted secondary education, interview): *Ja na fronc'e vajavala/ u m'an'e čatyre m'edal'i/ četyre m'idal'i u m'in'a...//*

(I was in the front lines, I have four medals (= *u m'an'e čatyre m'edal'i*)... four medals I have (= *četyre m'idal'i u m'in'a...//*)

(4) Speaker (female. approx. 40 yo, public transport;): *U jaγo mnoγa dź'en'eγ [...] vel'm'i śmat [...] jon γrośy n'i śčytajec'//*

(He has lots (= *mnoγa*) of money (=*dź'en'eγ*)...very much (= *śmat*)... he is rolling in money (= *γrośy*))

(5) Speaker (female, approx. 50 yo, hospital): *Ei dź'ed, k vam pryśl'i//n'i slyśa /ei dź'adul'a//n'a čuje stary/ ei dźed/ da vas prujśli/*

(Hey, grandpa, you have a visitor (= *k vam pryśl'i*), doesn't hear (= *n'i slyśa*), hey, grandpa, doesn't hear (= *n'a čuje*), an old man, hey grandpa, you have a visitor (= *da vas prujśli*))

If we compare these examples, we will realise that while being similar on the surface, they differ in the underlying strategies they employ. Examples (1) and (2) did not show any signs of self-correction; they represent free distribution of elements with the same meaning, with their choice sometimes being motivated, probably, by topic, as, e.g., in the example (2) – the Belarusian elements here are used in the part referring to the informant's rural life experience.

Example (3), on the other hand, is the obvious case of simple, or discourse-based, language management (in terms of J. Neustupný (1994)) revealing the informant's awareness of language matters. The self-correction here evidently is triggered by the interlocutor's speech (Standard Russian); it demonstrates the speaker's wish to use a standard, more prestigious variant. Similar examples are numerous in all interviews with T-speakers in our corpus, which, as Hentschel (2017) points out, is only to be expected when T-speakers communicate with R-speaking researchers. The same strategy but with the reverse target language can be seen in the situation when R-speakers try to speak Belarusian (see below).

However, self-corrections can be found also in the spontaneous speech of T-speakers, as is shown in the examples (4) and (5), recorded during communication between T-speakers. In the latter example, the T-speaking woman gradually modifies her speech by replacing all Russian elements in it with Belarusian ones while trying to be understood by an old man who as she had guessed was a T-speaker.

Despite the high level of variation, Trasyanka is by no means an ad hoc mixture of elements from two standard languages. Hentschel's suggestion (2017) that it is a systematic variety regulated by its own norms, even if less strict and explicit, can be supported by the results of a small-scale metalinguistic experiment. In the course of the interviews with T-speakers, they were presented with different words and were asked if they were acceptable in Trasyanka. Among actual words regularly used by speakers, there were artificially constructed ones, **druγujuc'* and **družuc'* (= 'to be friends'), which were combinations of Russian stem *drug-* ('friend') with Belarusian verb endings for 3rd person plural present *-uc'/juc'*. Both variants were found unacceptable by informants, confirming, therefore, the existence of some shared norms:

Russian: dru**ž**at (they are friends)
Belarusian: s'ab**ru**juc'
Trasyanka: dru**ž**ac', dru**ž**at, s'ab**ru**juc'
Constructed variants: ★dru**ž**uc', ★druɣujuc' – unaccepted by informants.

Summing up, Trasyanka can be described as a mixed variety, tending to use mainly Russian lexemes in combination with Belarusian phonology and mixed morphology and syntax, with a preference for Belarusian ones. It is characterised by high level of variability, which is, though, restricted by usage norms present in speakers' minds. In terms of Meyers-Scotton (2002), it can be, with some reservations, described as matrix Belarusian and embedded Russian; however, the likeness between these two closely related languages makes using these terms even more problematic. Employing Muysken's approach (2000), it is possible to view Trasyanka as a case of congruent lexicalisation.

Cychun (2000) explains the origin of Trasyanka in the following way: it 'appears as a result of spontaneous studying Russian in the process of language relations with its speakers but not in the process of institutionalised step-by-step learning Russian by people brought up in rural Belarusian-speaking surrounding' (Cychun 2000: 57). This explanation can be supported by self-reports of T-speakers in our data: people describe their experience of shifting to Russian after moving to the city from their native Belarusian-speaking villages.

Despite some attempts to find historical roots of Trasyanka (see Mechkovskaja 2014), modern Trasyanka, as stated above, emerged in the process of urbanisation. It exists not in a dialectal continuum but on the scene domineered by two standard languages, with Russian being significantly more powerful. In this world, Trasyanka has been developing as a transitional phenomenon of Russian urban speech of rural migrants, native speakers of Belarusian dialects, who were trying to adjust to the Russian-speaking majority. Starting, therefore, as a form of interlanguage (according to Selinker's definition, 1972), against the background of two standard languages, Trasyanka nowadays looks like a combination of Russian vocabulary with Belarusian phonetics, prosodics, syntax and morphology. Time has passed, and this variety has become the mother tongue for children born in T-speaking families (see Hentschel 2017); when moving to a predominantly Russian-speaking environment, they can either shift to Russian (retaining some Trasyanka features), or stick to their native vernacular.

The last decades have seen a new phenomenon: Trasyanka spoken by R-speakers, who use it instead of Belarusian due to lack of oral practice. It happens when the situation, for some reasons, demands the use of Belarusian. In such cases, R-speakers, who normally have no problems with passive understanding of Standard Belarusian but lack fluency in speaking it, would fail to remember correct Belarusian words and make use of Russian words trying to make them sound 'Belarusian' (usually choosing wrong endings as well).

> (6) Informant (male, approx. 30 yo, university degree, interview): *Ya v'el'm'i dobra yavaru*[B =razmawl'**a**yu] *pa-b'ilarusk'i [B= pa-b'ilarusku]//*
> (I speak Belarusian very well).
>
> U. Liankievič obtained many examples of this kind while performing his experiment (see Liankievič 2013).
>
> This new Trasyanka sometimes is used even in written form. Belarusian media sources quote the following examples:
>
> (7) [Stamp on a passport] *U vjezde adkazana* (cf.: BL *U vjezdze admowlena*, RL: *V vjezde otkazano*)
> (Entry [to the country] is denied).
>
> (8) [Official sign in the airport] *Chyrvony karidor* (cf.: BL *chervony kalidor*, RL *krasnyi koridor*)
> (red corridor [at the customs])[1]

Trasyanka, therefore, is a wide-spread speech variety in Belarus which can be used in various domains. However, longitudinal observations done between 2000 and 2019 show a consecutive decline in usage of Trasyanka among Minsk dwellers. Our observations certify the finding obtained by researchers working in this field (see Woolhiser 2011; Kittel et al. 2010; Hetschel 2013; Liankievič 2013; Liankevich 2014). At the same time, as can be seen from the studies, Minsk, being the biggest and by far the most Russian-speaking city in Belarus, leads this trend, with Trasyanka becoming obsolete here much faster than in other parts of the country.

To understand the reasons for this decline in Trasyanka use, we need to consider the sociolinguistic status of this variety, the social meanings ascribed to it by speakers. To reveal their impact on everyday communication in Minsk, we will focus on attitudes to Trasyanka typical for members of the three above-mentioned main groups of speakers – R-speakers, B-speakers, and T-speakers residing in Minsk.

11.4 Attitudes to Trasyanka

11.4.1 Russian speakers

Russian speakers, as already mentioned, constitute the biggest part of Minsk citizens. Their attitudes to Trasyanka, in most cases, are overtly negative as is evident from their interviews in our data and from the observations made by A. Liankevich. According to her doctoral research, 69% of the respondents expressed negative attitudes towards Trasyanka, while only 15% were indifferent and 16% were positive (Liankevich 2014: 12). Certainly, any attitude represents a complex phenomenon and includes many components. It is a common practice in language attitude studies to distinguish two main factors: status and solidarity, since negative evaluation of speakers of a certain variety in terms of social status does not necessarily mean the same low evaluation on the scale of solidarity; usually, this fact can explain relative stability of low-prestige dialects (see Peterson 2020, ch. 5).

In regard to the social status scale, it is very important to note that according to a very strong and persistent stereotype, usage of Trasyanka stigmatises its speaker as having a low educational level. This stereotype is based on the fact that higher education in Belarus (and the same was true for the situation during the Soviet times) could be obtained mostly in Russian. Consequently, any person while studying for a university degree or diploma of professional training in any field had more possibilities to acquire 'better' Russian (see below example 13). As a result, most former T-speakers and Belarusian dialects speakers shift to Russian in the process of education, and the majority of people still speaking Trasyanka are those with merely 7 or 8 years of school education received in rural Belarusian-language schools. Certainly, it does not mean that there is a full equivalence between speaking Trasyanka and poor education, and, as we will discuss later, someone's ability to speak Standard Russian does not imply an inevitable shift to it and using only Russian in any situation. However, the stereotype is very strong, and, most probably, a professor speaking Trasyanka, even outside classroom, will be treated suspiciously by his or her students, and a T-speaking doctor would not be able to get a position in a private medical clinic since well-to-do patients would have no trust in her or him. Personal stories of informants in our study confirm these assumptions, and in everyday conversations and discussions, people tend to express openly their prejudices against T-speakers as professionals.

(9) Speaker (male. approx. 60 yo, university degree, private conversation): *On iz t'ekh u kavo awdytoryja i trapka/takova uravn'a sp'icyal'ist.*

(He is one of those who had 'awdytoryja' and 'trapka' [R = auditor'ija, tr'apka], specialist of this level).

The stereotypes about T-speakers also ascribe to them such characteristics as low income, manual low-paid job, and overall low-class life-style reflected in certain clothes, eating habits, manners, etc. (see also Liankevich 2014). In other words, according to the stereotypes, T-speakers can be recognised by the way they behave and dress. Certainly, it does not mean the recognition would be accurate; what is important is if R-speakers would demonstrate similar presumptions about the strangers they encounter in the streets of Minsk. To test this hypothesis, a small-scale experiment was conducted by Irina Liskovets in 1999–2001.

Four R-speaking Minsk residents aged 20–35 (three females and one male, of whom two with university degrees, one student and one college graduate) were asked first to give a verbal portrait of a typical T-speaker. The attributes produced by all the experts were «деревенский» (rural), «некультурный» (uncultured), «примитивный» (primitive), and «язык малообразованных» (uneducated). It corresponds to C. Woolhiser's observation: 'For monolingual Russophones, Trasyanka is a mark of peasant origins, limited intelligence and a general lack of culture' (Woolhizer 2014: 111). A. Liankevichquotes her respondents' labelling Trasyanka as 'калгасны' (belonging to a collective farm, a term often used derogatorily about somebody's low-level habits and lifestyle) (Liankevich, 2014: 12).

Then the respondents were asked to guess what variant – Russian, Belarusian, or Trasyanka – would be used by a passer-by. After every guess, the researcher approached the person in question asking some question (in Russian since speaking Russian is a default choice for communication with strangers in Minsk). Overall, 20 subjects were evaluated in that way, and there was a clear pattern in experts' evaluations: while Russian was expected from young and well-dressed people, elder ones, especially in cheap and old-fashioned clothes, were guessed as T-speakers. In all six cases when two experts' opinions were elicited (individually) about the same person, their answers were identical.

Regarding the accuracy of the experts evaluations, in total there were three cases when they were wrong, and they confirm the same pattern. On the one hand, Trasyanka was erroneously attributed to two poorly dressed women in their fifties (and in one case there were two experts, and they expressed the same opinion); on the other hand, a young man in a suit and tie, who actually spoke Trasyanka, was mistaken for an R-speaker. This experiment proved the existence of a strong stereotype about the low social status of T-speakers.

In 2019, Irina Liskovets repeated this experiment with one of her former experts and got the same results: guesses about people's speech were based on their age and appearance. The only difference was that it turned out almost impossible to encounter actual T-speakers in the city center, and even in the outskirts of the city, in Zavodskoj district, where many recent migrants from rural areas reside, as only people over 50 answered in Trasyanka. In a way, the reality was brought in compliance with the stereotype turning it into a self-fulfilling predicament.

Another piece of evidence of the fact that R-speakers associate Trasyanka with a low social position can be found in the way they use it as a stylistic resort. By code-switching to Trasyanka when trying to portray certain people, R-speakers do not necessarily quote their speech as it is but can simply express their own lack of appreciation and negative feelings towards those people. In fact, as is often the case, those alleged T-speakers can speak Russian and not Trasyanka. This type of code switching, therefore, can be called linguistic appropriation. It can be illustrated by the following examples recorded during spontaneous interaction between Minsk R-speakers:

(10) Speaker (female, approx. 30–40 yo, university degree, private conversation, speaking about her neighbour): Kak babka na *bazare/ kol'ki stoic'*.
(Like a grandma at the farmers' market: how much is it)
(R = *na bazar'i: skol'ka stoit*, B = *na bazary: kol'ki kaštuje*.

(11) Speaker (female, approx. 30–40 yo, college graduate, private conversation, speaking about her Russian-speaking mother): *U γarošyk jej aboi nada // Ty by išč'o u cv'atočak kup'ila.*

(She needs <u>polka-dotted</u> wallpaper! Maybe you even need <u>flowery</u> ones!)

(R; v garo<u>šek, v</u> cv'itoč'ik, B= u γarošak, ukv 'etačku).

In both examples the speakers were actually R-speaking; however, to derogate them, the speakers used references both to their supposed low social status or 'bad taste' and to speaking Trasyanka, combining them in the stereotypical image of badly educated people of rural origin. This strategy – making an unpleasant and arrogant parody of somebody, especially one's political opponent, who speaks Trasyanka – is widely used in Belarusian popular culture (Woolhiser 2011: 43–45). The protests of 2020 use this technique rather widely, attributing Trasyanka to president Lukashenka, who does speak with a Belarusian accent but definitely not in Trasyanka per se. One of the popular memes of the year is the word '*aščuščenija*' *(feelings, R = ašč'ušč'enija, B =* adčuvann'i), pronounced in this way by Lukashenka in March 2020 and used as a banter at marches (see, e.g., Ivanov 2020).

In other words, attitudes to Trasyanka among R-speakers turn out to be negative on both status and solidarity scales – Trasyanka can be used as a means of alienation and distancing from the opponents, of construction their negative images.

Another interesting aspect of Minsk R-speakers' language attitudes concerns their notion of relations between Trasyanka and Belarusian, and some important changes can be revealed there. The majority of the respondents interviewed in 1999–2002 overtly expressed very favourable attitudes to Standard Belarusian; they considered it to be beautiful and elaborated while Trasyanka, in their opinions, definitely lacked these qualities. However, the following statement was extremely popular: Belarusian, being artificial and designed for official usage, is not, and cannot be, used in everyday communication. It meant it lacked certain registers, and, consequently, Trasyanka, an 'ugly' spoken variant, was seen as a substitute for these registers, the only option besides colloquial Russian. In this sense, Trasyanka could be mixed up with Belarusian in the eyes of R-speakers who used to have very little exposure to Standard Belarusian.

(12) Informant (Minsk-born male university student, interview): Many people consider that this [Belarusian] is a serf's language because many Belarusians who are from villages speak Trasyanka. And that's why many consider Trasyanka to be Belarusian.[2]

In this commentary, the use of a rather strong deteriorative epithet – 'kholopskij' (serfs') – in regard to the Belarusian language underlines not only its supposed rural origin but also low social position of its speakers.

However, some changes in this aspect can be attested if we consider recent data. During the follow-up interview with the same informant conducted in 2018, he, now a small business owner, claimed:

(13) [there is] too much of Belarusian around today. And you can easily say whether it is this filth [Trasyanka] or whether it is Belarusian.

This statement expressing, on the one hand, overtly negative attitudes to Trasyanka, on the other hand stresses the increase in exposure to Standard Belarusian and, as a consequence, higher awareness about the differences between Belarusian and Trasyanka among R-speakers, displayed as well by other respondents interviewed in 2018. Belarusian nowadays, as already mentioned, receives more support from nationally oriented youth activists, and its use, especially on the internet, became more popular, which promotes language awareness and helps to distinguish Standard Belarusian from Trasyanka even without actual knowledge of the language. Probably, public discussions on Trasyanka as a 'bad language' in the media and social networks contributed to the process as well. In this regard, R-speakers' attitudes to Trasyanka have become closer to the ideological discourse of Belarusian language activists.

11.4.2 Belarusian speakers

As already mentioned, Standard Belarusian in Minsk used to be spoken almost exclusively by the nationally oriented cultural elite and language activists. Representatives of Belarusian-speaking intellectuals regularly express strictly negative attitudes towards Trasyanka. They regard it as a danger to the very existence of Belarusian, stating Trasyanka would cast a black shadow over the Belarusian language. For instance, Henadz Buraukin, the former president of the Belarusian Language Society,[3] said in his interview to *Belorusskaya delovaya gazeta* (12 March 1999): 'Trasyanka is an index of crying ignorance, when two languages at once are rudely distorted: both the great Russian language and our own native Belarusian … it is what all normal cultured people should be ashamed of.' Trasyanka, therefore, is represented as an anomaly, challenging established cultural norms and dangerous for 'pure' languages. Moreover, as C. Woolhiser puts it, 'For many members of the Belarusophone opposition, Trasyanka has an even greater number of negative associations, including not only ignorance, but also conformism, opportunism, aggressiveness, and slavish deference to authority' [Woolhiser 2011: 50]. The words by a Belarusian author and activist M. Skobla, who called Trasyanka 'a Trojan horse of Russification',[4] can serve as evidence of this radical rejection of Trasyanka by the Belarusian intelligentsia (see more on this topic in: Liankevich 2014, Woolhiser 2014).

(14) Speaker (male, approx. 60 yo, University degree, interview): *γeta [Trasjanka] pav'inna pam'erc'i*

   (This [Trasjanka] must die).

(15) Speaker (female, approx. 40 yo, University degree, interview): *jany [T-speakers]... ni adnoj movy n'i v'edajuc'*.[5]

(They [T-speakers] don't know any language.)

More similar examples can be found in Liankievich (2011). However, not all Belarusian intellectuals are so radical in their disapproval of Trasyanka. Some of them, like Aleg Trusau, the former head of the Belarusian Language Society, express a more pragmatic attitude, regarding Trasyanka as a positive factor in deterring assimilation by Russian. According to this view, due to being a stage in shifting from Belarusian to Russian or vice versa (see above), Trasyanka can be instrumental in the gradual transition to Belarusian for Russian-speaking Belarusians providing them with several Belarusian elements and thus making the process easier: '*My advice* [to those who wish to transfer to Belarusian]: *speak Trasyanka. It is impossible to immediately start speaking* [Belarusian] *well. Time will pass and you will replace Russian words by Belarusian ones.*'[6] Trusau's view on the language shift in Belarus is also different from mainstream ones. Focusing on regional traits of Russian as spoken by Belarusians and separating it from 'mainland' Standard Russian, he argues that most people in Belarus in fact speak not Russian but Trasyanka, shifting, therefore, in the opposite direction, not towards Standard Russian but to the Belarusian language. Even if this position is not popular and looks more like wishful thinking, being expressed by an important public figure, it inevitably has some impact on public discussions about the linguistic situation in Belarus. Trasyanka, though, is not fully 'rehabilitated' by this approach; it is presented as something natural, inevitable and useful for the moment; however, as a transitional phenomenon, it is due to disappear in the future.

11.4.3 Trasyanka speakers

Attitudes to Trasyanka on the part of Russian and Belarusian speakers, i.e. those who never used it or have chosen to abandon it, are, therefore, extremely negative; it tends to be seen as a disgrace and even threat to 'proper' languages by outsiders. Moreover, this view, to a considerable extent, is interiorised by T-speakers.

Of all 18 Minsk T-speakers interviewed, 5 defined their speech as Belarusian and 13 as mixed speech, with nobody claiming to speak Russian. All of them had migrated to Minsk in the past, and all of them felt the difference between their speech and those of their urban-born neighbours. They did not claim to be bilingual; however, four informants mentioned their ability to vary their speech depending on their addressee and settings. Most importantly, all the respondents admitted shame to be their dominant feeling about Trasyanka. They referred to it as an incorrect, 'bad' language, which is appropriate to be used only with members of their circle (mostly the people of the same origin).

(16) Informant (female, rural-born, approx. 40–50 yo, uncompleted secondary education, interview): *Tak slovy jak'ija zabudź'eś dyk skažaś*

> b'ilaruskaje/ tože ž n'ačoɣa/ pajmuc' // ws'e ž tak//. tak w ɣoradź'e starajems'a kab pa-rusku / a doma tam / jak skažaš to i ladna / što ž tut// khto ž ne pajm'oc'// von ɣal'a ɣaradskaja naša /i to ws'o pan'imajec' i sam<u>ane l'ep'ej za nas</u> ɣavoryc'//
>
> Researcher: A doma kak gavar'**it'**e//
>
> Informant: Pa-b'ilarusk'i// čaɣo ž tam// u m'an'**e** mužyk z dź'arewn'i//
>
> Researcher: A d'**et'**i pa-rusk'i//
>
> Informant: Da// jany ž u ɣoradz'e naradz'**il'**is'a// u nas tak / khto u ɣoradz'e / tyja pa-rusk'i / khto u dz'arewn'i / tyje jak u dz'arewn'i// tak tol'k'i na l'**u**<u>dz'akh užo</u> <u>staraješs'a</u>//
>
> (– If you forget some words, you just say Belarusian ones – it is OK, they'll understand it anyway. Everybody does. It is in town where we try to say it in Russian but at home whatever you say it's OK, who won't understand? Even Galya, our city native, even she understands everything and speaks <u>not better than we do</u>.
> – And how do you speak at home?
> – Belarusian, why not? My husband is <u>from a village</u> as well.
> – And do children speak Russian?
> – Yes, they were born in the city. Here it is like this: who was born in the city they speak Russian, who was born in the village they speak like in the village, it is <u>only in public you try hard.</u>)

Trasyanka sounds stigmatising to the extent that a person whose parents speak Trasyanka may try to hide this fact, for example by not answering the interviewer's direct question about the language used in the family, or behaving as if offended by the question.

> (17) Speaker (female, 30 yo, university degree):
> Researcher: A doma kak gavar'**il'**i va<u>šy rad'it'il'</u>i//
> Informant: kak v s'imje gavar'**il'**i// stranny vapros// moj ac'ec v goradz'e davno žyv'ot…

(How did your parents speak?

My family language? Weird question. My dad has been an urban dweller for a long time).

(Later in the interview, the informant spokes about her embarrassment because of her father's 'improper' language).

It is not uncommon also to witness children being embarrassed by their T-speaking parents. When adult T-speakers are approached by R-speaking strangers somewhere outside, their children may tend to answer the questions on behalf of their parents rather than let them communicate by themselves though the same situation can hardly happen with R-speaking parents. During her fieldwork in the early 2000s, Irina Liskovets experimented with addressing several T-speaking women accompanied by their teenaged children with a simple question in Russian asking them to show the way to a supermarket or pharmacy nearby. In all cases, the children were those who answered instead of their mothers. The experiment was done in Zavodskoj district of Minsk where the share of new migrants from villages was the greatest in the city at that time.

Similar strong negative attitudes towards speakers of low prestige dialects were attested in different studies all over the world (see, e.g., Luhman 1990; Chand 2009; Clarke 2010). However, more revealing parallels can be found in the context of migration: the second-generation migrants with native or near-native competence in a majority language tend to be ashamed of their parents' poor language performance, and, consequently, there are 'tensions related to children's role as translators, mediators and interpreters' for their parents (Foner and Kasinitz 2007: 279). In the authors' personal experience, the same behaviour when children changed roles with their parents in dealing with strangers occurred in a Latino neighbourhood in Oakland, California, and in interaction with labour immigrants from Central Asia and their children in St. Petersburg, Russia.

Summing up, we can make a supposition that representatives of the three main groups of Minsk residents, despite being quite different in many other aspects and having different grounds for their motivations, share strongly negative attitudes towards Trasyanka. They ascribe the following characteristics to this variety:

- low prestige related to its rural origin;
- mixed and 'corrupted' linguistic nature;
- aesthetic ugliness;
- stigmatising role in marking its user as a native of rural area, a person with bad education and a primitive lifestyle.

In this sense, Trasyanka 'as a discursive object serves not merely to describe, but to stigmatize and reprove' [Woolhiser 2011: 50], it refers to the marginalised minority, formed not by ethnicity or social status themselves, but rather by the combination of its members' migrant past and their inability to comply in full with the linguistic norms of Belarusian capital, i.e. to shift to Russian. As a result, we may say that Trasyanka in Minsk is seen by many, including some of its speakers, as a transitional phenomenon; something one has to try to get rid of as soon as possible to avoid embarrassment. Unsurprisingly, being both transitional and stigmatised, Trasyanka is doomed to become an endangered variety.

11.5 Concluding discussion: The decline of Trasyanka

Field observations reveal that the share of people speaking Trasyanka in Minsk has been diminishing over the course of the last decades. There is an evident lessening of Trasyanka's presence in the city's soundscape: it is less heard in the streets and on public transport, in clinics and even markets. As already mentioned, it has become almost impossible to encounter T-speakers, at least those who are unable to 'pretend' to be R-speakers in public, in the city center, and even in the industrial districts where many former rural migrants work and live, Trasyanka is spoken mostly by elderly people.

As Yury Koryakov (2002), in his description of the distribution of languages in Belarus, once pointed out, the bigger the city, the stronger Russian is in it (see also Hetschel et al. 2015). Minsk nowadays is a big predominantly Russian-speaking place – so Russian is growing stronger and stronger there, pushing Trasyanka off the stage. On the one hand, it is part of the same process which is attested in many investigations in the whole country (Hetschel 2017; Kittel et al. 2010; Woolhiser 2011): there is a shift to Russian from dialect Belarusian and Trasyanka, going along with urbanisation and the increase of educational level, and this trend started long before 1991 when Belarus turned into an independent state. On the other hand, Minsk is, and always has been, a leader in this respect, with Russian being a default language here, and all deviations from it treated as a failure to become a city dweller, to urbanise 'properly'.

As a result of the general spread of Standard Russian in Belarus, newcomers to Minsk from other regions of the country, especially the younger ones, nowadays are less likely to lack proficiency in Russian. At the same time, there are less and less domains for speaking Trasyanka, which is both evidence of and a contribution to its decline.

During Irina Liskovets's research in the early 2000s, she encountered several cases revealing the effect of a workplace on attitudes and language practices. She discovered that R-speaking engineers who had had to abandon their professional careers to earn money as street vendors and small traders had changed their speech patterns and began to use certain elements of Trasyanka, such as fricative [ɣ] or 'wrong' stress. The number of Russian-Trasyanka code-switches also increased in their speech. In cases when such persons' mother tongue had been Belarusian, or, which was much more common, Trasyanka, and they had once transferred to Russian, the Trasyanka environment could easily make them reverse to Trasyanka. On the contrary, if the environment was R-speaking, the T-speakers were forced to 'watch their language' and speak 'proper' Russian, which led to a step-by-step abandoning of Trasyanka for good.

To compare data from different linguistic environments, the observations were made in two workshops of a big Minsk plant. The first one was manned by R-speakers, and the only T-speaking woman showed a great variance in her speech, with some utterances being almost Standard Russian. She also tended to start her utterances in Russian and gradually lessening the control over her speech, switching to Trasyanka. In the second workshop, Trasyanka was spoken by everyone including one woman born in Minsk to an R-speaking family (see example 16). The speech of this woman with her colleagues was indisputably Trasyanka, but during the interview with a Russian-speaking interviewer, she was speaking in Russian with minor dialect features, proving her full competence in it.

With more and more workplaces becoming mainly R-speaking, Trasyanka is being pushed out of the working place: the later observations done in 2018, 2019 and 2020 found absolutely no Trasyanka among traders working in the biggest Minsk farmers' market; Trasyanka was spoken only by the farmers from rural areas selling their own products and not by residents of Minsk.

Therefore, it seems obvious that Trasyanka in Minsk is dying. Partly, it is a part of a natural process of further language standardisation. First, in rural Belarusian schools, Standard Russian is taught better now, and the dominance of Russian mass media provides easy access to the language all over the country. Second, obligatory school teaching of Standard Belarusian seems to have resulted in better knowledge of it by the younger generation and better awareness of the differences between Belarusian and Trasyanka.

At the same time, this standardisation process is facilitated by very strong negative attitudes to Trasyanka inherent for all Minsk residents, including T-speakers themselves. The low, or, to be more precise, negative prestige of Trasyanka in terms of social status is not counterpoised by any warm feelings towards its speakers as members of some traditional/rural/local community. They are seen as migrants and are judged according to their relative success, including linguistic adaptation. Moreover, an important shift in the system of attitudes towards Russian and Belarusian also has an impact on the position of Trasyanka. As the researchers in this field have shown, Belarusian has become more respected, it is associated with ethnic history and identity and can, therefore, serve for the purpose of solidarity; the quality lacked by Trasyanka (see Woolhiser 2013; Liankievic 2013).

As a result, Trasyanka is confronted not just by one but by two standards and also by two ideologies. Belarusian national revival which is on the rise nowadays demands the use of 'pure' Belarusian, and if monolingualism in it is currently impossible, there should be stable bilingualism with a clear-cut distinction between Belarusian and Russian. The Russian normative orientation is also very strict; it is combined with a strong monolingual bias (Baranova and Fedorova 2020), and any deviations from Standard Russian are disregarded as a failure to achieve the high 'speech culture level' – a term invented by Soviet linguists to address the issues of social stratification. In some aspects, the status of Trasyanka in Minsk looks similar to the status of so-called *prostorechie* ('simple speech') in Russia (Fedorova 2020). *Prostorechie* is an urban phenomenon; the term refers to the speech of poorly educated city dwellers, often of rural origin, who are unable to master the *kodifitsirovannyj literaturnyj yazyk* (the codified literary language), the version of Standard Russian used in official communication. Like T-speakers, people speaking in *prostorechie* are treated as 'bad speakers', lacking certain linguistic skills. Both Trasyanka and *prostorechie* then are treated as deviations, not linguistic systems of their own, and, consequently, in this perspective, it is impossible to be bilingual in Trasyanka and Standard Russian since the only reason to keep speaking Trasyanka, according to popular attitudes, is inability to get rid of it.

In a sense, therefore, Trasyanka in Minsk is treated more like a transitional phenomenon on the way from a dialect to a standardised form of a language (cf. Trudgill 1986) but this transition occurs in very hostile and intolerant conditions, demanding fast and complete language shift. At the same time, the existence of two standards makes Trasyanka's hybrid nature evident for speakers. For linguists, Trasyanka is a good example that supports the idea formulated by François Grosjean (1989), Peter Muysken (2000), Peter Auer (2007), and others: namely, that the existence of individual isolated languages with clear-cut borders should not be taken for granted. However, for non-professionals, governed by the domineering standard language ideology, Trasyanka is an emblem of all possible linguistic and social vices: it is non-standard, non-pure, refers to a migrant origin, a poor education and a lack of socio-adaptive skills. In this perspective, Trasyanka looks very ambivalent. On the one hand, it definitely exists as a form of speech since there are those 'half-speakers' allegedly unable to speak purely; on the other hand, it does not exist as a linguistic object, as a language per se which can be learned and used alongside other, 'real', languages. Naturally, actual patterns of language use are not limited to this picture dictated by standard language bias but the force of linguistic prejudices is strong, and it leaves very little hope for Trasyanka in Minsk

Notes

1 More examples are provided in Budz'ma online magazine. See: https://budzma.by/news/mikhas-skobla-adkazaw-alyehu-trusavu-pra-trasyanku.html (accessed January 2, 2021).
2 Quotations from the interviews and other sources in Standard Russian without code switching are given in English translation.
3 Founded in 1989, Frantsishak Skaryna Belarusian Language Society has been organizing numerous campaigns of promotion of the Belarusian language.
4 See M. Skobla's Facebook post from October 2018 quoted by www.budzma.by website: https://budzma.by/news/mikhas-skobla-adkazaw-alyehu-trusavu-pra-trasyanku.html (accessed June 14, 2020).
5 Interestingly, this very remark deviates from the norms of Standard Belarusian: the speaker uses Russian form *ni adnoj* instead of *n'ivodnaj*.
6 See A. Trusau's interview of 2013 at: https://nn.by/?c=ar&i=103005 (accessed January 2, 2021).

References

Auer, Peter (2007). The monolingual bias in bilingualism research, or: why bilingual talk is (still) a challenge for linguistics. In: Heller, M. (ed.) *Bilingualism: A Social Approach*. Palgrave, pp. 319–339.
Baranova, Vlada and Fedorova, Kapitolina (2020). Overcoming aggressive monolingualism: prejudices and linguistic diversity in Russian megapolises. *Open Linguistics* 6, 672–689.
Blommaert, Jan (2010). *The Sociolinguistics of Globalization*. Cambridge: Cambridge University Press.

Chand, Vineeta (2009). [V]at is going on? Local and global ideologies about Indian English. *Language in Society* 38 (4), 393–419.

Clarke, Sandra (2010). *Newfoundland and Labrador English*. Edinburgh University Press.

Coupland, Nikolas (2000). Sociolinguistic prevarication about Standard English. *Journal of Sociolinguistics* 4 (4): 622–634.

Cychun, Henadz (2000). Крэалізаваны прадукт. Трасянка як аб'ект лінгвістычнага даследавання [Creolised product. Trasyanka as an object for linguistic research]. *Arche* 6, 2000. https://web.archive.org/web/20050501081414/http://arche.home.by/6-2000/cychu600.html (Accessed Jan. 2, 2021).

Fedorova, Kapitolina (2020). Prostorečie (Gorodskoe) [Simple speech]. In: Greenberg, Marc L. et al. (eds.). *Encyclopedia of Slavic Languages and Linguistics Online*. Brill. https://referenceworks.brillonline.com/entries/encyclopedia-of-slavic-languages-and-linguistics-online/prostorecie-gorodskoe-COM_031993 (Accessed Jan. 2, 2021).

Foner, Nancy, and Kasinitz, Philip (2007). The second generation. In: Waters, Mary C. and Ueda, Reed (eds.). *The New Americans: A Guide to Immigration since 1965*. Harvard University Press, pp. 270–282.

Grosjean, François (1989). Neurolinguists, beware! The bilingual is not two monolinguals in one person. *Brain and Language* 36, 3–15.

Hentschel, Gerd (2013). Белорусский, русский и белорусско-русская смешанная речь. [Belarusian, Russian and the Belarusian-Russian Mixed Speech]. *Вопросы языкознания* 2013 (1). 53–76.

Hentschel, Gerd (2017). Eleven questions and answers about Belarusian-Russian mixed speech ('Trasyanka'). *Russian Linguistics* 41 (1), 17–42.

Hentschel, Gerd, Brüggemann, Mark, Geiger, Hanna and Zeller, Yan Patrick (2015). The linguistic and political orientation of young Belarusian adults between East and West or Russian and Belarusian. *International Journal of the Sociology of Language* 236, 133–154.

Ivanov, Kirill (2020) *Ашчушчэния, тихари и Ніна. Краткий словарь белорусской революции* [Aščuščenija, tikhari and Nina. Short dictionary of Belarusian revolution]. https://gazetaby.com/post/ashchushcheniya-tixari-i-nina-kratkij-slovar-belor/169351/0/ (Accessed Jan. 2, 2021).

Kittel, Bernhard, Lindner, Diana, Tesch, Sviatlana and Hentschel, Gerd (2010). Mixed language usage in Belarus: the sociolinguistic background of language choice. *International Journal of the Sociology of Language* 206, 47–71.

Koryakov, Yury (2002). Языковая ситуация в Белоруссии [Language Situation in Belarus]. *Вопросы языкознания* 2002 (2), 109–127.

Luhman, Reid (1990). Appalachian English stereotypes: Language attitudes in Kentucky. *Language in Society* 19, 331–348.

Liankevich, Alena (2011). Стаўленне да беларускай літаратурнай мовы і змешанага маўлення ў медыя-дыскурсе (на матэрыяле публікацый у газеце «Звязда») [Attitude towards Belarusian literary language and mixed speech in media discouse on the materials of publications in newspaper Zvyazda]. In: Веснік БДУ. Сер. 4. 2011. № 3, 34–28.

Liankevich, Alena (2014). Беларуская мова і змешаныя коды ў сацыялінгвістычным і псіхалінгвістычным аспектах: катэгорыя адносін да мовы ў грамадстве [The Belarusian language and mixed codes in a sociocholinguistic and psycholinguistic perspectives: the category of language attitudes in the society]. PhD thesis. Minsk.

Liankievič Uladzimir (2013). Выбор языка и речевая (не) аккомодация условиях в двуязычной коммуникации в Беларуси: На основе полевых экспериментов в Минске и Дзержинске [Language Choice and (Non-)Accommodation in Bilingual Communication in Belarus: Based on Field Experiments in the Streets of Minsk and Dzyarzhynsk] Slavia - časopis pro slovanskou filologii 3: 333–346.

Mechkovskaja, Nina (2014). Die weißrussische Trasjanka und der ukrainische Suržyk: Quasi-ethnische, russifizierte Substandards in der Geschichte der sprachlichen Situation. In: Gerd Hentschel, Oleksandr Taranenko and SiarhejZaprudski (eds.). *Trasjanka und Suržyk – gemischte weißrussisch-russische und ukrainisch-russische Rede. Sprachlicher Inzest in Weißrussland und der Ukraine?* Frankfurt-am-Mein: Peter Lang. P. 53–89.

Milroy, James (2001). Language ideologies and the consequences of standardization. *Journal of Sociolinguistics* 5 (4): 530–555.

Muyskin, Pieter (2000). *Bilingual Speech. A Typology of Code Variety-Mixing.* Cambridge: Cambridge University Press.

Myers-Scotton, Carol (2002). *Contact Linguistics: Bilingual Encounters and Grammatical Outcomes.* Oxford: Oxford UP.

Neustupný, Jiří V. (1994). Problems in English contact discourse and language planning. In T. Kandiah and J. Kwan-Terry (eds.). *English and Language Planning: A Southeast Asian Contribution.* Singapore: Academic Press, pp. 50–69.

Peterson, Elizabeth (2020). *Making Sense of 'Bad English'. An Introduction to Language Attitudes and Ideologies.* Routledge.

Romaine, Suzanne (1988). *Pidgin and Creole Languages.* London: Longman.

Selinker, Larry (1972). Interlanguage. *International Review of Applied Linguistics in Language Teaching* 10 (1–4), 209–241.

Todd, Loreto (1990). *Pidgins and Creoles* (2nd edition). London: Routledge.

Trudgill, Peter (1986). *Dialects in Contact.* Oxford: Oxford UP.

Woolhiser, Curt (2011). 'Belarusian Russian': sociolinguistic status and discursive representations. In: Rudolf Muhr (ed.), *Non-dominating Varieties of Pluricentric Languages. Getting the Picture.* In memory of Prof. Michael Clyne. Wien et al., Peter Lang, pp. 11–50.

Woolhiser, Curt (2013). New Speakers of Belarusian: Metalinguistic Discourse, Social Identity, and Language Use. www.academia.edu/4611831/New_Speakers_of_Belarusian_Metalinguistic_Discourse_Social_Identity_and_Language_Use

Woolhiser, Curt (2014). The Russian Language in Belarus: Language Use, Speaker Identities and Metalinguistic Discourse. In L. Ryazanova (ed.), *The Russian Language Outside the Nation: Speakers and Identities.* Edinburgh: Edinburgh University Press.

Zaprudsky, Siarhej (2008). Маўленчая акамадацыя і пераключэнне кодаў у працэсе міжкультурнай камунікацыі: выпадак Беларусі [Speech accommodation and code-switching in the process of intercultural communication: the case of Belarus]. In: Hentschel, G. and Zaprudski, S. (eds.), *Studia Slavica Oldenburgensia 17: Belarusian Trasjanka and Ukrainian Suržyk: Structural and Social Aspects of Their Description and Categorization.* Oldenburg, pp. 57–97.

12 Language problems in interactions between locals and foreign tourists in the city of Prague

A language management study

V. Dovalil

12.1 Introduction: Background information and research questions

This chapter aims at analyzing the language use and language choices in the area of international tourism in the capital of the Czech Republic, which – along with the current migration and economic development – contributes to superdiversification of this country.[1] First, an overview of tourism is sketched drawing upon statistical data, which show the macro-perspective. Then, the micro-perspective is the focus. It concentrates on individual interactions in cafés and restaurants, including the problems and language management processes in which these problems are solved.

Generally speaking, the total number of tourists coming to the Czech Republic from abroad has been constantly growing since 1989. Disruptions of this global tendency in the late 1990s and after 2000 were only short interruptions of a continuous development as is shown in Figure 12.1.

Although the Czech Republic is not as prominent a member of the European group of international tourist destinations as are France, Italy, the Canary Islands, Spain or Croatia, tourism represents a stable source of income of the Czech economy in the tertiary sector. Its proportion amounts to 2.9% of the GDP, which is a higher proportion than in the case of agriculture. The average foreign exchange revenues from tourism have been reaching more than 7 billion USD every year since 2008 (Palatková and Zichová 2014: 209). Before the corona pandemic in 2020, which will have a severe impact on the economy of international tourism, this income amounted to 164.9 billion Czech crowns (CZK) in 2018 and to 168.5 billion CZK (= 7.5 billion USD) in 2019.[2]

According to the Czech Statistical Office, 10.9 million foreign tourists visited the Czech Republic in 2019, which slightly exceeded the total population of the country with 10.639.939 inhabitants (as of December 31, 2019). The corresponding total number of foreign tourists for 2018 amounted to 10.635.645, which represented an increase by 5.6% in comparison with 2017. More than 2 million tourists came from Germany in 2019, representing almost one fifth of all foreign tourists. This proportion has remained stable for many

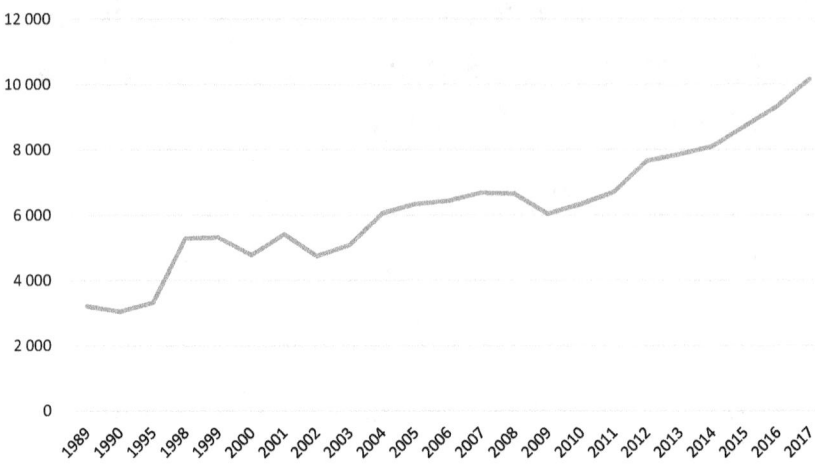

Figure 12.1 Foreign tourists in the Czech Republic since 1989 (in thousands). (Source: Czech Statistical Office).

years. Two other neighboring countries follow with a substantial distance – Slovakia with almost 750.000 and Poland with over 670.000 visitors. The last neighboring country, Austria, was represented among the top ten countries with almost 300.000 tourists only in 2018. Ukraine, from where almost 272.000 tourists arrived, occupied the tenth position in 2019. This country recorded the most dynamic increase in 2019 (by more than one quarter). In contrast to the stable growth during the previous years, the total number of visitors coming from China and South Korea decreased by 1% and 7.4% respectively.

The regional distribution of foreign visitors within the Czech Republic is far from balanced. The capital Prague was the most visited administrative unit with 6.786.151 tourists in 2019. This is an increase by 1.4 % when compared with the year 2018. Related to the total number of 1.324.277 inhabitants as of March 2020, Prague is one of the most visited cities in Europe ever, with one resident getting more than five foreign tourists. Thus, two out of three foreign tourists coming to the Czech Republic visit its capital. The second, third and fourth regions were the South-Moravian (756.416 tourists), the Karlsbad (719.328 tourists) and the South-Bohemian regions (636.206 tourists) respectively.

As these basic statistics show, it can be expected that everyday interactions between tourists and the local staff of restaurants and cafés have become commonplace, which may generate manifold language problems. Regarding language management theory, language problems are defined by social actors' noting a deviation from their expectations and by evaluating these noted deviations negatively.[3] Hence, language problems are not objective phenomena. Drawing upon these circumstances, the following research questions are raised:

Table. 12.1 Foreign tourists in the Czech Republic in 2019 and in 2018 (top 10 countries)

Country	Number of tourists 2019 (in total)	Number of tourists 2018 (in total)	Change (%) 2019/2018	Change (%) 2018/2017
Germany	2.075.956	2.033.065	2.2	3.6
Slovakia	749.977	734.910	2.6	7.8
Poland	672.571	620.414	8.4	7.8
China	612.048	619.877	-1.0	26.5
USA	583.614	555.736	5.3	2.8
Russia	564.794	545.406	3.8	-0.5
Great Britain	495.572	496.807	0.1	5.7
Italy	409.623	409.903	0.3	5.2
South Korea	384.532	416.243	-7.4	0.2
Ukraine	271.933	211.292	28.7	
Austria	not among top 10	299.162		2.8

(Source: Czech Statistical Office, March 2020).

1) How do foreign tourists solve their language problems in Prague when they need to communicate with local employees of restaurants, cafés or tourism agencies, and vice versa?
2) Which languages are chosen, or preferred in these interactions?

12.2 Theoretical basis and method of data collection: Participant observation

Language choices are results of decision-making processes, which are influenced both by individual experiences and by social structures. Therefore, it is necessary to have a theoretical framework that is able to cover the dynamics of such processes, and to structure them in transparent phases. For these reasons, language management theory is particularly useful (Nekvapil and Sherman 2015; Nekvapil 2016; Dovalil and Šichová 2017; Fairbrother et al. 2018; Kimura and Fairbrother 2020; Marriott 1991). It is sometimes designated as a theory concerning language problems.

The crucial notion of language management is defined as behavior toward language, which is metalinguistic in nature. Language management theory differentiates between the generation of utterances (including their perception) on the one hand, and their management on the other. Language management processes are based on the actors' mutual expectations – if they are fulfilled, there is nothing to manage and the actors achieve their communication goals. The management process is triggered when a deviation from these expectations is noted. Once it is noted, it may be evaluated, or not. The evaluative phase may turn out positive (gratification of the deviation) or negative. The latter may bring about the necessity to design an adjustment to solve the problem. And if adjustments are designed, they may be implemented in interactions, or not. This concise description indicates that the management process may finish in each phase, and it also manifests its cyclic nature. Given this overview, it is useful to add that language problems may also be anticipated before the actors experience them (more details concerning this pre-interaction management are provided by Nekvapil and Sherman 2009).

The whole process may take place both at the micro-level (simple management), or it may involve institutions at the macro-level in some phases (organised management). Three levels influencing the successful course in terms of accomplishing the actors' goals are identified – (1) management of socioeconomic circumstances, under which the process takes place, (2) communicative management, and (3) management of the language structures, i.e. linguistic management in the narrow sense. The linguistic management (third level) – which applies to the knowledge of vocabulary, grammar, pronunciation, or spelling – may fail when it is blocked by circumstances at the first or second level (for more details elaborating on the aspects as sketched above, see Nekvapil and Sherman 2015; Nekvapil 2016; Dovalil and Šichová 2017; Fairbrother et al. 2018; Kimura and Fairbrother 2020; Marriott 1991).[4]

All these crucial features of language management are present in the decision-making processes in which individual actors at the micro-level choose a language to accomplish their communication goals in their individual interactions. To project the aforementioned theoretical basis into the research questions, the analysis concentrates on the simple management of language problems occurring in communication between foreign tourists and the staff of restaurants (cafés) as the main actors participating in these processes. Their fundamental expectations consist in making themselves understood. In terms of their social status, these actors are endowed with approximately equal power. However, this equality may be disrupted, e.g., in critical situations in which the staff depends on the customers' cooperative behavior. What is referred to in this context are disputes between the customers and the staff in which a customer is not willing to pay the bill and the staff has to call in police to restore the power relations. This kind of dependence may also have an impact on the language choices.

The data consists of 30 participant observations of interactions, 19 interactions with the actors of the participant observations and three conversations with tourism agency employees. 27 observations were conducted in the city and three observations in a restaurant in a shopping mall in the outskirts of Prague.

In terms of the classification of this method, my role mostly corresponded to the concealed observer (Lamnek 2010: 511). My identity as a researcher, including the real purpose of my presence in these situations, did not have to be revealed. I entered the easily accessible field of observation of cafés and restaurants (Lamnek 2010: 531–534) and acted like a regular customer. Having sat down at a table and ordered some meal or drink, I usually started reading a book or a newspaper, or working with my computer. Behaving like a normal customer, I could begin to observe what was happening around me. I was able to maintain both a necessary detachment and personal involvement (Lamnek

2010: 529). In this respect, my role can be classified as complete identification with the field, or complete participation ('vollständige Identifikation mit dem Feld (vollständige Teilnahme)' in German; Lamnek 2010: 524), according to which the observed persons do not know the real identity of the researcher. In this situation, the researcher is allowed to interact with the observed persons in as natural a way as possible.[5] I usually remained passive and did not intervene in interactions of the observed persons. I concentrated on their language use and foreign-language choices. Hence, no sociological data characterising the observed persons were gathered. The relevant data were recorded by means of field notes, which could be written down immediately during the observation. According to the recommendations summarised by Lamnek (2010: 559–560), the usual data were recorded: time and place of the observation and the main points of the summary of the event. Particularly important parts of sequences or expressions were noted down as exactly as possible. However, not each of the observations turned out to be equally relevant, of course. The length of a typical observation depended on suitable opportunities and varied between 15 minutes and one hour and a half.

Another set of important data represents my own occasional interactions with the actors of the participant observations. In such situations, the focus of my role moved toward the type of the participator as observer: I became primarily participator of the situation and secondarily observer (Lamnek 2010: 525). These interactions could not be planned in advance and depended on appropriate situations. Overall, this happened 19 times. The interactions with the tourists took place in English as a lingua franca, with the exception of German-speaking persons, which I addressed in German.[6] Conversations with the Czech employees were held in Czech. Opportunities to enter the interactions between waiters and tourists arose typically when a problem was being solved. I could take advantage of acting like a regular customer who was willing to help, which enabled me to maintain a relatively natural contact with both actors (staff and tourists) after the problem had been solved. In this way, it was possible to continue communicating and to add several questions to gather some more data.

Surprisingly enough, some Asian or German-speaking tourists as well as waiters who were not too busy outside lunch or dinner time were quite talkative. In such situations, I asked the employees about how often they needed to use foreign languages and which ones, or which language problems they had experienced. Continuing the talks with tourists, I concentrated on their experiences with foreign languages in the Czech Republic. In order to legitimise my interest in nine cases, I just said I worked as a linguist in the end. Thus, I revealed a part of my real identity, but I did not communicate the main purpose of the small talk anyway. After that, I said goodbye, left the situation and put down the field notes.

The smallest part of the data comes from my conversations with employees of three tourism agencies operating in Prague. I addressed them as a person organising a program on behalf of a group of foreign tourists coming from various countries. With this identity of a complete participator, I was interested in sightseeing tours in Prague and a trip to the Karlštejn castle. I focused on how flexible the agencies were in terms of language accommodation.

The data were collected in two phases. The first period took place in the spring and summer of 2017, the second one in December 2018 and January 2019. Several individual observations were added accidentally in October, November and December 2019.

12.3 Language accommodation in international tourism: Language problems and language choices

International tourism represents one of the largest international trades in the world; it is a global cultural industry, mobilising people, culture and money (Heller et al. 2014: 427). Since this branch is essentially influenced by the interplay of demand and supply, we can raise the question of the extent to which a country comes up with which competitive advances. Heller et al. (2014: 430) refer to 'monetizing the touristic potential' in this context. As aforementioned, foreign tourists come to the Czech Republic in order to visit Prague above all. Apart from its capital, they visit other historical towns, castles, chateaus, galleries and museums.[7] Yet another important reason is doing shopping.[8] In terms of such competitive advances, Austria is taken to be the main competitor of the Czech Republic (Palatková and Zichová 2014: 210).

The findings of the research are structured as follows: First, the economic basis of the supply-demand-interplay is discussed in connection with the socio-economic management. Then, concrete results of the observations showing specific patterns of language use are analyzed. They start with the issue of the language of the first contact and go on to German-related aspects. Findings concerning interactions with Russian- and Slovak-speaking tourists are presented afterwards. The next part is devoted to observations of the interactions of persons coming from Asian countries, after which avoidance strategies are analyzed. The last part of the analyses deals with various functions of Czech.

12.3.1 Supply and demand as crucial features of socio-economic management

It is evident that foreign language skills play an important role as a part of this competition in the post-modern era of globalisation and that international tourism represents one of the prototypical domains in which languages are commodified (Heller, Pujolar and Duchêne 2014; Heller 2010: 108). The economic value of foreign language skills plays a prominent role in these processes (Ammon 2015: 853–864; Costa 2019: 201–202; Marriott 1991). Heller, Pulolar and Duchêne (2014) point out that not only (foreign) languages, but also local identities and cultures are commodified. Heller et al. (2014: 441) see local languages 'being, in the first instance, fully commodified as an exotic marker of Otherness, and, in the second instance, "spectacularised" as a performance of place-based authenticity by a local'.

Good supply-sided foreign language knowledge is an unambiguous expression of the socioeconomic management which stimulates the establishment of (not necessarily only short-term) social networks of enterpreneurs/employees and their customers (level of communicative management; see Dovalil and Šichová 2017: 22–23).[9] As it does pay off to have a good command of foreign languages in these networks, it often makes the people working in international tourism improve their competence in foreign languages. In other words, the linguistic management in the narrow sense is further driven.

Using the customers' language in terms of *the customer is the king* represents a stable component of polite behavior toward foreign tourists, which substantially influences their contentment and comfort (Ammon 2018: 14–15). At the same time, Ammon (2018: 17) warns against any simplistic interpretation of this principle, because foreign visitors may also want to use local languages, or do not wish to be discouraged from speaking them (for approaches applying the concept of face, see O'Driscoll 2001). Politeness depends on individual contexts, and it is a standard factor of the economics of tourism (Palatková and Zichová 2014: 210). These authors refer to their qualitative research according to which foreign visitors coming to the Czech Republic consider as factors of satisfaction above all the culture-related activities, sport events, quality of catering, and the attitudes of local people toward the foreign tourists. On the other hand, the most frequent causes of dissatisfaction on the part of tourists are the relatively low foreign language skills of the local population, quality of communication services, the price level in terms of the price-performance ratio, and the quality of information services (ibid.). All these aspects co-determine the socioeconomic management.

The language accommodation strategies are considered by Prague tourism agencies as obvious. If possible, they try to avoid lingua franca communication (for details, see Costa 2019: 202). They operate – not only online – in the following 10 languages: English, German, Chinese, Japanese, Russian, Italian, Spanish, French, Portuguese and Polish. However, guided sightseeing tours and other parts of programs for tourists in Prague (trips, organisation of visits of culture events such as concerts, exhibitions etc.) are available in several more additional languages (e.g., in Dutch, Hungarian, Korean or Danish). Electronic devices with recorded basic information as well as detailed lectures and commentaries about historic sights and works of art in the form of apps have become a part of standard equipment of big agencies. These apps no longer represent additional costs for the suppliers of these services.

Entrepreneurs in other branches which primarily depend on tourism (restaurant services) act similarly. As an expression of pre-interaction management, menus in restaurants and cafés are – not only in the city of Prague – regularly translated into English, approximately in every fifth restaurant also into German and/or Russian.[10] This goes hand in hand with the required foreign language skills on the part of local employees. Prague waiters consider basic knowledge of English as 'standard' or 'obvious'.[11] From time to time, the employees also have some knowledge of German or Russian, because 'it also pays off'. Combinations of languages without English were not encountered. Interestingly enough, the knowledge of German is commented on with restraint and its command seems to be underestimated. This also holds for domains other than the language use in restaurant services in which restrained attitudes toward German come out (more details concerning, e.g., international research projects can be found in Dovalil and Sherman 2010).

12.3.2 Language of the first contact as a problem and German-related observations

What may cause problems at the very beginning is the question 'how one is supposed to recognise at all' which tourists are going to use which language. Obviously, this applies to the German-related cases, particularly when the local staff is willing to speak German. The employees mentioned the habits of German-speaking tourists to start the conversation in English and to switch – potentially – to German on the initiative of the staff. The problem of choosing a language other than English for the first contact does not arise in such situations in which a waiter hears (and understands) the language of those who are entering the restaurant and he himself prefers German to English. This pattern can also be observed in the case of Russian.

However, with the exceptions mentioned above, the language of the first contact is regularly English. Foreign tourists as well as the employees of the restaurants and cafés share the general expectation that English as a lingua franca will be the most reliable language to start communication. Mutual interactions begin with greetings 'hi' or 'hello'. German-speaking tourists fall into this type of behavior toward language, too. What might play a specific role in their case are their relatively weak language loyalty to German and its rather low prestige abroad. They think that it would look 'impolite' if they expected the command of German on the part of the Czech population to be good enough to communicate fluently in German.[12] The asymmetric relations between Czechs and German-speaking tourists underlied one remarkable commentary according to which 'Germans do not learn Czech at all, do they? So why should Czechs learn German?' English is believed to be 'equally foreign' for both and it does not bring any communicative advance for anyone. A relatively low command of German is considered to be 'absolutely normal' overall, which also applies to the Czech Republic as a neighboring country of Germany and Austria.

What can be observed as common practice is the fact that although Czech employees open their conversations with German-speaking customers in German in some cases, these customers indicate that 'We can speak English' and prefer English to German. However, re-negotiations of languages are definitely possible. They depend on tenacity on the part of the local staff. If a waiter continues using German and his command of this language sounds good enough, then the German-speaking customers switch back to German. Moreover,

Czech staff with a good command of German got compliments from German-speaking customers.

12.3.3 Slavic contexts

Russian-speaking tourists represent another specific group of customers. Referring to Russian, it needs to be taken into consideration that this language is used not only by Russians, but also by many other citizens of the former Soviet Union. Thus, Ukrainians, Belorussians, Kazakhs, and members of other nationalities coming from this region usually speak Russian abroad (Sloboda 2016: 158).

Although many Russian-speaking tourists also use English as the language of the first contact, it is possible in some cases for Czechs and Russians to interact 'in their own respective language', as was mentioned by one Czech waitress. This constellation, designated as semicommunication, can be regularly observed in interactions with Slovaks. Semicommunication takes place when a Czech speaker addresses a Slovak in Czech and is able to understand his/her counterpart's Slovak. This holds for the other way around as well (for more details concerning the question of mutual intelligibility, see Gooskens et al. 2018: 174–175 and 182–187). However, in spite of the structural proximity of Czech and Slovak, it cannot be claimed that Czech-Slovak receptive bilingualism would work wihout any problems (Sloboda 2004; Nábělková 2016; Sloboda and Nábělková 2013: 203–205).

Unlike Slovak, which is not systematically taught as a foreign language in the Czech education system, Russian is one of such languages. As for the sociocultural management of Russian, it had the status of the first mandatory foreign language in Czechoslovakia before 1990. This may still explain the remnants of the knowledge of Russian among the older and middle-aged people in the Czech Republic. In most cases though, Czech employees rather tend to mix both languages in that they try to accommodate Czech to Russian (and vice versa) on the phonetical, morphological as well as lexical level. Somewhat more rarely, this also applies to mixing Czech and Slovak (for more details concerning 'Czechoslovak', see Nábělková 2007). However, when compared with Slovak, the structural distance between Czech and Russian is much bigger. Hence, the Czech-Russian semicommunication is only possible in limited lexical areas.

A group of Russian-speaking tourists noted that Russian was 'quite present' in the public space. From their point of view, this perception aroused an impression that 'Czechs seem to be willing' to communicate in Russian.[13] This impression may lead to misunderstandings in individual cases, which a waiter experienced in a café. A group of tourists – categorised as Russians by him – was said to have insisted on Russian in interactions with this employee, although he 'signaled that he does not speak Russian' and 'asked them to switch to English'. It was very difficult for this waiter to re-negotiate 'broken English' instead of Russian in order to make these tourists pay the bill in the end. The waiter recalled this situation as a very 'stressful experience', because he was afraid of the tourists leaving without paying.

12.3.4 Language problems in interactions with tourists coming from Asia

The problems occurring in English-based interactions with visitors who come from East and South East Asia are more often phonetic in nature. In these cases, in which communication fails due to an incomprehensible foreign accent, the interlocutors reach for a piece of paper or an electronic device. Otherwise, no difficulties emerge when the language problems have to do with a sum of money, because the customers see the bills. Local staff of restaurants and cafés also refer to Asian tourists who use various translation applications to solve language problems. They show a phrase that is translated from the respective language either into English, or even into Czech. Using electronic devices represents an adjustment design which enables rapid implementation.

12.3.5 Topics of unsolved problems and avoidance strategies

As for the topics which are communicated in foreign languages, the waitresses and waiters claim that the repertoire is 'quite small' and that they need to be able to speak about orders and payments. Many problems are solved immediately by a reference to the menu. Lexically difficult explanations concerning ingredients or somewhat more precise descriptions of meals are not communicated under all circumstances. If a first attempt to explain such contents fails, further efforts to provide the customer with the adequate information are often given up. Although these – mostly lexical – problems remain unsolved, new cycles of simple management with more appropriate adjustment designs are not triggered. The staff member is not always interested in, or showing willingness towards, answering the customers' questions, because it is quite busy anyway and 'does not have enough time to explain all details'. The staff indirectly counts upon the fact that 'it will always turn out fine', because the foreign tourists 'will see soon what they have ordered anyway'. Such forms of behavior correspond to a strategy of not dealing with the identified deviations from the expectations: the management process is interrupted in the phase of negative evaluation, but no adjustment designs follow. Rather exceptionally, adjustment design and implementation may consist in calling a colleague for help. Obviously, this interaction between two Czech employees takes place in Czech. However, their critical remarks concerning 'how demanding the tourists are' illustrate the function of Czech as a secret language, because the tourists are not supposed to understand them.

Other topics appearing in interactions are more rare. The tourists sometimes ask for a taxi or inquire about the direction how to get to a certain place.

12.3.6 Further aspects of the use of Czech as a local language

The reversed perspective according to which foreign tourists would like to open their interactions in Czech can also be observed. Given this happens and the Czech employees hear non-native Czech, they almost immediately switch into English. A German tourist with a good command of Czech experienced in one situation how intensely a waitress refused to accept his 'non-native Czech', no matter how much this German wished to continue speaking Czech. He had expected that it would have been 'normal to speak Czech in Prague' and evaluated this deviation negatively as 'quite impolite' (for analyses of several cases of this kind, reproducing the hegemonic position of English, see Sherman 2009: 85–93). O'Driscoll (2001: 256) interprets this kind of behavior consisting in 'the desire to practice' the other interlocutor's language as 'selfish'. That corresponds to Ammon's (2018: 17) argument. He exemplifies this constellation by means of an Italian hotelier who insists on speaking German with a German-speaking guest who would like to speak Italian:

> So wirkt z. B. ein italienischer Hotelier nicht wirklich höflich, wenn er mit einem deutschsprachigen Gast hartnäckig Deutsch spricht, der seine mühsam erlernten Italienischkenntnisse anwenden möchte (Ammon 2018: 17).
>
> [Thus, an Italian hotel manager does not sound very polite when he obstinately insists on speaking German with a German-speaking guest who would like to use Italian which he has acquired with difficulties.]
> (my translation, V.D.)

In Ammon's opinion, a lingua franca could be a compromise.

Apparently, the Czech people's competence in foreigner talk is still rather low. Many Czechs do not know how exactly they should accommodate linguistically to non-native speakers in terms of reducing the lexical and grammatical complexity of their utterances. This also holds true for slower and more careful pronunciation, which would be another appropriate component of an adjustment design. Nekvapil (2013) connects this behavior with the language ideology of Czech being believed to be a small language used only by Czechs:

> Czechs [...] do not expect the foreigners (tourists and expatriates, in particular) to be able to communicate in Czech. Consequently, Czechs find it difficult to communicate with foreigners who are trying to use the Czech language. [...] They do not feel that they should communicate in Czech with foreigners, offering them (or even forcing upon them) their English or German, [no matter how] poor it may be. In the last instance, this means that Czechs indirectly discourage foreigners from learning their language, something that is occasionally noted by the foreigners themselves.
> (Nekvapil 2013: 26)

On the other hand, Czech does not have to be enough for someone to succeed in interacting with the employees of the restaurants and cafés under all circumstances. One café might seek out employees with English as the first language (my estimation, V.D.). A waitress who claimed that she did not understand either Czech or Slovak insisted on using English only. She argued that 'everybody speaks English after all' these days, which was believed to mitigate the negative evaluation. Thus, this case was noted as a clear deviation from the expectation of what is polite behavior.

Suffice it to note that difficulties in making oneself understood in the official language of the respective country are by no means specifically Czech. They are recorded in bigger language communities as well, e.g., in the German one. One example for others in which a German with good knowledge of English complains about the necessity to use English in a hostel in Berlin:

> Ich fand es leicht sonderbar, dass wenn man in Deutschland (wo Deutsch gesprochen wird), in die JH [Jugendherberge] eincheckt, von Personal empfangen wird, das[s] die deutsche Sprache nicht wirklich beherrscht hat und beinahe darauf bestanden wurde, dass ich hier in Deutschland, meinem Heimatland, das Gefühl vermittelt bekomme, nicht Deutsch sprechen zu 'dürfen'[,] sondern Englisch im deutschen Hostel[.] Ich spreche gut und gerne Englisch, aber ich sollte hier problemlos meine Sprache sprechen dürfen in einer öffentlichen Einrichtung! (booking.com, Berlin, August 19, 2018).

> [I considered it slightly weird that when someone checks in at a youth hostel in Germany (where German is spoken) one is received by staff whose command of German is not good and who almost insists on that I get an impression here in Germany, in my homeland, not to be 'allowed' to speak German, but English in a German hostel. I like speaking English and I speak it well, but I should be allowed to speak my language without problems here, in a public facility.]
>
> (my translation, V.D.)

12.4 Conclusion and prospects for future research

The global character of tourism in the twenty-first century gives rise to enormously heterogeneous language problems and language contacts among people with very different mother tongues. As a solution in terms of pre-interaction management, this heterogeneity is usually overcome by choosing English as a lingua franca. Socio-economic features of international tourism bolster up the necessity of learning this as well as other foreign languages (particularly in the case of tourism agencies). This, in turn, is reflected in very easy establishment of rather short-term networks (or communities of contact) in which English and other foreign language knowledge does pay off. The communicative management stimulates the linguistic management in the narrow sense. However, differences in the implementation at this third level are obvious. Although the foreign language skills of the Czech population are reported to be relatively modest in the European context, this branch of the national economy does not seem to suffer from this level immediately.[14] This observation applies to such occupations which are important for tourism, but which – at the same time – are not primarily conditioned by high proficiency in foreign languages. Unlike employees of cafés and restaurants, tourist guides' command of foreign languages is expected to be very high (Costa 2018: 4).

The dominant position of English in international tourism in Prague goes hand in hand with expectations toward this language both on the part of the local staff and on the part of the visitors coming from abroad. Complying with one of language ideologies, English is enough in the vast majority of situations, indeed. This observation can be projected onto the gradually harmonised expectations of both groups of actors. Mutually harmonised expectations in favor of English limit potential deviations and essentially reduce the necessity of triggering language management activities. The use of a language other than English in terms of a lingua franca could not be reliably proven in the collected data.

By choosing English as a lingua franca, foreign tourists intend to avoid potential language problems. Related to language management theory, tourists' behavior allows us to infer that they expect this language to be the most frequently chosen foreign language in the Czech Republic. This inference corresponds to the aforementioned pre-interaction management. Choosing English as a lingua franca means designing an optimal adjustment whose implementation most often enables avoidance of difficulties. However, this choice does not have to guarantee communicative success in all circumstances (Phillipson 2003: 167; Phillipson 2017). German and Russian are negotiable alternative adjustment designs in interactions with German-speaking or Russian-speaking customers.

When interlocutors encounter phonetic problems, they try to use written media. They count on electronic translators nowadays. These implemented adjustments confirm that writing represents a reliable basis for solutions to problems occurring in spoken language. Electronic devices with translators enormously extend the possibilities of designing adjustments in various languages, including the implementation thereof. Using electronic devices in these interactions definitely deserves further research.

As an element of socio-cultural management working in favor of German, no specific impact of neighborhood can be proven, which would potentially reflect, e.g., the fact that the Czech Republic, Austria and Germany are geographically as well as culturally closely related neighbors, and that this should preferably play a role in the process of language choices. This can partially be explained by the fact that the participant observations took place only in Prague, and not in the border regions, which would have been more germane to such a question. With the exception of the aforementioned spa triangle in West Bohemia, there are no comparable hotspots of international tourism located along the Czech-German or Czech-Austrian border. Seemingly paradoxically enough, this spa triangle was mentioned in one case in connection with the influence of the linguistic landscape on the foreign language choices (in favor of Russian, and not of German, though).

Leaving language problems unsolved means that interlocutors are not able to find an appropriate adjustment design. In other words, the management process finishes in the phase of negative evaluation in such cases. If customers do not express their dissatisfaction sufficiently, they often do not make the staff deal with their problems. The management process finishes by noting a deviation, or unclear evaluation.

Obviously, the insight into the choices of foreign languages in international tourism in the capital of the Czech Republic, as presented in this chapter, could not cover many other branches of services and communication domains, which play an essential role in feelings of contentment of every foreign tourist. Thus, future research should explore their interactions with employees of public transportation services (bus drivers, conductors, ticket inspectors), but also with policemen, or with shop assistants. Another very important communication domain is represented by medical staff.

12.5 Acknowledgments

This work was supported by the European Regional Development Fund-Project 'Creativity and Adaptability as Conditions of the Success of Europe in an Interrelated World' (No. CZ.02.1.01/0.0/0.0/16_019/0000734). Thanks are also due to the editors of the volume for their valuable comments in various phases of the work on this chapter.

Notes

1 For a recent overview of the gradual development of superdiversity in the Czech Republic during the last 25 years as well as the factors working against this general tendency, see Sloboda 2016.
2 This sum is derived from the current exchange rate 1 USD = 22,5 CZK. However, this rate has been moving between approximately 1:40 and 1:16 since 2000.
3 This is only a simplified version of the conceptualisation of language problems drawing upon the management process. Elaborating on this issue, Lanstyák (2014: 327–328) refers to a difference between a 'problem token' in terms of *hic et nunc*, which is designated as language inadequacy in this theoretical framework, and a more generalized 'problem type'. More thorough discussions on the concept of language problem can be found in Neustupný (2002: 432–436), Nekvapil (2009: 5–6) and Jernudd (2020: 39–43).
4 An overview of this theory including an extensive bibliography is also available at the website languagemanagement.ff.cuni.cz. It is administered by the Language Management Research Group at the Faculty of Arts of Charles University in Prague.
5 Describing the roles of the observer, Lamnek (2010: 523–531) classifies four possibilities: complete participation, participator as observer, observer as participator, and complete observation. However, he points out that these roles are primarily only prototypes, which hardly occur in social reality as such. Rather, they should be interpreted as specific points of a continuum with several well identifiable grades.
6 Considering the issue of accentedness, I realize that having 'an accent' may be an important factor in how people react. Admittedly, a German tourist might praise,

or complain about, different matters when speaking with another German in a restaurant in Prague than when speaking with a Czech. For more details concerning the significance of phonetic vs. grammatic variation for speakers' evaluation, see Hanulíková (2019) or Hendriks et al. (2018).
7 The aspects of organisation of tourism in the Czech Republic, its administration as well as its goverment and regional policies cannot be described thoroughly in this chapter. For more details, see www.czechtourism.com and Palatková and Zichová (2014: 224–240).
8 See the overviews put together by the Czech Statistical Office: www.czso.cz/csu/czso/cestovni_ruch. As Sloboda (2016: 144–145) points out, the motivation of foreign tourists to visit the Czech Republic may be manifold, indeed. Tourists coming from East Asia are attracted, e.g., by movies which are shot in the Old Town or the Lesser Town of the city of Prague.
9 The duration and stability of contacts between foreign tourists and locals within these networks, or the establishment of 'communities of contact', are discussed by Heller et al. (2014: 426 and 428) and Costa (2018: 3–4). Without having elaborated on this issue, I take the contacts in cafés and restaurants for rather fleeting and fugitive moments.
10 This estimation is based on personal experience (V.D.). The quality of the translation would deserve a specific inquiry, though. It varies considerably. Interestingly enough, my participant observation does not contain any situations in which language mistakes in the menus would have been commented on negatively.
11 Here as well as in the following passages of the chapter, the quotation marks indicate that the expressions or parts of utterances are authentic and were used by the persons themselves. If originally uttered in German or Czech, these words are translated into English.
12 The evaluation as impolite is relative, of course. In one case, a German-speaking tourist even said that she would experience 'unpleasant feelings' if she should 'impose' her language on Czechs.
13 This utterance was recorded in Prague, but the remark about the presence of Russian in the public space applied to the West-Bohemian spa triangle (Karlsbad, Marienbad and Franzensbad). Sloboda (2016: 158) also refers to the evident presence of this language in the tourist hotspots in the Czech Republic: '[…] Russian is probably most frequently heard in tourist sites and tourism-related services […]'.
14 More details concerning the foreign language competence in the European comparison are available at http://ec.europa.eu/eurostat/statistics-explained/index.php/Foreign_language_skills_statistics. The results of this survey were published in April 2019. An overview of foreign language teaching in the educational systems of various European countries, which is one of the general preconditions of foreign language skills, is provided by Ammon and Wright (2010). Dovalil (2018) and Dovalil (2017) deal with the position of English and German in the Czech Republic.

References

Ammon, Ulrich (2018) Prinzipien der Sprachwahl im Tourismus, mit Schwerpunkt auf sprachlicher Höflichkeit. In: *Sprachwahl im Tourismus – mit Schwerpunkt Europa / Language Choice in Tourism – with the Focus on Europe* (= Sociolinguistica 32). Ulrich Ammon and Marcella Costa (eds.), 13–21. Berlin: Walter de Gruyter.

Ammon, Ulrich (2015) *Die Stellung der deutschen Sprache in der Welt*. Berlin: Walter de Gruyter.

Ammon, Ulrich and Sue Wright (eds.) (2010) *Fremdsprachen an den Schulen der Europäischen Union* (= Sociolinguistica 24). Berlin: Walter de Gruyter.

Costa, Marcella (2018) Sprachwahl im Gesprächsprozess. In: *Sprachwahl im Tourismus – mit Schwerpunkt Europa / Language Choice in Tourism – with the Focus on Europe* (= Sociolinguistica32). Ulrich Ammon and Marcella Costa (eds.), 3–12. Berlin: Walter de Gruyter.

Costa, Marcella (2019) Deutsch als Fremdsprache für den internationalen Tourismus. In *Förderung der deutschen Sprache weltweit: Vorschläge, Ansätze und Konzepte*. Ulrich Ammon and Gabriele Schmidt (eds.), 201–213. Berlin: Walter de Gruyter.

Dovalil, Vít (2017) Deutsch in Tschechien als aktuelles bildungspolitisches Problem. In: *Akten des XIII. Internationalen Germanistenkongresses Shanghai 2015 – Germanistik zwischen Tradition und Innovation* Band 5. Jianhua Zhu Zhu, Jin Zhao and Michael Szurawitzki (eds.), 93–98. Frankfurt am Main: Peter Lang.

Dovalil, Vít (2018) Qual der Wahl, or spoiled for choice? English and German as the subject of decision-making processes in the Czech Republic. In: *English in Business and Commerce. Interactions and Policies*. Tamah Sherman and Jiří Nekvapil (eds.), 276–309. Berlin: Mouton de Gruyter.

Dovalil, Vít and Tamah Sherman (2010) *Language Management in European Research Projects: Case Studies*. Presentation at Sociolinguistics Symposium 18, 2 September 2010, Southampton.

Dovalil, Vít and Kateřina Šichová (2017) *Sprach(en)politik, Sprachplanung und Sprachmanagement*. Heidelberg: Winter.

Fairbrother, Lisa, Jiří Nekvapil and Marián Sloboda (eds.) (2018) *The Language Management Approach. A Focus on Research Methodology*. Berlin: Peter Lang.

Gooskens, Charlotte, Vincent van Heuven, Jelena Golubović, Anja Schüppert, Femke Swarte, Femke and Stefanie Voigt (2018) Mutual intelligibility between closely related languages in Europe. *International Journal of Multilingualism* 15(2): 169–193.

Hanulíková, Adriana (2019) Bewertung und Grammatikalität regionaler Syntax. Eine empirische Untersuchung zur Rolle der Sprecher Innen und Hörer Innen. *Linguistik Online* 98(5): 197–218.

Heller, Monica (2010) The Commodification of Language. *Annual Review of Anthropology* 39: 101–114.

Heller, Monica, Adam Jaworski and Crispin Thurlow (2014) Introduction: Sociolinguistics and tourism – mobilities, markets, multilingualism. *Journal of Sociolinguistics* 18(4): 425–458.

Heller, Monica, Juan Pujolar and Alexandre Duchêne (2014) Linguistic commodification in tourism. *Journal of Sociolinguistics* 18(4): 539–566.

Hendriks, Berna, Frank van Meurs and Ann-Katrin Reimer (2018) The evaluation of lecturers' nonnative-accented English: Dutch and German students' evaluations of different degrees of Dutch-accented and German-accented English of lecturers in higher education. *Journal of English for Academic Purposes* 34: 28–45.

Jernudd, Björn (2020) The origin and development of a language management framework. In: *A Language Management Approach to Language Problems: Integrating Macro and Micro Dimensions*. Goro Kimura and Lisa Fairbrother (eds), 31–48. Amsterdam: John Benjamins.

Kimura, Goro and Lisa Fairbrother (eds.) (2020) *A Language Management Approach to Language Problems: Integrating Macro and Micro Dimensions*. (= Studies in World Language Problems 7). Amsterdam: John Benjamins.
Lamnek, Siegfried (⁵2010) *Qualitative Sozialforschung*. Basel: Beltz.
Lanstyák, István (2014) On the process of language problem management. *Slovo a slovesnost* 75(4): 325–351.
Marriott, Helen E. (1991) Language planning and language management for tourism shopping situations. *Australian Review of Applied Linguistics*. Supplement Series 8(1): 191–222.
Nábělková, Mira (2016) Česko-slovenský jazykový kontakt [Czech-Slovak language contact]. In: *Nový encyklopedický slovník češtiny* [New Encyclopedic Dictionary of Czech]. Petr Karlík, Marek Nekula and Jana Pleskalová (eds.), 223–236. Praha: Lidové noviny.
Nábělková, Mira (2007) Closely-related languages in contact: Czech, Slovak, 'Czechoslovak'. *International Journal of the Sociology of Language* 183: 83–73.
Nekvapil, Jiří (2016) Language Management Theory as one approach in Language Policy and Planning. *Current Issues in Language Planning* 17(1): 11–22.
Nekvapil, Jiří (2013) The main challenges facing Czech as a medium-sized language: The state of affairs at the beginning of the 21st century. In: *Survival and Development of Language Communities. Prospects and Challenges*. F. Xavier Vila (ed.), 18–37. Toronto: Multilingual Matters.
Nekvapil, Jiří (2009) The integrative potential of Language Management Theory. In: *Language Management in Contact Situations: Perspectives from Three Continents*. Jiří Nekvapil and Tamah Sherman (eds.), 1–9. Frankfurt/Main: Peter Lang.
Nekvapil, Jiří and Tamah Sherman (2009) Pre-interaction management in multinational companies in Central Europe. *Current Issues in Language Planning* 10(2): 181–198.
Nekvapil, Jiří and Tamah Sherman (eds.) (2015) The Language Management Approach: Perspectives on the Interplay of Bottom-Up and Top-Down. *International Journal of the Sociology of Language (special issue)* 232.
Neustupný, Jiří (2002) Sociolingvistika a jazykový management. [Sociolinguistics and language management]. *Sociologický časopis / Czech Sociological Review* 38(4): 429–442.
O'Driscoll, Jim (2001) A face model of language choices. *Multilingua* 20(3): 245–268.
Palatková, Monika and Jitka Zichová (2014) *Ekonomika turismu. Turismus České republiky*. [Economics of tourism. The tourism of the Czech Republic]. Praha: Grada Publishing.
Phillipson, Robert (2017) Myths and realities of 'global' English. *Language Policy* 16(3): 313–331.
Phillipson, Robert (2003) *English-Only Europe? Challenging Language Policy*. London: Routledge.
Sherman, Tamah (2009) Managing hegemony: Native English speakers in the Czech Republic. In: *Language Management in Contact Situations. Perspectives from Three Continents*. Jiří Nekvapil and Tamah Sherman (eds.), 75–96. Frankfurt/Main: Peter Lang.
Sloboda, Marián (2004) Slovensko-česká (semi)komunikace a vzájemná (ne)srozumitelnost. [Slovak-Czech (semi-)communication and the mutual (un)intelligibility]. *Čeština doma a ve světě* [Czech at home and in the world] 12(3–4): 208–220.
Sloboda, Marián (2016) Transition to super-diversity in the Czech Republic: Its emergence and resistance. In: *Sociolinguistic Transition in Former Eastern Bloc Countries. Two*

Decades after the Regime Change. Marián Sloboda, Petteri Laihonen and Anastassia Zabrodskaja (eds.), 141–183. Frankfurt am Main: Peter Lang.

Sloboda, Marián and Mira Nábělková (2013) Receptive multilingualism in 'monolingual' media: Managing the presence of Slovak on Czech websites. *International Journal of Multilingualism* 10(2): 196–213.

Internet and data sources

Statistics of tourism and the Czech population (Czech Statistical Office):
URL: www.czso.cz/csu/czso/cri/cestovni-ruch-4-ctvrtleti-2018
URL: www.czso.cz/csu/czso/obyvatelstvo_lide
URL: www.czso.cz/csu/czso/satelitni_ucet_cestovniho_ruchu
(last accessed on January 20, 2020)

Agency Czechtourism:
URL: www.czechtourism.com (last accessed on May 20, 2020)

Language Management Research Group at Charles University in Prague:
URL: languagemanagement.ff.cuni.cz (last accessed on October 30, 2020)

Foreign language skills in Europe
URL: http://ec.europa.eu/eurostat/statistics-explained/index.php/Foreign_language_skills_statistics
(last accessed on October 30, 2020)

Part IV
Linguistic landscapes

13 'Non-identical twins'

Monolingual bias and linguistic landscapes of the twin cities of Ivangorod/Narva

K. Fedorova and V. Baranova

13.1 Introduction

Studies on linguistic landscapes – written language usage in public spaces – started in a systematic way about twenty years ago,[1] mostly as an instrument to measure language diversity in certain areas and, therefore, to evaluate linguistic vitality and/or suggest specific measures for language policy (Blommaert and Maly 2014). Later studies changed the focus to power relations between different social and ethnic groups as well as to domineering language ideologies (Gorter 2006; Blackwood et al. 2016). Linguistic landscapes do not necessarily provide precise reflections of multilingual speech practices typical for the area; some languages can be underrepresented, especially in the public space. Sometimes such cases can be easily explained by quite an overt restrictive language policy implemented by the state trying to suppress politically active ethnic minorities, as was the case, e.g., in Barcelona during Franko's dictatorship (Miller and Miller 1996). More often though, mismatches between spoken multilingualism and its visual representation have causes that are more complex. For example, in Tabriz, Iran, populated by many ethnic Azeri, the visual absence of the Azerbaijani language in public places is evident in both official 'top-down' signs and in 'bottom-up' signs produced by business owners despite the fact there are no legal restrictions on using other languages than Farsi in public communication (Mirvahedi 2016). Similar examples can be found all over the world; including post-Soviet countries (see, e.g., Marten 2010 on underrepresentation of minority languages – Latgalian and Russian – in Latvia).

According to Long and Nakai (2014: 229), linguistic landscapes affect people's 'sense of being in a particular place' and perception of that place. In the modern world, the visual environment is to a large degree constituted by written words: where medieval city dwellers would do with an image of a barrel or a barber's scissors, we expect to read 'bar' or 'hairdresser', alongside additional information such as open hours, menus, or list of services. Indeed, 'in going about their ordinary daily life, people today are constantly encountering literacy' (Barton 1994: 3). A ubiquitous linguistic landscape demands at least some linguistic proficiency, and being unable to read its signs one inevitably turns out to be excluded from and deprived of basic everyday activities. Excluding

DOI: 10.4324/9780429348037-17

certain languages from written public communication, therefore, not only reflects exclusion of their speakers from public life but also helps to maintain the existing state of affairs. 'Linguistic invisibility' both represents and creates inequality, certainly, not directly but via the language ideology it both reflects and (re)produces (Hult 2018). In this sense, it is true that 'emplacement, or entextualisation, of linguistic signs is indeed a metadiscursive, and of necessity, an ideological act' (Jaworski and Thurlow 2010a: 12); by placing signs failing to represent minority languages, the majority states its dominance and refusal to accept others as their equals.

Border communities present a rather interesting case for studies on multilingualism. Usually in places situated in close proximity to state borders, linguistic landscapes demonstrate more diversity than in other areas. As Gerst and Klessmann (2015: 2) state it in their study on the German-Polish border cities, 'border towns, and especially twin cities, create multilingual spaces of language contact and linguistic demarcations that distinguish them from cities located further from the border'. However, Russian border cities do not necessarily comply with this principle, and visual linguistic diversity there can be even less than in other places, especially such global cities as Moscow and St. Petersburg. Ivangorod, a small city on the border with Estonia, presents an interesting case for analysis, especially in comparison with its twin city of Narva on the other side of the border. The linguistic landscapes of these two cities, analyzed in this chapter, reveal different patterns of interplay between official language policy (monolingual in both countries) and bottom-up language management.

This chapter is structured as follows: first, we deal with some theoretical concepts important for this study and describe in short the socio-economic context for border-crossing activities in Russia; in the next section, the research methodology is discussed; Section 13.4 is dedicated to Ivangorod's economic and social background; then, Ivangorod's relations with its twin city of Narva are discussed; the results of the study on Ivangorod's and Narva's linguistic landscapes are presented in Sections 13.6 and 13.7, respectively; in the *Concluding discussion* section, we compare the data from two border cities, summarise our findings and try to suggest possible explanations for the situation we discovered there.

13.2 Border cities, migration, and linguistic landscapes: Theoretical and empirical background

Transformations in linguistic landscapes are usually associated with migration processes. The mobility of people and consequent changes in the ethnic and social composition of settlements – be it a village, a small town, or modern megapolisis – inevitably lead to changes in speech practices, both oral and written; usually there is an increase in 'the visibility of differences' (Blommaert 2010: 133). Unsurprisingly, in sociolinguistics interest in globalisation and its effects on communication results in the growing interest in space and its interaction with language (Vigouroux 2009; Johnstone 2011). In their analysis of changes in the linguistic landscape of Rabot neighborhood in Ghent, Blommaert and Maly (2014) show how recent migration flows introduced new languages (Bulgarian, Spanish, Chinese, Arabic, etc.) to the streets where Turkish and Dutch had been co-used for several decades. At the same time, alongside the obvious increase in linguistic diversity, the rise of English in the area was observed, contributing to a movement towards a global commercial culture. What is important, all these multilingual signs do not exist separately; they are 'placed', i.e. incorporated into specific urban context, and should be analyzed in their relations with the city's infrastructure and people creating and reading them. The emergence of English and French words in the window of a Turkish kebab restaurant signals its owner's attempts to address a new type of clients – the student population of Ghent; at the same time it means that these new clients, mostly Dutch-speaking, position themselves as a part of a global world.

When addressing issues of relations between linguistic landscape and migration, it is important to take into account that migration processes include not only permanent or seasonal labour migration often implied by the term but also various forms of tourism. Recent studies on tourism show it as instrumental in organising and reorganising the socioeconomic order (Thurlow and Jaworski 2010), and its influence on speech practices is undoubtedly important. However, there is no unanimity of opinions among researchers regarding the nature of such influence on and its results for multilingualism. While, on the one hand, tourism promotes globalisation and increases cosmopolitan tolerance for diversity (see e.g. Hannerz 1996), the same process is responsible for the global spread of English, a (perceived) 'killer language' (Phillipson 2009: 20–21) forcing out other languages from many spheres and taking over their fundamental functions. The same is certainly true for different aspects of local cultures – those that turn out to be attractive for tourists are maintained; others can be neglected. The neocolonialist nature of modern tourism (Hall and Tucker 2004) and globalisation demands commodification of many practices, including linguistic ones (Jaworski and Thurlow 2010b; Heller 2010). The increase in the use of English is inevitably observed wherever tourism is flourishing, be it post-Olympic Beijing (Xiao 2018) or a traditional Hongcun village in China (Lu, Li and Xu 2020). Minority languages, especially those with a high symbolic value, can also be promoted in a tourist area, as is the case, e.g., with Irish in Dingle (Moriarty 2014), or, on the contrary, get less visibility, as Catalan in Mallorca (Bruyèl-Olmedo and Juan-Garau 2015).

Naturally, tourism tends to have the biggest impact on the situation in border areas. Serving, on the one hand, as a gate and starting point for many migrants moving further, on the other hand, border cities often become tourist destinations on their own. Moreover, in border cities tourism can lose its 'elitist' character and become an everyday activity for significant numbers of people. While elsewhere to travel abroad means spending a lot of money on transportation and accommodation, in close proximity to the border people can make short trips to the other side rather often, even on a daily basis. So-called 'shopping tourism' (see Wachowiak 2006: 176–179) sometimes becomes an important part of the regional economy, often with local people involved in various forms of small-scale half-legal trade and smuggling (van Schendel 2005). Also, a completely new infrastructure is created to provide services for tourists: hotels, restaurants, shopping malls, tourist agencies, car rentals, money exchange offices, etc., and these enterprises draw labour migration from other parts of the country. Thus, many Mexican border cities, such as Tijuana, Nogales and Juárez, at the beginning of the twentieth century were merely small frontier towns but began to expand in the second half of the century with the growth of tourism from the United States (Enríquez Acosta 2009). Evidently, the greatest impact of borders on the lives of local dwellers can be witnessed in those regions where there is a significant social, political and economic disparity between bordering countries while the borders between them are not impenetrable. Then the border can be turned into a resource – the borders' 'existence as barriers to movement can simultaneously create reasons to cross them' (Donnan and Wilson 1999: 87). Unsurprisingly, such borders attract more attention from researchers: as Paul Nugent states, 'the most studied border regions are those where the disparities between one country and the next manifest themselves in contrasting physical aspects <…> and differential levels of state presence on opposite sides of the line' (Nugent 2012: 557). Twin cities, often historically united and later divided by new state borders, present even more interesting cases for analysis (see, e.g., Garrard and Mikhailova 2019).

Cross-border practices involve people from both sides of the state borderline and brings mutual benefits as well as inconveniences for people divided by this line. Moreover, cross-border practices inevitably lead to interethnic communication: borderland dwellers have to deal with the people 'from the other side' trying to find their ways to interact with them. Changes in linguistic landscapes, therefore, can be seen as a part of such adjustment to the situation of language contact.

After the collapse of the Soviet Union, many new state borders – between former Soviet republics and now independent states – came into existence. Moreover, state borders, unlike those of the USSR, the famous 'iron curtain', became more or less permeable, creating in the process new arenas for cross-border activities and interethnic communication (see, e.g., Fedorova 2011; Gurova and Ratilainen 2016; Holzlehner 2014; Laine 2017; Stern 2016; Zotova et al. 2018). Unfortunately, the borderlands of Russia remain under-researched in terms of linguistic landscape studies, and especially in a comparative perspective. There are only a few publications on the bordering areas of the Baltic States. Ruzaitė (2017) compares multilingual signs in Polish and Lithuanian resorts and discovers interesting differences with respect to the ways in which languages of tourists – mostly English, Russian and German – are used there. In both countries in the resorts studied, the vast majority of multilingual signs are created by private sectors, mostly restaurants and shops, and not by governments; in Lithuania, though, these multilingual signs belong to independent shops and not to those that are part of a national or international chain. In Poland, independent and chain-owned shops contribute to the multilingual landscape with almost the same frequency (Ruzaitė 2017: 207–208). Marten et al. (2012) studied six places – two in every country – in Lithuania, Latvia and Estonia and did quantitative research on the languages used in public signs, complementing it with interviews with locals. The mismatch between quantitative and qualitative data led them to state that Russian is by far more important in the region than its reflection in the linguistic landscapes presumes. Both these investigations are important for our study since they reveal two crucial points: unexpected lower visibility of a certain foreign language, due to a strict language policy and ideology, and a focus on agents creating linguistic landscape. Our research, addressing both the Russian and Estonian sides of the border, aims at describing linguistic landscape in this – actor-oriented – perspective and in the context of language ideologies. Our study in Ivangorod and Narva is a part of a broader project focusing on linguistic landscapes of several Russian cities; another case – the city of Vyborg, on the border with Finland – is also presented in this book (see Chapter 14).

13.3 Research methodology and data

Our data analysis is based on Blommaert's methodology of ELLA (Ethnographic Linguistic Landscape Analysis), treating elements of linguistic landscape as embedded in communication (Blommaert 2013; Blommaert and Maly 2014); this approach focuses on actors responsible for creating written signs and placing them in the public space, as well as these actors' attitudes and motivations. Also fundamental for this study is a semiotic reading of landscapes (Jaworski and Thurlow 2010a). Linguistic signs do not exist separately; they are incorporated in certain places, in practices occurring in these places, and in discourses referring to these practices and places.

More specifically, when analyzing written texts placed in the public space the following factors should be considered alongside linguistic forms: materiality of signs – their size, colour, the material they are made of; their positions relative to other signs and details of landscapes; their functions – the audience they address and the effect they should have on that audience. Certainly, a proper understanding of the functions of signs is impossible without paying close attention to actors responsible for creating these signs. In his analysis of signs on ethnic Korean businesses in Oakland, Malinowski (2009) focuses on the notion of linguistic landscape authorship and tries to go beyond the simple distinction between 'top-down' and 'bottom-up' signs: indeed, advertisements produced individually by a local shop owner and by an international retail corporation demonstrate very different kinds of authorship; the authors' control over the meaning customers will read from them can be different as well. In order to perform such a complex analysis it is important to obtain the most contextualised data, i.e. pictures of signs should be collected alongside a lot of metalinguistic information. Moreover, other methods of collecting data on societal treatment (see Garret 2010, ch. 3) of linguistic landscapes can be used, such as observations, discussions of linguistic landscapes with their creators and users, and searching for such discussions on internet forums and in social media.

For this study, fieldwork in Ivangorod and Narva was conducted in October 2018. We made digital photos of street signs, advertisements, announcements, graffiti, etc. (108 photos overall). For obtaining additional information on these twin cities' everyday practices and context, we used academic publications (Brednikova 2007; Nikiforova 2004; Brednikova and Voronkov 1999), local news web-portals, tourist blogs and reviews, and comments on internet forums and social media.

13.4 Ivangorod and Narva: Political and economic background

Ivangorod is a town in the Kingisepp district of the Leningrad region. It is located on the river Narva, which divides Russian and Estonian territories. In January 2019, 9,816 citizens were registered there (Petrostat 2019: 4). Ivangorod was founded in 1492 right in front of the castle of Narva (Hermann Castle at that time) to form a bulwark against the Teutonic Order during the war; later it was destroyed and rebuilt exchanging hands several times during the sixteenth and seventeenth centuries (for more details see Vlasov and El'kin 2011). Since the eighteenth century, both Ivangorod and Narva have been incorporated into the Russian Empire, and Ivangorod was treated as a suburb of Narva's. After the 1917 October Revolution, Estonia took control of the territory including Ivangorod. In 1944–1991, the river Narva served as a formal border between the Estonian Soviet Socialist Republic and the Russian Soviet Federative Socialist Republic. *De jure*, the twin cities had separate administrations but *de facto* they functioned as one urban agglomeration (Pfoser 2017: 29–30); their citizens shared their day-to-day life, e.g. by residing in Narva and working in Ivangorod or going to school in Ivangorod and attending evening musical classes in Narva. It is important to mention, that most of Narva's citizens were and still are ethnically Russian and native Russian speakers, and Narva nowadays has the unofficial title of 'the most Russian' Estonian city.

Narva's population during the Soviet period increased due to the industrial migration from other regions of the USSR from 6,600 in 1954 to 82,200 in 1990 (Nikiforova 2004: 151). Most of the newly arrived people and their children spoke Russian as their first or second language and had no knowledge of Estonian, although Estonian was taught in schools. After Estonia became an independent state in 1991, the number of city dwellers has been reducing due to the decline of local industries, migration and other economic and political reasons. In the early 1990s, Narva became a center of the movement for regional autonomy; in 1993, a referendum was held here; however, its results were not recognised by the State Court. Despite the fact that studies on Russian-Estonian language contacts show an obvious increase in Russian-Estonian bilingualism among the young Estonian population in the last decades

Figure 13.1 Ivangorod Fortress and Narva Castle facing each other across the Narva river.

(Verschik 2002; Ehala and Zabrodskaja 2014), the Northeast part of the country (Narva and its region) is still predominantly Russian-speaking.

Since 1991, Ivangorod-Narva territory is a part of the state borderline between Estonia and the Russian Federation. The two fortresses – Ivangorod Fortress in Russia and Narva Castle in Estonia – are facing each other across the river, and the bridge between them[2] is a no-man's land (Figure 13.1). According to the Russian legislation, border areas are regulated by a so-called 'border regime' demanding any non-residents to obtain a permit from the Ministry of Internal Affairs if they plan to visit these areas. Therefore, to come to Ivangorod Russian citizens not residing there need either to apply for such a permit or to have a valid Schengen visa proving they make a stop there on their way to Estonia.[3] Living in a so-called 'closed', or 'forbidden' city in a border zone, Ivangorod's residents are engaged mostly at the hydroelectric power plant and in textile, food and timber industries partly inherited from the Soviet period. The economic level of Ivangorod is relatively low, its budget is subsidised by the regional budget.

From 1992 and until 2000, a simplified (visa-free) border-crossing regime between Russia and Estonia for citizens of Ivangorod and Narva had been operating (Nikiforova 2004: 159). Then it was revoked, and nowadays local residents, the same way as other Russian citizens, need a Schengen visa to cross the border; most of them, however, can easily obtain a five-year multi-entry visa. What is more, up to 30% of Narva residents have Russian citizenship and an Estonian residence permit so they are eligible to cross the border any time as well. Unlike many other border checkpoints in Russia, in Ivangorod it is possible to cross the border on foot,[4] without vehicles (therefore, quickly and without additional taxes and insurances for the car). Consequently, there is a continuous flow of people through the border; an average number of border crossing is 12,000 per day. In front of the checkpoint, many cars can be seen during the day waiting for their owners at an unofficial parking. People from both sides visit relatives; Narva residents buy gasoline and some other cheaper goods in Ivangorod; people from the Russian side mostly bring from Narva food and clothes. In addition to individual consumption, local dwellers with resident permits or with long-term visas take part in an informal economy of small-scale smuggling. For the sake of small payment, they include some goods (gasoline, alcohol, cigarettes, food) in their non-declared baggage and then, passing a cargo to its owners, they visit their friends or return for the next portion immediately. Obviously, such practices are evident for everyone; nevertheless, it is hard to prove they are illegal, and so border and customs officers prefer not to pay attention to them. Some people can keep moving from one side to the other for the whole day. The border, therefore, significantly contributes to consuming practices of local citizens and their everyday routine. Moreover, its presence transforms the organisation of the cities' space. In Ivangorod, it is the border, rather than central streets, that is the local center of gravity; symbolic value of the border for the public image of Ivangorod is also very important.

13.5 The symbolic construction of twin cities

The picturesque face-off of two 'divided cities', or 'twin cities', Ivangorod and Narva, is quite popular among journalists and ordinary tourists. Unsurprisingly, all bloggers and journalists emphasise the contrast between 'two towers face to face' and 'the West and the East'.[5] In contrast to the more prosperous Narva, Ivangorod is usually depicted as an unattractive, poor and dirty place.[6] Authors of travel blogs note that the 'border regime' has a negative impact on both cities' development. The media mostly consider the twin cities in terms of instability and potential conflicts. In Russian official media, the most popular topics over the last decades were territorial disputes between Russia and Estonia and the accession of the EU and NATO (Brednikova and Nikiforova 2018). The representation of Narva in Estonian and European media is 'orientalised', and its citizens are often presented as strongly oriented to Russia (Erbsen 2020), although some studies show that the Russian-speaking community in Estonia consists of different subgroups, and they are not homogeneous in their attitudes to Russia (Ehala and Zabrodskaja 2014: 183). The personal narratives of both Ivangorod's and Narva's inhabitants use, as Pfoser (2017) shows, categories from dominant discourse, like the *East and West* dichotomy and the 'peripheral' imagination of the place – each city is depicted as provincial, remote from the centers of power (Moscow / St. Petersburg or Tallinn), and opposed both to them and to its immediate neighbour.

Being very close to each other geographically and historically, Narva and Ivangorod share a lot: their architectural styles, patterns of social stratification, and the educational level of their residents are quite similar. For example, some Soviet monuments are preserved both in Ivangorod and in Narva, as well as Soviet-style five-floors apartment buildings ('*Khrushchevki*'). Naturally, these similarities between two cities were even bigger just after the collapse of the

Soviet Union, but later their urban landscapes partly diverged: Brednikova (2007: 51–53) analyzes the construction of new monuments in Narva representing 'a Swedish part of the history' of the city. The identities of Ivangorod and Narva, as we see them nowadays, became divergent by appealing to different periods of the historical past and tying themselves to different images and traditions. Starting from Anderson's seminal study (1983), museums are considered to be an important part of the way to 'imagine' a community, and studies comparing museums in the twin cities of Ivangorod and Narva reveal very different strategies of representation of local history. Okunev and Tislenko state (2017: 602–603) that a symbol of a 'fortress' prevails the exposition of the Ivangorod city museum. They associate it with 'antagonism to the external neighbor' while Narva's narrative has a more diverse character and uses different metaphors for different historical periods.

13.6 Ivangorod's linguistic landscape: An outpost of monolingualism

Overall, the visibility of the border and trans-border practices in Ivangorod are extremely high in terms of organisation of space as well as people's behaviour. At the same time, against all expectations, the city's linguistic landscape can prevent newcomers from recognising the place as a border area. The city virtually exists on the border, with many of its citizens crossing the border every day; however, it looks like a place very far away from other countries and languages. Certainly, it is not an easy task to illustrate the absence of some phenomenon, including multilingualism, but we should state that Ivangorod is a predominantly monolingual place. Beyond the checkpoint itself and one main street leading to the city's art museum, only Russian can be observed in all the signs and advertisements. There is no English signs or transliteration of any kind, let alone Estonian. At the checkpoint, official signs are bilingual in Russian (placed on the top) and English; Estonian is not used.[7] An unofficial sign on the door with a rather tricky door handle instructing how to open it is in Russian only. Tourist information near the border and the museum – city map and poster of Ivangorod art museum – are available in Russian and in English, but not in Estonian (Figures 13.2 and 13.3). Interestingly, the museum poster states that its production was financed by one of the European Union programs – The Estonia-Latvia-Russia Cross Border Cooperation Program – and is a part of the Via Hanseatica cultural project so its existence has not that much to do with the efforts of the city's or museum's administration. All practical information about the museum near its entrance, including the home-printed note about it being closed for reconstruction, is provided only in Russian (Figure 13.4). Everything looks like foreigners are not welcome, or even expected, in Ivangorod. Moreover, any references to Estonian – the official language of the neighbours – are absent from the city's linguistic landscape.

There is an interesting example of this 'hostile' attitude to Estonia expressed linguistically on a bilingual road sign near the border (Figure 13.5). It shows the

Figure 13.2 Tourist map of Ivangorod.

direction and distance to the capital of Estonia, with its name written both in Cyrillic and in Roman characters. However, the latter is spelled with one 'n' – 'Tallin' instead of 'Tallinn'. This trivial omission of one letter has serious political implications. Estonians insist on spelling the name of their capital with double

Figure 13.3 Poster of Ivangorod Art Museum.

final 'nn' to represent an etymological connection with the word *linn*, 'city'. International maps and official documents follow this spelling. At the same time, in Russian it was traditionally spelled with one final 'n', following the transcription (as it is pronounced) and not transliteration. The demand for a change from 'Tallin' to 'Tallinn' in official Russian documents became an important symbol of the Estonian fight for independence from the Soviet Union at the end of the 1980s. As a result, the choice between the spelling according to Russian orthographic conventions or to original Estonian norms is a sensitive issue. 'Tallin' on the road sign in question, therefore, should be seen not as an international geographical name but rather as a reverse transliteration from the Russian version of it, the same way as if Paris were spelled as *Parizh*. By applying this spelling, an ordinary road sign turns into a political statement; it represents Ivangorod's refusal to comply with Estonian rules. Even more striking is the fact that the same city name is spelled differently in Ivangorod and in other places in Russia. In St. Petersburg, e.g., on the road signs showing directions to different cities it is written as *Таллин* in Russian but as *Tallinn* in Latin script.

Ivangorod, therefore, looks somewhat paradoxical. It is a city that is semi-closed for internal tourists and its only resource for further touristic development is international – Estonian – tourism. Nevertheless, neither municipal authorities, nor local businesses attempt to use Estonian, or even English, to

Figure 13.4 Ivangorod Art Museum's entrance.

attract foreign visitors or somehow acknowledge the city's bordering status. All signs are in Russian only, and even the directions for transit cars going to Tallinn follow the 'internal' Russian norms. Official and private actors put up a united monolingual front. During our survey of the city's streets, we managed

Figure 13.5 Road sign near the border, Ivangorod.

to find only one multilingual advertisement of a commercial establishment (Figure 13.6) – a huge poster inviting to visit hotel and restaurant 'King' in Narva. Technically, it can be defined as trilingual: most information is provided in Russian, but the name is in English, as well as the words *hotel and restaurant*, and the Estonian words *baar* and *restoran* are visible on the photo of the building placed in the center of the poster. The hotel's address contains the Estonian street name (*Lavretsovi*) but the country's name is given in English (*Estonia*) rather than in Estonian (*Eesti*). Thus, the use of Estonian is involuntary – it is presented only if it cannot be avoided.

13.7 Ivangorod's twin city of Narva: So close, so different

The nearest place to Ivangorod, Narva across the river of the same name, presents a very different picture in terms of visible multilingualism. Due to the city's turbulent past and complicated relations with the rest of Estonia, very different elements coexist in Narva's symbolic landscape, defining the city simultaneously as 'Soviet', 'Estonian', 'European', 'Russian', and uniquely 'local' (Martínez 2018: 155–158).

The Urban landscape is created via infrastructure, and the old infrastructure can preserve images and signs from the past, thus forming a background to the

Figure 13.6 The advertisement of Narva hotel and restaurant 'King', Ivangorod.

city's linguistic landscape. Such inconspicuous multilingualism is represented in some areas of Narva as a legacy from Soviet times. As mentioned above, Narva consists of typical Soviet-style buildings. Some of such cheaper houses were partly renovated but still they are marked with signs in Russian (Figure 13.7). Some other historical signs in Russian, such as inscriptions on monuments, probably were left intentionally as memorabilia of the Soviet Estonia period of history or references to Russian culture. In addition, on some buildings old bilingual signs from the early 1990s can still be found. In these signs, Estonian street names are accompanied by Cyrillic transliterations. An example can be found in Figure 13.8, where the bottom line reads Космонауди and not ул. Космонавтов ('Astronauts' street') as it was called in the Soviet period.

Apart from these relics of the dominance of Russian in the USSR and the former less strict language policy of the Estonian government after independence, all new governmental signs in the city nowadays, including road and street signs, are monolingual in Estonian. The only exception is tourist information: signs providing it are either bilingual in Estonian and English or use Russian as well and are trilingual, as shown by the city map on Figure 13.9. Interestingly, this map mentions the same Via Hanseatica project as the museum poster in Ivangorod discussed in the previous section, but while the poster is bilingual in Russian and English, the map is not only trilingual but also refers to the

Figure 13.7 An entrance to an apartment building, Narva.

website and mobile application in five languages – German and Latvian as well. Evidently, Narva is treated by international culture management responsible for publishing this map as considerably more multilingual than Ivangorod. Moreover, on the Estonian side of the border checkpoint, all signs are also

Figure 13.8 Old street sign, Narva.

trilingual and use Russian while on the Russian side, as already mentioned, Estonian is never used.

Away from the border and Narva Castle, though, there are no more traces of such tolerance to multilingualism on the part of officials, and Estonian totally

'Non-identical twins' 229

Figure 13.9 Tourist map of Narva.

dominates the official signage. At the same time, official Estonian monolingualism here comes into collision with everyday communication practices of Narva's predominantly Russian-speaking population. As a result, there is a large gap between *top-down* language planning in linguistic landscape and a *bottom-up* perspective. All small local businesses use both Russian and Estonian for their signs and advertisements. Moreover, many home-printed signs inside small shops are only in Russian (Figure 13.10). Some of them represent a local non-standard variety of Russian, possibly, influenced by the Estonian language. Thus, e.g., the text on Figure 13.11 ('Glasses') *Очки для зрения*, lit. 'glasses for vision', sounds strange in Standard Russian; the preposition *для* 'for' can co-occur with a noun *очки* 'glasses' only when marking the concrete purpose (*очки для чтения,* 'glasses for reading', or *очки для вождения* 'glasses for driving'). Such signs are part of internal communication between local citizens conducted in Russian.

Other places where Russian is widely used include numerous shopping centers. Here, Russian is used to address both local city dwellers and shopping tourist from the other side of the border. In some cases, as in Figure 13.12, it is evident that the outsider's point of view becomes more important: *Товары из Эстонии* 'Goods from Estonia' means not just 'Estonian goods' but 'goods brought from Estonia', i.e. sold not in Estonia but somewhere else. It is either a

Figure 13.10 Hand-written sign ('The shop is open') inside a local shop, Narva.

poor translation made by the Estonian speaker who is non-local to Narva, or an attempt to appeal to the idea that Narva, or at least this particular supermarket, actually is not part of Estonia.

There are also many advertisements of Russian pop-stars and classical music concerts and performances that include Narva as part of the Russian cultural

Figure 13.11 Home-printed signs ('Glasses for vision', 'Glasses for 6.50 €') inside a local shop, Narva.

scene. Figure 13.13 depicts a bulletin board placed in a shopping center. All posters but one are bilingual in Estonian and Russian, and 4 of the 10 refer to events involving guest performers from Russia. Such elements of Narva's linguistic landscape help to maintain the city's Russian identity and represent its close ties with the country across the border.

13.8 Concluding discussion

Contrary to expectations, the situation on the Russian side of the border, in Ivangorod, can hardly be described as a true 'multilingual space of language contact' (Gerst and Klessmann 2015: 2): the linguistic landscape there demonstrates less visual linguistic diversity than that of St. Petersburg and significantly less than that of Narva, Ivangorod's twin city in Estonia. Despite the fact that for many people living in Ivangorod border-crossing practices and interethnic communication are a necessary part of everyday activities, very few adjustments to this reality can be found in the streets of the city. There is a sharp contrast between bordering areas: the Estonian side reveals more typical multilingual patterns for border areas, with 'bottom-up' language management playing a major role in transforming linguistic landscapes. In Ivangorod, nobody, it seems, is trying to make any efforts to address non-Russian speakers;

Figure 13.12 Trilingual advertisement in a supermarket, Narva.

monolingual signs totally prevail. What could explain this lack of linguistic diversity in the urban space? To answer this question, we should firstly consider the ethno-social differences between our two cases; then we will be able to discuss reasons of a more general character.

Naturally, the main reasons for the lack of multilingualism are purely pragmatic. First, Ivangorod's twin city Narva is basically Russian-speaking, which means that most visitors from the other side have no problems with using only Russian. Second, these cities have a different status in terms of touristic attractiveness: Ivangorod has very few – apart from a fortress – to offer to both foreign and Russian tourists, and many of them view it as an optional addition to visiting Narva; the situation is aggravated by the status of a restricted city – Russian citizens, as was already mentioned, can come there only if they have an official permission or Schengen visa. However, there are a few evidences of serious attempts, on the part of local cultural management, to change this situation. It would be possible to make Ivangorod more tourist-friendly, creating, among other measures, a more culturally and linguistically diverse image of the border city. Presumably, local actors lack both ambitions and resources to do so. Instead of promoting multilingualism, Ivangorod retains its image of a 'guardian of Russianness' opposing any foreign influence, be it the Estonian way to spell the name of the country's capital, or refusal to use Estonian alongside English

Figure 13.13 Advertisements of cultural events on a billboard, Narva.

in official signage at the checkpoint. The ideology of monolingualism turns out to be equated with patriotic feelings and nationalism.

Pragmatic reasons, therefore, are not necessarily determinative in this case. Political and symbolic considerations undoubtedly should also be taken into account. Estonian citizens, regardless of their actual linguistic skills, are expected to understand Russian; they are still considered to be a part of the perished Soviet Empire. Another factor is an image of Estonia as a hostile state maintained by official Russian propaganda. Estonian national policy, strict monolingualism and an unwillingness to acknowledge linguistic rights of Russian-speaking residents have been hot topics in Russian media since the beginning of the 1990s (Brednikova and Nikiforova 2018). This scary image of a totalitarian state oppressing a Russian minority still dominates the discourse related to Estonia in Russia despite the fact that, as academic research shows (Berezkina 2015), Russian retains its function of an important linguistic resource and is used widely even by state institutions. Moreover, during their routine visits to Narva for shopping, Ivangorod citizens can actually see for themselves that nobody forbids anyone to use Russian in signs and advertisement there. In Narva's small shops and other local businesses they can observe a consistent use of local Russian addressed to city-dwellers and Russian tourists. This corresponds to attitudes of Russian-speaking residents of Estonia to the Estonian language policy as revealed in interviews in Skerrett (2012): they did not demand their language to have any official status but wanted to see more use of Russian 'on the ground'. However, these factual evidences, as it seems, do not change the generally negative assumptions of people in Russia, especially officials, with regard to Estonia since Russian mass media depict Estonia's language policy towards Russian speakers as extremely hostile. As a result, a monolingual bias and hostile attitudes still dominate the scene in Ivangorod, making the Estonian language *persona non grata* in the city literally living on and economically surviving with the help of the border.

Notes

1. On earlier studies in Japan and Israel see Backhaus 2019 and Gorter and Cenoz 2008 respectively.
2. The bridge was officially named *Druzhba*, 'Friendship' which was quite a popular name in the Soviet Union; e.g., the railroad bridge linking Russia and North Korea is called *Most Druzhby*, 'Bridge of Friendship'.
3. Admission rules for Ivangorod:www.ivangorod.ru/travelers/border-zone/444.html (retrieved 18 Oct. 2019). The history of border zones forbidden for non-residents goes back to the Soviet legislation and restrictions on free movement of people in the country (see Matthews 1989: 118).
4. Actually, there are two check-points for pedestrians but the second one, in Parusinka, an old industrial island district, is less used.
5. E.g. https://uritsk.livejournal.com/188572.html
6. See, e.g., https://puerrtto.livejournal.com/157255.html;https://varlamov.ru/2434012.html and https://varlamov.ru/2435613.html.
7. Unfortunately, it is forbidden to take pictures at checkpoints in Russia so no illustrations can be provided here.

References

Backhaus, P. 2019. Linguistic landscape. In: P. Heinrich and Yu. Ohara (eds.), *Routledge Handbook of Japanese Sociolinguistics*. Routledge, pp. 158–169.

Barton, D. 1994. *Literacy: An Introduction to the Ecology of Written Language*. Oxford: Blackwell.

Berezkina, M. 2015. Russian in Estonia's public sector: 'Playing on the borderline' between official policy and real-life needs. *International Journal of Bilingual Education and Bilingualism*. http://dx.doi.org/10.1080/13670050.2015.1115004

Blackwood, R., Lanza, E. and Woldemariam, H. (eds.). 2016. *Negotiating and Contesting Identities in Linguistic Landscapes*. Oxford: Bloomsbury Academic.

Blommaert, J. 2010. *The Sociolinguistics of Globalization*. Cambridge: Cambridge University Press.

Blommaert, J. 2013. *Ethnography, Superdiversity, and Linguistic Landscapes: Chronicles of Complexity*. Bristol: Multilingual Matters.

Blommaert, J. and Maly, I. 2014. Ethnographic linguistic landscape analysis and social change: A case study. *Tilburg Papers in Culture Studies*100. URL: www.tilburguniversity.edu/upload/6b650494-3bf9-4dd9-904a-5331a0bcf35b_TPCS_100_Blommaert-Maly.pdf

Brednikova, O. 2007. Windows' project ad marginem or the «Divided History» of divided cities? A case study of the Russian-Estonian borderland. In: Ts. Darieva and W. Kaschuba (eds.). *Representations on the Margins of Europe. Politics and Identities in the Baltic and South Caucasian States*. Frankfurt, New York: Campus Verlag, pp. 43–64.

Brednikova, O. and Nikiforova, E. 2018. 'Familiar others': Russian-Finnish and Russian-Estonian borderscapes in the Russian media. In: Ju. Laine, I. Liikanen and J.W. Scott (eds.), *Post-Cold War Borders: Reframing Political Space in Eastern Europe*. Routledge, pp. 110–127.

Brednijova, O. and Voronkov, V. 1999. Граница и реструктурирование социального пространства (случай Нарвы-Ивангорода) [The borders and restructuring of the social space (the case of Narva-Ivangorod)]. In: Brednijova, O. and Voronkov, V. (eds.), Кочующие границы. Сб. статей по материалам международного семинара (Нарва, 12—16 ноября 1998). St. Petersburg: CICR, pp. 19–25.

Bruyèl-Olmedo, A. and Juan-Garau, M. 2015. Minority languages in the linguistic landscape of tourism: The case of Catalan in Mallorca. *Journal of Multilingual and Multicultural Development* 36 (6), 598–619.

Donnan, H. and Wilson, T. M. 1999. *Borders: Frontiers of Identity, Nation and State*. Oxford: Berg Publishers.

Ehala, M. and Zabrodskaja, A. 2014. Ethnolinguistic vitality and acculturation orientations of Russian-speakers in Estonia. In: L. Ryazanova-Clarke (ed.), *Russian Language Outside the Nation*. Edinburgh: Edinburgh University Press, pp. 166–188.

Enríquez Acosta, J. A. 2009. Migration and urbanization in northwest Mexico's border cities. *Journal of the Southwest* 51 (4), 445–455.

Erbsen, H. 2020. Orientalism and Russian speaking minority regions in Europe: representing Narva, *National Identities* 22(1), 151–172.

Fedorova, K. 2011. Transborder trade on the Russian-Chinese border: Problems of interethnic communication. In: B. Bruns and J. P. Miggelbrink (eds.), *Subverting Borders. Doing Research on Smuggling and Small-scale Trade*. Wiesbaden: Verlag für Sozialwissenschaften, Springer, pp. 107–128.

Garret, P. 2010. *Attitudes to Language*. Cambridge University Press.
Garrord, J. and Mikhailova, E. 2019. *Twin Cities. Urban Communities, Borders and Relationships over Time*. London; New York: Routledge.
Gerst, D. and Klessmann, M. 2015. Multilingualism and linguistic demarcations in border regions. The linguistic border landscape of the German-Polish twin cities Frankfurt (Oder) and Słubice. Реторика и комуникации *(Rhetoric and Communications Journal)* 15. URL: http://rhetoric.bg/wp-content/uploads/2015/02/Gerst_Klessmann_-_Linguistic_Border_Landscape-PhD-issue-15-January-2015-last.pdf
Gorter, D. (ed.). 2006. *Linguistic Landscape: A New Approach to Multilingualism*. Clevedon; Buffalo; Toronto: Multilingual matters.
Gorter, D. and Cenoz, J. 2008. Knowledge about language and linguistic landscape. In: N. H. Hornberger (ed.). *Encyclopedia of Language and Education*, 2nd revised edition. Berlin: Springer Science, pp. 343–355.
Gurova, O. and Ratilainen, S. 2016. From shuttle traders to middle-class consumers: Russian tourists in Finnish newspaper discourse between the years 1990 and 2014. *Scandinavian Journal of Hospitality and Tourism* 16 (1), 51–65.
Hall, M. and Tucker, H. (2004). Tourism and postcolonialism. An introduction. In: M. Hall and H. Tucker (eds.), *Tourism and Postcolonialism. Contested Discourses, Identities and Representations*. London; New York: Routledge, pp. 1–24.
Hannerz, U. 1996. *Transnational Connections: Culture, People, Places*. London: Routledge.
Heller, M. 2010. The commodification of language. *Annual Review of Anthropology* 39, 101–114.
Holzlehner, T. 2014. Trading against the state: il/legal cross-border networks in the Russian Far East. *Etnofoor* 26 (1), 13–38.
Hult, F. M. 2018. Language policy and planning and linguistic landscapes. In: J. W. Tollefson and M. Pérez-Milans (eds.), *Oxford Handbook of Language Policy and Planning*. New York: Oxford University Press, pp. 333–351.
Jaworski, A. and Thurlow, C. 2010a. Introducing semiotic landscapes. In: A. Jaworski and C. Thurlow (eds.), *Semiotic Landscapes. Language, Image, Space*. Continuum International Publishing Group, pp. 1–40.
Jaworski, A. and Thurlow, C. 2010b. Language and the globalizing habitus of tourism: Toward a sociolinguistics of fleeting relationships. In: N. Coupland (ed.), *The Handbook of Language and Globalization*. Wiley-Blackwell, pp. 255–286.
Johnstone, B. 2011. Language and place. In: R. Mesthrie (ed.), *The Cambridge Handbook of Sociolinguistics*. Cambridge University Press, pp. 203–217.
Laine, J. 2017. Finnish-Russian border mobility and tourism: Localism overruled by geopolitics. In: D. Hall (ed.) *Tourism and Geopolitics: Issues and Concepts from Central and Eastern Europe*. CABI, Wallingford, pp. 182–195.
Long, D. and Nakai, S. 2014. Researching non-standard dialect usage in linguistic landscapes. In: A. Barysevich, A. D'Arcy and D. Heap (eds.), *Proceedings of the 14th International Conference on Methods in Dialectology*. Frankfurt: Peter Lang, pp. 228–235.
Lu, S., Li, G. and Xu, M. 2020. The linguistic landscape in rural destinations: A case study of Hongcun Village in China. *Tourism Management* 77, 1–9. https://doi.org/10.1016/j.tourman.2019.104005
Malinowski, D. 2009. Authorship in the linguistic landscape. A multimodal-performative view. In: E. Shohamy and D. Gorter (eds.) *Linguistic Landscape. Expanding the Scenery*. New York; London: Routledge, pp. 107–125.
Marten, H. F. 2010. Linguistic landscape under strict state language policy: Reversing the Soviet legacy in a regional centre in Latvia. In: Ben-Rafael, E., Shohamy, E. and

Barni M. (eds.), *Linguistic Landscape in the City*. Bristol: Multilingual Matters, pp. 115–132.

Marten, H. F., Lazdiņa, S., Pošeiko, P. and Marinska, S. 2012. Between old and new killer languages? Linguistic transformation, linguae francae and languages of tourism in the Baltic states. In: C. Hélot, M. Barni, R. Janssens and C. Bagna (eds.), *Linguistic Landscapes, Multilingualism and Social Change*. Frankfurt am Main: Peter Lang, pp.. 289–308.

Martínez, F. 2018. *Remains of the Soviet Past in Estonia. An Anthropology of Forgetting, Repair and Urban Traces*. London: UCL Press.

Matthews.M. (ed.). 1989. *Party, State, and Citizen in the Soviet Union. A Collection of Documents*. Armonk; London: M. E. Sharpe, Inc.

Miller, H. and Miller, K. 1996. Language policy and identity: The case of Catalonia. *International Studies in Sociology of Education* 6 (1), 113–128.

Mirvahedi, S. H. 2016. Linguistic landscaping in Tabriz, Iran: A discursive transformation of a bilingual space into monolingual place. *International Journal of the Sociology of Language* 242, 195–216.

Moriarty, M. 2014. Contesting language ideologies in the linguistic landscape of an Irish tourist town. *International Journal of Bilingualism* 18 (5), 464–477.

Nikiforova, E. 2004. The disruption of social and geographic space in Narva. In: R. Alapuro, I. Liikanen and M. Lonkila (eds.), *Beyond Post-Soviet Transition: Micro Perspectives on Challenge and Survival in Russia and Estonia*. Saarijärvi: Kikimora Publications, pp. 148–164.

Nugent, P. 2012. Border towns and cities in comparative perspective. In: Th. M. Wilson and H. Donnan (eds.). *A Companion to Border Studies*. Oxford: Wiley-Blackwell, pp. 557–572.

Pertostat [Official website of Federal State Statistic Service for St. Petersburg's and Leningrad region]. 2019. Численность постоянного населения Ленинградской области в разрезе муниципальных образований по состоянию на 1 января 2019 года. [The number of permanent residents of Leningrad region by municipal districts up to January 1, 2019] http://petrostat.gks.ru/wps/wcm/connect/rosstat_ts/petrostat/resources/7dabbe8049a8aaf29788df3fbd401489/%D0%9B%D0%9E+%D1%87%D0%B8%D1%81%D0%BB++%D0%BD%D0%B0+01.01.2019+.pdf

Pfoser, A. 2017. Nested peripheralisation: Remaking the East–West border in the Russian–Estonian borderland. *East European Politics and Societies* 31(1), 26–43.

Philipson, R. 2009. *Linguistic Imperialism Continued*. New York; London: Routledge.

Ruzaitė, J. 2017. The linguistic landscape of tourism: Multilingual signs in Lithuanian and Polish resorts. *Eesti ja Soome-Ugri Keeleteaduse Ajakiri* 8 (1), 197–220.

Skerrett, D. M. 2012. How normal is normalization? The discourses shaping Finnish and Russian speakers' attitudes toward Estonian Language policy. *Journal of Baltic Studies* 43(3), 363–388.

Stern, D. 2016. Negotiating goods and language on cross-border retail markets in the post-socialist space. In: Kamusella, T., Nomachi, M. and Gibson, C. (eds.), *The Palgrave Handbook of Slavic Languages, Identities and Borders*. Palgrave Macmillan, London. pp. 495–523.

Thurlow, C. and Jaworski, A. 2010. Silence is golden: The 'anti-communicational' linguascaping of super-elite mobility. In: A. Jaworski and C. Thurlow (eds.), *Semiotic Landscapes. Language, Image, Space*. Continuum International Publishing Group, pp. 187–218.

Tislenko, M. and Okunev, I. 2017. Geopolitical positioning of twin cities: A case study of Narva/Ivangorod, Valga/Valka, and Blagoveshchensk/Heihe. *Teorija in Praksa* 54 (3/4), 592–702.

van Schendel, W. 2005. Spaces of engagement: How borderlands, illicit flows, and territorial states interlock. In: W. van Schendel and I. Abraham (eds.), *Illicit Flows and Criminal Things, States, Borders, and the Other Side of Globalisation*. Bloomington: Indiana University Press, pp. 38–68.

Verschik, A. 2002. Russian-Estonian language contacts and interference mechanisms. *Trames* 6 (56/57), 3, 245–265.

Vigouroux, C. 2009. A relational understanding of language practice: Interacting timespaces in a single ethnographic site. In: J. Collins, S. Slembrouck and M. Baynham. *Globalization and Language in Contact. Scale, Migration and Communicative Practices*. London & New York: Continuum International Publishing Group, pp. 62–84.

Vlasov, A. S. and El'kin, G. N. 2011. *Древнерусские крепости Северо-Запада* [Ancient Russian Fortresses of the North-West]. St. Petersburg: Paritet.

Wachowiak, H. (ed.). 2006. *Tourism and Borders. Contemporary Issues, Policies and International Research*. Aldershot: Ashgate Publishing Company.

Xiao, R. 2018. The Linguistic landscape of Beijing tourism spots: A field-based sociolinguistic approach. *International Journal of Languages, Literature and Linguistics* 4 (1), 23–28.

Zotova, M., Gritsenko, A. and Sebentsov, A. 2018. Повседневная жизнь в российском пограничье: мотивы и факторы трансграничных практик [Everyday life in Russian borderland: motives and factors of trans-border practices]. *Мир России / Universe of Russia* 27 (4), 56–77.

14 'Nothing personal, just business'

Individuals as actors in changing monolingual linguistic landscapes in Vyborg, Russia

V. Baranova and K. Fedorova

14.1 Introduction

Linguistic landscapes existing in certain geographical places and historical times can be seen as static pictures, collections of written texts naming different objects, prescribing or forbidding some activities, explaining rules, advertising services, etc. Undoubtedly, they can serve as a valuable source of information on societal practices and norms of language use. At the same time, we can look at these 'spatially embedded' texts with a different perspective, seeing them as a result of someone's actions. In this sense, every sign, announcement, or advertisement is created by someone driven by their own reasons, goals, and ambitions.

The issue of agency, i.e. the capacity of individuals responsible for creating the signs to act independently, is highly important for linguistic landscape studies; it is related to issues of literacy, language rights, and identity (Woldemariam and Lanza 2014). If taken out of its social context, it may appear as representing merely an individual taste. For instance, analyzing linguistic landscape and visual resources in Leeds Kirkgate Market, Adami (2020) emphasises its creators' obvious freedom in choosing décor, fonts, colors, etc., focusing on semiotic diversity produced from below. However, in more complicated cases, where, e.g., non-fully accepted minority languages and their scripts are involved, we see that what looks on the surface as merely individual tastes can in fact be interpreted as shaped by societal norms, beliefs, and prejudices. Recent studies show 'how individual and collective identities are manifested and contested in the L[inguistic]L[andscapes] of contemporary urban spaces' (Blackwood et al. 2016: xvii). When placing some signboards or advertisement at their premises, business owners can consciously try to represent linguistic diversity and use multiple tools for that, or deliberately choose to avoid some 'problematic' languages, or simply follow monolingual ideology without any reflection. Different strategies of minority languages usage in linguistic landscape can be analyzed in terms of 'the management of linguistic landscape' (Sloboda et al. 2010). Moreover, these strategies can provoke different reactions from potential clients. Recent research in Cheboksary, the capital of Chuvash Republic in Russia (Alòs i Font 2019), focuses on the impact on linguistic landscape by citizens who are actively involved in inspecting how the law on minority language usage is executed: they report places where official bilingual signs are lacking. Recipients, therefore, can also shape linguistic landscapes; they can support multilingualism and promote the visibility of minority languages, or they can reject usage of some languages due to their stereotypes about 'suitability' of these languages, or their written forms, for public areas.

As our previous studies show (Fedorova and Baranova 2018; Baranova and Fedorova 2019), big Russian cities tend to maintain a 'monolingual façade' misrepresenting their actual multilingualism. Notwithstanding some detailed restricting measures, such as regulation of the font size of signboards in Moscow, in general language management in Moscow and St. Petersburg is implemented under the conditions of a 'no-policy policy' (Fishman 2006: 318) which always favors the stronger – majority – party on the scene. Migrant workers, speakers of different languages, have to comply with implicit rules demanding not to use languages other than Russian in public spaces (Baranova and Fedorova 2018). Written communication in the languages used by migrants, therefore, is usually limited to in-group communication and tends to occur in places hidden from the eyes of the Russian-speaking majority (Baranova and Fedorova 2019). However, migrants are not the only group affected by such negligence of their language problems. Foreign tourists to Russia also experience many language-based problems in their daily activities: everything, from navigating around the city to obtaining medical treatment, is more demanding if one does not speak and read Russian. Thus, e.g., street signs in central St. Petersburg do show transliterated street names but written in a font three times smaller than their Cyrillic versions (Figure 14.1), and outside the city center all such signs are monolingual. Despite the fact that English as an international language is becoming more and more popular and trendy, and therefore is used in many brand names and advertisements, practical information provided in English is usually insufficient.

On the other hand, some increase in the number of multilingual signs can be witnessed in recent years, as well as some subtle changes in language attitudes (Baranova and Fedorova 2020). Going behind the simple statement of this fact, we can try to address the problem of changes in linguistic landscapes as a part of more general transformations in a language regime, with a focus on agents of these transformations. Linguistic landscapes are not static and stable; they change along with the situation. Even more importantly, all these changes are implemented by people acting under their own agendas. However, their actions, motivations and attitudes are not arbitrary; they are based on certain sets of norms and beliefs existing in a given society. At the same time, conventional norms can come into conflict with socio-economic reasons. Then, while pursuing their own business goals, individuals may start to challenge those conventional norms.

Border cities, i.e. cities situated in a close proximity to state borders and using them as important economic resources, are usually seen as places of intensive

Figure 14.1 Street sign for Shpalernaya str., St. Petersburg.

cultural and linguistic contacts (for more details on border cities studies see Fedorova and Baranova (this volume). One should expect them to be more culturally diverse and visually multilingual than the rest of the country. However, when looking at the linguistic landscape of Vyborg, a city in the Leningrad region situated at a one-hour distance by train from St. Petersburg (121 km) and 30 km from the Russian-Finnish border, one can inevitably conclude that visual linguistic diversity there is significantly less than, e.g., in St. Petersburg. In this chapter, we will try to explain this phenomenon by examining the data on the linguistic landscape of this border city, with a focus on agency and grass-roots language management, and ideological frameworks they come into conflict with.

The chapter is structured as follows: first, in the next section, our data and research methodology are explained; the section after that describes in short the socio-economic context for border-crossing activities in the Russian-Finnish border area; the subsequent section is dedicated to linguistic landscape data in Vyborg. Data from interviews are presented after that; in the concluding section, we summarise our findings, try to suggest possible explanations, with the focus on agency in language management, and outline further perspectives for gradual transformations in language regime as a result of individual efforts.

14.2 Method and data

The chapter focuses on Vyborg's linguistic landscape and the changes it has been undergoing in recent years. In particular, our research aims at evaluating the temporal dynamic in the spreading of multilingual signs as well as its possible causes. The well-known limitation of linguistic landscape studies is underrepresentation of such a temporal dimension: a synchronous 'snapshot' of visual images often fails to reveal development and transformation of linguistic landscapes. At the same time, due to different social or political factors, typical patterns of representation or ways of transcribing linguistic contents may change rather rapidly and drastically. Discussing the linguistic landscape of Tokyo in a diachronic perspective, P. Backhaus points out the phenomenon of 'layering', or coexistence of different multilingual signs. A possible 'way of detecting changes in the linguistic landscape when data from only one point in time are available is to concentrate on the coexistence of older and newer versions of a certain sign' (Backhaus 2005: 106). Following this methodology, we were also able to use comparative data, including pictures made in the same places in Vyborg with an eight-year interval. Our recent linguistic landscape data were collected in May 2018; we made digital photos of all multilingual and some monolingual signs (street signs, advertisements, announcements, graffiti, etc.; overall 70 photos) in areas around Vyborg railway station, Sobornaya square, Vyborg Castle and central streets. We have similar data (28 photos) from the previous project conducted in 2010 and reported in Fedorova and Gavrilova (2010). By analyzing and comparing our data from different decades, we try to understand what circumstances could be conducive to further changes. We also used other methods of obtaining data: we observed interactions in public places and tried to elicit reactions to the elements of linguistic landscapes from some Vyborg citizens.

Another research question for us is about the further possible development of the linguistic landscape and, more broadly, multilingualism in the city. What potential changes related to multilingualism can occur there, and what factors can advance these changes? What actors are involved in maintaining or challenging the monolingual linguistic landscape and spreading multilingual awareness? The language management framework (Language Management Theory) is a broad approach focusing on actors and their actions towards language (Spolsky 2009). Such actions may be divided into macro (organised management) am micro (simple management) levels of efforts (Nekvapil 2016). In situations like those described in this chapter, where organised management does not manifest itself explicitly, micro-level management becomes even more important. In our analysis, we try to go beyond the surface of linguistic landscape and understand if different motivations of the involved actors could result in promoting linguistic diversity and challenging the existing monolingual ideology. For understanding this issue, we interviewed Vyborg residents in August 2019. Additional sources of information, such as, web sites, travel blogs, and discussions on internet forums and in social media were used to supplement data for analysis. A focus on agents creating linguistic landscape presupposes the attention to the authors' intention when creating signs, and recipients' reading of them. In our approach to linguistic landscape, we follow Blommaert's methodology of ELLA (Ethnographic Linguistic Landscape Analysis), which examines written signs as a part of the communication process (Blommaert 2013; Blommaert and Maly 2014); this analysis aims at revealing motivations and attitudes of actors influencing linguistic landscape and can provide us with a deeper understanding of processes behind language use.

14.3 Political and economic background of Vyborg

Vyborg is a city in the Leningrad region situated 30 km from the Finnish-Russian border. In January 2019, it had 76,389 residents (Pertostat 2019: 3). Thus, it is a relatively large city (before 1940 it was the second big city in Finland, to which it belonged at that time). Vyborg was founded as a Swedish fortress in Karelia at the end of the thirteenth century; its later history reflected changes in dominance of different groups, states and languages in the area but mostly it is associated with Finns and Finnish. Thus, Finnish has a controversial status in the region: at the same time, it is a language of a local minority, Ingrian Finns (speaking several dialects of Finnish), and the language of the neighboring state. Vyborg Castle is the most famous and well-preserved European medieval fortress in Russia, making the city a popular weekend destination for tourists from St. Petersburg. Nowadays Vyborg exists as both an industrial (there are ship-repair yards and factories producing farm machinery and electrical equipment) and a touristic center.

In the 1990s, Finnish citizens could come to Vyborg for one day without visas, and these 'drunken' tours – christened in this way due to tourists' strong interest in consuming cheap Russian alcoholic drinks – were quite popular. Later border regulations became less flexible, and the tourist flow decreased. Nevertheless, many dwellers of Lappeenranta and other Finnish border cities and towns obtain Russian multi-entry visas and make regular short trips to the Russian side of the border to buy much cheaper petrol, cigarettes and alcohol. Shopping trips from Russia to Lappeenranta, Imatra and other Finnish cities are also extremely popular, especially because many residents of the St. Petersburg and Leningrad region obtain their Schengen visas from the General Consulate of Finland; in order to use them to travel all around Europe they have to 'check in' in Finland, making at least one short trip there. While the overall level of shopping tourism from Northwestern Russia to Finland has been rather stable during three decades, the specific purposes of such short trips changed several times. In the 1990s, many Russians from St. Petersburg and Vyborg were involved in the trans-border shuttle trade; nowadays most tourists are buying Finnish goods for themselves. As Gurova and Ratilainen (2016) state, these changes were discussed in Finnish media as a change from 'shuttle traders' to 'middle-class consumers'. At the same time, there are semi-legal schemes of wholesale purchases and deliveries for customers making online orders for Finnish food items banned in Russia, and such schemes probably involve hired buyers.

Vyborg, the same way as Ivangorod (see Chapter 13), serves as a stepping stone on the way to the bordering state: the fast train *Allegro* linking St. Petersburg with Helsinki makes a stop here, and there is a border checkpoint at Vyborg railway station; many tourist buses going to Finland from St. Petersburg also make a stop in front of the railway station, and direct buses and minibuses from Vyborg to different Finnish destinations start from the same point. The railway station, therefore, occupies a prominent position in the city's semiotic landscape. Another important place emphasising closeness to Finland is Vyborg's market, situated on Sobornaya Square in the building constructed with the same architecture who built Hakaniemi market in Helsinki. After its completion at the beginning of the twentieth century, Vyborg's market was considered the biggest in Scandinavia. Nowadays it is the place where most tourists buy souvenirs and local products.

14.4 Vyborg's linguistic landscape: controversial tendencies

It is natural to start the discussion of Vyborg's linguistic landscape from its main tourist place, the market. It is divided in two parts: an open space, with temporary market stalls on the square in front of the historical building, and the indoor market inside it. The market is serving mostly Russian and Finnish tourists; it is no surprise, therefore, that only these two languages are used here, and English or, e.g., Chinese – main touristic languages in St. Petersburg (see Baranova and Fedorova 2020) – are absent from its linguistic landscape. All the signs using Finnish, though, are found inside while on the square everything is advertised exclusively in Russian, including those products that can be attractive for foreign tourists – e.g., traditional Russian beverages and jams. Indoors, there are two types of Finnish signs which can be differentiated; on the one hand, by their authors and their level of authority, and on the other hand, by their material/techniques. First, there are permanent bilingual billboards installed by the market administration; they provide the same information in both Russian and Finnish. Printed in one style and using the same green-yellow colors, these signs mark an entrance to the market, its exit, toilets and cafés as well as different sections of the market listing the products sold in them (Figure 14.2). Second, there are handwritten or home-printed signs made by sellers or owners of small shops. They advertise their products and prices (Figure 14.3). These signs may also serve as a signal for Finnish customers that they can expect to be able to communicate in Finnish in such places (Figure 14.4). During our fieldwork in 2018, we never had a chance to witness any interaction between Finnish and Russian speakers. In 2010, such dialogues were recorded; Russian sellers used some basic 'market Finnish' and tried to learn new words from their customers (see Fedorova and Gavrilova 2010). Official bilingual billboards had already been installed in 2010; they stayed in the same places in 2018. One more place

Figure 14.2 Bilingual sign inside Central Market, Vyborg.

where Finnish was present was the stall with unlicensed DVDs; among Russian and American movies there, there were also some Finnish (and in Finnish) ones sold, probably; much cheaper than in Finland and attractive therefore for some not-so-law-abiding Finnish tourists.

Figure 14.3 Home-printed sign ('Fresh bread') inside Central Market, Vyborg.

Against all expectations and in contrast with the rather wide use of Finnish in the indoor market, other Vyborg places that are potentially attractive for foreigners look overwhelmingly monolingual. Vyborg Castle, a natural point of attraction for every city visitor, is a prime example of this tendency. All information on the museum provided there, such as opening hours or ticket prices, are only in Russian, and direction signs are stylised to look like ancient road signs and are also monolingual (Figure 14.5). The only multilingual – and even trilingual – sign found in the vicinity of the castle is an advertisement for a souvenir shop, and it uses English and Chinese but not Finnish (Figure 14.6). Most other shops around the city do not employ foreign languages to advertise themselves and attract non-Russian customers. The same is true for various services such as bicycle or boat rentals – it looks like no one tries to sell anything to foreigners beyond the market and it serves as the only place assigned for such trade. Restaurants and cafés show a different approach to foreigners. The budget ones tend to ignore them the same way as shops but ones that are more expensive do make some adjustments for potential foreign clients. Some, usually midrange cafés, use Finnish (and not English) in their signs; e.g., adding to their name besides the Russian word кафе, 'café', its Finnish equivalent *kahvila*. However, that is the limit to their efforts in promoting multilingualism: all practical information, including menus, is only in Russian. It may be

Figure 14.4 Hand-written sign ('We serve in Finnish') inside Central Market, Vyborg.

interpreted also as a sign that here you can be served in Finnish because some of the Vyborg dwellers can speak Finnish a little bit; however, it is not necessarily the case. More often, it is merely a symbolic gesture, a 'welcome' sign; it aims to show hospitality but could be misleading if some tourists decide they wish to find a menu and other information in Finnish there. Similar cases of the purely symbolic use of languages other than Russian are typical for businesses trying to target new – migrant – audiences in our St. Petersburg data (Baranova and Fedorova 2019).

More complex multilingual strategies are found at the most posh places. In such hotels and hotel restaurants, menus and leaflets listing services and prices are usually trilingual – in Russian, English, and Finnish (Figure 14.7), and sometimes bilingual and trilingual signs (e.g., with information about opening hours) can also be found there. At the same time, there are certain limits to their level of multilingualism. Thus, situated just across the market hotel named *Виктория*, 'Victoria', where the photo from Figure 14.7 was taken, runs its web site in Russian and in English but not in Finnish. An even more interesting case is represented by the restaurant *Круглая башня*, 'The round turret', also situated in close proximity to the Central market. On a historical map of Vyborg's fortifications painted on the wall at the entrance hall (Figure 14.8), notations are given in Russian, Finnish, and Sweden, referring to the languages

Figure 14.5 Direction sign in Vyborg Castle.

and cultures that for centuries determined the city's destiny. Strikingly, the city's name on the top is written only in Finnish and Swedish and not even in Russian. The menu is also trilingual but in a more conventional way; it uses English, not Swedish. The same trilingual menu can be found on the restaurant

Figure 14.6 Trilingual souvenir shop's advertisement near Vyborg Castle.

website; how anyone not speaking Russian can obtain that menu is unclear, though – apart from the menu itself, the web site is purely monolingual, and to get to the page with this 'main menu' (*основное меню*) one needs to navigate in Russian. Moreover, there are two types of group menus, one for Russian

Figure 14.7 Trilingual menu, restaurant Вкус ('Taste'), hotel Victoria, Vyborg.

Figure 14.8 Historic map of Vyborg on the wall of the restaurant Круглая башня ('The round turret').

tourists and one for foreigners (with prices twice as high); these are written only in Russian. Probably, all group visits for Finnish tourists are organised via Russian tourist agencies.

In the case where we can compare our new data with those from 2010 from the same place – café *Глория* 'Gloria' – it is evident that its management moved forward on the way to multilingualism. In 2010, Finnish was used there only symbolically: several words in Finnish such as *Salateja* 'salads' and *Liha* 'meat' were added on the otherwise Russian billboard near its entrance (Figure 14.9).

Figure 14.9 Billboard near café Gloria, Vyborg, 2010.

Figure 14.10 Official trilingual sign, Vyborg railway station, 2010.

but there was no any other information in Finnish available inside. In 2018, still not all epyinformation available in Russian was presented in Finnish, but menus in English and in Finnish has appeared.

Evidently, at least some businesses in Vyborg do try to create a more diverse linguistic landscape. However, at and near the railway station, this natural hub of all travelers going to and via Vyborg, the opposite tendencies are discovered. First, while in 2010 official signage at the station was trilingual in Russian, English, and Finnish, nowadays these trilingual signs are substituted by new bilingual ones using only Russian and English. (Figure 14.10 and 14.11).

Moreover, Finnish was not only substituted by English as the only foreign language; it was literally erased from the linguistic landscape! On the photos presented in Figure 14.12 and 14.13 and taken in 2010 and in 2018, consequently, we can see the same sign for a car wash placed in front of the railway station. In 2010, it was bilingual; in 2018, there are no traces of Finnish apart from an empty space. Next-door café Jorma underwent the same transformation: the Finnish text was erased from its sign. Such an awkward retreat to monolingualism can hardly be explained by the initiative of local businessmen; most probably, they had to follow the orders from local administration. Unlike the cases of similar erasure of Polish from the signs in Czechia described in Sloboda et al. (2010), there is no evident conflict between official language

Figure 14.11 Bilingual sign for tourist information centre, Vyborg railway station, 2018.

Figure 14.12 Car wash in front of the railway station, Vyborg, 2010.

Figure 14.13 The same car wash in front of the railway station, Vyborg, 2018.

policy and grass-root actions; moreover, the issues of language policy are not discussed in the open.

14.5 Individual efforts, challenges and failures

Viborg's linguistics landscape, therefore, at first glance looks monolingual with rare elements of multilingualism aimed at tourists, mostly, but not exclusively, Finnish. However, the comparison between the data collected in 2010 and in 2018 reveals a more controversial pattern. In the 1990s and early 2000s, Vyborg was more oriented towards Finnish visitors, not only regular tourists but also 'nostalgic tourists', i.e., people whose families had moved to Finland after 1940. These tourists aiming to have a look at the place of their or their parent's birth had started to come to Vyborg in the early 1980s, several years before Perestroika and lessening of international tensions were declared by Gorbachev in 1985; they influenced the formation of Vyborg's new identity as a city for foreigners (Shikalov 2016). In the 1990s, signs in Finnish represented both the city's hospitality to visitors from the neighboring country and, at the same time, the identity of Vyborg as a Finnish city. Nowadays, the new image of Vyborg as a romantic medieval city is promoted by its government and media. This image is designed mostly for the purpose of inner tourism and has no need for the Finnish language.

Thus, the development of Vyborg's linguistic landscape reveals a turn (at the official level) from approved Russian-Finnish bilingualism to more hostile attitudes to Finnish. English is used in some official signs as a neutral international language for all non-Russian-speaking tourists. In practical terms, for most tourists from Finland English is enough; nevertheless, discarding Finnish, Vyborg inevitably loses its identity of a border city, 'a bridge' between Russia and Finland. In these circumstances, any changes in the linguistic landscape favoring Finnish and multilingualism in general can only be done by actors still trying to benefit from the vicinity to the border. Indeed, language planning is implemented not only by top-down efforts; as shown above, all elements of Vyborg's linguistic landscape employing Finnish – be it handwritten Finnish signs at Vyborg's market or menus at posh restaurants – are examples of micro-level language management exercised by business owners and individuals involved in business interactions with Finns.

Another interesting case of such individual contributions to the progress of multilingualism is an attempt to organise Finnish language courses in Vyborg. Our informants, a mixed Russian-Finnish family, after spending 15 years in Lappeenranta, moved their business to Vyborg. In Finland, besides providing services for Russian speakers, they conducted courses of Russian for local business employees, border officers, and other categories of people dealing with Russians. These courses were supported and partly financed by the city's administration. After moving to Vyborg, they had an ambition to implement a similar project there. They started to advertise Finnish classes aiming at two categories of clients: people planning to emigrate to Finland, and hotel and restaurant staff. For the latter they designed a special course; 'Finnish for business'. Despite many interested responses, they never managed to gather a group for this course while a 'general' Finnish course was quite successful. In Finland, hotels and restaurants contributed to their employees' education by paying half of the fee. In Vyborg, nobody was ready to pay the full price just to become more efficient at their work with Finnish tourists while employers, although expressing the ardent wish to provide better services for Finnish clients, were not eager to pay either. According to our informants, in general, all Vyborg's citizen they ever contacted displayed very positive attitudes to the Finnish language and would not mind its more visible presence in the city. Moreover, as Svetlana, our respondent, put it, 'any second Vyborg's dweller some way or other will be able to say something in Finnish'. However, the lack of support at the governmental level and poor economic situation in the city prevent further growth of multilingualism. Still, as a newcomer in the city, she testifies to the recent increase in the number of signs in Finnish, and all this increase should be attributed to the efforts of business owners and individual entrepreneurs. Her observations, therefore, confirm our conclusions based on the linguistic landscape data.

14.5 Concluding discussion

Our study, therefore, reveals crucial differences between top-down and bottom-up approaches to language management; this opposition, often discussed in relation to language policy studies, turns out to be extremely important in the case of Vyborg. In the absence of official support to multilingualism, local business still tries to use more languages in its day-to-day work with clients. When creating the linguistic landscape, at least some Russian business establishments in Vyborg use Finnish in their signs as a marker of hospitality for tourists; however, their efforts are at variance with the official policy of municipal administration using English as the only 'foreign' language. Moreover, as our comparison of the data from 2010 and 2018 shows, Finnish was used by Vyborg officials before; nowadays, though, its existence in the linguistic landscape is not supported by them anymore, or is probably even frowned upon, which could explain the disappearance of Finnish from the commercial signs around the railway station. Interestingly, as anthropological studies show, cross-border cooperation between Finnish and European Union cultural organisations, on the one hand, and Russian authorities, on the other hand, in most cases was not very successful and even problematic due to the latter's lack of interest to Finnish cultural heritage, as is visible in the case of the Alvar Aalto library in Vyborg (Kiiskinen 2012). Most probably, any references to the former Finnish presence at the territory are seen as potentially politically dangerous and consequently unwelcome. Moreover, as Jauhiainen (2002: 174) states, 'From the viewpoint of the state, cross-border cooperation should not challenge the 'taken-for-granted' idea of a state as the most significant territorial power'. Control over the territory can be implemented in different ways, and regulation of languages used in the linguistic landscape is a graphic example of such attempts at control.

If we compare our data on linguistic landscape in Vyborg to our study of another Russian border area, Ivangorod, co-existing with its Estonian 'twin', Narva (see Chapter 13), it becomes evident that in both these cases, close proximity to the border *per se* does not determine tendencies of linguistic landscape development. Neither Ivangorod, nor Vyborg, despite being the cities profiting by the borders, can be described as visually multilingual and diverse. Nevertheless, while Ivangorod looks like a total outpost of monolingualism, in the case of Vyborg, there are some manifestations of gradual changes not totally disguised by its monolingual façade. To analyze them properly we need to take into consideration the following. The influence borders may have on changes in linguistic practices is by no means direct: after the 'opening' of the border in the beginning of the 1990s, Vyborg citizens became more mobile; unlike the Soviet times, many of them are involved in border-crossing activities and can observe how urban spaces are organised in other places. Attempts, even unsuccessful, to transfer business and cultural models and apply them in Russia, as in the case of language courses in Vyborg, are very important. They demonstrate, on the one hand, problems faced by actors trying to oppose monolingual dominance; on the other hand, the very fact of their existence means there is some interaction between two opposing views of language regimes prevailing in Russia and Finland.

Summing up, our study on Vyborg's linguistic landscape leads to several conclusions. First, the existence of visual multilingualism in Vyborg totally depends on efforts of individuals and business owners. While registering multilingual texts placed in the city's landscape, we should always bear in mind that behind any such texts there are individual actors who are responsible for creating them. By pursuing their own – purely commercial – goals, they, probably unintentionally, have to challenge dominating patterns of language attitudes and monolingual ideology in general. Such an actor-based approach is in line with the recent shift of focus in language management studies to the efforts of local actors involved in language planning on the micro-level (Liddicoat and Baldauf 2008). The concept of authorship (Malinowski 2009) is important for linguistic landscape studies, especially in situations where bottom-up efforts contradict both top-down official policy and a well-established tradition of monolingualism.

Second, linguistic landscapes tend to be very fluid and flexible on the surface. Temporal dimension of linguistic landscape, therefore, cannot be ignored; deep, or 'thick', in Geertzian terms, an ethnographic description of a multilingual city is necessary to go beyond momentary imprints and surface observations. At any historical moment, linguistic landscape consists of several 'layers', sometimes contradicting each other, as, e.g., is the case with old Soviet signs on buildings in Narva, or old signs containing Finnish and new, Finnish-free, signs in Vyborg. To understand if such signs are 'the traces of the past' or 'the green shoots of the future' is impossible without a longitudinal perspective and inclusion of insider information obtained not from landscapes but from people who create, use, and change them.

References

Adami, E. 2020. Shaping public spaces from below: the vernacular semiotics of Leeds Kirkgate Market, *Social Semiotics*, 30:1, 89–113, DOI: 10.1080/10350330.2018.1531515

Alòs i Font, H. 2019. Russian, Chuvash and English: Minority-language activism, tourism promotion and the evolution of municipal advertisements in Shupashkar/Cheboksary (2015-2018). A. Nikunlassi and E. Protassova (eds.), *Russian Language in the Multilingual World*. Slavica Helsingiensia 52. Helsinki: University of Helsinki: 68–86.

Backhaus, P. 2005. Signs of multilingualism in Tokyo – a diachronic look at the linguistic landscape. *International Journal of the Sociology of Language*, 2005(103–121). doi:10.1515/ijsl.2005.2005.175-176.103

Baranova, V. and Fedorova, K. 2018. Многоязычие в городе: языковая политика, дискурсы и практика [Urban multilingualism: language policy, discourses, and practice]. *Труды Института лингвистических исследований (Acta Linguistica Petropolitana)* 14 (3), 38–56.

Baranova, V. and Fedorova, K. 2019. 'Invisible minorities' and 'hidden diversity' in St. Petersburg's linguistic landscape. *Language & Communication* 68: 17–27. https://doi.org/10.1016/j.langcom.2018.10.013

Baranova, V. and Fedorova, K. 2020. Видимо-невидимо: миграция и трансформация языкового ландшафта Санкт-Петербурга [(In)visibility: Migration and transformation of St. Petersburg's linguistic landscape]. *Laboratorium: Russian Review of Social Research* 12 (1), 105–137.

Blackwood, R., Lanza, E. and H. Woldemariam. 2016. Preface. Negotiating and contesting identities in linguistic landscapes. In: Blackwood, R., Lanza, E. and Woldemariam, H. (eds.), *Negotiating and Contesting Identities in Linguistic Landscapes*. Oxford: Bloomsbury Academic, XVI–XXIV.

Blommaert, J. 2013. *Ethnography, Superdiversity, and Linguistic Landscapes: Chronicles of Complexity*. Bristol: Multilingual Matters.

Blommaert, J. and Maly, I. 2014. Ethnographic linguistic landscape analysis and social change: A case study. *Tilburg Papers in Culture Studies* 100. URL: www.tilburguniversity.edu/upload/6b650494-3bf9-4dd9-904a-5331a0bcf35b_TPCS_100_Blommaert-Maly.pdf

Fedorova, K. and Baranova, V. 2018. Moscow: diversity in disguise. In: P. Heinrich and D. Smakman (eds.), *Urban Sociolinguistics. The City as a Linguistic Process and Experience*. Routledge, pp. 221–237.

Fedorova, K. and Gavrilova, T. 2010. Native speakers of Russian in interethnic communication: Sociolinguistic situations and linguistic strategies. In: A. Mustajoki, E. Protassova and N. Vakhtin (eds.), *Slavica Helsingiensia 40. Instrumentarium of linguistics. Sociolinguistic approaches to non-standard Russian*. Helsinki: Helsinki University Press, pp. 52–67.

Fishman, J. A. 2006. Language policy and language shift. In: T. Ricento (ed.), *An Introduction to Language Policy: Theory and Method*. New York: Blackwell, pp. 311–328.

Gurova, O. and Ratilainen, S. 2016. From shuttle traders to middle-class consumers: Russian tourists in Finnish newspaper discourse between the years 1990 and 2014. *Scandinavian Journal of Hospitality and Tourism* 16 (1), 51–65.

Jauhiainen, J. 2002. Territoriality and topocracy of cross-border networks. *Journal of Baltic Studies* 33 (2), 156–176.

Kiiskinen, K. 2012. Border/land sustainability: Communities at the external border of the European Union. *Anthropological Journal of European Cultures* 21 (1), 22–40.

Liddicoat, A. J. and Baldauf, R. B. 2008. Language planning in local contexts: Agents, contexts and interactions. In: A. J. Liddicoat and R. B. Baldauf (eds.), *Language Planning in Local Contexts*. Clevedon: Multilingual Matters, pp. 3–17.

Malinowski, D. 2009. Authorship in the linguistic landscape. A multimodal-performative view. In: E. Shohamy and D. Gorter (eds.), *Linguistic Landscape. Expanding the Scenery.* New York; London: Routledge, pp. 107–125.

Nekvapil, J. 2016. Language management theory as one approach in language policy and planning, *Current Issues in Language Planning*, 17 (1), 11–22. DOI: 10.1080/14664208.2016.1108481

Pertostat [Official website of Federal State Statistic Service for St. Petersburg's and Leningrad region]. 2019. Численность постоянного населения Ленинградской области в разрезе муниципальных образований по состоянию на 1 января 2019 года. [The number of permanent residents of Leningrad region by municipal districts up to January 1, 2019] http://petrostat.gks.ru/wps/wcm/connect/rosstat_ts/petrostat/resources/7dabbe8049a8aaf29788df3fbd401489/%D0%9B%D0%9E+%D1%87%D0%B8%D1%81%D0%BB++%D0%BD%D0%B0+01.01.2019+.pdf

Sloboda, M., Szabó-Gilinger, E., Vigers, D. and L. Šimičić. 2010. Carrying out a language policy change: Advocacy coalitions and the management of linguistic landscape. *Current Issues in Language Planning*, 11 (2), 95–113, DOI: 10.1080/14664208.2010.50506

Shikalov, Yu. G. 2016. История в формировании региональной идентичности жителей г. Выборга в советский и постсоветский периоды [History and regional identity formation in Soviet and post-Soviet Vyborg]. *Ученые записки Петрозаводско гогосударственного университета* 158, 13–20.

Spolsky, B. 2009. *Language Management*. Cambridge: Cambridge University Press.

Woldemariam, H. and Lanza, E. 2014. Language contact, agency and power in the linguistic landscape of two regional capitals of Ethiopia. *International Journal of the Sociology of Language*, 228, 79–103.

15 Behind the linguistic landscape

An interview-based study of business owners' reasons for choosing business names in the German city of Mainz

F. van Meurs, B. Planken and N. Lasarzewski

15.1 Introduction

Third Wave sociolinguistics is interested in individuals' agency in constructing meaning and expressing identity (Eckert 2016; Hernandez-Campoy 2016). This postmodernist approach emphasises the individual, rather than group, perspective on language use. That is, it aims to gain insights into different actors' 'situated knowledge' in a specific social context (Pennycook 2006: 63). The present study applies this approach to investigating language use in an urban setting, namely by exploring how individual business owners' language choice constructs meaning and expresses their identity. Specifically, this study investigates the motivations underlying business naming practices.

The use of a single language or multiple languages in business names is an aspect of the linguistic landscape, which has been defined as 'The language of public road signs, advertising billboards, street names, place names, commercial shop signs, and public signs on government buildings [...] in a given territory, region, or urban agglomeration' (Landry and Bourhis 1997: 25). In the linguistic landscape, for instance, in an urban space, various types of actors shape and consume signage to co-construct meaning. These actors may include authors of signs and readers of signs, for example, those who reside in, work in or visit the linguistic landscape (Huebner 2016). Generally speaking, linguistic landscape has been studied from three angles. Some studies have investigated the frequency of use of different languages in a specific setting and linked this to factors such as type of business (e.g. Nikolaou 2017; Schlick 2003). Other studies have gauged how certain actors in the linguistic landscape respond to language use (e.g. Aiestaran et al. 2010; Garvin 2010). A third type of study has explored the reasons authors have for choosing certain languages, for instance, for signage (e.g. Bletzer 2003; Selvi 2016).

A number of researchers and scholars have pointed out the need for investigations of the third type in particular, that is, the need for studies that involve the authors' perspective (e.g. Malinowski 2009; Thistlethwaite and Sebba 2015). Hult (2009), for example, remarks that 'although the focus of linguistic landscape research has tended to be on the object produced by these

DOI: 10.4324/9780429348037-19

actors, it may also be useful to focus on what takes place behind the scenes, what makes an individual choose to create […] a linguistic object in a certain way' (p. 94). Blommaert (2013) underlines the need to gain insight into how the linguistic landscape comes into being: 'We can only understand signs […] by reading back into their genesis and their trajectories of becoming' (p. 118). The aim of the current study is to contribute to existing studies of the linguistic landscape in this respect by interviewing authors of commercial signage in an urban space with regard to their motivations for choosing a particular name for their business.

In the present investigation, the theoretical framework for classifying the reasons given by authors is based on earlier linguistic landscape studies. Ben-Rafael et al. (2006), for example, used three perspectives on language choice derived from general sociological theories of social action to study language dominance in bottom-up and top-down signage in the linguistic landscape in a number of Israeli towns and cities. The first perspective, *power relations*, relates to whether language choice in the linguistic landscape is determined by dominant groups in society. The second perspective, *presentation of self*, assumes that an author's language choice in the linguistic landscape expresses his or her identity. Finally, Ben-Rafael et al. used a third perspective, *theory of good reason*, to interpret how language choice reflects 'the interests of LL [Linguistic Landscape] actors vis-à-vis the public – i.e. the attractiveness and expected influence of signs on eventual clients' (2006: 10). Given the commercial nature of the urban space that was the setting for the present study, we expected reasons that could be explained by the *theory of good reason* to be mentioned by the business owners interviewed. Furthermore, language-product congruence, that is, the match between products and the languages used to describe them, has been found to be an important mechanism underlying language choice in advertising (Hornikx and van Meurs 2017, 2020; Kelly-Holmes 2005). It has also been commented on in relation to the linguistic landscape, with, for instance, French shop names being used for businesses selling typically French products (MacGregor 2003). Therefore, we also expected language-product congruence to feature as a reason for language choice.

15.2 Method

Interviews were conducted in German with 30 business owners in the city of Mainz, Germany, between 5 and 8 May 2014. The interviewer was the third author of this chapter, who is a native speaker of German. Mainz is an example of a multicultural and multilingual western European city, with a population of ca. 220,000 (Landeshauptstadt Mainz 2022). A preliminary corpus study of the languages used in 459 business names (i.e. in shop signs) in the city centre showed that 58% were in German (e.g. *Schokoladenhaus am Dom*), 22% were in English (e.g. *Superfly*), 20% were in other languages, for instance Italian (e.g. *La Pizzetta*), French (e.g. *L'Arcade*), Spanish (e.g. *La Danza*) and Turkish (e.g. *Hünkar*). Language mixing occurred in 21% of the business names, of which

93% combined two languages (e.g. *Per la Donna – exclusiv*) and the remaining 7% three languages (e.g. *Sakura Sushi – Running – Viet-Thai-Küche*). A convenience sample of 51 business owners in the city centre was subsequently approached for interviews, of whom 30 were available. The others were busy at the time they were approached and had no time for an interview. Chain or franchise stores were not included in the sample, as chain store managers and franchisees usually do not have any influence in naming the store. The interviews with the business owners were conducted at their place of business. Table 15.1 shows the interviewee numbers, the language(s) used in the names of businesses owned by the interviewees, and the types of business. Business names are given only in instances where business owners gave explicit permission to mention them in a published article.

German was the language that appeared most frequently in the names of the businesses owned by the interviewees, followed by English, Italian and French. Other languages that occurred were Thai and Spanish. English, German and Italian occurred in combination with other languages. The 30 shops offered a wide range of products, from fashion to art and interior and food. All but two of the interviewees were German and spoke German as their mother tongue. Interviewee 1 was American and spoke English as a first language, while interviewee 27 was an Italian whose mother tongue was Italian.

The interviews were semi-structured and covered several topics. For the present study, we analyzed interviewees' answers relating to their reasons for choosing a specific name for their business, as we wanted to provide insights into individual agency and how it shapes the linguistic landscape. Most of the interviews were recorded and transcribed. Nine business owners did not want to be recorded, so the researcher took notes during the interviews. The 21 recorded interviews lasted an average of 2 minutes, 50 seconds (range: 1 minute, 24 seconds to 4 minutes, 16 seconds).

The quotations given in the Results section were all taken from the transcribed interviews. They were translated into English from the original German. In all cases, we have omitted information that could identify businesses and owners to guarantee anonymity and protect their privacy. All interviewees consented to the interview data being used for this study, but only nine explicitly consented to the business name being mentioned in a published article (see Table 15.1).

The analysis of the transcriptions and notes started with the selection of fragments from the interviews on specific themes, which were then labelled and grouped, using the qualitative analysis software ATLAS.ti. The labelling and grouping codes were based on reasons for naming businesses discussed in the literature we studied prior to the analysis and what emerged from the data during analysis (Boeije 2009: 107). As this was an exploratory study and we were interested in the motivations of individual business owners for naming their business, we regarded any instance of a particular motivation as a manifestation of a reason. In other words, our primary aim was not to quantify the frequency with which reasons were manifested, only whether they occurred.

Table 15.1 Characteristics of the businesses whose owners were interviewed

Interviewee/ *business name	Language 1 in business name	Language 2 in business name	Business type
1	English	German	art and interior
2	English	German	pub
3	English		fashion
4	English	German	assorted goods and specialty shops
5 Coco: Beauty	French	English	healthcare
6	French	German	fashion
7	French	German	food
8	French	German	accessories and decoration
9	German		fashion
10	German	English	fashion
11 Gaumenschnaus: Wein trifft…	German		restaurant
12	German		accessories and decoration
13	German		art and interior
14 Laufsteg 11	German		fashion
15	German		assorted goods and specialty shops
16 Schokophonie [S is written as a clef]	German		food
17	German	English	sports
18	German	Italian	art and interior
19 Tandaradei	German		accessories and decoration
20	German		art and interior
21	German		books
22	Italian	German	assorted goods and specialty shops
23	Italian		fashion
24 Mondo: Ruhe Raum Gute Form	Italian	German	art and interior
25 Monteverde: Naomi Grünberg Mode	Italian	German	fashion
26 Per la Donna, Exclusiv	Italian	German	fashion
27	Italian		food
28	Italian	German	fashion
29 Nosostros Lichtstudio	Spanish	German	art and interior
30	Thai		fashion

*The business name is only mentioned if business owners gave explicit permission to mention it in a published article.

Once we had labelled and grouped the reasons, we then searched the linguistic landscape literature more broadly to see if these 'emergent' reasons were mentioned. Every fragment was assigned at least one code, and in some cases multiple codes. The overarching (grouping) codes that were used to categorise the reasons related to:

- *presentation of self*, e.g. for the name's capacity to express aspects of the owners' identity (Ben-Rafael et al. 2006);
- *theory of good reason*, e.g. for the name's capacity to attract potential clients' attention (Ben-Rafael et al. 2006);
- *properties of the name*, such as its 'good' sound (cf. Pošeiko 2018: 114) or its brevity (cf. Papen 2012: 66);
- *the link between the language(s) used for the name and products sold* (cf. MacGregor 2003: 21; Selvi 2016: 34);
- *trends in naming* (cf. Manan et al. 2017: 656);
- *references to the owners' or family members' names* (cf. Bogatto and Hélot 2010: 281; Coluzzi 2017: 114; Knospe 2016: 209);
- *references to the city or the location of a shop*.

In our interpretation of the reasoning of interviewees, we tried to stay as close as possible to the individual's literal wording. For instance, only when a business owner explicitly referred to an effect on potential clients did we code the reason as relating to *theory of good reason*, and only when an interviewee said he or she chose a name to express part of his or her identity did we code it as *presentation of self*. As a result, reasons relating to *properties of the name* were coded as different from *theory of good reason*, because, even though a name sounding good could lead to positive effects on potential customers, such effects were not explicitly mentioned by the interviewees. Similarly, reasons linked to *references to the owners' or family members' names* were coded as different from *presentation of self*, because the interviewees did not explicitly refer to such names expressing their identity.

All the data were coded by the third author, a native speaker of German. A random subsample of four interviews was coded by a second coder, also a native speaker of German, to determine intercoder reliability (Boeije 2009: 106; Neuendorf 2002: 134). She was provided with the coding scheme and a summary of the main theoretical perspectives that informed the creation of categories. After coding one practice interview together with the first coder, the second coder coded the four randomly selected interviews on her own. Cohen's Kappa was calculated to measure interrater reliability, that is, the extent to which coders agree in their coding. Cohen's Kappa can range from 0 (agreement equivalent to chance) to 1 (perfect agreement) (Glen 2014). Kappas for the overarching codes in this study ranged from .65 to .85, indicating substantial agreement between the two coders in their labelling of the reasons.

15.3 Results

The reasons business owners gave for naming their business did not relate to Ben-Rafael et al.'s (2006) *power relations* perspective. None of the business owners mentioned local language policy or restrictions on naming their business imposed by local or national authorities.

Business owners gave a number of reasons that related to the perspective of *presentation of self* (Ben-Rafael et al. 2006). One owner (interviewee 1) explained that the name she created was an expression of how she approached life at the time: 'At that time it meant to me breaking out. Just run a riot, live what you haven't dared before'. Another noted that the business name he chose referred to a particular decade that was important to him: 'So I said, well, my music will be played, from [that decade], and that's why I called the pub [after that decade]' (interviewee 2). Another business owner remarked 'So, I am, I have a fondness for Italy and speak a bit of Italian and also used to pass through Italy a lot in the past, also professionally, and when I became self-employed, it was clear to me, I had a firm in mind, that I could in any case incorporate in my shop, and that was an Italian firm. And as a result I have it then – the name was the thing that I knew right at the beginning' (interviewee 23).

A number of reasons for naming businesses mentioned by the interviewees can be linked to the *theory of good reason* perspective, in the sense that they aimed to bring about a certain effect on customers. For example, three business owners remarked that the name was meant to attract the customers' attention. The first (interviewee 30) said: 'So, we wanted to stand out a bit by having something extraordinary', while the second (interviewee 22) said: '[…] because you make the customer curious. Why exactly is the shop called what it is? Or how is it pronounced? What's the meaning behind it?' Interviewee 1 noted that 'I wanted to have something with a unique selling point, so people should really stand in front of it and say what is this, what does it mean, which in turn leads to them coming in and asking about the background [of the name]'. A second effect that played a role in naming businesses was to create more clarity about the products or services offered. For example, one business owner (interviewee 29) added a clarification in German, *Lichtstudio* [light studio], to the main Spanish name: 'Yes, of course I have to provide some reference. *Nosostros* has nothing to do with the name 'light' – like *la luche* […] I think it's stupid to write a name on a car and then no one can make out the meaning – what do they actually do? Do they sell atomic bombs or hand-knitted socks?'. A third effect business owners mentioned was that the name given to the business would be easy to remember for customers. Interviewee 29, for example, said: 'in my view it is very memorable [*einprägend*, which can also be translated as 'catchy']'.

While some of the reasons could be linked to two of the three perspectives distinguished in Ben-Rafael et al. (2006), a number of reasons given by business owners were not explicitly linked to any of the three perspectives. A first set of reasons reflected *properties of the name itself*, such as how it sounded and its brevity. With respect to sound, one business owner explained the choice of a French name as follows: 'Yes, I think the French sounds more beautiful' (interviewee 8), while another said: 'we just translated it [our family name *Grünberg*, which literally means 'green mountain'] into Italian [*Monteverde*] because it sounds better' (interviewee 25). As for brevity, two owners indicated this was a reason: 'short and to the point' (interviewee 13) and 'Because it [*Nosostros*] was a name which describes in a short form: us. That's all' (interviewee 29).

A second set of reasons related to *the link between the name and the products sold by the business*. One owner explained the choice of a French name by saying 'and they are French specialties. Therefore French' (interviewee 7). Another noted that he chose an Italian name, *Mondo*, for his furniture shop as 'It also has to do with the fact that expensive, well, trendsetter furniture comes from Italy a lot' (interviewee 24). The owner of *Per la Donna* (Interviewee 26) said 'I mainly have Italian brands. And this was actually the main reason [for choosing an Italian name].' While the previous three examples reflect a clear country-language-product fit, another reason that was given linked the meaning of the name and products sold in the shop in another way: 'because [the word's meaning] includes simply everything. And you are free to sell something different at any time' (interviewee 8).

A third type of reason can be related to certain *trends relating to foreign languages* at the time when the name was chosen. One owner gave the following reason for his parents choosing a German rather than an English name: 'Well, I mean, maybe you could justify it with the background at that time. And my parents had no ambition whatsoever, to use anything English. I think it just wasn't that up-to-date then' (interviewee 12). Another owner explained his parents' choice for an Italian name as follows: 'Some 10, 20 years ago […] it was just very in then' (interviewee 20).

A fourth type of reason for choosing a name relates to the desire to include *references to the owners' or family members' names*. Interviewee 11 noted that the name for his restaurant, *Gaumenschnaus*, incorporated a play on words on his last name to suggest fine taste. The word *Gaumenschmaus*, meaning culinary delight, was changed to *Gaumenschnaus*, *Schnaus* being the surname of the founder. Another owner explained that the Italian name of his business (three words) included his wife's first name (interviewee 28). The owner of a delicatessen mentioned that the French name of her business, denoting a spice, was a translation of her German last name (interviewee 7). The owner of a clothes shop explained the choice of a name incorporating a word from the 'Pacific region' as follows: 'because the original shop owner also has a very unusual first name, which also comes from Persian, and therefore they have had a tendency in the family already to this unusual name' (interviewee 30).

Finally, a number of reasons for naming businesses would seem to indicate a *desire to reflect references to the location of a business*. For instance, one owner said: 'So, it's [street name, number]' (interviewee 13). A second owner noted that 'and the [first part of the name] is a real word; it comes from the Pacific region and means island. And because we're located in the Island street, we have more or less put these two words together' (interviewee 30). A third explained: 'And that's why [...] we then added 11 [to the name *Laufsteg*, which translates as 'catwalk'] because this is house number 11 and because I had something to do with *Fastnacht [local cultural event]*' (interviewee 14).

15.4 Discussion

In line with the postmodernist interest in individual agency, the aim of this study was to gain insight into the language use of a particular group of actors in an urban community. More specifically, we investigated the motivations underlying business naming practices of shop and restaurant owners in the commercial quarter of a Western European city. Interviews with individual owners were used to shed light on these actors' own perspective on how they contribute to an urban linguistic landscape.

A qualitative analysis of the interviews showed that business owners would seem to have diverse reasons for deciding what to name their business. These could, to some extent, be related to the theoretical perspectives on language use in urban environments distinguished in Ben-Rafael et al. (2006), namely the *presentation of self* perspective and the *theory of good reason*. In line with the first perspective, some of the reasons mentioned explicitly by the business owners indicated that they used the name of their business to express parts of their identity. With respect to the *theory of good reason*, some reasons reflected that a particular name was given to create a certain effect on potential customers. None of the reasons could be linked to the *power relations* perspective, which may be explained by the fact that language use is situated, in the sense that it may be influenced to a greater or lesser extent by the political context in a particular setting. In Ben-Rafael et al.'s (2006) study, *power relations* were found to play an important role in the language use (e.g. Arabic versus Hebrew) in a number of urban contexts in Israel, where ethnic relations and language policy were found to be clearly intertwined. In Germany, the setting for the present study, the political situation is relatively less charged with respect to relations between minority and majority groups in society. In addition, the sample of interviewees in the present study included only very few business owners that belonged to ethnic minority groups. Future research might focus on reasoning behind language use in names of businesses owned by speakers of minority languages.

Business owners in the present study gave a number of reasons that could not be explicitly related to the three theoretical perspectives in Ben-Rafael et al. (2006), at least not in the way the interviewees expressed them. These reasons could, however, be linked to motivations for language use in the linguistic landscape identified in the literature. For example, one set of reasons reflected *properties of the name*, that is, that it sounded good or that it was brief (cf. Papen 2012; Pošeiko 2018). A second set of reasons aimed to establish a *link between the business name and the products offered* (cf. Hornikx and van Meurs

2020: 172; MacGregor 2003; Selvi 2016), while a third set reflected *trends in foreign language use* at the time the business was named (cf. Manan et al. 2017). A fourth set of reasons related to the business owners' wish to *incorporate their or a family member's name in the business name* (cf. Bogatto and Hélot 2010; Coluzzi 2017; Knospe 2016).

One set of reasons would seem to be new in the sense that we have not encountered them in the linguistic landscape literature. They related to the business owners' desire to *reference the location of the business in the business name*. This shows the added value of gaining insight into the authors' perspective on the linguistic landscape.

All of the reasons provided by the individual business owners, by their very nature, reflected their individual agency. The individuality of reasons for naming practices is underlined by the fact that some reasons could be linked to the *presentation of self* perspective and by the finding that in some cases a specific name was motivated by the desire to *incorporate the owners' or their relatives' own name*. These reasons could be said to reflect highly particular aspects of the business owner's background or personal circumstances. While we have identified abstract overarching reasons that were shared across a number of individual business owners, each business owner mentioned concrete reasons that were specific to him or her. In all cases, the reasons led to a linguistic choice for a business name that was different for each individual business owner. Thus, our study suggests that actual naming practices and specific reasons for choosing business names are a matter of *individual* agency, while the overarching reasons under which the individual reasons can be subsumed apply at the level of the *group* of business owners. In this sense, our analysis ties in with other approaches to sociolinguistic variation – in our case in business naming practices – that 'attempt to link individual speaker behavior with the study of the community' (Walker and Meyerhoff 2013: 2).

An interview study such as this is worthwhile in the context of research into the linguistic landscape, because it has been shown to yield insiders' perspectives into individual practices in language use. Such insights can complement outcomes from observational analyses of language use in the linguistic landscape and from studies of actors' responses to such language use. For example, the desire to *allude to an owner's or their family members' personal names* as a factor in naming a business can probably only emerge from interviews with authors, although it may also be known to other actors close to the business owner, and it may even be indicated in the linguistic landscape signage itself (as in the case of Interviewee 25's shop name *Monteverde*, which was displayed in combination with the owner's German surname, *Grünberg*, of which the Italian shop name is a translation). The current study has provided insights into a diverse set of mechanisms that shape the linguistic landscape in a commercial urban space. However, we did not investigate to what extent other actors, such as potential clients of commercial businesses, interpret the meanings and effects of business names as they are intended by the authors. Future studies might therefore employ a multi-method approach to yield insights from different actors that interact to construct the linguistic landscape, that is, for example, by combining corpus analyses of signs, interviews with makers of signs, and interviews, experiments or focus groups involving recipients of signs. In a number of cases, for instance, it could be argued that the signs employ a foreign language to communicate with potential customers who do not speak this language, a practice which has been described as 'commodification of language', meaning that languages are used 'as 'things' that can be transformed into commodities that in turn help to sell/advertise other commodities' (Banda and Mokwena 2019: 180). In such cases, it has been suggested that the foreign language expression is not primarily used for its referential meaning, but for its symbolic meaning (see also Kelly-Holmes 2005, 2014). Future studies could explore how makers of commercial signs and potential customers view instances of signs that use foreign languages in this way.

Finally, it is worth noting that the reasons given by the business owners in the present study did not always relate to the *choice* of (foreign) language but to the *meaning* of the words used, regardless of what language(s) the name was in. This is also mentioned explicitly by a number of the business owners. As one of them noted, 'It might just as well have been Greek, I wouldn't have cared. I don't care that it's Spanish either. It was only about the word' (interviewee 29). Another owner, whose shop had a German name, mentioned: 'If I'd wanted to, I could also have taken an English or a French name' (interviewee 13). This again shows the added value of gaining an insider's perspective: the choice of a business name in a linguistic landscape may be about more than choosing a particular language.

15.5 Acknowledgements

We would like to thank the reviewers for their useful comments.

References

Aiestaran, J., Cenoz, J. and Gorter, D. (2010). Multilingual cityscapes: Perceptions and preferences of the inhabitants of the city of Donostia-San Sebastian. In E. Shohamy, E. Ben-Rafael and M. Barni (eds.), *Linguistic landscape in the city* (pp. 219–234). Bristol: Multilingual Matters.

Banda, F. and Mokwena, L. (2019). Commodification of African languages in linguistic landscapes of rural Northern Cape Province, South Africa. *International Journal of the Sociology of Language*, 260, 177–198.

Ben-Rafael, E., Shohamy, E., Amara, M. H. and Trumper-Hecht, N. (2006). Linguistic landscape as symbolic construction of the public space: The case of Israel. *International Journal of Multilingualism*, 3(1), 7–30.

Bletzer, K.V. (2003). Latino naming practices of small-town businesses in rural southern Florida. *Ethnology*, 42, 209–235.

Blommaert, J. (2013). *Ethnography, Superdiversity, and Linguistic Landscapes: Chronicles of Complexity.* Bristol: Multilingual Matters.

Boeije, H. (2009). *Analysis in Qualitative Research.* Los Angeles: Sage.

Bogatto, F., and Hélot, C. (2010). Linguistic landscape and language diversity in Strasbourg: The 'Quartier Gare'. In E. Shohamy, E. Ben-Rafael and M. Barni (eds.), *Linguistic Landscape in the City* (pp. 275–291). Bristol: Multilingual Matters.

Coluzzi, P. (2017). Italian in the linguistic landscape of Kuala Lumpur (Malaysia). *International Journal of Multilingualism*, 14(2), 109–123. DOI: 10.1080/14790718.2016.1151883

Eckert, P. (2016). Third wave variationism. *Oxford Handbooks Online*. DOI: 10.1093/oxfordhb/9780199935345.013.27

Garvin, T. R. (2010). Responses to the linguistic landscape in Memphis, Tennessee: An urban space in transition. In E. Shohamy, E. Ben-Rafael and M. Barni (eds.), *Linguistic Landscape in the City* (pp. 252–271). Bristol: Multilingual Matters.

Glen, S. (2014). Cohen's Kappa statistic. Retrieved 9 November 2020 from www.statisticshowto.com/cohens-kappa-statistic/

Hernández-Campoy, J. M. (2016). *Sociolinguistic Styles*. Hoboken, NJ: Wiley-Blackwell.

Hornikx, J. and van Meurs, F. (2017). Foreign languages in advertising as implicit Country-of-Origin cues: Mechanism, associations, and effectiveness. *Journal of International Consumer Marketing*, 29(2), 60–73.

Hornikx, J. and van Meurs, F. (2020). *Foreign Languages in Advertising: Linguistic and Marketing Perspectives*. Cham, Switzerland: Palgrave Macmillan.

Huebner, T. H. (2016). Linguistic landscape: History, trajectory and pedagogy. *MANUSYA: Journal of Humanities*, 22, 1–11.

Hult, F. (2009). Landscape ecology and linguistic landscape analysis. In E. Shohamy and D. Gorter (eds.), *Linguistic Landscape: Expanding the Scenery* (pp. 88–103). New York, NY: Routledge.

Kelly-Holmes, H. (2005). *Advertising as Multilingual Communication*. Basingstoke: Palgrave Macmillan.

Kelly-Holmes, H. (2014). Linguistic fetish: The sociolinguistics of visual multilingualism. In D. Machin (ed.), *Visual Communication* (pp. 135–151). Berlin: De Gruyter.

Knospe, S. (2016). Through the cognitive looking glass: Studying bilingual wordplay in public signage. In S. Knospe, A. Onysko and M. Goth (eds.), *Crossing Languages to Play with Words: Multidisciplinary Perspectives* (pp. 195–230). Berlin: De Gruyter.

Landeshauptstadt Mainz (2022). 'Mainz in Zahlen.' Accessed 3 February 2022. www.mainz.de/tourismus/stadtportraet/mainz-in-zahlen.php.

Landry, R. and Bourhis, R. Y. (1997). Linguistic landscape and ethnolinguistic vitality: An empirical study. *Journal of Language and Social Psychology*, 16(1), 23–49.

Malinowski, D. (2009). Authorship in the linguistic landscape: A multimodal-performative view. In E. Shohamy and D. Gorter (eds.), *Linguistic Landscape: Expanding the Scenery* (pp. 107–125). New York, NY: Routledge.

MacGregor, L. (2003). The language of shop signs in Tokyo: A report on the salient role of English in Japan's complex commercial signs. *English Today*, 19(1), 18–23.

Manan, S. A., David, M. K., Dumanig, F. P. and Channa, L. A. (2017). The glocalization of English in the Pakistan linguistic landscape. *World Englishes*, 36(4), 645–665.

Neuendorf, K. A. (2002). *The Content Analysis Guidebook*. Thousand Oaks, CA: Sage.

Nikolaou, A. (2017). Mapping the linguistic landscape of Athens: The case of shop signs. *International Journal of Multilingualism*, 14(2), 160–182.

Papen, U. (2012). Commercial discourses, gentrification and citizens' protest: The linguistic landscape of PrenzlauerBerg, Berlin. *Journal of Sociolinguistics*, 16(1), 56–80.

Pennycook, A. (2006). Postmodernism in language policy. In T. Ricento (ed.), *An Introduction to Language Policy: Theory and Method* (pp. 60–75). Malden, MA: Blackwell.

Pošeiko, S. (2018). 'Following in the footsteps of names': Commercial ergonymia in linguistic landscape of the Baltic countries. In P. Cotticelli Kurras and A. Rizza (eds.), *Language, Media and Economy in Virtual and Real Life: New Perspectives* (pp. 99–123). Newcastle upon Tyne: Cambridge Scholars.

Schlick, M. (2003). The English of shop signs in Europe. *English Today, 19*(1), 3–17.

Selvi, A. F. (2016). English as the language of marketspeak: Reflections from the linguistic landscape of Turkey. *English Today 32*(4), 33–39.

Thistlethwaite, J. and Sebba, M. (2015). The passive exclusion of Irish in the linguistic landscape: A nexus analysis. In R. Rubdy and S. Ben Said (eds.), *Conflict, Exclusion and Dissent in the Linguistic Landscape* (pp. 27–51). London: Palgrave Macmillan.

Walker, J. A. and Meyerhoff, M. (2013). Studies of the community and the individual. In R. Bayley, R. Cameron and C. Lucas (eds.), *Oxford Handbook of Sociolinguistics*. Oxford: Oxford University Press. DOI: 10.1093/oxfordhb/9780199744084.013.0009

Part V
Global processes and sound change

16 Rhotics frequency in Beijing

H. Hu and D. Smakman

16.1 Beijing rhoticity

The Chinese city of Beijing attracts many speakers from all over the country. The approximate number of native Beijingers is now 6 million, which means that most of this city's 20 million (Beijing Municipal Bureau Statistics and Survey Office of the National Bureau of Statistics in Beijing 2020) inhabitants are newcomers. Beijing is where one can build a better future for oneself and one's family, and this attracts many other newcomers. Through their jobs and in their personal lives, these migrants come in contact with native Beijingers and with newcomers like themselves. They are on a daily basis made aware of their own language use and of the communicative habits of the people they communicate with. Part of this experience is the frequent presence of the rather prominent postvocalic *r* in the Beijing accent. Native Beijingers typically use this feature in their pronunciation, while immigrants often adopt and spread this feature and in the process influence pronunciation norm formation.

Indeed, rhoticity is one of the most characteristic features of the Beijing accent (Duanmu 1990; Huang and Liao 2017; Lin 2007). Even those who don't speak Mandarin Chinese will recognise this salient rhotic ring in certain syllables. In Standard Chinese, a limited number of rhotics exists (Huang and Liao 2017; Lin 2007), but in Beijing Mandarin, its phonetic basis, the extensive occurrence of rhotic words is widely considered to be one of its typical features. Rhotic words also widely exist in other Mandarin dialects, but in most varieties spoken in southern China, rhotics barely exist. For Chinese speakers who are not originally from Beijing to imitate this city's typical accent, they will need to produce this feature in their daily speech. Some newcomers to the city will be more likely and even more capable of doing this, because rhoticity is part of their own native Chinese dialect. For speakers of non-rhotic dialects, rhoticity is a relatively alien concept that they need to learn. Some other immigrants simply need to produce more rhotic rhymes than they are used to. While with a speaker's dialect background comes a certain natural inclination to produce rhotics, rhotic tendencies are also influenced by lexical and grammatical factors.

So, the required effort to emulate Beijing postvocalic *r* is therefore different for speakers with different dialect backgrounds. Social factors are another source of influence. Notably, age is a likely social variable determining the use of this feature, and gender, too, is a likely factor (Zhang 2008). The current chapter describes the frequencies of rhotics in the speech of speakers of the various rhotic and non-rhotic dialects who have joined the Beijing speech community and it considers the effects of age and gender on the general production of rhotics.

16.2 Methodology

16.2.1 Data source

This investigation is based on frequency counts of the number of rhotics per person per 1,000 words; i.e. 'rhotics frequency'. These count data were obtained from the recordings of pair talking sessions in Beijing that took place in 2015 and 2017. These recordings took place either in a recording studio or a quiet room in the speakers' homes.

16.2.2 Participants

As mentioned, three social variables pertaining to the speakers were examined in this study:

- Native dialect background: Beijing dialect ('Beijing Mandarin'), non-Beijing rhotic dialect ('With-r dialect'), non-Beijing non-rhotic dialect ('Non-r dialect').
- Gender: female or male. Almost all participants indicated belonging to one of these two groups. The (low) number of speakers who did not fill in this question were not considered.
- Age groups with ten-year gaps between them were created: 'Young' (18–27 years old), 'Middle' (38–47 years old), and 'Old' (58 years or older).

The participants were asked to participate and in many cases given a small sum of money for their participation. They themselves indicated what their dialect background was and whether they were native Beijingers or not. In addition to these statements, the participants indicated when and where they were born and raised, and if applicable, how long they used to live in other places, except Beijing and their hometown. Table 16.1 contains an overview of the participants.

16.2.3 Procedure

Each participant's speech was firstly transcribed into Chinese texts, starting from the 11th minute of each recording. This was done to avoid the effects of possible speaker discomfort during the beginnings of the pair talks. From this point onwards, words were written out and the number of rhotic words counted for 1,000 words. The instances of rhoticised syllables were easily detectable and

Table 16.1 The speaker groups ($N = 76$), split up on the basis of gender, age and dialect background

Gender	Age	Beijing Mandarin	With-r dialect	Non-r dialect
Male	Young	8	4	4
	Middle	4	4	4
	Old	4	4	2
Female	Young	7	4	5
	Middle	4	4	3
	Old	4	2	5
Total		31	22	23

were therefore determined aurally by the first author of this chapter, a native speaker of Mandarin Chinese. The considerations for taking number of words as a basis for counting (and not time or number of syllables) were the following:

- The inter-speaker speech rates differed dramatically from each other; some speakers simply talked faster and with fewer silences (perhaps because of their personalities) than others and probably produced more rhotics because of this rate, not because of their tendency to rhotacise. This made a time measurement problematic.
- The recordings were pair talks and speech overlaps often occurred, which made the timing difficult.
- Counting syllables was not considered feasible or useful. Mandarin Chinese is often referred to as a monosyllabic language, and most morphemes are monosyllabic, while words can be both monosyllabic or polysyllabic (Lin 2007). Different from postvocalic 'r' in some western languages, including English, in Beijing Mandarin it is used as a suffixation and also has a diminutive function. In the minds of speakers, they use a rhotic word as a lexically meaningful unit. Therefore, when dealing with such data, we should focus on words, not syllables.

16.2.4 Statistical treatment

In this chapter, both parametric and nonparametric statistical tests were used. Normality tests were done with a combination of visual inspection and a significance test in R (R Core Team 2020). We used the ggpbur package (Kassambara 2020) in R to do the visual inspection and Shapiro-Wilk's test to do the significance test. The datasets of Beijing native speakers were normally distributed. Thus, parametric statistical tests – t-tests and one-way ANOVA – were mainly used. The total participant dataset, however, was not normally distributed, according to the Shapiro-Wilk's test in R, and therefore nonparametric statistics was also used. It should be noted that in nonparametric statistics, data are not required to fit a normal distribution. The nonparametric methods usually apply to data sets in which the number and nature of the parameters are flexible and not fixed in advance. The Kruskal-Wallis test by rank is a non-parametric alternative to a one-way ANOVA, which extends the unpaired two-samples Wilcoxon test (also known as the Mann-Whitney U test) in the situation where there are more than two groups. It is used when the assumptions of a one-way ANOVA test are not met. Therefore, the Kruskal-Wallis test and Wilcoxon test were applied to deal with the nonparametric dataset.

16.3 Results

16.3.1 Overall rhotics distribution

Table 16.2 shows the number of participants, the sum of rhotic words, and the average rhotics frequency per participant over each social variable.

The total number of counted words is 76,000 (76 participants times 1,000 words), and 3,402 rhotacised syllables were encountered. This means that about 4.5 percent of all the words taken into consideration were rhotacised.

To show the effects of the various social variables, boxplots are particularly convenient. Besides average tendencies, distributions are considered relevant. Boxplots can be used to present the distribution of the number of rhotic words across the social variables. The x-axis indicates speakers by the social variables, and the y-axis indicates the number of rhotic words produced by each group. The top and bottom ends of the box are the upper and lower quartiles, which means that the boxes as a whole span the interquartile range. The median is marked by the dark horizontal line inside the box. The 'whiskers' extend to the highest and lowest observations. Outliers are represented by single dots. These outliers are not part of the statistical calculations. In this study, the boxplots were made by the ggplot2 package (Wickham 2016) in R. Figure 16.1 shows the

Table 16.2 Number of rhotics ($N = 3,402$) per 1,000 words for the various speaker groups ($N = 76$)

Gender	Age	Beijing Mandarin			With-r dialect			Non-r dialect		
		p n	*r n*	*average*	*p n*	*r n*	*average*	*p n*	*r n*	*average*
Male	Young	8	466	58	4	139	35	4	13	3
	Middle	4	282	71	4	137	34	4	62	16
	Old	4	435	109	4	108	27	2	2	1
Female	Young	7	450	64	4	173	43	5	51	10
	Middle	4	376	94	4	134	34	3	57	19
	Old	4	394	99	2	74	37	5	49	10
Total		31	2403	78	22	765	35	23	234	10

Note: *p n* refers to the number of participants; *r n* refers to total number of rhotic words per 1,000 words by participants in each sub-group; *average* is the number of rhotic words per 1,000 words per participant in each sub-group. *Beijing Mandarin, With-r dialect* and *Non-r dialect* refer to the three dialect backgrounds of participants.

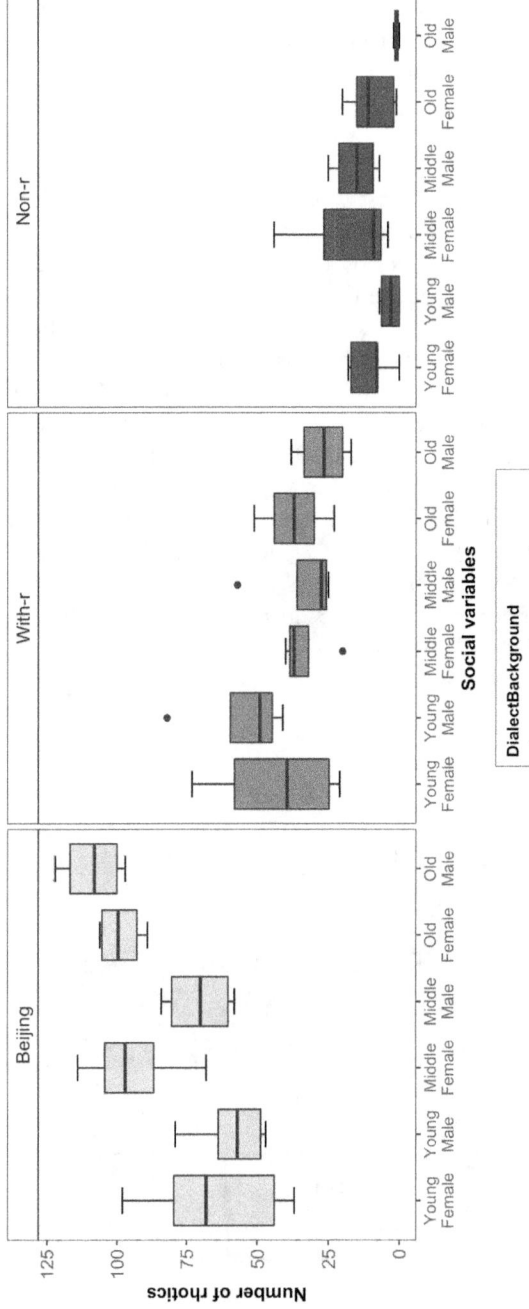

Figure 16.1 Distribution of rhotics ($N=3{,}402$) across the speaker groups ($N=76$).

Note: *BJ* refers to speakers having a dialect background of Beijing Mandarin; *With-r* and *Non-r* respectively refer to speakers from rhotic and non-rhotic areas; *F* and *M* refer to female and male.

overall distribution of rhotics across the social variables. The subsequent figures show the statistical results.

The figure shows that, combined and independently, the three social variables affect the tendency of speakers towards rhotacisation. The specific effects of these social variables are considered next.

16.3.2 Gender[1]

An independent two-samples *t*-test was conducted to examine if the variable *Gender* is a factor among the *Beijing* native speakers. Figure 16.2 presents the boxplot of the number of rhotics by two gender groups and the alpha value. The big horizontal brackets above the boxplots below indicate that the difference of the two groups is tested and asterisks are used to show the *p*-value and significance level. The smaller the *p*-value is, the more significant the difference will be; 'ns' means that the comparisons are not significant. One asterisk means that $.01 < p < .05$ and the significance level is .05. Two asterisks means that $.001 < p < .01$ and the significance level is .01. If the *p* value is smaller than .001, then three asterisks will be shown and its significance level is .001.

The result shows that there was no significant difference in the number of rhotics for *Female* ($M = 81.3$, $SD = 24.7$) and *Male* native speakers ($M = 73.9$, $SD = 24$); $t(29) = 0.84$, p $= .41$. It suggests that the social variable *Gender* has no effect on the number of rhotics by *Beijing* native speakers. The detailed *t*-test results are summarised in Table 16.3.

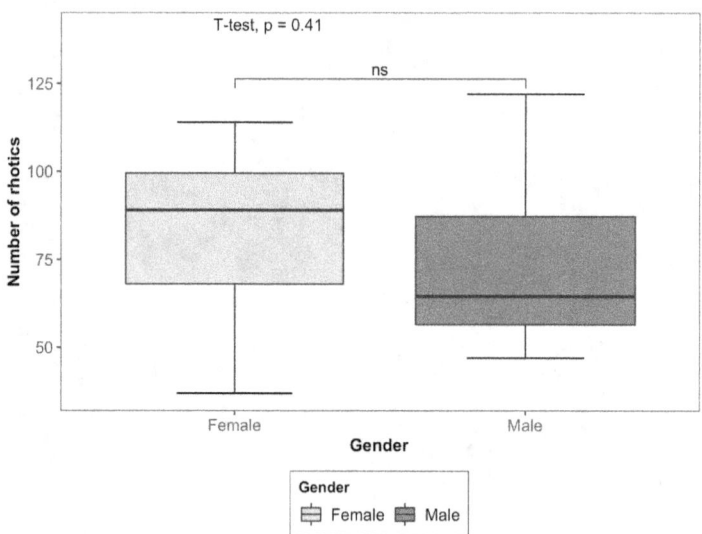

Figure 16.2 Number of rhotics ($N = 2{,}403$) of each gender *(female, $N = 15$; male, $N = 16$)*.

Table 16.3 Summary of the independent *t*-test on the number of rhotics types by female and male *Beijing* native speakers

Gender	N	Mean	SD	Se
Female	15	81.3	24.7	6.38
Male	16	73.9	24.0	6.01

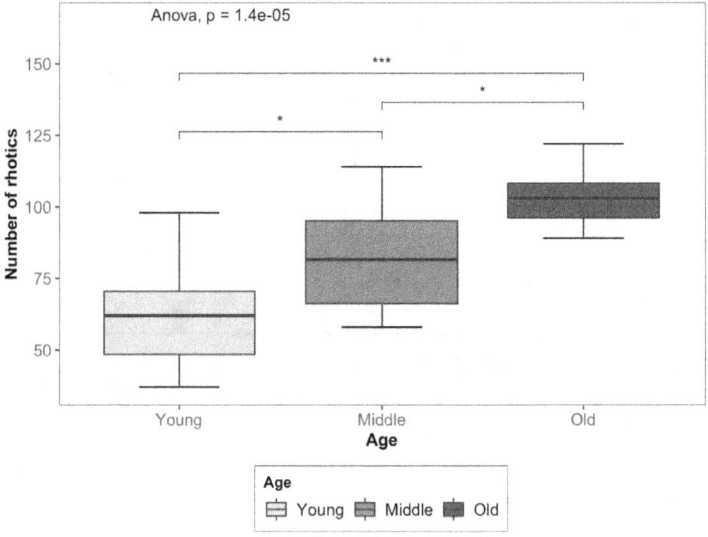

Figure 16.3 Number of rhotics ($N = 2{,}403$) of each age group of *Beijing* Speakers ($N = 31$).

When comparing the gender differences between Beijing speakers of the same generation, we find no significant differences. The number of rhotics by both *Female* and *Male Beijing* speakers in the same generation is not significantly different from each other ($p = .53, p = .09, p = .204$).

16.3.3 Age²

A one-way ANOVA test was conducted to examine if *Age* is an effective factor. Figure 16.3 presents the boxplot of the number of rhotics by three age groups and the alpha value.

The results of the one-way ANOVA test show that there was a significant effect of *Age* on the number of rhotics at the $p < .01$ level for the three conditions [$F(2, 28) = 17.07, p = .000$]. Post hoc comparisons using the Tukey HSD test indicate that the *Young Beijing* native speakers ($M = 61.1, SD = 17.7$)

Table 16.4 Summary of the independent *t*-test on the number of rhotics by female and male *Beijing* native speakers (N = 31)

Age	N	Mean	SD	Se
Young	15	61.1	17.7	4.57
Middle	8	82.2	19.8	6.98
Old	8	104	10.9	3.85

Table 16.5 *p*-values of pairwise comparisons of three age groups of *female Beijing* native speakers (N = 15)

Young Beijing female speakers	Middle Beijing female speakers	Old Beijing female speakers
Young Beijing female speakers	.063	.023
	Middle Beijing Sp.	.685
		Old Beijing female speakers

Table 16.6 *p*-values of pairwise comparisons of three age groups of *male Beijing* native speakers (N = 16)

Young Beijing male speakers	Middle Beijing male speakers	Old Beijing male speakers
Young Beijing male speakers	.12	.000
	Middle Beijing male speakers	.004
		Old Beijing male speakers

produced significantly fewer rhotics than the *Middle* ($M = 82.2$, $SD = 19.8$) and the *Old* ($M = 104$, $SD = 10.9$) speakers. *Middle Beijing* native speakers ($M = 82.2$, $SD = 19.8$) also produced significantly fewer rhotics than *Old Beijing* native speakers ($M = 104$, $SD = 10.9$). Table 16.4 lists the summary of the results.

As *Age* turned out to be an effective variable, an independent *t*-test was conducted to test the generational difference among *Female* and *Male Beijing* native speakers among the three age groups. The results are shown in Table 16.5 (females) and Table 16.6 (males).

Young Beijing Female native speakers and *Old Beijing Female* speakers had significantly different rhotics productions; $t(9) = 2.74$, $p = .023$. The difference between the *Young* and *Middle Beijing Female* speakers is not significant, $t(9) = 2.12$, $p = .063$, nor was the difference between *Middle* and *Old Beijing Female* $t(6) = -0.43$, $p = .685$. The number of rhotics by *Young* and *Middle Male Beijing* native speakers respectively were significantly different from that by *Old Beijing Male* speakers, $t(10) = 1.7$, $p = .000$; $t(6) = -4.38$, $p = .004$, while there was no significant difference between *Young* and *Middle Beijing Male* speakers; $t(10) = 1.7$, $p = .12$.

16.3.4 Dialect background

Next, the nonparametric tests Kruskal-Wallis test and Wilcoxon test were conducted due to the non-normal distribution of the total dataset. The results are shown in Figure 16.4.

The results reveal a significant difference on at least one non-paired comparison (Kruskal-Wallis chi-squared = 56.554, df = 2, p = .000). This shows *Dialect Background* is a crucial social variable. Wilcoxon tests were conducted to test which pair of groups is significantly different. The figure (the horizontal lines with asterisks) shows that all pairs of groups are significantly different. The number of rhotics is greater for *Beijing* native speakers (n = 79) than for *With-r* Dialect speakers (n = 37), U = 199, p = .01, and *Non-r* Dialect speakers (n = 7), U = 771, p = .000. *With-r* Dialect speakers (n=37) also produce significantly more rhotics than *Non-r* Dialect speakers (n = 7), U = 25, p = .000. Thus, speakers with a *Beijing* dialect background produced the highest number of rhotic words in their natural speech, while the *Non-r* speakers produced the least.

Wilcoxon tests were conducted to test the rhotics difference of *Beijing* native speakers and speakers from *With-r* areas of the same generation. The difference of the number of rhotic words produced by the *Young*, *Middle* and *Old* speakers in these two dialect groups are tested and the *p*-values are shown in Table 16.7.

There exists a significant difference in the number of rhotic words between *Middle Beijing* native speakers (n = 8) and *Middle With-r* speakers (n = 8), U = 64, p = .000, and between *Old Beijing* native speakers (n = 8) and *Old With-r*

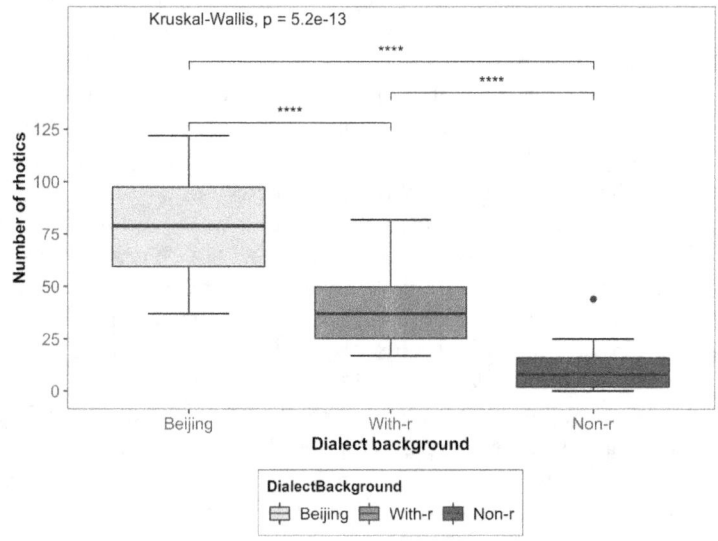

Figure 16.4 Number of rhotics (N = 2,403) of each dialect background group (N = 76).

Table 16.7 *p*-values of pairwise comparisons of *Beijing* native speakers (N = 31) and With-*r* speakers (N =22) of three generations

Young With-*r* speakers	Middle With-*r* speakers	Old With-*r* speakers
.258	.000	.000
Young Beijing speakers	Middle Beijing speakers	Old Beijing speakers

speakers ($n = 6$), $U = 48, p = .000$. The number of rhotic words by *Young Beijing* native speakers ($n = 15$) was not significantly different from that by *Young With-r* speakers ($n = 8$), $U = 78, p = .258$.

16.4 Discussion and conclusion

This investigation is reminiscent of Labov's famous New York City department store study, which also focused on the frequency of postvocalic *r* by various groups of speakers (Labov 2006). His Rapid Anonymous Survey gave the answer to this question. In Beijing, this approach was never likely to lead to any such clear-cut answers. One reason is that an anonymous survey would fail to provide information on speaker-specific social factors. Estimates as to speakers' gender and age could be made, but because so many Beijingers are immigrants, the most important determinant of accent – i.e., dialect background – would remain unknown. The situation in New York City was such that predictions as to the speakers' geographical background were predictable, but this is quite the opposite in Beijing nowadays (and difficult in New York City nowadays too, for that matter). Class distinctions in Beijing are also less predictable than they were in 1960s New York; and less relevant even. An alternative to Labov's approach is the frequency counts as presented in this chapter, which provide more reliable information in several ways.

Another difference that warrants a different approach is the likely frequency of postvocalic *r*. Not only would a predictable answer to a fixed question (Labov's approach) probably not yield a natural postvocalic *r* that was directly reflective of the dialect background of the speaker, the natural number of rhotic syllables in Beijing Chinese is also naturally lower. As was mentioned before, in Standard Chinese the number of rhotic words is likely to be much lower from the number in Beijing Mandarin. This determines the degree of markedness of the feature. In the speech of all rhotic speakers in this experiment, including Beijing native speakers and speakers from other rhotic areas, it turned out that the rhotic words constituted less than 4.5% if the words. We did a quick calculation of the number of rhotics in an online discourse by two native English (rhotic) speakers, and it showed that more than 15 percent of their words were rhotic. This means that the salience of this feature is likely to be different in the two places, at least from a frequency point of view. More research is needed to confirm this.

16.4.1 Striking results

Among the three variables, *Gender* has no effects on the number of rhotics among Beijing native speakers. There was nevertheless a significant difference across *Age* groups. That is, the *Young* generation produced significantly fewer rhotics than their *Middle* counterpart; the *Middle* generation produced significantly fewer rhotic words than the *Old* speakers did. A striking factor regarding *Dialect Background* was that three dialect groups were significantly different from each other in rhotic frequency.

In addition, among the *Dialect Background* groups, there was a significant difference between *Beijing* and *With-r* speakers in general. However, there is no statistical difference among the *Young Beijing* speakers and the *Young With-r* speakers. This contrast, to some extent, suggests that compared to its *Middle* and *Old* counterparts, the speech of the Young generation of *Beijing* native speakers is probably undergoing a process of de-rhotacisation in the sense of the number of rhotic words.

16.4.2 Discussion

Beijing native speakers produce more rhotic words in their spontaneous speech than speakers with other dialect backgrounds. The results thus provide statistical evidence that the extensive occurrence of rhotic words is characteristic of Beijing Mandarin. Speakers from a non-rhotic dialect background produce the lowest number of rhotic words in their natural speech, but they do appear to adopt this feature that is not natural to them. In addition, it is impressive to see that the number of rhotic words by *YoungBeijing* native speakers is not statistically different from those by *Young* speakers with rhotic dialect backgrounds, while there is a significant difference between their counterparts of *Old* generations on the number of rhotics.

16.4.3 Sound change

These results suggest that an intergenerational change in the natural speech of Beijingers may be taking place; a process of de-rhotacisation. The promotion of Standard Chinese, the long-term and profound social and language link between Beijing natives and migrants, as well as the population superiority of migrants are all possible causes of such observed de-rhotacisation.

Notes

1 For *Gender*, only the gender differences among the Beijing native speakers were studied. *Dialect Background* was not analyzed. In this study, speakers from other rhotic and non-rhotic areas usually come from varied towns and cities in varied provinces in China. Their original accents and dialects are also very different from each other.

So, there is no comparability across those speakers and the results of comparison will not be too valuable, due to the heterogeneous nature of the group of non-native speakers.

2 As was the case for *Gender*, no statistical tests were done to examine the effects of *Age* among the group of 'rhotic speakers' (With-r) and 'non-rhotic speakers' (Without-r), due to the heterogeneous nature of the group of non-native speakers.

References

Beijing Municipal Bureau Statistics, and Survey Office of the National Bureau of Statistics in Beijing. (2020). *Beijing Statistical Yearbook 2020* (1st ed.). China Statistics Press. http://nj.tjj.beijing.gov.cn/nj/main/2020-tjnj/zk/indexeh.htm

Duanmu, S. (1990). *A formal study of syllable, tone, stress and domain in Chinese languages* [Doctoral dissertation, Massachusetts Institute of Technology]. https://dspace.mit.edu/bitstream/handle/1721.1/13646/24289692-MIT.pdf?sequence=2

Huang, B. and Liao, X. (2017). *Xiandai hanyu [Modern Chinese]* (6th ed., Vol. 1). Gaodeng jiaoyu chubanshe.

Kassambara, A. (2020). *ggpubr: 'ggplot2' Based Publication Ready Plots.* https://CRAN.R-project.org/package=ggpubr

Labov, W. (2006). *The Social Stratification of English in New York City* (2nd ed). Cambridge University Press.

Lin, Y.-H. (2007). *The Sounds of Chinese with Audio CD* (Vol. 1). Cambridge University Press.

R Core Team. (2020). *R: A Language and Environment for Statistical Computing.* R Foundation for Statistical Computing. www.R-project.org/

Wickham, H. (2016). *ggplot2: Elegant Graphics for Data Analysis.* Springer-Verlag, New York. https://ggplot2.tidyverse.org

Zhang, Q. (2008). Rhotacization and the 'Beijing Smooth Operator': The social meaning of a linguistic variable. *Journal of Sociolinguistics, 12*(2), 201–222. https://doi.org/10.1111/j.1467-9841.2008.00362.x

17 Reacting to urbanisation in Morocco

New language practices, old discourses?

J. Falchetta

Since Blanc's (1964) early work *Communal dialects in Baghdad*, Arabic linguists have been working with socio-historical data in order to examine socially motivated differences in language use in the Arabic-speaking region, particularly in urban areas. In the 1980s, Arabic urban sociolinguistics started flourishing as a well-distinguished branch of Arabic dialectology, with studies such as those of Abd-El-Jawad (1986), Abu-Haidar (1992), Al-Khatib (1988), Haeri (1996), Jabeur (1987), Walters (1989) and others.[1] Most of these works, which aimed at explaining language variation in the light of the mainstream sociolinguistic theories of the time – sometimes questioning them – supported their analysis with an historical and/or social description of the urban community studied.[2] Even in subsequent works in this strand, socio-historical context has always proven essential in making sense of the variation observed in the field (cf. also works by Al-Wer, e.g. 1999, 2007). Recent studies (such as Bassiouney 2014, Germanos 2009, Hachimi 2005, 2007, 2012, and the contributions found in Bassiouney 2018) have also drawn on the latest developments in anthropological linguistics[3] to examine the interaction between the speakers' language use, social meaning and identity.

In the present chapter, I shall focus on the town of Temara, Morocco, showing how the linguistic choices of younger (38 or younger) male speakers have evolved with respect to those of the older generations (39 or older) of men residing in Temara, at least as far as two ongoing phenomena of language change are concerned. These are a phonological switch (from /g/ to /q/) that is spreading in the form of lexical diffusion[4] and the progressive lenition of the phoneme /t/. In doing this, I will follow the example of the urban sociolinguistic works cited above, in that, before talking about the linguistic data themselves, I shall make a brief historical sketch of the town's urbanisation, also highlighting the consequences that this has had on the residents' lifestyles. However, I will then go beyond the linguistic analysis by contrasting the observed evolution of language use with the conservativeness characterising the attitudes of several of my (even younger) informants towards some of the social consequences of urbanisation.

DOI: 10.4324/9780429348037-22

17.1 Temara's rural-to-urban progression

During the French Protectorate in Morocco (1912–1956), several cities on the Atlantic coast started attracting huge immigration fluxes, as the French administrative and economic policies chose Casablanca as the economic pole and Rabat as the administrative capital of French Morocco. These immigration flows, which continue uninterruptedly to this day, have led to the dramatic demographic growth expressed in the figures in Table 17.1.

The same phenomenon involved Temara, which, before the Protectorate, used to be a part of Rabat's rural *banlieue* (outskirts), and was only populated by a few thousand dwellers who lived according to a tribal system (Mission Scientifique du Maroc 1918). Starting in the 1930s, the urbanisation of Temara progressed through different stages, each of them characterised by a growth in size and an increase of the regional diversification of the population, mainly due to immigration fluxes from rural areas. The steepest demographic growth took place between the early 1970s, when just about 20,000 people lived in Temara (cfr. Table 17.1), and 1982, when as many as 78,727 residents were counted (1982 census Aït Mouloud 1998). Up to that point, the vast majority of Temara's residents lived in shacks, as very few could afford renting, buying or building a brick house.

Temara's shift from being a conglomerate of *dwāwər* (a plural Moroccan Arabic word indicating 'bidonvilles', the singular being *dəwwāṛ*) to an urban centre mostly made of modern residential and commercial areas occurred under two main thrusts. The first one came from the local tribes, who decided to sell pieces of their land to companies willing to develop real estate projects on them; the second one came from the government, which, after switching Temara's status from rural to urban municipality in 1983, launched several campaigns for the relocation of the slums occupiers onto land parcels, which were offered to them at convenient prices. Today, Temara can be considered an urban centre for all means and purposes, both for the modern look which its districts have acquired (thanks to the proliferation of brick housing) and for the quality of the services and living conditions that it offers to its residents.

Table 17.1 Evolution of the population in four central Moroccan cities

	1890s – 1910s	1970s	2014
Sale	ca. 20,000*	ca. 159,000**	973,418†
Rabat	ca. 27,000††	ca. 374,800††	572,717†
Casablanca	ca. 20,500˙	1,506,373˙˙	3,343,642†
Temara	ca. 3,000⁵ ▸	22,233˙˙	312,246†

Sources: *El Himer (2015: 68); ** RGPH 1971 in Fadloullah (2005); †RGPH 2014;⁶ †† RGPH 1971 in Camara (2009: 24); ˙Cohen and Eleb (2002: 286 in Hachimi 2005: 22); ˙˙Lfarakh (1993: 170); ▸Mission Scientifique du Maroc (1918); ˙˙RGPH 1971 in Aït Mouloud (1998: 25).

17.2 Language change and social background

The data on which the following discussion is based are taken from the corpus I collected in Temara between September 2015 and August 2017, in the course of two field studies. The corpus consists of 37.5 hours of recorded Moroccan Arabic speech, including four different types of communicative events: spontaneous conversations among native speakers, group interviews with me in the interviewer's role, individual interviews with a native collaborator in the interviewer's role, and a guided elicitation test during which native speakers were requested to perform verbal tasks. In total, 53 speakers from Temara were included in the corpus, and were divided into 38 'younger' (i.e. younger than 39) and 15 'older' informants (i.e. 39 or older). This division is field-based: while I recruited all informants younger than 39 (henceforth simply 'younger') from my personal networks, all informants older than 38 (henceforth simply 'older') were recruited by asking other people to put me in contact with a relative or acquaintance of that age range. The different recruiting methods should obviously be kept in mind as one of the factors that may have biased the data. Another such factor is the different upbringing environment of the members of the two groups: all younger informants, except one (who moved to Temara from a big city, Marrakesh, at the age of 24), either had arrived in the by now urbanised Temara before the age of 18, or had been born and still lived there; this implies that all of them had either always lived or spent at least a part of their 'formative years for dialect formation'[7] in an urban environment. On the other hand, most older informants were either locals raised in Temara when it was still a rural community, or immigrants raised in other rural areas.[8] As all younger informants were men and only two of the older ones were women, the following discussion will be limited to male speakers, to obviate the bias that would derive from the under-representation of the female population in the informants' sample.

The aim of the study was to identify how Moroccan Arabic speakers communicating within a linguistically and socially diversified environment, such as Temara, interpreted the social meanings of three linguistic features that appeared to vary in the language use of the community studied. Two of these cases of language variation were mentioned above (oscillation between /g/ and /q/ and affrication of /t/); the third one was the lexical alternation between /dwa/ and /hdərˁ/ (both corresponding to the English verbs 'to talk' or 'to speak') and will be excluded from the following discussion as it did not present a clear inter-generational bias. In order to identify these social meanings, it was decided to address the speakers' *implicit* evaluations on linguistic variation that could be inferred from their language use: by consequence, all the discussion below is entirely based on inferences on such evaluations corroborated by the linguistic data.

The first phenomenon analysed was the speakers' alternative assignment of a restricted set of lexemes to one of two phonological classes: /g/ and /q/. The two phonemes are the most recurrent historical reflexes of Old Arabic /q/

(which corresponds to <ق> in the Arabic script) in today's Moroccan Arabic varieties; another, much less common one is the glottal stop /ʔ/ (in some varieties, a pharyngealised variant /ʔˤ/ is also found), which did not occur at all in my data. The synchronic distribution of /g/ and /q/ is quite complex, as which lexeme is assigned to which of the two phonological classes depends on a wide range of factors, including the speaker's social class, regional origin (or place of upbringing), social network and stylistic choices (cf. Moumine 1990 for a variationist study on this variable). In traditional Moroccan dialectology, /q/ (in alternation with /ʔ/) is ascribed to old urban (mdīnī) varieties and /g/ to rural (ʕrūbī) or Bedouin varieties; however, it is unlikely that this distribution has ever been clear-cut in any historical period since the Arabisation of North Africa,[9] due to the constant population movements that have continued until our days (Lévy 1998). Nevertheless, it appears from recent studies (e.g., Hachimi 2007, 2011; Sánchez and Vicente 2012) that urban and rural connotations are still respectively associated with the use of either phoneme in today's Moroccan urban society. Temara is therefore one of many areas in which, while some lexemes are invariably pronounced with /g/ or /q/, others vary between the two both at the inter- and at the intra-individual level. An analysis conducted on five of the variable lexemes showed that younger speakers prefer assigning these to /q/ more often than older ones, which suggests that /g/ is regressive in the community studied (cf. Figure 17.1). The lexemes chosen are reported in Table 17.2.[10]:

In the attempt to identify the younger speakers' social evaluations connected to these two variants, the second field study was specifically dedicated to the collection of data on the targeted lexemes. A guided elicitation test was conducted with the aim of inducing my younger informants to produce the targeted lexemes while performing a verbal task (describing silent hidden-camera videos); thus, their verbal productions constituted a database in which the use-in-context of such lexemes could be analyzed. The results showed that /q/ appeared to be chosen more frequently by those speakers whose social networks and backgrounds suggested either a greater contact with bigger urban areas, or an active engagement in activities implying an upgrade of their own social status (e.g. work in Western companies, participation in 'modern' types of entertainment such as skating, rave parties, etc.). In parallel, it was observed that, when a test-taker alternated the two phonemes for the same lexeme during a single test session, /q/ was usually preferred in communicative acts in which the scientific task of the test was more salient (e.g. when the informant describing the video was providing new information to the listener[11]). These two facts led to positing that /q/ was a variant that speakers associated with out-group norms – i.e. with language norms picked up out of the social milieu (family, friends, neighbourhood peers, etc.) that had influenced their dialect acquisition – and that their accommodating to /q/ was tantamount to the adoption of a language register connected to urban and/or upgraded social environments.[12] This hypothesis is compatible with the fact that the older speakers, who – on average – had spent a greater part of their lives in rural areas

Reacting to urbanisation in Morocco 291

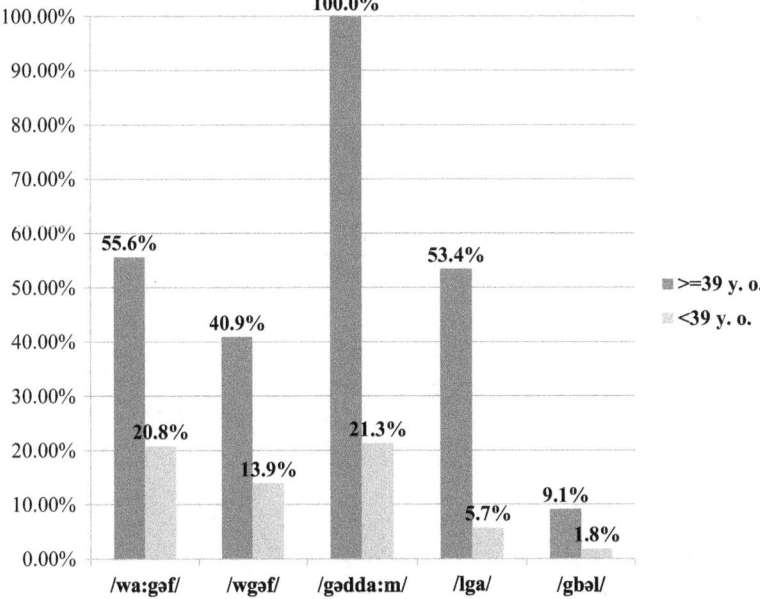

Figure 17.1 Variation of phonological assignments between two generations of informants. The percentages indicate the frequency with which that particular lexeme was pronounced with a /g/ by any of the speakers of that generation.

and had lived in Temara in a time in which connections with the nearby Rabat were much scarcer, *less frequently* assigned the five analyzed lexemes to /q/. This seems to suggest that the evolution of the variable in real time is connected to an increase of its saliency, in the sense that, for the younger generation, it concurs in the attribution – or denial – of prestige to one's speech, while the older generation does not seem to give it the same amount of importance (at least not in the lexemes concerned).

The second variable is the phonetic realisation of the phoneme /t/, which is often affricated or fricatised in Maghrebi Arabic varieties (for an old but still useful account of the geographical distribution of /t/ allophones, cf. Cantineau 1960: 37). Here, too, the variation appears to be very complex: on the one hand, different speakers may use different sets of allophones, particularly according to their age and place of upbringing; on the other, the same speaker may vary her/his pronunciation of the phoneme even in the same linguistic environments. However, a radical evolution is globally observed at the inter-generational level, as younger informants do not only sensibly reduce the repertoire of allophones found in the older informants' speech (from seven to four, two of which include 90% of the /t/ occurrences among the younger; cf. Table 17.3), but also appear to radically change the quality of the alveo-palatal affrication, which they quite

Table 17.2 The chosen lexemes

Lexeme (produced with /g/ and /q/ respectively)	Grammatical function	Corresponding English lexemes/meanings
/waːgəf/ - /waːqəf/	Active participle or adjective	'Standing', 'still'
/wgəf/ - /wqəf/	Verb	'To stop'
/gəddaːm/ - /qəddaːm/	Preposition or adverb	'In front of' (prep.), 'in front' (adv.), 'forward' (adv.).
/lga/ - /lqa/	Verb	'To find'
/gbəl/ - /qbəl/	Preposition or adverb	'Before' (prep. and adv.)

Table 17.3 Frequency of each allophone in the two age ranges

/t/ allophone	Occurrence rate in the over-39's speech	Occurrence rate in the under-39's speech
/t/	25%	4.5%
/tˢ/	17.3%	2.6%
/tʃ/	2.8%	0%
/t͡ʃ/	34.8%	51.2%
/ʃ/	8.8%	41.6%
/tˢ/	3.4%	0%
/t͡s/	7.2%	0%
/s/	0.8%	0%

often push as far as [ʃ] (i.e. an almost completely fricatised allophone), whereas only two older informants (out of 15) did this regularly. On the other hand, speakers over 38, who also present an alveo-palatal type of affrication in their speech, occasionally produce it in a distinctly more advanced place than [t͡ʃ] (resulting in an allophone that I transcribe as [t͡ʃ]). The fact that the latter realisation is totally absent from my younger informants' speech seems to suggest that the affrication of the younger informants implies a more advanced stage of lenition and, therefore, is qualitatively different from that of the older ones.

In my work (Falchetta 2019), I interpret such qualitative innovation as indicating that my younger informants *borrowed* the feature from another social group rather than acquired it from the older generation(s) of Temara residents. This interpretation is also supported by the fact that Ziamari et al. (2020) trace back this kind of affrication to Casablanca lower classes. In any case, even though explicit language attitudes have not been elicited, some comments informally collected during and after the field studies seem to confirm that the feature is stigmatised: when it was brought to the attention of a young informant from Fez, who had lived in Casablanca for two years, that he had affricated /t/ while saying /fhəmti/ ('Did you understand?'), he reacted: 'I need to stop talking like that!' In a totally unrelated episode, a Moroccan student from Rabat, who was attending a communication on the present research in a seminar in Paris, openly declared that hearing the marked [t͡ʃ] was a 'pain for [her] ears'. Similar comments are occasionally found on Facebook as well, such as the following, posted (in English) by an English teacher from, and working in, Casablanca (informally: 'Casa'):

'Students in Casa be like:
TEACHER: have you finished?
STUDENTS: notch yetch.' (Aziz Ghannaj 2019)

From these metalinguistic statements, the affricated pronunciation [t͡ʃ] of what is expected to sound closer to a stop [t] (even when speaking foreign languages, as in the case of the Facebook post) appears either to cause annoyance or to attract mockery.

Considering now both variation phenomena, two contrasting tendencies appear to emerge: on the one hand, young Temarese speakers have moved towards the adoption of a feature (/q/) that responds to out-group norms, which they apparently follow to sound more 'desirable' outside of their social milieu; on the other, they have adopted (probably through borrowing) another feature (the more lenited affrication of /t/) that is ostensibly stigmatised by virtue of its association to marginalised social groups. In fact, two characteristics of Temara may explain this seeming contradiction: its diversified social tissue and its integration in a wider social conurbation including the city of Rabat. These two features possibly affect Temarese youth in different and partly conflicting manners. On the one hand, the capital of Morocco offers many opportunities for Temarese youth to improve their economic and social status, and exploiting such opportunities requires extending their networks out of Temara, which in turn presumably pushes them to accommodate to a different way of speaking so as to access those networks (hence the increase in the assignment of *at least* a part of their lexical repertoire to /q/). On the other hand, social diversification *within* Temara – where modern residential areas have been built quite abruptly right next to old slums – inevitably brings youth of different social backgrounds in contact with each other. This, at a certain point in Temara's history, has probably led young speakers to become familiar with marginalised social groups' language practices, some of which (such as the lenited /t/ affrication) may be shared with those of Casablanca lower classes; following such contact, the feature may have acquired covert prestige (Trudgill 1972) and witnessed a general spread in the speech of Temarese youth. Such wide diffusion could be the reason why, unlike /g/, my younger informants do not appear to level out this feature in any communicative context. Nonetheless, its association with marginalised groups apparently survives, as is inferred from its ongoing stigmatisation.

It therefore emerged that, for the two variables discussed, the younger generations' linguistic choices concerning these features differed more or less radically from those of older generations, and that this seemed to reflect – at least in part – the attribution of different social connotations to those features by older and younger speakers. Even though these partial conclusions are only based on the analysis of two variable features, other differences in speech repertoire that could be observed between younger and older speakers seem to confirm them. However, since providing further examples would excessively lengthen the discussion, I have chosen these two cases as they both involve features that recur in my informants' speech quite often, and thus arguably illustrate linguistic trends found today among urban Moroccans and the social motivations underlying these linguistic choices.

17.3 The evolution of material conditions and the preservation of ethical values

As it has emerged above, the evolution of Temara residents' living and socio-economic conditions appears to be responsible for the differences observed between the language practices of the younger and the older Temareses. However, a comparison between the discourses of the two generations suggests that, while the youth's linguistic choices indicate their acceptance of, and adaptation to, the requirements of Temara's urban life in terms of language behaviour, their *stances* do not necessarily express their approval towards the social and moral changes that urbanisation has brought about. Indeed, these stances appear to partially reproduce, in several aspects, those of the older generation, who ostensibly disapprove such changes. However, as we will see below, the discourses produced by the youth are inevitably adjusted to the social background in which this generation have been raised.

The following discussion is based on a part of the corpus collected in Temara, i.e. on the individual and group interviews: all the latter involved younger informants, while all the individual interviews were addressed to older informants.

The purpose of the interviews was to maximise each informant's verbal performances and, by consequence, the amount of linguistic data available for analysis (as is the classical procedure in variationist sociolinguistics; cf. e.g. Labov et al. 1968): for this reason, the interview content was organised differently for the two sub-populations. Concerning the older informants (individual interviews), I followed a suggestion from Reda, the native interviewer, inviting interviewees to compare today's economic and social life with that of past times (usually the 1950s–70s); this because it was (correctly) expected that this type of topic would arise lengthy nostalgic and/or indignant comments from people who had witnessed the relatively radical social changes brought about by urbanisation. As for the group interviews, which I conducted on my own, the subjects of the interviews mainly revolved around the lives and aspirations of the informants, who nonetheless often expanded spontaneously to other topics of their choice, including social and political issues; this made it unnecessary to focus on the choice of specific contents that would help maximise their verbal productions.

Despite the interviews being mainly aimed at collecting samples of speech, the topics proposed by the interviewer caused a specific kind of discourse to emerge during most of the interviews with older informants, which I call here 'nostalgic discourse'. The arguments supported through this kind of discourse included some non-cultural-specific stances, such as the view of the young generations as failing to live up to general standards of respect (towards the family and the elder) or decency (e.g. through the use of vulgarities and profanities in their language). Other common subjects of complaint were the lack of safety in public places and the rise of the cost of living. However, some issues were also raised that not only were strictly linked to the urban and/or cultural context in which their proponents had been living, but also criticised some aspects of the socio-economic development that Moroccan society had been going through specifically; as shall be seen, these are social phenomena that are usually positively evaluated by the mainstream media and by major national and international political actors. In the rest of this chapter, I shall tentatively show how the ethics that support my older informants' 'nostalgic discourse' also inform the views of the youth, although the discourses of the latter ostensibly bear the marking of the (arguably) improved material conditions in which the younger Tamareses have been raised.

As was mentioned above, one of the key stages of Temara's urbanisation was the government's relocation of slum dwellers to cheap land parcels. The aim of this policy was to demolish the emptied slums and enhance Temara's living conditions and urban landscape; as a consequence, the relocated residents were requested to build houses that responded to official standards of safety and sanitation. For this reason, modern brick houses soon replaced shacks in most of Temara. The changes in urban planning also brought about some other, socio-cultural ones, as many of my older informants who had once inhabited a shack (like **MW** below) or still did (like **HN3** below) described the *dwāwər* as a socially serene environment, in which solidarity and commonality would form the bases of living together, and by no means considered them a degraded and/or unhealthy place for living.

MW[13] **(70, retired public employee):** *'In the dəwwāṛ there were like 12 shacks or 15 tents. (…) In the evening, everybody used to gather in the same tent and smile, chat and so on; nobody was against anybody… There was no mistrust or anything like that: everybody would eat and drink, everybody would smile, everybody! Now it's different: your neighbour eats, you don't!'*

HN3 (47, carpenter): *Even though it was the slums, we were well-bred. (…) We could enter any house we wanted, and after we moved to modern housing (…) we've kept on having lunch in everybody's home until now (…) like we're one family (…) Why this? Because we were raised like that! Now, you and I can even be friends without knowing much about each other.*

Indirectly connected to the rise of individualism is that of consumerism: according to older people, today's youth are spoilt by the overt availability of food and other types of material goods – some even unnecessary. In the excerpt below, another informant, **AL** (a then 39 year-old small business manager) makes this point in support of Reda (who was 32 years old) observing the existence of a generational gap in the familiarity with the use of technology. In **AL**'s account of how *he* used to play when he was young, very simple objects such as nails, spinning tops and even faeces (each of these highlighted in bold in the text[14]) are contrasted to telephones and computers. In order to summarise the concept expressed by **AL**, Reda uses a typical Moroccan Arabic idiom, i.e. 'to create happiness out of nothing' (/ka:-təχləq s-saːʕaːda mən la ʃaːjʔ/, as per the original text). This expression, as shall be seen, is also employed by younger informants in reference to their own leisure practices – although these are evidence of quite better-off material conditions.

Reda: *I know a guy whose son is three or maybe four, and he unblocks his father's telephone pattern! And why this? It's the influence of technology, of globalization; we [=our generation] never saw a computer…*

AL: *We used to take a* **nail** *this long, trace lines in the soil and draw squares, and then you started [throwing it]: if you thrusted it in the ground, you'd win! (…) Then came* **spinning tops** *(…) Then marbles! And we didn't even have those… I remember what we used to do here: marbles were expensive, so we'd go search for… The Ghzawis lived next to us and they [owned] livestock; and those animals'* **excrement** *was like…*

R: *Marbles!*

AL: *Yeah, so we gathered it and played with it!*
(…)

R: *And you were happy: happiness used to be created out of nothing!*

During my field study, I could personally ascertain how my younger informants' standards of living partially confirmed the argumentations supported by the 'nostalgic discourse', in that their housing conditions, consumption patterns and leisure opportunities approached very closely those commonly found among Western middle or lower middle classes.[15] Nevertheless, not all of them appeared to be 'blinded' by their own well-being; in fact, some of them made clear how they valued sobriety over the quest for superfluous material commodities. In the following excerpt, **SI** and **DS** regret the time when students could attend classes with poor equipment without being taunted.

SI (21, university student): *When I used to study in primary school, Moroccans had an asset, like… people would never go as far as laughing at you or something like that. Like, for example, someone wearing broken sandals… Back then there was poverty… (…)*

DS (21, university student): *Some used to carry books in a plastic bag… A bag made of plastic, to carry books!*

SI: *Yeah, you'd carry your books in a plastic bag at that time… Back then, only those who really had money would own a backpack. And the good thing, better than now,* was that even though there was poverty, everybody was poor! Like, for example, no one would mock you in the classroom. Like, children today... If you send your son and he's wearing broken sandals, they can laugh at him and traumatize him!

Later in the same group interview, talking about their leisure activities, all the participants agreed in praising the ability of 'creating happiness out of nothing' (cf. excerpt below), significantly evoking the same idiom used by Reda during our interview with **AL**. However, the hobbies and activities mentioned by these young students (playing guitar, rap, combat sports, pigeon breeding) are clear indices of a more sophisticated and partly westernised lifestyle, and sharply contrast with the humble games mentioned by **AL** – who is less than 20 years older – in reference to his childhood. Therefore, while the ethics that supports the two types of discourse (the nostalgic and the youth's) is the same, what blatantly emerges are the different material conditions in which such ethics has been acquired. The words in bold in the excerpt below show concrete manifestations of this changed material context in the form of modern leisure commodities and activities:

SI (21, university student): *If you're in Europe or another place you need something to create happiness... [Whereas in Morocco] you've got zero dirhams. Not zero dirhams for a day or... You have zero dirhams the whole month and you keep smiling!*
(...)
GG (26, vocational student): *Each of us [has got a hobby]: one plays* **guitar**, *the other may enjoy doing* **full-contact**... *The other is into 'Hiroshima'...*
PT (20, university student): *That's a* **Facebook** *group (...) He [=GG]* **raps**, *sits in front of the sea, writes a couple of lyrics...*
SI: *And he [=PT] is into* **pigeon breeding**!

Another recurring argument of the older informants' 'nostalgic discourse' is the re-assessment of schooling and, particularly, the downplaying of its usefulness in daily life. Most of those who supported this argument were men of little or no schooling, who nonetheless had found a job and achieved a stable financial situation in their lives, a fact that may partly explain their stance. **HN3** – a 47-year-old carpenter who was cited above – aptly summarised this concept by saying: '*Thank God, I didn't study!*'. Another informant, one of whose daughters was completing a PhD at the time, made the same point more exhaustively:

OUL (68, retired clerk): *For example, you see, when I'm sitting and my daughter's there, I tell my children:* **'It's not enough to have diplomas!'** *(...) [The real question is,] is there something in your brain that makes it work, that makes those diplomas work? (...) Now you've become a 'doctor', now you have to go and run a community! A city! A tribe! And how would you run it? Will you bring your diploma, hang it there in front of them and tell them: 'Here you are, now I'll go to my village [and run it]...'?* **You need to go there with some experience**, with an overall view, with some planning skills... this way, your knowledge will come out! (...) I swear I sit with them every day, saying: 'Look, don't come to me with diplomas! Diplomas alone mean nothing: **you have to teach yourselves**, know what you're doing, what has to be done!' This is what they need to come to terms with!

Quite predictably, a different position with respect to schooling was adopted by my younger informants, as most of them were students who expressed great concern about the quality of their education and the shortcomings of the Moroccan school system. However, some of them also explicitly subordinated schooling to the exigency of finding a job, which is obviously a preoccupation common to youth across the world. Still, it is interesting to notice that some of my younger informants spontaneously insisted on the insufficiency of a type of knowledge limited to what is taught in schools and universities, and that they did so in a way that partially echoes my older informants' open aversion for schooling-based expertise. In the excerpt below, **DS** illustrates this in the most exhaustive manner.

DS (21, university student): *...because you've got two kinds of people: those who take studying as a **means** and those who take it as a **goal**, you know. If you ask most young people here: 'How do you take studying, as a means or as a goal?', they'll answer:* **'As a means!'** *They take it like they want to study [in order to] get somewhere, they want to get a diploma to work with;* **they don't take it as a goal just to improve their own knowledge. They want to make use of it afterwards.**

In spite of these stances, what emerges from the youth's discussions on their own life paths and ambitions is that school plays a very important role in the young Moroccans' lives nowadays. In fact, it can sometimes be inferred between the lines that such role goes beyond the mere fact of enabling someone to stabilise their own financial situation: in the following excerpt, **PG**, a mechanic who was interviewed with his friends – some of whom were students – *justifies* his not having completed his studies by explaining how repairing cars makes one acquire a way of thinking that is just as complex as 'a 3D vision', which is a concept acquired from schooling. Although **PG**'s point may recall **HN3**'s words '*Thank God, I didn't study*', his taking school as a term of comparison to show the value of his working expertise may be seen as an implicit acknowledgement of school education as a model that legitimises other sources of knowledge by converse, HN3 made no such acknowledgement at any moment of his interview.

PG (29): *I've spent thirteen years doing this job. Thirteen years! No study and stuff, I've just studied a little (...) up to the 1ˢᵗ grade of Middle School, I may have completed just over half of it, then, boom! I switched straight to mechanics.* **But auto mechanics teaches you some things in life**, *you know like what?*

*Like **you get a 3D vision**, you see things from all their angles. You don't see just one side, you see this and this side... Like when you're holding a piece of a car, analyze it...*

17.4 Conclusion

The linguistic analyses of the /q/-versus-/g/ and of the /t/-affrication variables have brought to light two clear innovation tendencies in the speech of men under 39 residing in Temara, as opposed to that of men over 38: a phonological relocation of a portion of the lexical repertoire from /g/ to /q/, and a radical change of affrication through the adoption of a lenited alveo-palatal allophone [tʃ] (sometimes fricatised to [ʃ]) for the phoneme /t/. As I argued above, these linguistic choices seem to be linked to the evolution of the urban environment surrounding my younger informants, who have been raised in a social and material context that is radically different from that in which older generations of Temara residents grew up. More specifically, the younger:

a) have all been living in a modernly equipped town, and in dwellings that matched the governmental standards of safety and sanitation (with very few exceptions) at least since their early childhood
b) have been raised while Temara's demographic growth was at its highest (i.e. in the 1990s–2000s), and consequently came in contact with a much more regionally and socially differentiated population
c) have got more chances and, at the same time, need to diversify their professional and/or socialising opportunities by extending their social networks to other urban centres – most notably Rabat

However, while the orientations observed in the language use – and pursuit of better living – by the youth appear to indicate that they are willing (or compelled?) to adapt to the new social constraints and modernising trends linked to urbanisation, this does not necessarily exclude that some of them may adopt a more conservative stance with respect to the ethical values and life priorities associated with this type of modernisation. In fact, what emerges from my group interviews is that youth *can* endorse some of the arguments supported through what I called 'nostalgic discourse' – such as the disapproval of materialism and excess, or the prioritisation of work-oriented knowledge over knowledge as an end in itself – and re-adjust them to the new social context in which they have grown up. Even though my data are limited and do not allow to verify how widespread such stances are among young Temareses, the discourses recorded in my interviews prove at least that such discursive re-adaptations *are possible* in the Temarese and, more generally, the Moroccan context. This suggests that discourses play an important role in widening the gap between the evolution of social and linguistic habits, on the one hand, and the people's attitudes towards them, on the other, and therefore require an in-depth analysis that rests on a combination of different approaches.

Notes

1 Cfr. Miller (2007) and Caubet & Miller (2009) for a more detailed overview of these and other early works in Arabic sociolinguistics.
2 This was also done in the main Anglo-American variationist studies in dialect contact that were the references of these authors, such as William Labov (1963, 1966), Peter Trudgill (1972, 1986) and Lesley Milroy (1980).
3 Particularly in the works of Penelope Eckert (e.g. 2000, 2003, 2008), and Michael Silverstein (2003).
4 My use of this term follows the description given by Wang (1969: 12–18) of the phenomenon it refers to.
5 The number, reported by the French Scientific Mission in Morocco, only refers to the Ūdāya, one of the two tribes that occupied the area of Temara, which was a territorial subdivision of the Rabat municipality at the time. As for the other tribe, called the ʕrəb, its territory was split among several areas, among which was Temara. It therefore seems reasonable to believe that the Ūdāya formed the bulk of Temara's population when the Protectorate was established.
6 RGPH stands for the *Recensement Général de la Population de l'Habitat* ('General Census of Population and Housing'), which was conducted at irregular intervals in Morocco until 1994, and every 10 years since then. The institution responsible for conducting the census is the public *Haut Commissariat au Plan*. The source for the RGPH data cited here is the website hcp.ma, except where another source is noted.
7 Chambers (2002: 368) defines the age from eight to eighteen as 'formative years for accent and dialect formation'.
8 The social salience of the urban-rural dichotomy is a very important one in Moroccan society, and its reflections on language variation in the urban centres have been illustrated by Messaoudi (2002) and El Himer (2015).
9 For an account of the two phases of the spread of spoken Arabic varieties in North Africa, cf. Marçais (1961) who bases his reconstruction on ancient Arabic sources.
10 The five lexemes were chosen following the first field study, by cross-checking which lexemes oscillated between the two phonemes both in the corpus I had collected and in the language used in a selection of Moroccan TV and YouTube series which addressed a pan-Moroccan audience.
11 For a definition of what constitutes 'focused' (i.e. 'new') and 'presupposed' (i.e. 'not new' or 'given') information in a discourse analysis perspective, cf. Ward and Birner (2001: 120).
12 For more details, cf. Falchetta (2019).
13 I use two- or three-letter codes, with the occasional addition of numbers, in order to preserve my informants' anonymity.
14 Except here and where differently noted, words or statements highlighted in bold in the excerpts are the key ones that convey the overall message of the text.
15 I'm obviously referring to the informants of my sample, who were recruited in two modern residential areas of the town. The stardands of living of many other Moroccans, especially those living in rural areas, are quite different.

References

Abd-El-Jawad, Hassan Rashid (1986) The emergence of an urban dialect in the Jordanian urban centers. *International Journal of the Sociology of Language*, 61(1), 53–64.

Abu-Haidar, Farida (1992) Shifting boundaries: The effect of modern standard Arabic on dialect convergence in Baghdad. *Perspectives on Arabic linguistics*, 4, 91–106.

Aït Mouloud, Hassan (1998) *Urbanisation et aménagement de Témara*, Mémoire pour l'obtention du diplôme des études supérieures en Aménagement et Urbanisme, Rabat: Institut National d'Aménagement et d'Urbanisme.

Al-Khatib, Mahmoud Abed Ahmed (1988) *Sociolinguistic Change in an Expanding Urban Context: A Case Study of Irbid City, Jordan*, Doctoral dissertation, Durham University.

Al-Wer, Enam (1999) Why do different variables behave differently? Data from Arabic. In *Language and Society in the Middle East and North Africa*, 38–57.

Al-Wer, Enam (2007) The formation of the dialect of Amman: From chaos to order. In Miller Catherine, Al-Wer, Enam, Caubet, Dominique and Watson, Janet C. E. (eds.), *Arabic in the City: Issues in Dialect Contact and Language Variation*, London and New York: Routledge, pp. 69–90

AzizGhannaj. Facebook status. *Facebook*, 30 October 2019, 9.40 p.m., www.facebook.com/permalink.php?story_fbid=1516588075174207&id=100004690873164

Bassiouney, Reem (2014) *Language and Identity in Modern Egypt*. Edinburgh: Edinburgh University Press.

Bassiouney, Reem (2018) *Identity and Dialect Performance. A Study of Communities and Dialects*. London and New York: Routledge.

Blanc, Haim (1964) *Communal Dialects in Baghdad*, Cambridge, MA: Centre for Middle Eastern Studies.

Camara, Salim (2009) *Ville périphérique et centralité urbaine: cas de la Municipalité de Temara*, Mémoire pour l'obtention du diplôme des études supérieures en Aménagement et Urbanisme, Rabat: Institut National d'Aménagement et d'Urbanisme.

Cantineau, Jean (1960) *Cours de phonétique arabe. Suivi de notions générales de phonétique et de phonologie*. Paris: Klincksiek.

Caubet, Dominique and Miller, Catherine (2009) Arabic sociolinguistics in the Middle East and North Africa. In Ball, Martin J. (ed.), *The Routledge Handbook of Sociolinguistics around the World*. London and New York: Routledge, pp. 238–256

Chambers, Jack (2002) Patterns of variation including change. In Chambers, J. K., Schilling-Estes, N. and Trudgill, P. (eds.), *The Handbook of Language, Variation and Change*. Oxford: Blackwell.

Cohen, Jean-Louis and Eleb, Monique (2002) *Casablanca: Colonial Myths and Architectural Ventures*. New York: Monacelli Press.

El Himer, Mohammed (2015) *Dynamique linguistique dans la ville marocaine: l'espace urbain de Salé*. Rabat: Rabat Net.

Fadloullah, Abdellatif (2005) Explosion urbaine et maîtrise de la croissance des grandes agglomérations marocaines: le cas de la capitale, *colloque Les villes au défi du développement durable: Quelle maîtrise de l'étalement urbain et des ségrégations associées*, 24–27 novembre 2005, Sfax, Université de Sfax (laboratoire SYFACTE).

Falchetta, Jacopo (2019) *The social connotation of linguistic variation in a Moroccan urban context: the case of Temara*, PhD thesis, Aix-Marseille Université, https://tel.archives-ouvertes.fr/tel-02571596.

Germanos, Marie-Aimée (2009) *Identification et emploi de quelques stéréotypes, traits saillants et autres variables sociolinguistiques à Beyrouth (Liban)*, thèse de doctorat, Université de la Sorbonne Nouvelle (Paris 3).

Hachimi, Atiqa (2005) *Dialect leveling, maintenance and urban identitiy in Morocco Fessi immigrants in Casablanca* (Doctoral dissertation).

Hachimi, Atiqa (2007) Becoming Casablancan. In Miller, Catherine, Al-Wer, Enam, Caubet, Dominique and Watson, Janet C. E. (eds.), *Arabic in the City: Issues in Dialect Contact and Language Variation*, London and New York: Routledge, 97–122.

Hachimi, Atiqa (2011) Réinterprétation sociale d'un vieux parler citadin maghrébin à Casablanca, *Langage et société (4)*, 21–42.

Hachimi, Atiqa (2012) The urban and the urbane: Identities, language ideologies, and Arabic dialects in Morocco. *Language in Society*, *41*(03), 321–341.

Haeri, Niloofar (1996) *The Sociolinguistic Market of Cairo: Gender, Class, and Education*, London and New York: Kegan Paul International.

Heath, Jeffrey (2002) *Jewish and Muslim Dialects of Moroccan Arabic*. New York: Routledge Curzon.

Jabeur, Mohamed (1987) *A Sociolinguistic Study in Tunisia: Rades,* Diss. University of Reading.

Labov, William (1963). The social motivation of a sound change. *Word*, *19*(3), 273–309.

Labov, William (1966) *The Social Stratification of New York City*. Washington, DC: Center for Applied Linguistics.

Labov, William, Cohen, Paul, Robbins, Clarence and Lewis, John (1968) *A Study of the Non standard English of Negro and Puerto Rican speakers in New York City. Volume I – Phonological and Grammatical Analysis*. New York City: Columbia University.

Lévy, Simon (1998) 'Problématique historique du processus d'arabisation au Maroc. Pour une histoire linguistique du Maroc', in Aguadé, Jordi, Cressier, Patrice andVicente, Angeles (eds.), *Peuplement et arabisation au Maghreb occidental. Dialectologie et histoire*. Madrid-Zaragoza: Casa de Velazquez, Universidad de Zaragoza

Lfarakh, Abdellatif (1993) Croissance démographique et dynamique urbaine au Maroc (1960–1982). In AIDELF no. 5, *Croissance démographique et urbanisation. Politiques de peuplement et aménagement du territoire*. Paris: Presses Universitaires de France, 167–176.

Marçais, William (1961) Comment l'Afrique du nord a été arabisée. In *Articles et conférences*. Paris: Adrien-Maisonneuve, 171–192.

Messaoudi, Leila (2002) Le parler ancien de Rabat face à l'urbanisation linguistique. In *Aspects of the Dialects of Arabic Today. Proceedings of the 4th International Arabic Dialectology Association, Marrakesh Apr. 1-4 2000*, Amapatril (Rabat).

Miller, Catherine (2007) Arabic urban vernaculars. Development and change. In Al-Wer, Enam, Caubet, Dominique, Miller, Catherine and Watson, Janet C. E. (eds.), *Arabic in the City: Issues in Dialect Contact and Language Variation*, London and New York: Routledge, 1–31.

Milroy, Lesley (1980) *Language and Social Networks*, Baltimore: Univ. Park.

Mission Scientifique du Maroc (1918) *Villes et tribus du Maroc. Rabat et sa région. Tome I – Les villes avant la conquête*, Paris: Ernest Leroux.

Moumine, El Amine M. (1990) *Sociolinguistic Variation in Casablanca Moroccan Arabic*. Doctoral Dissertation Thesis. Universite Mohammed V, Facultes des Lettres.

Sánchez, Pablo and Vicente, Ángeles (2012) Variación dialectal en árabe marroquí: əl-haḍra š-šāmālīya u la-hḍra l-maṛṛākšīya. In Barontini, Alexandrine, Pereira, Christophe, Vicente, Ángeles and Ziamari, Karima, (eds.), *Dynamiques langagières en Arabophonie: variations, contacts, migrations et créations artistiques*, Universidad de Zaragoza, Área de Estudios Árabes e Islámicos, Zaragoza, 223–251.

Trudgill, Peter (1972) Sex, covert prestige and linguistic change in the urban British English of Norwich. *Language in Society*, *1*(02), 179–195.

Trudgill, Peter (1986) *Dialects in Contact*. Oxford: Blackwell.

Walters, Keith (1989) *Social Change and Linguistic Variation in Korba, a Small Tunisian Town.* Ph.D. dissertation. University of Texas, Austin.

Wang, William S.-Y. (1969) Competing changes as a cause of residue. *Language,* 45(1), March, 9–25.

Ward, Gregory and Birner, Betty J. (2001) Discourse and information structure. In Schiffrin, D., Tannen, D. and Hamilton, H. E. (eds.), *The Handbook of Discourse Analysis,* Oxford: Blackwell, 119–137.

Ziamari, Karima, Caubet, Dominique, Miller, Catherine, and Vicente, Ángeles (2020) Matériaux d'enquêtes autour des 'usages jeunes' dans quatre villes marocaines Casablanca, Meknès, Tétouan, Marrakech. In Trimaille, C. et al. (eds.), *Sociolinguistique des pratiques langagières de jeunes. Faire genre, faire style, faire groupe autour de la méditerranée.* Grenoble: UGA Éditions.

18 The dynamic sociophonetics of Bulgarian /l/

The quiet transition from [l] to [ŭ]

S. Mitsova, G. Padareva-Ilieva and D. Smakman

18.1 Introduction

An increasingly frequent characteristic in many languages across the globe is the realisation of /l/ as vocalised rather than [l]. In Bulgarian, too, /l/ vocalisation (in both the onset and coda) is heard, including in the daily speech of speakers associated with standard Bulgarian. The existence of this realisation is old (Stoykov 1961; Holiolchev 1974) but within approximately the last four decades it seems to have lost much of its markedness and has even come to be associated with the standard language, according to certain estimates (Naydenova 1998; Murdarov 2001; Murdarov 2003; Mladenov and Sotirov 1992; Padareva-Ilieva and Mitsova 2012; Padareva-Ilieva and Mitsova 2014; Zhobov 2004; Soroka, 2013; etc.). Although some Bulgarian linguists have been commenting on it, and despite the fact that the phenomenon is heard in the public space and in the media, a systematic phonetic description as well as an analysis of the sociolinguistic relevance of this perceptually salient articulatory phenomenon does not yet exist. Both ordinary speakers of Bulgarian and Bulgarian linguists are struggling with this rather prominent phenomenon by on the one hand tacitly tolerating and even embracing (using) it while on the other hand not wholly accepting it in their meta-discourses about the topic.

This chapter will present the transition in both the pronunciation of this /l/-variant and in the way society, individual speakers, and linguists have reacted to it. It draws parallels with how similar sociophonetic transitions have taken places in other languages. The social and linguistic factors that have likely effectuated the change will be described. This chapter comments on the current position of the 'new' allophone [ŭ] in Bulgarian society; how it is discussed in the media and online and what its status as an identity marker is. A 'societal treatment' approach (cf. Smakman 2018) is taken; in social media, newspapers, magazines, blogs, and on websites, people spontaneously express their ideas about certain language issues, and this meta-discourse reveals society's attitude towards linguistic phenomena. We will reveal the workings of /l/ vocalisation in the daily lives of speakers of Bulgarian, both within and outside Sofia, the capital of Bulgaria, including some seemingly mundane and practical ramifications, such as spelling issues, which actually provide much sociolinguistic information.

DOI: 10.4324/9780429348037-23

18.2 The phenomenon

In mainstream literature, /l/ is usually characterised as coronal, as it involves contact between the flexible front part of the tongue and the alveolar ridge. It is also described as an approximant, in that the airflow is narrowed by this contact and is allowed only to pass through the two sides of the tongue (or one side, for some speakers). Viewed globally, the vocalisation of /l/ often involves replacing lateral approximant [l] by a vowel or glide. The substituting vowel is often a high back vowel [u], but other replacements are also possible. It is usually phonologically conditioned. Interestingly, it is also associated with developmental constraints, as children are known to go through stages in which this phoneme is vocalised (Gnanadesikan 2004; Pater 1997). It is therefore likely that vocalised /l/ has a high ease of articulation, and that this ease may be a factor in the move of grown-ups towards vocalised realisations. In a previous paper concerning Bulgarian /l/ (Padareva-Ilieva and Mitsova 2014), it was already discussed that this vocalised pronunciation fits into the frame of coarticulation models and the principle of speech economy. Farnetani and Recasens (1999) explained that '…when [articulatory precision is not needed] speakers tend to under-articulate and economize energy' (p. 34). The phenomenon at hand is thus generally considered to be a natural phenomenon, and this conclusion is supported by the fact that it is progressing in various groups of languages across the globe.

When comparing this phenomenon in various languages, it should be noted that the various sources are not always clear about which articulatory feature is referred to. Various terms are used to qualify the same or a similar effect. Transcription-wise, there is also some variation. Besides [ŭ], the transcriptions [w], [o], [ɰ], and [ɫ] can sometimes be found in the literature, followed by qualifications like 'vocalised', 'velarised' and 'dark'. This variation is likely to be due to different perception tendencies of researchers, their native tongue(s), local transcription conventions, and the stage at which the change is in a certain language. The literature does generally agree on /l/ moving towards a less obstructed realisation in many languages across the globe.

Recasens (2012) performed acoustic measurements of /l/ in a set of languages. Many of the 'dark' /l/'s found could be qualified as vocalised, on the basis of the measurements. He explained how different phonetic contexts strongly affected type of dark /l/. Leemann, Kolly, Britain, Werlen and Studer-Joho (2014) also emphasised the role of phonetic/phonological context as a determinant of the nature of /l/ variation.

18.3 /l/ vocalisation across the globe

As said, /l/ vocalisation can be found in languages across the globe (Leemann et al. 2014). Amongst these languages are Germanic languages like Dutch and German (Jongkind and van Reenen 2007; van Reenen and Jongkind 2000). Swiss German has also been undergoing vocalisation; a change that started in dialects near the city of Bern (Leemann et al. 2014). Recasens (2012) found that dark /l/ occurs in areally dispersed and mutually independent language varieties. Examples of varieties in which dark /l/ occurred in his research were Majorcan Catalan, Portuguese and Russian. He also encountered this phenomenon in Mid-Western American English and Leeds British English. Indeed, vocalisation is common in many varieties of English across the globe, like British dialects (Tollfree 1999; Trudgill 1986) but also American dialects (Pedersen 2001) as well as Australian and New Zealand English (Borowsky 2001; Horvath and Horvath 2001). Sudbury (2001) noticed this phenomenon on the relatively isolated English-speaking community on the Falkland Islands, even. Johnson and Britain (2007) encountered similar /l/ changes in the South-East English Fens area.

Bulgarian is not the only South-Slavic language in which vocalisation is common. In Slovenian (Chepar 2011), for instance, the process is said to have begun in the nineteenth century already (Merkù 1983). In Serbian, the process is already completed and leads to the phonetic transition of the consonant [l] to the vowel [o].[1] In other Slavic regions, this phenomenon has also been noted. The process is taking place in Ukrainian (Albul and Soroka 2012), for instance, which is an East-Slavic language. In Polish (Padareva-Ilieva and Mitsova 2014), a West-Slavic language, a similar pronunciation is standardised, even in the same morphophonemic positions (Naydenova 1998).

18.4 /l/ vocalisation in Bulgaria

The standard phonemes of Bulgarian have largely been codified. In addition, the various realisations of standard Bulgarian vowels and consonants have been noticed and are being documented. In contemporary Bulgarian speech, several salient and dynamic pronunciation processes can be observed; each with its own sociolinguistic relevance. The phonetic change of Bulgarian /l/ has been one of the most expansive and dynamic ones in the last few decades. Its sociolinguistic status relative to the standard language is yet unclear. On the one hand, it is used in standard Bulgarian. On the other hand, it is subject to critical debate.

Early publications described standard Bulgarian /l/ prescriptively (Stoykov 1961; Grammar of Contemporary Bulgarian Language, V.1 'Phonetics', 1983; Boyadzhiev and Tilkov 1999). In these and other publications (Pashov 2002; Boyadzhiev, Kutsarov and Penchev 1999), this phoneme is described as having various different realisations, like [lʷ, ľ, ɫ], depending on phonological position and dialect. Interestingly, the [ŭ] realisation is not amongst them, although it is nowadays one of the most common realisations of /l/.

18.5 Phonetic/phonological features of Bulgarian [ŭ]

The literature on the Bulgarian standard language asserts that the realisation of /l/ should be as an alveodental lateral laminal consonant /l/, i.e. [l̪] (we will use the '[l]' transcription henceforth, to avoid normative suggestions regarding the difference between [l̪] and [ɫ] and other variants of [l] like [lʷ]), and is

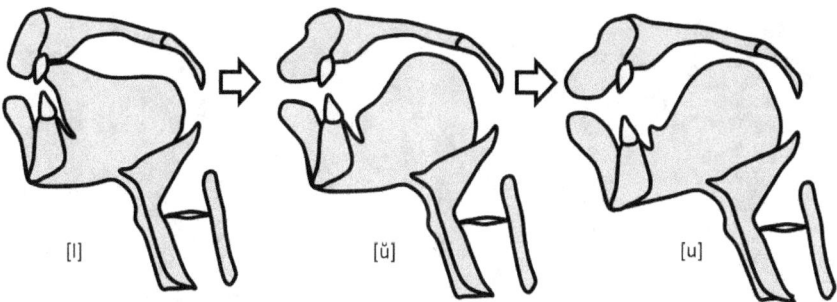

Figure 18.1 Articulatory configurations of [l], [ŭ] and [u].

articulated by creating an obstruction with the blade of the tongue placed between the alveolar ridge and the upper teeth. The mid-part of the tongue forms lateral openings. The lips do not take part in the articulation (Stoykov 1961; Boyadzhiev and Tilkov 1999; Pashov 2002; Boyadzhiev, Kutsarov and Penchev 1999; Zhobov 2004).

The 'new' articulation of /l/ (Padareva-Ilieva and Mitsova 2014), namely [ŭ], is similar in pronunciation and perception to IPA /w/, which is noted down in Bulgarian linguistic literature as a short labiovelar sound [ў].[2] Typical for this articulation is the participation of the lips (lips rounded), while the tongue blade does not create an obstruction, but is loosened behind the bottom teeth as in the articulation of the high back vowel [u]. The result is a sound which can be indicated as [ŭ]. Figure 18.1 is our tentative assessment of tongue/lip position pronouncing Bulgarian consonant [l], variant [ŭ], and vowel [u], created for this chapter.

Figure 18.2 and Table 18.1 show the acoustic differences between [l], [ŭ], and [u], i.e. the continuum from consonantal to vocalised and vowel. In Bulgarian phonetic literature, there are acoustic measurements of F1 and F2 of Bulgarian consonant [l] (Zhobov 2004; Stoykov 1961; Marinov 2019) and vowel [u] (Zhobov 2004; Stoykov 1961), but there are no acoustic measurements of the variant [ŭ]. Below, in Figure 18.2, we present a spectrogram and measurements of F1 and F2 of [ŭ], pronounced by a 40-year-old Bulgarian female with Praat Software (Boersma and Weenick 2016).

The formant values of the above visual representations are in Table 18.1.

It is important to mention that lips are rounded only during the articulation of the vowel [u] and the variant [ŭ]. This is the reason for the low frequencies of both the F1 and F2 for [u] and [ŭ], as it is distinguishable in the spectrograms (Figure 18.2) and visible in Table 18.1. It should also be noted that it is difficult to pronounce [ŭ] isolated, which illustrates the ambiguous phonological status of this sound. Its pronunciation is dependent on phonetic/phonological position. The same is true for [l]. This is the reason why in Figure 18.2 [l] and [ŭ] are excerpted from the Bulgarian word лампа[lampə, ŭampə]. [u] as a vowel

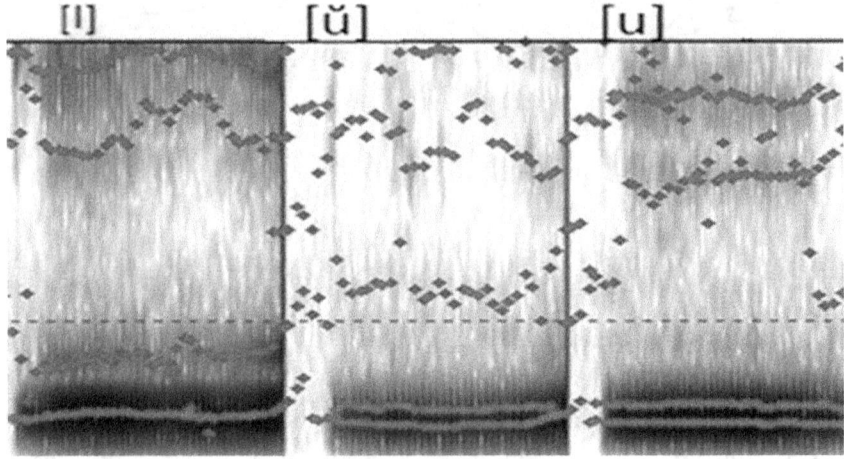

Figure 18.2 Spectrogram of [l], [ŭ], and [u].

Table 18.1 Formant frequencies (mean value F1 and F2) of [l] (isolated from the word [lɑmpə]), [ŭ] (isolated from the word [ŭɑmpə]) and [u]

	F1	F2
[l]	506 Hz	1067 Hz
[u]	382Hz	595 Hz
[ŭ]	367Hz	532Hz

could be pronounced in isolation and using this isolated phoneme here we illustrate how close in articulation [ŭ] and [u] are. However, it seems unlikely that [ŭ] is moving towards [u], because they occupy different phonological positions. To be clear, [ŭ] is similar in articulation to vowel [u],[3] but it appears as a variant of consonant /l/.

18.6 Variants of /l/ in Bulgarian

The /l/ is in the literature described as the only lateral consonant in standard Bulgarian and as having two main allophones: rounded (labialised) [lʷ] before the rounded vowels /ɔ, u/, and palatalised [lʲ] before front unrounded vowels /i, ɛ/ (Stoykov 1961; Boyadzhiev and Tilkov 1999; Boyadzhiev, Kutsarov and Penchev 1999). In addition, Bulgarian lateral /l/ has a soft correlate, i.e. [lʲ], realised before central and back vowels /ɑ, ɜ, ɔ, u/. [lʷ] is a result of an assimilation process. This allophone is influenced by the following /ɔ,u/, which are rounded sounds that induce the pronunciation of labialised [lʷ]. During this co-articulation process, the pronunciation of [lʷ] maintains the tongue blade obstruction placed between the alveolar ridge and the upper teeth but the lips are rounded ([lʷuna, lʷuk]). The palatalised allophone appears when /l/ is in a position before front vowels /i, ɛ/, e.g. [lʲɛn] and [lʲilaf] (see Table 18.2). So the allophone [lʲ] differs from the soft correlate of /l/, because they appear in different phonological positions. The soft correlate of /l/ appears only before central and back vowels as in [lʲaf] and [lʲut].

[ŭ] as a variant of /l/ appears before the central /a, ɜ/ vowels as well as before back vowels /ɔ, u/ (see Table 18.2), independently of the consonant environment. It is not overtly accepted as a regular allophone of /l/, although some phoneticians have noticed it (Zhobov 2004; Holiolchev 1974; Soroka 2013; Padareva-Ilieva and Mitsova 2014; Naydenova 1998; Mladenov and Sotirov 1992 etc.). A short survey of [ŭ]-like realisations in different phonological positions can be found in Padareva-Ilieva and Mitsova (2014).

18.7 Historic/regional dispersion

Some linguists consider the vocalised articulation to be a dialectal characteristic (Stoykov 1956, 1961; Kochev 2007; Burov 2013). They claim that its origin is a velar allophone [ɫ], which is very typical for many Bulgarian dialects, especially those spoken in the south-western part of the country. This is the reason why these linguists claim that [ŭ] is common for speakers from West Bulgaria rather than those from the East. For example, Stoykov (1962) noticed the variant in unstressed syllables at the end of the word that was close to the approximant [ɰ] (Zhobov 2004: 66). Even linguists have been known to link [ŭ] to the velar allophone [ɫ], and to another dialectal variant of /l/ pronounced as [ŭ], which is a dialect feature of Pernik (a Bulgarian town situated near the capital). Such a comparison does not hold because these two variants appear in completely different positions than [ŭ] (see Table 18.2). It should be noted that the feature may be both regional and non-regional and that these two realisations may have developed independently from each other in different parts of the region.

18.8 Onset of non-regionality associations

Bulgarian linguists (Holiolchev 1974; Naydenova 1998; Murdarov 2003; Mladenov and Sotirov 1992; Tanev 1995) define the production of [ŭ] instead of [l] as 'a new one', 'modern' or 'mincing' (Naydenova 1998: 197; Soroka 2013: 104; Murdarov 2003: 19). Tanev (1995), Zhobov (2004), Soroka (2013) and Mladenov and Sotirov (1992) noticed that the pronunciation of /l/ as [ŭ] is an expansive tendency in youth speech from the 1980s until the present. Most of the studies referred to above just mention the phenomenon or present general observations, not data. In 2014, Padareva-Ilieva and Mitsova started the first sociophonetic project in Bulgaria concerning the phenomenon at hand, based on empirical data (Padareva-Ilieva and Mitsova 2014).

Table 18.2 Realisations of /l/ in prevocalic position. The pluses show the possibility of appearance of the specific /l/ allophones in prevocalic position and the minuses show the absence of such a possibility

	Vowels					
Soft consonant /l/ and [l] realisations	[i]	[ɛ]	[ɑ]	[ɜ]	[ɔ]	[u]
/lʲ/ (soft consonant)	−	−	+ [lʲɑf]	+ [vɛsɛlʲɜ]	+ [mɛdʌlʲɔn]	+ [lʲut]
[lʲ] (palatalised variant)	+ [lʲilɑf]	+ [lʲɛn]	−	−	−	−
[lʷ] (labialised variant)	−	−	−	−	+ [lʷɔm]	+ [lʷuk]
[ŭ] (dialectal variant)	+ [piŭɛ]	+ [zɛŭɛ]	−	−	−	−
[ł] (dialectal velar variant)	+ [łipɑ]	+ [łɛk]	−	−	−	−
[ŭ] (vocalised [l])	−	−	+ [ŭɑmpə]	+ [ŭɜf]	+ [ŭɔm]	+ [ŭuk]

Two lines of socio-geographic dispersion of modern-day Bulgarian /l/ vocalisation are likely. First of all, we hypothesise that it is spreading through youth slang. In addition, the media seems to be taking part in the growing acceptance of this allophone.

Linguistic observations in Bulgaria so far indicate that /l/ vocalisation concerns especially young Bulgarians (Tanev 1995; Zhobov 2004; Mladenov and Sotirov 1992; Padareva-Ilieva and Mitsova 2014; Aleksova 2016). While investigating its roots in Bulgarian, we found that the first note is from the late 60s and 70s (e.g., by Holiolchev 1974). We hypothesise that the roots of this process of /l/ vocalisation lie in the youth slang of the capital city of Sofia of the early 1970s and in the subsequent decades it spread across other areas. Sofia is not only the administrative capital city of Bulgaria, it is a cultural hub and centre of modernity, dictating the latest social trends. That is why the youth slang of Sofia is considered as prestigious in the other parts of the country. Young people who move to Sofia to study or work commonly strive to imitate the speech habits of native Sofian youths. One of the distinctive markers of this slang is exactly the vocalised /l/ (Mladenov and Sotirov 1992; Tanev 1995). Therefore, we could define vocalised /l/ at that time as a temporary prestige marker. Even if it is not a prestige marker now, it can be heard increasingly often in the daily speech of both speakers within and outside Sofia in all Bulgarian regions, and it occurs in all phonological positions except before front vowels /ɛ/ and /i/.

This pronunciation has even been introduced and tolerated in media speech (Holiolchev 1974; Bozhanina 2014), which has always been associated with standard and prestigious Bulgarian speech, including high social status speech. It is important to mention that since the 1970s and 80s the national broadcasting has been situated in Sofia, and these were for a long time the only television and radio in the country. We believe that when /l/ vocalisation started to occur in this speech considered as the proper one, Bulgarians began to copy it in their everyday speech. Therefore, this media model of [ŭ] instead of [l] forms the other line of /l/ vocalisation amplification. That way, media speech may gradually change the individual's attitude towards this variant from being deviant/regional to regular/non-regional.

18.9 The current sociolinguistic status of [ŭ] and practical ramifications

In the past few decades, this vocalised realisation has been gaining momentum as an unmarked form. We believe that nowadays, /l/ vocalisation does not function as an identity marker in daily discourse anymore, although it probably did in the 1970s. We are currently developing sociolinguistic research that could confirm or contradict this suggestion. Most speakers who used to pronounce [ŭ] seem to have a low awareness of this ongoing change. In fact, we could tentatively divide Bulgarian speakers into two groups – without and with [ŭ] awareness. Some of those who are aware of the difference between the [l] and [ŭ] pronunciation emphasise [ŭ] when speaking and even when writing by replacing the letters Л/У; it might happen that Cyrillic letter У, representing phoneme/u/, is used instead of letter Л, which represents phoneme/l/. They seem to be doing this to mark the speech practice of /l/ vocalisation with a sense of irony. This is mostly evident in online communication, especially in social media. Users wittingly type words with wrong spelling replacing the letter Л with У or vice versa in some words, like чаЛ / *chal* / 'ciao' and ЛоЛпейпър / *lolpeipar* / 'wallpaper'. 'Ciao' is a well-established loan word in Bulgarian, 'wallpaper' is used in code-switching. The readers will realise that such users know the spelling because of the capitalised wrong letter Л. Language play seems to be taking place, and a stance such as annoyance regarding vocalisation may be at the root of this. The above mentioned sociolinguistic research in progress could enlighten this assumption too. Another motivation may be identity; gaining some kind of popularity through this phonostylistic effect. As an illustration, a famous Bulgarian rap band have chosen their name to be СкандаУ [skʌndau], which in English is 'Scandal'. They purposely perform a language play writing the band name with a spelling mistake – letter У instead of the correct letter Л – which mirrors the process of /l/-vocalisation.

The low-aware individuals seem to constitute the larger of the two groups.[4] A viable reason is that this new variant of /l/ has been spreading geographically and socially, and for increasing numbers of Bulgarians it is nowadays the only option for pronouncing [l] in particular in prevocalic positions (see Table 18.2). We suppose that today's school age children are the first generation to produce this [ŭ] as a default and relatively unmarked allophone of /l/ rather than the standard unvocalised [l]. In fact, many Bulgarian teenagers have rarely heard a pronunciation of [l] other than the vocalised one, in case the adults in their social environment also pronounce vocalised /l/. This intensifies the process of acceptance. Many young speakers even seem to be considering the standard realisation of /l/ as deviant. In a conversation on this topic, after mentioning the standard [l] articulation by the researchers, a young Bulgarian (25 years of age) who has always pronounced [ŭ] instead of [l] argues: 'I have always thought that I pronounce it correctly and I even try to articulate it like this.' This type of response to this allophone can commonly be observed amongst younger speakers.

18.10 Research and observations on /l/ realisation

Besides informal and incidental observations, there are also some experiments that have tried to capture the sociophonetic dynamics of this phenomenon. Padareva-Ilieva and Mitsova (2014) randomly selected thirty students studying Linguistics or Speech Therapy to participate in an experiment. The main goal of the experiment was to verify what the real number of individuals is who pronounce [ŭ] instead of [l]. The subjects were not informed about the purpose of the investigation so as to obtain their authentic pronunciation. The students were asked to read five previously composed sentences containing words with different in-word positions of /l/. Every speaker was recorded on a separate audio file by using a USB microphone on Praat software (Boersma and Weenick 2010). Auditory analyses were done by the researchers, who were native speakers of Bulgarian and able to categorise the various realisations. The results show that none of the subjects produced [l] in all investigated word positions, 30% of the speakers never produced the standard [l] at all, and 93% of them produced [ŭ] and another /l/ variant in over 75% of the words. At that stage of investigation, the impression was that this variant was close to a high back non-rounded cardinal vowel [ɯ]. Future acoustic analyses could reveal more about this assumption.

We presume that the subjects who are students specialising in Linguistics and Speech therapy will intuitively follow the language norm while doing the recording. It is also true that in official communication, which includes public institutions such as universities and media, nonstandard varieties are less acceptable. All of this would mean that students' language choices represent a modern, progressive form of the norm. A tentative conclusion might be that their obvious preference towards vocalised realisations shows not only a lack of markedness of this realisation but even the tacit acceptance into the standard pronunciation of Bulgarian. This is confirmed by Bozhanina, who found that in 68.4% of the analysed samples of media speech [ŭ] instead of [l] is produced (Bozhanina 2014, 2016). These data are based on the observation of 16 speakers from six Bulgarian media – radio and television within the period of May 2013 until February 2014.

In the second half of the twentieth century, media speakers were subjected to mandatory pronunciation training, with standard realisations as the object of training. This policy is not applied as strictly nowadays. The non-vocalised

/l/ realisation is nevertheless covertly a requirement still, and speech-language therapists are hired to stimulate [l] articulation. In an interview concerning this issue held in 2012 by Mitsova and Padareva-Ilieva, a speech therapist working in Sofia claimed that some media speakers are her clients and that the purpose of the therapy was to correct the [ŭ] towards the alveodental [l] pronunciation. The therapist communicated that most of her clients seek therapy by recommendation of their producers. Oftentimes, they neglect the use of the articulation that is perceived as 'proper' ([l]) and do not find it important to do so. Nevertheless, some media speakers found it easy to change to 'proper' alveodental [l]. Despite these efforts, [ŭ] instead of [l] is still commonly heard on television and other media.

Not only media speakers are sometimes sent to speech therapists. There are cases of parents who insist on the standard articulation and send their children to speech therapy to correct the vocalised /l/. They send their children to speech experts because of their awareness of allophonic variation and awareness that their own idiolects contain 'wrong' [ŭ]. Indeed, this realisation is interpreted by the speech therapists only as an aberration qualified as 'labial lambdacism' (Todorova and Atanasova 2010: 268), which comes down to some kind of articulatory condition almost. Approximately until the first decade of this century, the 'proper', standard pronunciation was covertly or overtly required when applying for certain professions (teachers, journalists, newsreaders, etc.) and when applying for certain academic programs (Pedagogy, Logopedics and Journalism, for instance). In fact, it was obligatorily when applying for these academic programs to pass a compulsory exam that included the proper [l] pronunciation.

18.11 Spelling issues

Experiments have revealed an evident tendency towards numerous spelling mistakes (Padareva-Ilieva and Mitsova 2012), probably as a result of the increasing normalcy of the [ŭ] use. This seems to have affected spelling in loan words and neologisms especially but not exclusively. Examples are '*salna*' vs. '*sauna*'; '*Windols*' vs. '*Windows*'; '*lord*' vs. '*ward*'; '*one*' vs. '*lan*'. This issue shows up in writing either in Latin or Cyrillic script. The spelling mistakes seem to be expanding socially and do not seem to be representative of young people only. In the same vein, many Bulgarians write Cyrillic letter У (/u/) instead of letter Л (/l/) and vice versa as in '*Ауцхаймер*' vs.'*Адцхаймер*', 'Alzheimer'.

In order to generate more detailed data concerning spelling, two more experiments were held. The participants were 82 pupils (11–12 year old) (Padareva-Ilieva and Mitsova 2016; Mitsova and Padareva-Ilieva 2017). These pupils were chosen on purpose from two Bulgarian dialectal regions to exclude any dialectal reasons. The students were asked to write five sentences containing words with Л (which represents the phoneme /l/) in different word positions under dictation by a teacher clearly pronouncing standard [l]. The results showed that 84.9% of the respondents made spelling mistakes concerning letters Л (/l/)

and У (which represents the phoneme /u/). This means that only 15.1% of the respondents did not make any spelling mistake concerning the confusion of letters Л and У and between the phonemes /l/ and /u/. These findings show that the allophone under investigation has spread to places across the country.

The situation is particularly confusing for teachers teaching the first and second grade. At the age of seven, Bulgarian children start primary school. In the first year, they study letters, phonemes, spelling and writing. When studying the letter Л and its sound value, teachers face the problem of explaining that [л]/[l] is a consonant, not a vowel. An illustration of this issue was found in an informal interview held by Mitsova and Padareva-Ilieva with a first grade teacher. She answered positively to the question whether she experienced difficulties when teaching consonant /l/ and the letter л. She pointed out that the major issue is '[…] the incorrect articulation of the alveodental sound /l/. Many students of age 7 pronounce it as a bilabial sound without a closure and because of that they define it as a vowel.' This teacher pronounced standard [l] herself and revealed some sensitivity towards the vocalised variant. She affirmed that she paid special attention in her classes to /l/ vocalisation, which leads to fewer spelling mistakes concerning the confusion of Bulgarian letters Л/У amongst her students (Padareva-Ilieva and Mitsova 2020).

18.12 Semantic disambiguation

Another interesting linguistic manifestation concerning /l/ vocalisation in Bulgarian is semantic (dis)ambiguation. This problem is aggravated by the fact that it does not merely concern articulation. In daily situations, the articulation of [l] as [ŭ] and the confusion in perception of /l/ and /u/ lead to homophony. In the examples below, we give samples of two Bulgarian minimal pairs.

In *блуза* ('blouse'), there is consonant /l/ (represented in the spelling as л) but the other word, *буза* ('cheek'), does not contain /l/. When pronouncing the word *блуза* ('blouse') with vocalised /l/ and a lax articulation, the word could be heard as *буза* ('cheek'). The examples below include the minimal pair *(блуза – буза)* in Cyrillic alphabet with a Latin transliteration *(bluza – buza)*, followed by two sentences in Bulgarian, their Latin transliteration, and the translation in English.

Момичето със синята <u>блуза</u>.	vs.	Момичето със синята <u>буза</u>.
Momicheto sas sinyata <u>bluza</u>.		*Momicheto sas sinyata <u>buza</u>.*
The girl with the blue <u>blouse</u>.		The girl with the blue <u>cheek</u>.

Another example is the verb pair 'receive' (*Получавам / poluchavam*), and 'preach' (*поучавам / pouchavam*), as the examples below illustrate:

Той <u>получава</u>.	vs.	Той <u>поучава</u>.
Toy <u>poluchava</u>.		*Toy <u>pouchava</u>.*
He <u>receives</u>.		He <u>preaches</u>.

Examples of this type are not that many in Bulgarian, which is a likely reason why many people, including linguists, do not consider /l/ vocalisation as a substantial communicative issue. English language teachers in Bulgaria have nevertheless indicated this problem. An issue is that [ŭ] has a pronunciation similar to the English approximant [w]. It is important to first mention that for most Bulgarians L2 English learners it is difficult to pronounce the English apical /l/. Usually they replace it with Bulgarian alveodental laminal /l/, which is easier for them. But at that stage the discussed articulation issue occurs, i.e. the articulation of [ŭ] instead of laminal /l/. As it was mentioned already [ŭ] is similar in pronunciation to the English approximant [w]. This replacement may cause spelling and sometimes semantic issues, such as: 'wife'/'life', 'why'/'lie', 'white'/'light', 'walk'/'lock', 'one'/'lan', 'ward'/'lord'.

In this respect, we will discuss here the above-mentioned spelling issues from another angle. Online written communication nowadays generates many examples of semantic ambiguity. An interesting example from a Facebook group is a shared picture of a shampoo price tag, 'Wash and Go', transcribed in Cyrillic as *Лош & Гол*, which in English would be translated as 'Bad and Naked'.[5] See Figure 18.3.

The [l]/[ŭ] confusion also causes comical situations in the traditional media. In the Bulgarian variant of the popular TV show 'Who wants to be a millionaire?', the question was 'What expresses the abbreviation LOL?' (pronounced as

Figure 18.3 Лош & Гол.

a word). The possible answers were: 'Shared love'; 'A big surprise', 'Laughing out loud' and 'Strong anger'. In Bulgarian, this abbreviation could be read as [lɔl], but the participant in the game pronounced it as [wow], which is the way some Bulgarians pronounce the exclamation 'wow!'. This is the reason why the candidate gave the wrong answer, 'A big surprise', for the abbreviation LOL, not 'Laugh out loud'. Examples of this kind are becoming more and more frequent and lead to critical debates on the issue at hand.

18.13 A language management perspective

The issue with the status of Bulgarian 'l' and its contemporary articulation can also be viewed from a Language Management perspective (Nekvapil 2011, 2016). According to Language Management Theory, the language phenomenon that deviates from the formal norm (standard) may pass through four stages constituting the 'language management process': (1) noting; (2) evaluation; (3) adjustment design; and (4) implementation of the adjustment design. Language Management typically takes place at two levels: a microlevel in case of 'simple management' and a macrolevel in case of 'organised management'.

We can first interpret the individual experiences with /l/ vocalisation as instances of simple management. We assign these experiences to different groups. Personal communication and experience or spontaneous observations, first of all, led to noting (Stage 1) the phenomenon. Conversations on the topic and conscious surveillance come down to evaluation (Stage 2). These two stages are followed by individual decisions to adjust the /l/ vocalisation in accordance with the prevailing norm (Stage 3). The decision of media producers to prescribe speech therapy to media speakers, or parents' decision to correct their children when pronouncing [ŭ], etc. can be placed in this stage. Participation in speech therapy or self-correcting represent Stage 4 – implementation.

Organised management is realised with the participation of the so-called 'language institutions' that can provoke a public discussion on language issues and after systematic observations and analyses can implement a regulation in contemporary language. The vocalisation of /l/ thus far seems to be embraced naturally, to such an extent that it may well be formalised at some point.

18.14 Conclusion

Vocalised /l/ in Bulgarian is an interesting phenomenon for several reasons. Historically, the process can be viewed as a part of /l/ vocalisation in Indo-European languages, for one. There are, however, no strong indications that the exceptional status of this 'mispronunciation' has sociophonetic equivalents in other countries. More research is needed to see whether a reason for vocalisation is the lack of noting and the ease of articulation that it seems to be subject to. Vocalisation did not progress in earlier stages of the Bulgarian language, as was the case in nearby and surrounding languages, despite ease of articulation. Indeed, the recency of this phenomenon is another interesting aspect, as change in progress can be observed in real time, almost. It may be used as an illustration of modern mechanisms of sound change, which may defy historical patterns.

The change at hand is all the more interesting as a consonant seems to be changing into a vowel-like pronunciation, and this may affect the phonology of Bulgarian in the long run, unless it becomes part of the group of semi-vowels that behave like consonants. It seems to be going in that direction, which means that a possible merger with the /u/ (always the nucleus) is not likely for the [ŭ] realisation.

Future research should not only monitor the sociolinguistic development of vocalised /l/ in Bulgarian but the situation in neighbouring countries with similar and dissimilar languages. An important question is what happens to a phoneme that is articulatorily and perceptively easily confusable with an adjacent/similar phoneme. Are sociolinguistic mechanisms active when two such phonemes push or pull each other, merge, or move away from each other when they get 'too close'.

Somehow, this new usage change escaped corrective attention for a long time, amongst others because prototypical speakers of the standard language also seemed to be pronouncing /l/ 'wrongly'. Two groups of individuals can now be discerned: aware and less aware of their own pronunciation and perception. Their individual experience when using or perceiving this speech issue is different. Some aware individuals know that they do pronounce [ŭ] rather than [l] but they feel confident in doing so. Others try to change their own articulation according to the standard norm. Less aware speakers may be oblivious to specific evaluations by their interlocutors triggered by the vocalisation. The high rate of occurrence of /l/ and the tendency of large groups of speakers to produce [ŭ] affects the status of this variant as a notable linguistic marker. It carries both connotations of progressive city speech and of being an aberration. Its conscious use and its conscious and subconscious perception and evaluation depend on which group of speakers the speakers belong to in discourse in which this sound occurs.

In their ground-breaking book 'Language Contact, Creolization, and Genetic Linguistics', Thomason and Kaufman (1988) explained how for well over a hundred years system-internal motivations and mechanisms have been used to explain language change, and that intrasystemic causes underlie virtually all language change. They emphasised that 'the history of a language is a function of the history of its speakers, and not an independent phenomenon that can be thoroughly studied without reference to the social context in which it is embedded' (4). This means that linguistic factors may be overridden by social factors. The Bulgarian case described in this chapter indeed provides food for thought, as linguistic factors do not seem to be the main determinants of its future.

Notes

1 For example *Beograd* is the name of the Serbian capital city. It is a word made from two roots – *beo* (white) and *grad* (city). We can see the /l/ vocalisation at the end of the Slavic word [bʲal]; in Serbian [bel] transformed to [beo].
2 Bulgarian linguists often use Cyrillic symbols in transcription (Kochev 2007).
3 In Bulgarian vowel and consonant charts there isn`t a sound similar to the English [w], so the vowel /u/ is the closest in articulation and perception to the /l/ variant [ŭ].
4 This assumption is a result of our pilot observations which are part of a sociolinguistic research project in progress.
5 We need to point out that this example is not a common practice for transcribing names and titles from the Latin alphabet. It is just a single example of an individual`s low literacy which indicates his/her perception and pronunciation of Bulgarian [l] and English [w].

References

Albul, O. and Soroka, O. (2012) Manifestations of language fashion in the contemporary Bulgarian language discourse. In V. A. Zarva (ed.), *Materials International Scientific and Methodological Seminar on Bulgarian Language, Literature, Culture and History*. Berdyansk: Berdyansk state Pedagogical University, pp. 27–31. [Вияви мовної моди у сучасному болгарському мовному дискурсі. Зарва В. А. (Ред.), Матеріали міжнародного науково-методичного семінару з болгарської мови, літератури, культури та історії (cc. 27–31). Бердянськ: Бердянський державний педагогічний університет]

Aleksova, K. (2016) *Sociolinguistic Perception, Language Attitudes and Social Identification on Speech*. Sofia: Paradigma. [Социолингвистична перцепция, езикови нагласи и социална идентификация по речта. София: Парадигма]

Boersma & Weenick, (2010). Praat: Doing phonetics by computer, Version 5.0.38. Retrieved from www.praat.org.

Boersma and Weenick (2016). Praat: Doing phonetics by computer, Version 5.3.56. Retrieved from www.praat.org.

Borowsky, T. (2001). The vocalisation of dark-l in Australian English. In D. Blair and P. Collins (eds.), *English in Australia*. Amsterdam/Philadelphia: John Benjamins, pp. 69–87.

Boyadzhiev, T. and Tilkov, D. (1999). *Phonetics of Bulgarian Standard Language*. Veliko Tarnovo: Abagar. [Фонетика на българския книжовен език. Велико Търново: Абагар]

Boyadzhiev, T., Kutsarov, Iv. and Penchev, Y. (1999) *Contemporary Bulgarian Language*. Sofia: Petar Beron [Съвременен български език. София: Петър Берон]

Bozhanina, S. (2014) The pronunciation of the alveodental consonant L as U in contemporary Bulgarian media speech. *Ezikov Svyat*, 12 (2), 15–22. [Изговорът на алвеоденталната съгласна л като ў в съвременната българска медийна реч. *Езиков свят*, 12 (2), 15–22]

Bozhanina, S. (2016) On inaccurate pronunciation of alveodental consonant l as u in contemporary bulgarian speech. *Наука. Мысль*, 8-1 [Вопрос о произношении альвеодентального согласного [л] как [ў] в современном болгарском языке. *Наука. Мысль, 8-1*] Retrieved fromhttp://wwenews.esrae.ru/39-446 [Accessed on 20.09.2019].

Burov, St. (2013) About two norms of Bulgarian oral standard speech. In M. Ilieva (ed.), *Speech Communication Issues,* 9 (1), 42–74. Veliko Tarnovo: University Publishing'Sv. Sv. Kril I Metodiy' [За две норми на българската устна книжовна реч (Предварителни бележки). *Проблеми устната комуникация,* 9 (1), 42–74]

Chepar, M. (2011) The first Bulgarian-Slovenian phrasebook. *Balgarska Rech,* 17(1), 63–66. [Първи българско-словенски разговорник. *Българска реч,* 17(1), 63–66.

Farnetani, E.and Recasens, D. (1999) Coarticulation models in recent speech production theories. In Hardcastle, W. J. and Hewlett, N. (eds.), *Coarticulation: Theory, Data and Techniques.* NY: Cambridge University Press, pp. 31–68.

Gnanadesikan, Amalia E. (2004) Markedness and faithfulness constraints in child phonology. In R. Kager, J. Pater and W. Zonneveld (eds.), *Constraints in Phonological Acquisition.* Cambridge: Cambridge University Press, pp. 73–108.

Grammar of Contemporary Bulgarian Language, V. 1 Phonetics. (1983) D. Tilkov (ed.), Sofia: BAN [*Граматика на съвременния български език. Том 1 Фонетика.* Д. Тилков (Ред.), София: БАН]

Holiolchev, Hr. (1974) About the speech of newsreaders, editors, reporters and correspondents of Radio Sofia. In L. Andreychin (ed.), *Issues of Bulgarian Contemporary Speech,* Sofiya, pp. 30–37. [За речта на говорителите, редакторите, репортьорите и кореспондентите на радио София. В Л. Андрейчин (Ред.), *Проблеми на българската книжовна реч.* София: Наука и изкуство, 30–37]

Horvath, B. and Horvath, R. (2001) A multilocality study of a sound change in progress: The case of /l/ vocalisation in New Zealand and Australian English. *Language Variation and Change,* 13, 37–57.

Jongkind, Anke P. and Van Reenen, Pieter. (2007) The vocalization of /l/ in standard Dutch. In A. Timuska (ed.), *Proceedings of the IVth International Conference of Dialectologists and Geolinguists,* University of Latvia, Riga, 28.7.2003. Riga: Latvian Language Institute, pp. 1–6.

Johnson, Wyn and Britain, David. (2007) L-vocalisation as a natural phenomenon. Explorations in sociophonology. *Language Sciences,* 29, 294–315.

Kochev, Iv. (2007) The liquid consonants in Bulgarian language. *Ezikov Svyat,* 3, 19–22. [Плавните съгласни в българския език. *Езиков свят,* 3, 19–22]

Leemann, Adrian, Kolly, Marie-José, Britain, David, Werlen, Iwar and Studer-Joho, Dieter. (2014) The diffusion of /l/-vocalization in Swiss German. *Language Variation and Change,* 26(2), 191–218.

Marinov, Vl. (2019) Acoustic characteristics of the consonants l and l' in Bulgarian and l and l' in the Wallachian dialect. In M. Ilieva (ed.), *Aut inveniam viam, aut faciam. Proceedings in honor of prof. Stoyan Burov.* Veliko Tarnovo: University Publishing, pp. 316–326. 'Sv. sv. Kiril i Metodiy' [Акустични характеристики на консонантите л и л' в българския език и l ил' във влашкия диалект. В М. Илиева (Ред.), *Aut inveniam viam, aut faciam.* Сборник в чест на чл. к-р проф. д.ф.н. Стоян Буров (316–326). Велико Търново: университетско издателство „Св. Св. Кирил и Методий']

Merkù, P. (1983) Prehod l>u v Tržaški slovenščini. *Slavistična Revija,* Letnic 31/83, 3, 260–262.

Mitsova, S. and Padareva-Ilieva, G. (2017) Incorrect articulation of consonant l, perception, spelling mistakes. *Bulgarian Language and Literature,* 59 (5), 495–503. [Некоректна артикулация на алвеодента́лната съгласна л: перцепция, правописни грешки. *Български език и литература,* 59 (5), 495–503].

Mladenov, Hr. and Sotirov, P. (1992) Towards the problem of the phonostylistic description of the language variation. *Balgarski Ezik*, 61 (1), 62–67. [Към проблема за фоностилистичното описание на езиковата вариативност. *Български език*, 61 (1), 62–67].

Murdarov, V. (2001) *99 Language Advises*. Sofiya: Prosveta [*99 езикови съвета*. София: Просвета].

Murdarov, V. (2003) *More 99 Language Advises*. Sofiya: Prosveta [*Още 99 езикови съвета*. София: Просвета].

Naydenova, V. (1998). A 'modern' tendency of phonetic level in the contemporary Bulgarian language. *Research Papers, Philology*, 36 (1) 197–200. [Една 'модна' тенденция на фонетично равнище в съвременния български език. *Научни трудове, Филологии*, 36 (1) 197–200].

Nekvapil, Jiří. (2011) The history and theory of language planning. In Eli Hinkel (ed.), *Handbook of Research in Second Language Teaching and Learning*. Vol. 2. New York and London: Routledge, pp. 871–887.

Nekvapil, Jiří. (2016) Language Management Theory as one approach in language policy and planning. *Current Issues in Language Planning*, 17 (1), 11–22.

Padareva-Ilieva, G. and Mitsova, S. (2012) Towards the question aboutў instead of L in contemporary Bulgarian speech. *Bulgarski Ezik*, 59 (3), 99–104. [Към въпроса за ў вместо л в речта на съвременния българин. *Български език*, 59 (3), 99–104]

Padareva-Ilieva, G. and Mitsova, S. (2014) Is Bulgarian language losing its alveodental consonant [l]? *International Journal of Linguistics and Communication*, 2 (1), 45–65.

Padareva-Ilieva, G. and Mitsova, S. (2016). Does the incorrect articulation and perception of consonant l lead to spelling mistakes? *Bulgarian Language and Literature*, 58 (3), 307–314. [Води ли неправилната атикулация и перцепция на съгласната Л до грешки присане? *Български език и литература*, 58 (3), 307–314]

Padareva-Ilieva, G. and Mitsova, S. (2020). Is it time for discussion concerning the problem l as ŭ at school? (Based on an experiment on spelling of words containing letters л and у at secondary school). *Bulgarian Language and Literature*, 62 (1), 43–54. [Време ли е за дискусии относно проблема л като ў в училище? (въз основа на експеримент в начален курс върху правописа на думи, съдържащи л и у). *Български език и литература*, 62 (1), 43–54]

Pater, Joe. (1997) Minimal violation and phonological development. *Language Acquisition*, 6, 201–253.

Pashov, P. (2002) *Bulgarian Grammar*. Sofia: Hermes [*Българска граматика*. София: Хермес]

Pedersen, Inge Lise. (2001) Dialects. In J. Algeo (ed.), *Cambridge History of the English Language: English in North America* (Vol. VI). Cambridge: Cambridge University Press, pp. 253–290.

Recasens, Daniel. (2012) A cross-language acoustic study of initial and final allophones of /l/. *Speech Communication*, 54, 368–383.

Smakman, D. (2018) *Discovering Sociolinguistics. From Theory to Practice*. London: Palgrave.

Soroka, O. (2013) About a phonetic phenomenon in the contemporary Bulgarian speech through the ear of the foreigner. *Speech Communication Issues*, 9 (1), pp. 104–122. Veliko Tarnovo: University Publishing 'Sv. Sv. Kril I Metodiy'. [За едно фонетично явление в съвременната българска разговорна реч през ухото на чужденеца. Проблеми на устната комуникация, 9 (1) (104–122). Велико Търново: УИ „Св. Св. Кирил и Методий']

Stoykov, St. (1962) In addition to the dialect consonantism in Bulgarian language. *Bugarski Ezik*, 1–2. [Към диалектния консонантизъм в български език. *Български език*, 1–2]

Stoykov, St. (1961) *Introduction to Bulgarian Phonetics*. Sofia: Nauka i izkustvo. [*Увод в българската фонетика*. София: Наука и изкуство]

Stoykov, St. (1956) A new change of the consonant l in Bulgarian language. *Bulgarski Ezik*, 8, 239–244. [Една нова промяна на съгласната л в българския език. *Български език*, 8, 239–244]

Sudbury, A. (2001) Falkland Islands English: A Southern Hemisphere variety? *English World-Wide*, 22, 55–80.

Tanev, M. (1995) Let's save the sound richness of Bulgarian language. *Ezik I Literatura*, 1, 85–91. [Да опазим звуковото богатство на българския език. *Език и литература*, 1, 85–91]

Thomason, Sarah and Kaufman, Terrence (1988) *Language Contact, Creolization and Genetic Linguistics*. Berkeley: University of California Press.

Todorova, E. and Atanasova, E. (2010) Production, automation and differentiation of sonorous sounds [l] и [R]. In V.V. Matanova (ed.), *Articulation Disorders:Therapy Guide*. Sofia: New Bulgarian University, pp. 267–308. [Постановка, автоматизация и диференциация на сонорните звукове [Л] и [R]. В В.Матанова (Ред.), *Артикулационни нарушения: ръководство за терапия* (267–308). София: Нов Български Университет]

Tollfree, L. (1999) South East London English: discrete versus continuous modelling of consonantal reduction. In Paul Foulkes and Gerard Docherty (eds.), *Urban Voices*. London: Arnold, pp. 163–184.

Trudgill, Peter. (1986) *Dialects in Contact*. Oxford: Blackwell.

Van Reenen, Pieter and Jongkind, Anke P. (2000) De vocalisering van de /l/ in het Standaard-Nederlands. *Taal en Tongval*, 52, 189–199.

Zhobov, V. (2004). *Sounds in Bulgarian Language*. Sofia: Sema RSh [*Звуковете в българския език*. София: Сема РШ].

Index

Note: Locators in *italics* represent figures and **bold** indicate tables in the text.

Abdel-Jawad, Hassan Rashid 287
Abruzzo: CAS in 16, 26; dialect of **22**
Abu-Haidar, Farida 287
Adamawa family 49
Adamawa-Fulfulde 49, 53, 57
Adamawa province 49–50, 56–61
Adami, E. 239
Agha, Asif 86–87, 92
Algemeen Beschaafd Nederlands (ABN) 100
Al-Khatib, Mahmoud Abed Ahmed 287
allophones 291, **292**, 308–309
Altuna, O. 145
Ammon, Ulrich 199, 203
Amsterdam dialect 106, 108–110
Androutsopoulos, Jannis 42
anti-Roma racism 89–90
Arabic dialectology 287
Arabic linguists 287
Arabic urban sociolinguistics 287
Armstrong, T. 142, 149
Athens 104
ATLAS.ti 262
auditory analyses 312
Auer, Peter 26, 190
Austin, John L. 31, 38
authenticity 88
authorisation 27n7
autochthonous speaker group 61
autochthony 49
Azad Kashmir 17, 19

Backhaus, P. 242
Ball, R. 167
Balochistan 17
Baranova, Vlada 7–8, 10
Batavia 105
Bauer, Laurie 110

Baumgardner, Robert 17
Beijing, rhotics frequency in 275–276; age 281–283; data source 276; de-rhotacisation 285; dialect background 283–284; gender 280–281; independent *t*-test **282**; participants 276; procedure 276–277; rhotics distribution 278–280, *279*; statistical treatment 277–278
Belarusian language 6–7, 172–173
Belarusian Language Society 184–185
Belarusian-speaking intellectuals 184
Bělič, Jaromír 115
Bell, Allan 109
Ben-Rafael, E. 261, 265, 267
Bergroth, M. 159
Berruto, Gaetano 16
Beyer, Klaus 4
Bhattacharya, Bhargab B. 32
bietjie (a bit) 39
bilingualism 145, 168n3, 172
bilingualism in Finland 154; in action 160–162; Finland-Swedish identity 165–166; language contact and phonetic change 162–165; language ideology 159–160; language of education 160; language policy and identity 156; mother tongue 160; Swedish 154–156; urbanisation of southern Finland 158–159
bilingual municipalities 156, 168n3
bilingual signs 245
Birnie, Ingeborg 6, 142, 144
Blackledge, A. 134n2
Black Salami 92–93
Blanc, Haim 287
Blok, D. 103

Blommaert, Jan 261
Blommaert's methodology of ELLA 243
Bloomfield, Leonard F. 110
Bodó, Csanád 5
boosaaru 59
border regime 219–220
Bourhis, R. Y. 142, 144
Britain, David 305
Budapest Pride Marches 89
Budapest University Dormitory Corpus 88–89
Bulgarian /l/, sociophonetics of 304; historic/regional dispersion 309; language management perspective 316; linguistic observations 310; /l/ realisation 312–313; onset of non-regionality associations 309–311; phenomenon 305; phonetic/phonological features of Bulgarian [ŭ] 306–308; semantic disambiguation 314–316; sociolinguistic status of [ŭ] and practical ramifications 311–312; spelling issues 313–314; variants of /l/ in Bulgarian 308–309; vocalisation across the globe 305–306; vocalisation in Bulgaria 306
Bulgarian linguists 304, 309
Bulgarian speakers 9
business names in Mainz 260–262, 266–269; characteristics of businesses **263**; method 261–264; results 264–267

Calinescu, Matej 83
Cameron, Deborah 83
childhood bilingualism 163
Chi-squared test of independence 165
Chromý, J. 134n9
class-related linguistic patterns 1
CMC *see* computer-mediated communication (CMC)
code alternation 16
code-mixing 16
coding scheme 264
Cohen's Kappa 264
commercial culture 215
commodification 215
Common Czech 117, 128
communal dialects in Baghdad 287
communicative and management strategies 10
communicative commodities 2
communicative factors 2
communicative habits 2
communicative management 196
computer-mediated communication (CMC) 4, 31; based speech 44; German-Namibian 33; German-Namibian speech acts 39–41; intra-individual language choices 34–37; Namibian language practices 35, 42
Comune 27n8
contact phenomena: code alternation 24–26; code-mixing 23–24; within the refugee centre 22–26; in speech 16
conversation analysis (CA) 118, 122, 133
Copenhagen 104
Cornips, Leonie 102
Corona restrictions 10
Corona virus pandemic 9–11
Coster, Laurens Janszoon 105
Creese, A. 134n2
crime 107
critical discourse analysis (CDA) 69–70
cultural model of speech 87
cultural shame 18
Cychun, Henadz 179
Cyrillic transliterations 226
Czech declension system 128
Czech Linguistic Atlas 114–116
Czechoslovakia 116, 118
Czech Republic 114
Czech-Russian semicommunication 201
Czechs 127

Daan, J. 102–103
Data Services Agency (DVV) 158
Dejmek, Bohumír 116–117, 120
Delta Metropole 102
De Rooij, Vincent A. 102
dialects of Dutch 105
Diamaré 50
Diba, Rachel 30
Di Carlo, Pierpaolo 30
diffuse language systems 4
digital communication 10
dilalia 17
diverse public-space contexts 2
Dovalil, Vít 7, 10
drug abuse 107
Duchêne, Alexandre 198
Dunbar, R. 141–142
dwāwəɾ 295

East-Central Europe, political correctness (PC) in 5, 83–84, 95–96; analyses 89–95; Budapest University

Dormitory Corpus 88–89; defined 84; hate speech 85; in Hungary 84, 87; language 85; in post-socialist Budapest 84–86; voice and enregisterment 86–88
East-Slavic language 306
ECN-measures 56
economic centres in the Netherlands 110
ego-centred-networks (ECN) 4, 50–51
ei-index 55; of Ego1 55–57, *56*
Eindhoven 109
ELB-codes 55
ELLA (Ethnographic Linguistic Landscape Analysis) 217, 243
English 17; English-only social linguistic soundscape 142; lingua franca in Japan 72; social setting of community 142
English-based interactions 202
English-medium schools 19–20
enregisterment works through indexical processes 5, 84, 86–88, 91–92
Estonia 217–218
Estonia-Latvia-Russia Cross Border Cooperation Program 221
ethnic and non-ethnic identifications 4
ethnic identities 18, 75
ethno-linguistic background (ELB) 53
ethnomethodology 122
European migrant crisis 15–16; code alternation 24–26; code-mixing 23–24; contact phenomena within the refugee centre 22–26; language policy and language use in Pakistan 17–18; new variety 19–22; Punjabi language vitality 18–19; research objectives 16–17; sociolinguistic background 17–22

Facebook 33–34
Fairclough, Norman 70
Falchetta, Jacopo 9
family language policy (FLP) 74
Farnetani, E. 305
Fedorova, Kapitolina 6–8, 10
fennicisms 165–166
Fennomanian movement 155
Finland, bilingualism in 154; in action 160–162; Finland-Swedish identity 165–166; language contact and phonetic change 162–165; language ideology 159–160; language policy and identity 156; linguistic climate in 158; map *157*; Swedish 154–156; urbanisation of southern Finland 158–159

finlandisms 165–166
finlandssvenskar 168
Finland-Swedish 154; pronunciation and vocabulary 155
Finland-Swedish community 158
Finnish 8, 154; language identity 76; loanwords 156
Finns in Japan, language identities of: children's linguistic upbringing 74; critical discourse analysis (CDA) 69–70; data and method 69–70; Finnish language identity 76; identity 67–68; identity of multicultural children and heritage language speaker parents 74–76; informants 69; language choices as acts of identity 70–72; negotiation of 78; research questions 68–69; second-language speakers 75; self-positioning and identity 72–74; successful and non-successful linguistic upbringing 76–78
Fishman, Joshua A. 6
foreign anti-racist discourses 86
foreign language: choices. 197; skills 198
foreign visitors in Czech Republic 194
Fox, S. 115
Franzén, Anna Gradin 92, 95
French Protectorate in Morocco (1912–1956) 288
Fulfulde 49–52
Fulfulde-as-lingua franca environment **54**
Fulfulde community 57

Gaelic communities 141; language for social interactions 149; linguistic norm 147; young adult Gaelic speakers 149
Gaelic Language (Scotland) Act 141–142, 145
Gaelic language plan (GLP) 145
Gaelic management initiatives 149
Gaelic Medium Education 149
Gaelic-sector organisations 143
Gaelic speakers 141, 146
Gàidhealtachd 141
Gal, Susan 6, 87
Gemeinschaft 149
Gemeinschaft domains 147
General Data Protection Regulation (GDPR) 15–16
German language 30, 119, 126, 200
German-Namibian CMC 33, 44
German-Namibian community 43

German-Namibian speech acts in CMC: users of smaller urban and rural backgrounds 39–41; users of urban backgrounds 38–39
German-speaking minority 34
German-speaking Namibians 31–32
Gerst, D. 214
ggpbur package 277
Gilgit-Baltistan 17
globalisation 68
globalising sociolinguistics 2
Globalising Sociolinguistics conference 9
global migration 68
Goeman, Ton 107
Good, Jeff 30
Gooskens, Charlotte 6
Goudsblom, J. 109
Gravity Model 104
Grin, F. 150
Groningen 109
Grosjean, François 190
Gujranwala 19
Gurova, O. 243
Gypsy 86, 88

Haarlem Dutch 106
Haarlem legend 5; academic centre, not 109; administrative position 106; anonymity 107; arguments against 107–110; capital city, not 108; cities as norm space 103–104; first train connection 105; geographically peripheral 109; Johan Winkler's publication 105–106; language norm 100–102; linguistic status 5; measured dialect distance 106; no centre of broadcasting 109–110; no economic centre 110; no national/international cultural hub 108–109; not amongst the largest cities 109; political centre, not 108; printing, history of 105; *Randstad* area 102–103; *Randstad* region and norm 103; reasons in favour of 104–107; residence of MYSFs 107; royal residence, not 108; stereotypical image 106–107
Haeri, Niloofar 287
half-speakers 190
hate speech 85
Haugen, Einar 100
Hawkey, J. 167
Heinrich, Patrick 30, 115
Heller, Monica 156, 198

Helsinki 158
Henricson, S. 161
Hentschel, G. 178
Hermans, T. 110
high-growth agglomeration 32
Hill, J. H. 144
Hindko 19
History and Present of Hradec Králové in Street Names, The (Dejmek) 118
HK *see* Hradec Králové (HK)
Holocaust 87–88
Hradec Králové (HK) 114–115; Anglo- Western bias 115; city identity 123; Czechs 127; ethnicity in 127; foreign nationals in 124, **125**; individual languages, visibility of 126–132; interactions 118; linguistic landscape 125–133; management of communication in religious proselyting 121–122; multilingualism in 114, 123–125, 130; railway station, direction to 120; regional language variants 117; research into urban speech in Czech Republic 115–119; service encounters in Kiosk 120–121; Slovak 127; socio-cultural diversification 133; sociolinguistic situation 132; tourist information 126; Ukrainian 127; urban speech of 116–118; variationist approach 119
Hradec Králové, magazyn wolnego czasu 126
'Hradec Králové – the salon of the republic' 123
Hu, Han 8
Human Development Index 11
Hungary 84
hybrid systems of communication 167

identities: of cities 5–6, 123, 133; construction 70; of migrants 67; negotiations 67–68, 72
identity-related motivations 103
identity-work of various kinds 4
Iezzi, Luca 3
immigrants 3; Pakistani 23; tendencies of 8; urban 4
indigenous languages 17
individual voices 87
inertia condition of language choice 147
Ingrian Finns 243
in-group communication 6
innovative language uses 3
interactional processes 31

intercultural communication 7
interethnic communication 216
intergenerational transmission 142
intra-individual language 36; variation 34
Islamabad Capital Territory 17
Italy: refugees in 15; SPRAR *(Sistema di Protezione per Richiedenti Asilo e Rifugiati)* 15
Ivangorod 10, *222*
Ivangorod/Narva, monolingual bias and linguistic landscapes 213–214; Ivangorod's linguistic landscape 221–225; Narva 225–231; political and economic background 218–220; research methodology and data 217–218; symbolic construction of twin cities 220–221; theoretical and empirical background 214–217
Ivangorod-Narva territory 219

Jabeur, Mohamed 287
Jauhiainen, J. 251
Jonsson, Rickard 92, 95
Juárez 216
Junius, Hadrianus 105

Kale Neurkata 144
Khyber Pakhtunkhwa 17, 19
Kiezdeutsch 30
Klessmann, M. 214
Kloeke, G. G. 103
Kolly, Marie-José 305
Koryakov, Yury 188
Králové, Hradec 10
Kruskal-Wallis test 278, 283
Kuronen, M. 162–163, 167

Labov, William 9, 115–116
Labovian variationism 118
Lahore 19
Lamnek, Siegfried 197
Landry, R. 142
language: accommodation strategies 199; choices 68, 195; domains 71; of education 160; ideology 172; innovation 4; of interaction 16; management theory 7, 194–195; mixing 261; movements 18; shift 6, 142–143; structures, management 196; variation 114
language-based stratification 19

Language Contact, Creolization, and Genetic Linguistics (Thomason and Kaufman) 313
language identities of Finns in Japan 67, 73, 75; children's linguistic upbringing 74; construction 70; critical discourse analysis (CDA) 69–70; data and method 69–70; Finnish language identity 76; identity 67–68; identity of multicultural children and heritage language speaker parents 74–76; informants 69; language choices as acts of identity 70–72; of migrants 67; negotiation of 67–68; research questions 68–69; second-language speakers 75; self-positioning and identity 72–74; successful and non-successful linguistic upbringing 76–78
language problems in interactions between tourists in Prague: background information and research questions 193–195; Czech as local language 202–204; language accommodation in international tourism 198–204; language of first contact as problem and German-related observations 200–201; participant observation 195–198; Slavic contexts 201–202; socio-economic management 198–200; with tourists coming from Asia 202
language-product congruence 261
Larin, B. A. 134n6
Lasarzewski, Nadine 8
Latvia 217
Leemann, Adrian 305
legislative decree 27n2
Lehto, Liisa-Maria 4
Lenin, V. I. 134n4
Levinson, S. C. 120
lexemes 291, **292**
lexical diffusion 287
lexical transfer 167
Liankevich, Alena 185
lingua franca 24, 26
lingua franca communication 199
linguistic/communicative factors 2
linguistic: appropriation 182; behaviour in social network 51; changes 8; diversity 172, 239; ideologies 74; innovations 4; invisibility 214; landscape 7, 10, 125, 261; landscape and migration 215; landscape of Tokyo

242; marker 163; minorities 167; phenomena 2, 9; variables **52**; vitality 213
Liskovets, Irina 6, 172, 188
Lithuania 217
Li Wei 167
Lo Bianco, J. 150
Lojander-Visapää, C. 160
Lotzmann, G. 109
/l/ vocalisation *see* Bulgarian /l/, sociophonetics of

Mac an Tàilleir, I. 142
Mac Donnacha, S. 146
MacKinnon, K. 141, 149
macro-sociolinguistic situational analysis 16
Maghrebi Arabic varieties 291
Malinowski, D. 217
Mandarin 275
Mandarin Chinese 277
Mann- Whitney *U* test 278
Mansoor, Sabiha 17
Marley, J. 167
Marten, H. F. 217
Massey, Doreen B. 3, 103
Mbum 49, 53
McLeod, W. 141–142
McRae, K. D. 161
Melegh, Attila 85
membership categorisation analysis 122
Menongue in Angola 32
metalinguistics 195; activities 2; statements 293
metrolingualism 30
migrants mix language 3–4
Milani, Tommaso M. 92, 95
minority languages 215
Minsk 172
Minsk T-speakers 185
Mitsova, Sofiya 9, 312–313
mixed code 20, 22
Mladenov, Hr. 309
mobile younger suburban female (MYSF) 107
modern lifestyles 3
Mongolia 32
monolingual bias and linguistic landscapes of Ivangorod/Narva 213–214; Ivangorod's linguistic landscape 221–225; Narva 225–231; political and economic background 218–220; research methodology and data 217–218; symbolic construction of twin cities 220–221; theoretical and empirical background 214–217
monolingualism 7, 72, 118, 221; *see also* multilingualism
monolingual Japanese 71
monolingual linguistic landscapes in Vyborg, Russia 239–241; individual efforts, challenges and failures 255–256; method and data 242–243; political and economic background 243–244; Vyborg's linguistic landscape 244–255
monolingual municipality 168n3
monolingual policy 7
monolingual proficiency 167
Mooney, D. 167
Moroccan Arabic speakers 289
Moroccan Arabic varieties 290
morpho-syntactic structures 20
morpho-syntax 19
mother tongue 74, 160
motorcycle taxi drivers 4
motorcycle taxi drivers (MTD) in Ngaoundéré, Cameroon 49–50; ethno-linguistic background **54**; linguistic background, theory and method 50–53; linguistic variation 53–60
multilingual advertisements 225
multilingualism 8, 67–68, 118, 167, 213, 247, 251; among German-Namibians 4, 31; in Hradec Králové (HK) 114, 124–125; level of 247
multilingual language practices 32
multilingual migrants 68
multiple language in business names 260
Munro, G. 142–143, 149
Muysken, Pieter 16, 20, 22, 190
Myers-Scotton, Carol 179

Namdeutsch 32, 42
Namibian language practices 35, 41; lexical and syntactic implications 35–36; multilingual speech in comparison 37; population size and frequency **41**; urban and rural backgrounds, users of 36–37
Namibia-specific language 38
Narva 7, 10
national identities 75
National Romantic movement 155
negotiation of identities 67–68

328 Index

Nekvapil, Jiří 5, 10, 50, 120–123, 203
networked multilingualism 42
Networks of Exchange (NoE) 31
Ngaoundéré 49
NicAoidh, M. 142, 148
Ni Chualain, F. 146
Niedzielski, Nancy A. 110
Niemi, S. 162
Ni Sheaghdha, A. 146
Nogales 216
non-mobile older rural male (NORM) 107
noun-class agreement morphology 52
Nugent, Paul 216
null hypothesis 41

O'Brien, M. 146
obscenities 91–92
October Revolution, 1917 218
O Giollagain, C. 146
ÓhIfearnáin, T. 143
Old Town of Hradec Králové Tells Its Stories, The (Dejmek) 117
Oliver, J. 142–143
OLUS (observational language use surveys) 146, 148
one-way ANOVA test 281
on-line management of communication 50
onomastics 114
Orbán, Viktor 85
Ostrobothnia 158

Padareva-Ilieva, G. 312–313
paindu 18
Pakistan: capital culturel 17; language policy and language use 17–18; new variety 19–22; provinces 17–18; Punjabi language vitality 18–19; territories 17
Pakistani immigrants 23
Pakistani informants 15–16
Pakistani migrants in Italy 3
Pakistani refugees 15
Palviainen, Å. 159
Pedersen, Inge 104
Peyton, J. K. 150
Pfoser, A. 220
phenomenon of misplaced scale 144
phonetic realisation of phoneme 291
photo-elicited interviews (PEIs) 164
Planken, Brigitte 8
politeness 199

political correctness (PC) in East-Central Europe 5, 83–84, 95–96; analyses 89–95; Budapest University Dormitory Corpus 88–89; defined 84; hate speech 85; in Hungary 84, 87; language 85; in post-socialist Budapest 84–86; voice and enregisterment 86–88
political incorrectness 86, 94
politically incorrect language 89
postmodernism 2, 84
power relations 261, 265, 267
Praat software 164, 312
Prague 114
Prague, language problems in interactions between tourists in: background information and research questions 193–195; Czech as local language 202–204; language accommodation in international tourism 198–204; language of first contact as problem and German-related observations 200–201; participant observation 195–198; Slavic contexts 201–202; socio-economic management 198–200; with tourists coming from Asia 202
presentation of self 261, 265, 267
Preston, Dennis R. 110
private CAS 15
profughi 3, 15
pronunciation variation 8
prostitution 107
prostorechie (simple speech) 189
Protectorate 288
Pujolar, Juan 198
Punjab 17–18
Punjabi 18–19

Qadir, Ashequl 31, 38

racist dehumanisation 94
Radke, Henning 4
Randstad: area 102–103; region and norm 103
Ratilainen, S. 243
rawaandu 59
R Core Team 277
Recasens, D. 305–306
reception system in Italy 15
Renkonen 155
reverse diglossia 143
reverse transliteration 223
rhetoric of revolution/of continuity 114–115

Rhotics frequency in Beijing 275–276; age 281–283; data source 276; de-rhotacisation 285; dialect background 283–284; gender 280–281; independent *t*-test 282; participants 276; procedure 276–277; rhotics distribution 278–280, *279*; statistical treatment 277–278
Rhotic words 275
Riloff, Ellen 31, 38
Ring City 102
Rotterdam 109–110
R-package EgoR 56
R-speakers associate Trasyanka 182
runaway language shift 141
rural language 172
rural multilingualism 30–32; dataset 33–34; Facebook, discourse on 33–34; intra-individual language choices displayed in CMC 34–36; multilingual speech in comparison 37; Namibia, individuals from urban and rural areas in 32–33; Namibia-specific language practices, roles and functions 37–41; urban, rural or CMC practices 41–43; urban and rural backgrounds, users of 36–37
Russian language 172–173
Russian phonology 175
Russian-speaking community in Estonia 220
Russian urban speech of rural migrants 179

Sachdev, I. 144
Schegloff, E. A. 120, 134n7
Schjerfbeck, Helene 156
Searle, John R. 31, 38
semicommunication 201
semi-conscious pronunciation level 9
semiotic behaviour 2
sexual abuse 89
sexual objectification 94
Shapiro-Wilk's test 277
Sharma, D. 115
Sherman, Tamah 50, 121, 123
shopping tourism 215
Sibelius, Jean 156
Sindh 17
single language in business names 260
Skerrett, D. M. 226
Slavic languages 172
Slavonic languages 7

Slovak 127
Smakman, Dick 5, 8, 30, 102, 115
Smith-Christmas, C. 143, 149
social domains 87, 92
social identities 75
social interaction 114
social linguistic soundscape in Stornoway 141–143, 149; language use patterns 148–149; methodology 143–146; results and discussion 146–148
social/situational factors 2
social stigmatisation 7
social stratification 88
Social Stratification of English in New York City, The (Labov) 115
social taboo 92
social voices 87
'societal treatment' approach 304
socio-cultural management 205
socioeconomic circumstances, management 196
socio-economic management 198
sociolinguistics 1, 5, 117, 260; Anglo-western realm of influence 3; changes 67; interest in globalisation 214; knowledge 5; mobile semiotic resources 2; patterns 33; systems 30; uniqueness 11
sociophonetics of Bulgarian /l/ 304; allophone 308; articulatory configurations *307*; historic/regional dispersion 309; language management perspective 316; /l/ realisation 312–313; onset of non-regionality associations 309–311; phenomenon 305; phonetic/phonological features of Bulgarian [ŭ] 306–308; semantic disambiguation 314–316; sociolinguistic status of [ŭ] and practical ramifications 311–312; spectrogram *308*; spelling issues 313–314; variants of /l/ in Bulgarian 308–309; vocalisation across the globe 305–306; vocalisation in Bulgaria 306
Sorbian 30
Soroka, O. 309
Sotirov, P. 309
South-Slavic language 306
Speech Act Theory 31–32, 38
SPRAR *(Sistema di Protezione per Richiedenti Asilo e Rifugiati)* 15
standaardnederlands 100
Standard Civilised Dutch 100

standardisation 189
standard language ideology 172
Stoykov, St. 308
Straattaal 30
Strandberg, Janine A. E. 6, 163–165, 167
Studer-Joho, Dieter 305
Stylistic and Social Stratification of English in New York City, The (Labov) 115
superdiversification 193
superdiversity 114–115
supply-sided foreign language knowledge 199
S-V-structure 57
Sweden-Swedish 155
Swedish in Finland 6
Szabó, Gergely 5

Tanev, M. 309
Temara 293; language behaviour 294; urbanisation 294–295
The Hague 108–109
The Netherlands 100
theory of good reason 261, 265, 267
Thessaloniki 104
Tijuana 216
Tilburg 109
tourism 215
translanguaging 161–162, 167
transnationalism 68
Trasyanka 7, 172–173; Belarusian speakers 184–185; Belarusian stems in **176**; differences in syntax **177**; linguistic structure and patterns of usage 174–180; methods and data 173–174; paraphones **176**; R-speakers associate 182; Russian speakers 180–184; Russian stems in **176**; Trasyanka speakers 185–187; utterances in **175**; variety 7
Trasyanka-speakers 174, 177–178
Trudgill, Peter 103, 106, 110
Turai, Ráhel Katalin 5
Tzitzilis, Christos 104

Ukrainian 127
unnamed voices 87
urban communicative situations 3
urbanhood 32

urban immigrants 4, 68
urbanisation 299
urbanisation in Morocco 287; evolution of material conditions 294–299; language change and social background 289–294; Temara's rural-to-urban progression 288
urban language situation 50
urban variety 20
Urdu 17–18
Utěšený, S. 116
Utrecht 109
Uusimaa 158

Van Bree, C. 103
Vandeputte, O. 110
Van de Velde, Hans 109
van Meurs, Frank 8
van Meurs, Peter 105
velar allophone 308
Vincent, P. 110
virtual linguistics 10
visual linguistic diversity 241
voices of named individuals 87
Vyborg's linguistic landscape 242, 244–255

Walters, Keith 287
Warf, Barney 102
Web Scraper 33
Weckström, Lotta 71
Werlen, Iwar 305
western-type modernisation 88
West-Slavic language 306
Wilcoxon tests 278, 283
Will, V. K. A. 149
Windhoek 32

Yurramendi, Y. 145

Zappen-Thomson, Marianne 31, 43
Zaprudsky, S. 174
Zeman, J. 120, 123
Zhobov, V. 309
Zhu Hua 167
Ziamari, Karima 292
Zimmer, Christian 31
Zuidas 110

For Product Safety Concerns and Information please contact our EU
representative GPSR@taylorandfrancis.com
Taylor & Francis Verlag GmbH, Kaufingerstraße 24, 80331 München, Germany